To Lee —

Best Wishes —

Bob Dopp

Oct. 26, 2008

Hell Hawks!

Hell Hawks!

The Untold Story of
the American Fliers Who
Savaged Hitler's Wehrmacht

Robert F. Dorr and Thomas D. Jones

ZENITH PRESS

To the men of the Ninth Air Force
who flew and maintained the
P-47 Thunderbolt in combat.

First published in 2008 by Zenith Press, an imprint of MBI Publishing Company, 400 First Avenue North, Suite 300, Minneapolis, MN 55401 USA

Zenith Press titles are also available at discounts in bulk quantity for industrial or sales-promotional use. For details write to Special Sales Manager at MBI Publishing Company, 400 First Avenue North, Suite 300, Minneapolis, MN 55401 USA.

To find out more about our books, join us online at www.zenithpress.com.

Maps by: Thomas D. Jones with Brenda C. Canales

ON THE COVER: Main: Fighting a grim war on the European continent between Normandy and V-E Day transformed P-47 Thunderbolt pilots, mechanics, and armorers into a closely bonded aerial band of brothers. This Thunderbolt pilot is surrounded by the enlisted men who helped him fly and fight. Together, they took on primitive living conditions, a frigid winter, the German army, and the Battle of the Bulge. *U.S. Army via Jack Lambert* **(inset)** A P-47 Thunderbolt, or "Jug," of the 365th Fighter Group, the Hell Hawks, flies a combat mission behind German lines in Europe. The P-47 (here with the later "bubble" canopy) was fast and tough, able to defend itself in the air and to slug it out with German forces at treetop altitude. *William L. Ward*

ON THE BACK COVER: During the 1944–1945 fighting in the Ardennes, the Hell Hawks found winter as bitter an enemy as the Germans. Two Republic P-47 Thunderbolts of the 365th Fighter Group take off from their base, A-84 Chièvres, near Mons, Belgium, on a mission to bomb and strafe Wehrmacht forces. Three Thunderbolts of the 386th Fighter Squadron stand ready to follow. *U.S. Army* **Also featured:** A 9th Air Force patch and the Hell Hawks jacket patch.

ON THE SPINE: The leadership of the 365th Fighter Group in Metz, France, January 1945. From left to right: Maj. George R. Brooking (386th), Maj. John W. Motzenbecker (387th), Col. Ray J. Stecker (group commander), and Maj. Robert M. Fry (388th). *U.S. Army*

Library of Congress Cataloging-in-Publication Data

Dorr, Robert F.
Hell hawks! : the untold story of the American fliers who savaged Hitler's Wehrmacht / by Robert F. Dorr and Thomas D. Jones.
        p. cm.
Includes bibliographical references.
ISBN-13: 978-0-7603-2918-4 (hbk.)
ISBN-10: 0-7603-2918-4 (hbk.)

1. United States. Army Air Forces. Fighter Group, 365th.
2. World War, 1939-1945—Aerial operations, American.
3. World War, 1939-1945—Regimental histories—United States.
4. World War, 1939-1945—Campaigns—Western Front. I. Jones, Thomas D. II. Title.
D790.252365th .D67 2008
940.54'4973—dc22
                2007039558

Designer: Diana Boger

Printed in the United States of America

Contents

Chapter One

Hell Hawks over Normandy

H EADING EAST, LOW OVER the English Channel, four P-47D Thunderbolt fighter-bombers streaked toward the French coast. It was late in the day, well past 7:00 p.m., and the spring light softened as a high cirrus filtered the last hour of sun. Good light for bombing, thought Capt. James G. "Jimmy" Wells Jr., one of the four pilots in the formation. *The sun will be in their eyes.*

The enemy coast—the Pas-de-Calais—was visible ten miles ahead as the formation nosed over into a shallow dive. Wells was one of the Hell Hawks, the 365th Fighter Group, a Thunderbolt outfit based in England as part of the Ninth Air Force. Their specialty wasn't dogfighting, although they had already taken the measure of the Luftwaffe. Instead, their job was close-in ground attack, where you put your bombs right on top of your enemy, then circled back with machine guns and chewed up anything that still moved. From mere yards away you looked into the eyes of the German gunners, who hurled white-hot metal at you until you killed them—or they you.

All day on May 3, 1944, back at the Hell Hawks' base in Beaulieu, England, near Southampton, mechanics and armorers had swarmed over the pilots' Thunderbolts: heavy, bottle-shaped fighters with eighteen-cylinder power plants turning thirteen-foot propellers. Each plane carried a 108-gallon belly tank of high-octane gas, a pair of thousand-pound bombs slung under the wings, and eight heavy .50-caliber machine guns, commonly called "fifties." The P-47, believed the Hell Hawks pilots, was a flying tank.

Golden sunlight flickered off the green sea as Wells leveled off with Capt. William D. Ritchie, the flight leader, just a hundred feet above the waves. The beach flashed under the four olive-drab fighters, the pilots dropping back to either side of Ritchie as he picked up the final run-in heading to the target, an inconsequential French village named Vacqueriette, twenty miles inland. Just outside the hamlet was a military compound clustered around three narrow reinforced-concrete buildings, each with a curved end. In aerial photos the three bunkers resembled skis, viewed from their sides. Close by was a 160-foot-long concrete ramp, its long axis pointed straight at London. The mysterious installation was a nest for a flock of V-1 Buzz Bombs.

Allied intelligence knew that the V-1, a pilotless flying bomb with a 1,870-pound warhead of Amatol high explosive, was close to becoming operational. This suspected launch site, and others for the still-mysterious V-2 rocket, were called Noball sites; they were at the top of priority bombing lists as D-Day approached. Bombing raids from high and medium altitude on this and other V-1 sites had failed to destroy the installations. Ritchie, Wells, and their fellow Hell Hawks were ordered to knock them out from ground level.

"They asked for volunteers for a special mission," Wells said later. "I was foolish enough to stick my hand up and get picked, and they took us in and they told us about the buzz bomb. They had gotten hold of plans for an emplacement where they launched them, and these concrete buildings were about forty feet square and they were three-foot-thick reinforced concrete. But they really weren't sure just how they were used. The buzz bombs themselves—they weren't sure whether they were controlled or had an automatic timer or what on them." All Wells knew was that "they said we had to be going over 450 miles per hour when we released the bombs so that they would penetrate those concrete emplacements."

Those were the tactics. Wells followed Ritchie in his descent, throttle wide open, guns and bombs armed. One and a half miles from the village the four pilots were at deck level, the steeple on the village church visible above the trees. Wells picked out his assigned dull gray "ski" site and eased his speeding Thunderbolt lower.

Closer now, airspeed 450 miles per hour out of the dive, that big 2,430-horsepower Pratt & Whitney up front howled with emergency water-injection thrust. Wells triggered the first burst from his .50-calibers at a flak pit that was blasting what looked like glowing white coals past his canopy. More tracers came ripping up from gun positions and a flak tower ringing the site. *Ignore them.* What Wells couldn't ignore was what he'd seen in the recon target photos: a string of telephone poles around the target's perimeter. "We didn't know what it was, if it had antennas on it, or what."

Wells was at thirty-five feet, flattening barley fields and bending small trees in his wake, when he discovered the reason for the telephone poles—and the tough steel cables strung between them. They were there to kill him.

No time to evade—the four went under, or tried to. "I'd say we were at twenty-five feet; and then you had to pull up to keep from running into the target!" recalled Wells. "All of us made it under, except Captain Cornell. He ripped off the top of his rudder."

Wells let go of his bombs and screamed over the concrete buildings while the semi-armor-piercing thousand-pounders punched through the reinforced walls and detonated seconds later on a delayed fuse. Smoke, dust, and debris shot skyward, boiling up from the launch installations and gun emplacements. Chunks of concrete ripped across the compound, lacerating vehicles, buildings, and men.

Shooting up a flak tower and gun pits, Captain Ritchie was at fifteen feet when he hit a cable set twenty feet or so off the ground. He ripped through some telephone wires and sheared off a row of tree tops, denting and crumpling his P-47's air scoop and fuselage. Ritchie hugged the ground and turned west, into the setting sun, trailing behind a long length of phone wire that thrashed and slapped against the fuselage and tail.

Off the target, Wells rejoined his element leader and stared into the adjacent cockpit. Capt. William H. Cornell's face was covered in blood. "Some shrapnel came in and hit him in the head . . . blood was coming out, and he pulled his helmet off and started calling 'Mayday!' on the radio," said Wells.

The four Thunderbolts headed for Beaulieu (pronounced "Byew-lee"), medical help waiting alongside the runway. Cornell landed first; the medics leaned into the cockpit to find his uniform slick with blood from his scalp wound. "Turned out it just scratched him," said Jimmy Wells, "but he didn't know it." Stitched up, Cornell was back flying a few days later.

The post-strike photos showed that each Hell Hawk Thunderbolt, throwing a ton of bombs against each V-1 target building, had inflicted as much damage as the 1,947 tons per target dropped by the heavy bombers in the last two weeks of April. Jimmy Wells was satisfied with his single Noball mission: "I only did that one," he said. Once was plenty.

☆

Wells was awakened at 1:00 a.m. on June 6, 1944, in his Nissen hut at Beaulieu. "This was it! We had known the invasion was coming soon," remembered Wells. To help friendly gunners tell friend from foe, ground crews painted all Allied planes with alternating black and white stripes on wings and fuselage. "I helped paint the stripes on myself," said the Houston native.

The intelligence officer briefed the pilots on the airborne drops, already underway across the Channel, and of their role that morning. The Hell Hawks were to hit crossroads, bridges, and gun emplacements—targets that would knock out German defenders and impede their ability to bring up reinforcements. "We took off at 4:00 a.m.," said Wells, "into a coal black sky." The weather was overcast but clear enough to do the job. It was D-Day: the real reason for the Hell Hawks' existence. Their work was about to begin in earnest.

Wells couldn't believe the sight of the invasion fleet crowding the Channel. "We got down and it was just getting daylight, and I was looking down, and I don't know whether it was a battleship or a cruiser . . . they were firing at the coast. But, oh!—When they let that broadside go with the flames and smoke, it looked like the ship exploded." Only when the second broadside tore through the darkness did Wells realize what he was seeing.

☆

From the cockpit of his own P-47 Thunderbolt, Lt. Col. Robert Lewis Coffey Jr. looked down at a sight few men would witness and all would remember forever. It was about 5:50 a.m. on June 6, 1944, still almost dark, a gray, murky daylight beginning to define itself off Coffey's left shoulder high over the English Channel. Coffey was looking down at thousands of ships and boats in the armada, the main thrust of the Allied invasion of France, already underway. From the roomy cockpit of his robust fighter, leading forty-seven planes into battle, Coffey took in the size and scale of the armada. He did not see the fighting that was now unfolding on the shores ahead, where 176,000 Allied troops were pouring ashore at five Normandy invasion beaches: Juno, Sword, Gold, Utah, and Omaha. In fact he had little time for reflection. He was more pragmatic than philosophical anyway, and his job for the moment was to lead his big fighters, nicknamed "Jugs" because of their portly contours, to attack three targets that lay just inland, ahead of the invasion.

Coffey commanded the 388th Fighter Squadron, one of three in a group that would soon be in the middle of the war on the European continent, a fight both bloody and very personal. Later in his brief life Coffey would be a politician, and he looked the part, "a pretty sturdy guy with black hair and a mustache," a fellow pilot recalled later. "He was a good pilot. He was aggressive." Another pilot called Coffey "suave" and "debonair," and he was married to a beautiful Puerto Rican girl whom some of his buddies had met, admired, and maybe fantasized about. Coffey was just twenty-six years old but had been in uniform for almost two years before the United States entered the war. He was older and more mature than his fellow Hell Hawks, who were mostly younger men plucked from civilian life shortly after Pearl Harbor. Coffey was a leader. Today was the show.

Coffey was busy monitoring his formation, correcting his course, performing routine cockpit tasks, keeping his eye on fuel flow and RPMs, and listening to the throb of his eighteen-cylinder Double Wasp radial engine. He must have been too busy to think much about the greatest invasion in history, apart from his own role in it. Coffey's focus as he "coasted in" over Utah Beach on D-Day, one of the great days of history, was on his set of targets: a railroad bridge south-west of St.-Sauveur-de-Pierre-Pont, a culvert at Couperville, and an embankment at St.-Sauveur.

One pilot in Coffey's flight, 2nd Lt. Robert L. Saferite, recalled that the stormy weather of the day before had cleared late, when Saferite returned from a mission at dusk and glimpsed the invasion fleet below. Now, flying with Coffey, Saferite looked down at Utah Beach, where GIs rushing ashore faced only a fraction of the resistance turning the water red at Omaha. Utah was near Cherbourg on the Cotentin Peninsula; the beach itself was backed by numerous small villages, but Saferite was searching for the enemy, in the darkened fields below, and in the murky sky. "There were plenty of German guns ready for us there," said Saferite. "Our job was air-to-ground, but we were also looking around alertly for German aircraft in case we'd have to fight them." But his flight was seemingly alone in the sky. "We did not see a single German aircraft." Saferite and the rest of Coffey's flight bored in toward their targets.

☆

Coffey may have been in command of all the Hell Hawks in the air that morning, but the Group's 387th Fighter Squadron had already left the formation. The 387th was on the deck, barely 250 feet off the surface of the Channel, its dozen

Thunderbolts headed inland under the command of the squadron operations officer, Capt. Arlo C. Henry Jr. He was as experienced that morning as any man in a P-47 cockpit. One of his fellow pilots called him a "daring flier" who smoked a cigar on takeoff, against the rules. Another said simply that Henry was "stocky, but not fat, laid-back, with a round face" and that he "kind of ambled along." Henry also had nightmares and sometimes screamed out from his bunk in the darkness, but the group fielded no bolder, better-skilled fighter pilot. He dubbed his plane *Turnip Termite*, now in its final twenty-four hours of existence as a flying machine.

Henry's Thunderbolts each carried two one-thousand-pound bombs, one under each wing. Other Hell Hawks in the air that day were hauling three five-hundred-pounders, the additional bomb hung on the fuselage centerline.

Henry's wingman was 1st Lt. John H. Fetzer Jr. piloting a Thunderbolt with the name *The Madam* emblazoned in red letters across the nose. A Louisiana boy with the distinct drawl associated with Shreveport, Fetzer remembers that the Hell Hawks took off in darkness, found murky daylight over the Channel, and were en route to Normandy to "strafe or bomb anything, any German we found, a half-track, tanks, or infantry."

At Omaha Beach, Fetzer looked down at "vehicles and people everywhere, bodies lying all over." The formation of Jugs continued inland at near treetop level; visible everywhere was the aftermath of the nighttime Allied airborne assault that had kicked off the invasion. Fetzer saw an American paratrooper dangling from a tree, head down, inert. He saw gliders attempting to land and others strewn across the fields and hedgerows of Normandy. "The Germans had laid tree trunks to prevent gliders from landing. There was wreckage scattered everywhere, men scattered on the ground—horrible!" Parts of the invasion had begun badly, and if the Hell Hawks and their P-47 Thunderbolts were going to help those paratroopers and glidermen, they needed to make a dent in German defenses.

Beneath the murk, in the wet greenish brown fields of France, Arlo Henry came upon a formation of lead gray Tiger tanks. That's just what our boys on the beaches don't need, thought Fetzer, close on Henry's wing. If the panzers were shooting at them, Fetzer didn't notice it; anyway, the pilots had learned by now to ignore ground fire. Fetzer maintained that you never knew when you might get hit, and there was no purpose in dwelling on it.

One of the Tigers followed a standard armor tactic—driving into a large house, a chateau, really, and allowing the structure to collapse around him, providing camouflage and cover. Other Tigers were rumbling through the nearby village, one of them clearly a communications vehicle with an antenna fully thirty feet tall. The Thunderbolt pilots briefly exchanged words and hand signals, then Henry led the attack.

"Henry dropped two bombs into the chateau and blew it to pieces," said Fetzer. "It was an odd kind of destruction because there were two walls left standing, one at either end of the house, like bookends, but nothing but blackness and smoke in between." Fetzer was wary of the delay fuses on the thousand-pounders; he didn't want to get caught in his leader's bomb blasts. He gave his boss plenty of spacing and dove, putting the panzer at the center of his gunsight. "I came in behind Henry, made my pass, and released one bomb that skipped into a field. My second bomb went off behind another Tiger tank." Fetzer craned his head back over his shoulder in the pullout and watched in amazement the result of his drop. Sixty-three years later the memory is still vivid: "It flipped that tank over three or four times! Later in the day on my second mission, I destroyed a half-track with a thousand-pounder and nearly mushed into the tree when pulling out, but that was nothing to match the sight of a Tiger tank flipping over. That was my contribution to D-Day."

☆

Also airborne with the Thunderbolt pilots of the Hell Hawks' 387th Squadron that morning was 2nd Lt. Grant Stout, a husky, athletic farm boy who had wanted to fly since childhood. Stout looked like an all-American linebacker and had a sense of humor—he kept a pet duck named Zeke—but he also had a curious habit, not typical of fighter pilots, of talking as if something bad was going to happen to him. "He seemed to have a belief in fate," said another pilot. If Stout believed his future was already determined, that death was looking over his shoulder, he was one of the few who defied superstition by speaking about it. But this was D-Day, and all Stout could control that morning was how he did his job in the air.

Like Wells and Coffey, Henry and Fetzer, Stout was part of a special breed— the aerial band of brothers who piloted the mighty P-47 Thunderbolt, an aircraft that evoked fierce loyalty from its pilots. When first introduced to the Thunderbolt, Stout had written home: "Imagine landing at 130 miles per hour!" A few days later, he wrote: "This Thunderbolt is more like a rocket ship than an airplane. You have no idea how powerful those eighteen cylinders are until you get hold of the throttle, and then she really goes places."

Republic Aviation, the Farmingdale, New York, manufacturer of the P-47, had a reputation for building fighters that were big, fast, and rugged. The Thunderbolt took that tradition to new heights.

The typical P-47D flown on the European continent by Stout and other pilots was powered by a Pratt & Whitney R-2800-59W Double Wasp, an eighteen-cylinder, twin-row, air-cooled radial engine. The massive power plant produced more than two thousand horsepower and gave the P-47 a 17,500-pound takeoff weight. It was armed with eight .50-caliber (12.7mm) Browning M3 machine guns packing 250 to 350 rounds each.

P-47s rolled out of American factories in greater numbers than any other U.S. fighter in history. The total of 15,683 P-47s built tops the 15,486 P-51 Mustangs, 13,143 P-40 Warhawks, and 10,037 P-38 Lightnings produced for the Army Air Forces.

With their sturdy fighter, bristling with heavy machine guns, Grant Stout and his buddies fought their war down in the treetops, where they came face-to-face with the German foe. It was a dirty war, fought eyeball-to-eyeball, and it produced more than its fair share of grit, gristle, and gore. Consider, for example, the following citation awarded to P-47 pilots later that summer for destroying a column of German vehicles attempting to escape advancing Allied forces near Châteauroux, France:

"Thirty-six P-47s . . . raced south of the Loire River to find the road from Châteauroux to Issoudon clogged with military transport, horse drawn vehicles, horse drawn artillery, armored vehicles and personnel. Attacking this [German] concentration, at minimum altitude, in spite of accurate ground fire, the . . . pilots . . . made pass after pass until their bombs, rockets, and ammunition were expended. The road was blocked for fifteen miles with personnel casualties, wrecked and burning military transport. More than 300 enemy military vehicles were destroyed in this attack alone."

The citation continues: "The group returned to home base, and after being re-fueled and rearmed in minimum time, returned to the scene of the action. Before the enemy could reorganize and extract the remnants of his column, a further 187 vehicles, including 25 ammunition carriers, were attacked and destroyed. [All this was accomplished] in spite of intermittent rain and the hazard of landing at night on a slick tar paper runway. . . ."

Their war was far from antiseptic. The aftermath of such an assault was a road strewn with burning vehicles and the tangled, bloody carcasses of men and—even in 1944—horses. One of Grant Stout's fellow P-47 pilots remembered: "The horses were not our enemy, but our assignment was to prevent those columns from harming our troops." The gruesome sight of those innocent animals caught in their lethal guns sometimes made pilots physically ill.

But this bullet-churned chaos wasn't part of their war on D-Day. The vigorous Stout had a good day as Allied armies poured ashore. The more senior, experienced Arlo Henry later wrote to Stout's parents of their son's D-Day actions: Stout "shot up so many enemy supply vehicles that he had only one [.50-caliber] gun firing when he spotted four German soldiers firing at him . . . . He got three of them, and the last one was running along a wall, trying to make the corner. [Stout's gun-camera] film showed the bullets clipping the wall about two feet above the German's head as he ran."

☆

Over Normandy, Lt. Col. Coffey's Hell Hawks, part of the massive Allied air armada deployed to crack the roof of Hitler's "Fortress Europe," arrived over their first target. The 388th Squadron pilots dove to the deck about a mile out and from an altitude of twenty-five feet dropped their thousand-pounders on the road culvert at Couperville. Other Hell Hawks dropped their five-hundred-pound bombs in a dive from six hundred to eight hundred feet under the overcast, trying to cut the road and isolate the beaches from German reinforcements. Second Lieutenant Jack J. Martell deliberately dropped his bombs from just a few feet in the air, but the delay fuses malfunctioned. Martell's P-47 was caught by the debris and shrapnel from his own bomb blast.

First Lieutenant Zell Smith, another 388th Squadron pilot, witnessed Martell's Thunderbolt hurtling across the flat Normandy terrain at two hundred feet, guns blazing and one wing root on fire. Smith watched in horror as Martell passed the target trailing fire and smoke, then abruptly dove at full throttle into the ground. His P-47 exploded on impact in the western outskirts of St.-Lô-d'Ourville.

Hitting gun emplacements behind the beaches were Capt. Jimmy Wells and the 386th Squadron. Flying low to skip their five-hundred-pounders into the concrete emplacements, 1st Lt. Robert L. Shipe had just released when he was engulfed by the flash and blast of his own bombs. A second plane was so badly damaged that the pilot barely made it back to Beaulieu to execute a crash-landing. Near the village of St.-Sauveur-de-Pierre-Pont, a French family recovered Shipe's body and buried him in a field, tending the grave until American forces liberated the area.

In the dawn twilight, smoke, and mist, it was almost impossible to determine what had happened to Shipe, or even the results of their attack. Wells landed back at Beaulieu and was mobbed by his ground crew for news of the invasion. A group from the staff of the Allied supreme commander, Gen. Dwight D. Eisenhower, listened in. Wells recognized one of them, "a fellow who had been my commanding officer in the National Guard, when I was an enlisted man. Last time I had seen him he was giving me a couple weeks of KP for punishment."

The colonel remembered Wells and pumped him for anything he could say about the fate of the paratroopers and the invasion. Wells, now a fighter pilot just back from one of the first air strikes of D-Day, was exuberant: "We had a very good time talking to each other. He wasn't going to give me any more KP."

☆

Stout, Coffey, Henry, Fetzer, and Wells were flying from the airfield at Beaulieu, England, where the 365th Fighter Group had begun operations weeks earlier. There, the pilots were backed by almost a thousand men on the ground: the fighter group's crew chiefs, armorers, truck drivers, cooks, and orderly-room clerks. On June 6 they went about what German Field Marshal Erwin Rommel had already called history's "longest day," doing their jobs with an extra measure of dedication and skill. They knew that they would soon be going ashore in Normandy, right behind the infantry. At 1:00 p.m. on D-Day, the men each received an announcement from General Eisenhower, reminding them that soldiers, sailors, and airmen of the Allied Expeditionary Forces were embarking "upon the Great Crusade toward which we have striven these many months." Charles R. Johnson, one of the crew chiefs, reported that many of the Hell Hawks grinned, and "now and again someone would let out an uncontrollable whoop as he realized the importance of the day." Johnson added, "It was almost impossible to quell the questions that were pouring at the pilots from all sides."

The crews readied their P-47s, waiting until late afternoon for orders to strike the railroad bridge at Oissel. All three squadrons—thirty-six fighter-bombers—descended on the bridge in a forty-degree dive, carpeting the span with seventy-two thousand-pounders. When the churning column of mud and water collapsed back into the river, half of the southern span had been dropped, and another German reinforcement route was blocked.

Shortly after 9:00 p.m., the group launched another cross-Channel attack to hit artillery positions throwing shells onto the beaches. Despite smoke screens and heavy flak that damaged two aircraft, the Hell Hawks located, hit, and destroyed all three targets. The final Thunderbolt touched down at Beaulieu as darkness fell, just after 11:30 p.m.

For the Hell Hawks ground crews, their only rest on June 6 was a rare nap in the pup tents clustered near the flight line. Theirs had indeed been "the longest day." Working through the night as the GIs in France tried to hold onto their shallow beachheads, those lucky enough to sleep were awakened at 3:00 a.m. on June 7. The Hell Hawks—pilots and ground crews alike—rose to face what would be their costliest day of World War II.

☆

The Ninth Air Force on D-Day flew 2,312 fighter sorties, providing air cover, escorting bombers, flying armed reconnaissance missions, and striking invasion targets. The Ninth's eighteen fighter groups dropped 385 tons of bombs on bridges, gun emplacements, buildings, and rail choke points, and strafed anything that moved behind the beaches. Combat losses totaled seven fighter aircraft, two from the Hell Hawks.

This would be their war: a relentless campaign flown over the front lines, in the air every day to support the GIs' advance. Their first mission was to keep the Luftwaffe off the backs of the troops below, to sweep enemy fighters from the skies above the battlefield. Their second was to provide "flying artillery" for Eisenhower's ground troops, on call whenever precisely applied hitting power was needed. When possible, the Hell Hawks would be freed to range far in the enemy's rear, destroying airfields, transportation, supply dumps—anything that would cut the legs out from under the Werhmacht soldier. Stated simply, the Hell Hawks' job was to use the P-47 Thunderbolt to kill their German opponents whenever and wherever they found them. Everything the 365th Fighter Group did was geared toward that singular aim.

During the course of their fifteen months in combat, the Hell Hawks would follow the battle lines, shifting bases forward as the Allies liberated Europe. They lived in the field, sharing the GIs' food and spartan lifestyle. They grew close, pilots and ground crews alike, forging bonds that would remain strong six decades later. And each day they rose to ready their warplanes, knowing that *every* day, some would stare death in the face and discover how far their Thunderbolts, and their courage, would take them.

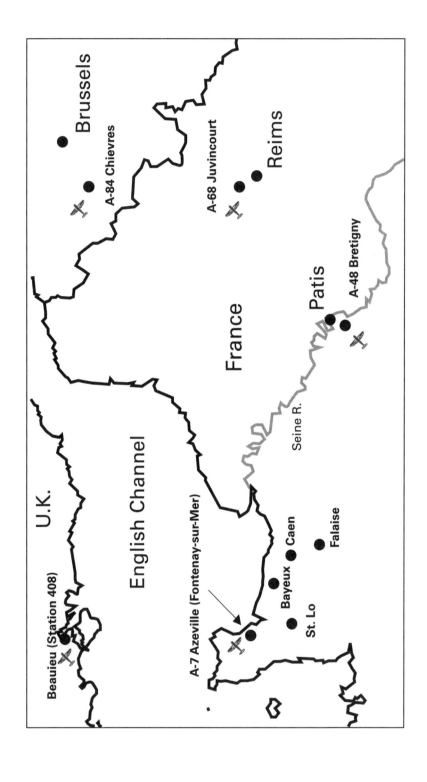

365th Fighter Group Airfields *March–December 1944*

Brussels

A-84 Chievres

A-68 Juvincourt

Reims

A-48 Bretigny

Patis

France

Seine R.

English Channel

U.K.

Beauieu (Station 408)

A-7 Azeville (Fontenay-sur-Mer)

Bayeux

Caen

St. Lo

Falaise

✪ *Chapter Two*

Over the Beach

W ITH THEIR THUNDERBOLTS back on the ground, crew chiefs, armorers, and repair teams labored through the damp hours of darkness to patch battle damage, refuel, rearm, and check out the aircraft for the coming day. Even lacking details of the invasion's progress, they knew the critical importance of the next twenty-four hours. Nearly 176,000 American, Canadian, and British soldiers had surged ashore by the time the landings ended around 10:00 p.m. on June 6, 1944. About 4,900 of those men were already dead, wounded, or captured by the German defenders. The beachhead established beyond the sands of Sword, Juno, Gold, Omaha, and Utah stretched along the Channel coast for over fifty-five miles. But the lodgment was a shallow one, nowhere more than six miles deep; at bloody Omaha, the GIs had penetrated barely one and a quarter miles after their horrific fight at the waterline against fierce Wehrmacht resistance. At daybreak, the fight to deepen the foothold in France would resume with grim determination.

On D-Day itself, the Allied tactical air forces had smothered German movement, isolating the battlefield and eliminating any possibility of the enemy bringing up men, guns, or tanks for a counterattack in strength. On D-Plus-One, June 7, the German army would strive to punch armored spearheads into the beachheads before the Allies could firmly establish themselves. To preempt this move, the Hell Hawks would join the other Ninth Air Force fighter-bomber units in extending their aerial umbrella, shutting out the Luftwaffe and delivering an avalanche of bombs and machine-gun fire on German countermoves.

Once again, pilots and ground crews lucky enough to sleep were awakened at 3:00 a.m. On the second of the group's "maximum effort" missions for the day, Lt. Col. Robert Coffey led fifteen Thunderbolts aloft from Beaulieu, just after 6:00 p.m. His 388th Squadron pilots, call sign ELWOOD, each lugged a pair of underwing thousand-pound bombs, targeted for the local transportation network and any enemy ground forces spotted. The bomb line—the boundary marked on their maps outside the Allied front lines, beyond which the P-47s could attack anything that moved—was two to five miles inland.

Coffey, the all-business fighter leader, led his Thunderbolts northeast over the main road between Bayeux and St.-Lô, the latter a vital road hub twenty-five miles south of Utah Beach. Peeling off into their dives from above ten thousand feet against the railroad bridge at La Molay, the pilots left the span in ruins and then shattered the highway bridge southwest of Bayeux. Free of the weight of their heavy bombs, Coffey's men swept low to shoot up a horse-drawn troop column and demolished nine armored cars in a hailstorm of .50-caliber slugs. Hedgehopping across Normandy, he and the rest of the Hell Hawks meant to destroy any traffic on the roads, freezing enemy reinforcements in place.

Major Donald E. Hillman led the 386th Fighter Squadron off from Beaulieu an hour behind Coffey's men. The Jug pilots noted with awe the invasion fleet lying offshore as they circled over St.-Lô. Lining up in a shallow dive from one thousand feet, the squadron put its TNT-filled thousand-pounders into the railroad near La Molay and wrecked the right-of-way. Catching more Wehrmacht traffic in the open, the squadron strafed with their heavy Brownings a dozen trucks and a motorcycle, then torched a gas truck and four railroad tank cars.

The Germans could scarcely move in the open without being attacked. General Fritz Bayerlein, commander of 12th SS Panzer Division, witnessed the aerial scourging his men endured at the hands of the *Jabos* (the Wehrmacht's evocative nickname for the fighter-bombers, short for *Jagdbomber*, or "hunting bomber"). He wrote of June 7: "By noon it was terrible; every vehicle was covered with tree branches and moved along hedges and the edges of woods. Road junctions were bombed and a bridge knocked out. By the end of the day I had lost forty tank trucks, carrying fuel, and ninety other vehicles. Five of my tanks were knocked out, and eighty-four half-tracks, prime movers, and self-propelled guns." It galled this aggressive panzer leader that the Thunderbolts exacted their toll before he could even engage his real objective: the GIs still struggling to expand their penetration beyond Omaha and Utah. Throughout the day, Gen. Omar Bradley's troops could look up into a Norman sky saturated with the bristling fighter-bombers of the Ninth Air Force.

One of Bayerlein's tormentors was Capt. John R. Murphy, back over Normandy with sixteen planes of the 388th Fighter Squadron. On this fifth Hell Hawks mission of June 7, Murphy's four flights of four demolished a railroad culvert, bombed a supply dump in the Forêt des Biards, and destroyed half a dozen trucks parked near Airel. Near St.-Martin-des-Besaces, Murphy ordered a dive-bombing attack on a railroad bridge, and the Hell Hawks bored in from 1,500 feet, lobbing their thousand-pound bombs at the span. The heavy bombs were timed to detonate eight to eleven seconds after impact, giving the pilots a chance to get clear, but as on D-Day, the delay fuses were tragically unreliable. First Lieutenant Edsel J. McKnight from Saratoga Springs, New York, was just beginning his pullout from his shallow dive when one of the bombs, just below him, exploded on impact. The blast caught McKnight's Thunderbolt and sent it hurtling out of control and into the ground, killing him instantly. He was the third Hell Hawk in two days to die in such a premature detonation. For the low-flying Jug pilots, there was no margin for error, human or mechanical.

On a sixth mission just after noon, Capt. William D. Ritchie led the 386th Squadron against the railroad bridge at St.-Sauveur-Lendelin. This time the Hell Hawks ran a gauntlet of German flak to deliver their ordnance.

The principal threat to the P-47 at low altitudes was the Wehrmacht's Flakvierling 38, a mobile cluster of four 20mm antiaircraft cannon. This ubiquitous "quad-20" weapon could hurl eight hundred explosive shells per minute to a height of over 7,200 feet. The 20mm rounds exploded on contact; if they missed, the shells were timed to detonate at altitude to prevent them from falling on the heads of friendly troops. A stream of these shells produced a rapidly blooming cloud of white smoke, what Jug pilots sometimes reported as a "wall of flak" over a target. Defending a fixed installation like a railroad bridge, the German gunners could throw a blizzard of fire into the path of Ritchie's squadron as they jinked their way down toward the target.

The Hell Hawks pressed through the tracers and dive-bombed accurately, bracketing the bridge and the tracks and sending great gouts of earth, shattered ties, and twisted rails into the air. But the flak gunners rapidly found the range. First Lieutenant Harold M. Jones's Thunderbolt was hit first, then, quickly, the P-47 flown by 2nd Lt. Coburn G. Arledge. The latter briefly radioed that Jones was hit and bailing out about a half mile north of the town, but no one else in the flight saw or heard from the two pilots again. The two Hell Hawks had vanished, and amid the vicious flak, Ritchie's squadron didn't have the luxury of searching for them. Not until American forces took the area was Jones' temporary grave located and his body recovered. Arledge wound up a German prisoner.

Near St.-Lô, the Jugs caught and wrecked more than a dozen trucks and shot up three trains in the marshalling yard of the crossroads town, soon to become the bloody focus of the fight to expand the Allied beachhead. Second Lieutenant John B. Fitzsimmonds rolled in on a group of German soldiers pinning down a platoon of American GIs; he dropped so low during his strafing run that he blasted his Thunderbolt straight through the crowns of some trees. Both his propeller and wing leading edges were heavily damaged, and he limped back to Beaulieu, his battered air scoop sporting scraps of pine boughs and needles.

Fitzsimmonds' near-fatal tree trimming didn't deter low-flying 2nd Lt. George T. Wark, who burst through another line of trees near Isigny. Wark was unhurt, but his P-47 was so badly crippled that he bellied in a mile west of the town, almost on top of the troops he'd been strafing. His element leader, 1st Lt. Herndon F. Williams, circled back in *Willie's Wagon* and strafed German gunners who were zeroing in on Lieutenant Wark's downed Thunderbolt. Williams' eight fifties silenced the enemy long enough to enable Wark to scramble to cover in the neighboring woodlot.

For covering Wark's escape, Williams earned the Distinguished Flying Cross. His citation noted that "although his own plane sustained serious damage from antiaircraft and small arms, Captain Williams* . . . circled his fallen comrade's plane, and by silencing machine gun nests and holding enemy ground troops at bay he enabled the pilot to escape into nearby woods." Despite Williams's efforts, the Germans quickly scooped up Lieutenant Wark, who remained a prisoner of war until the fighting ended in May 1945.

St.-Lô was a dangerous neighborhood for Captain Ritchie's 386th. Two miles north of town, 2nd Lt. Charles S. Voight Jr.'s plane caught fire while strafing; no

---

* Williams had been promoted by the time the citation was issued.

one saw him bail out of the flaming Thunderbolt. But Voight did jump, narrowly escaping into the hands of the underground and hiding with civilians huddled in the cellars of bombed-out Caen until the British liberated the town in early July. After Ritchie's squadron landed back at Beaulieu, the ground crews scanned the skies for more than thirty minutes, hoping that at least one of the four missing pilots would straggle in. Four Hell Hawks were gone.

None of the squadrons was spared on that June 7. Lieutenant Colonel Bob Coffey was back in the air with sixteen planes of the 387th just before 2:00 p.m. Ranging between Utah and Omaha Beaches on the west and Caen in front of the British sector, Coffey's planes made short work of a flak barge on the coast, bombed tracks and a marshalling yard, and caught and strafed ten half-tracks along a Norman road. Diving on this column, B Flight's leader, 2nd Lt. Mahlon T. Stelle, took several damaging hits. Stelle, from Burlington, Iowa, had been with the Hell Hawks since their inception at Richmond Army Air Base, Virginia, in May of the previous year. After nearly six months of combat, he was a popular leader with the pilots. They watched helplessly as Stelle's stricken Thunderbolt plunged into the ground and exploded, ten miles southwest of Villers-Bocage. Stelle was the third Hell Hawk to die that day.

Yet another 387th pilot ran into trouble on the sweep. Second Lieutenant Joseph R. "Dick" Miller, twenty-two, had just strafed a column of German tanks and scout cars when ground fire caused the propeller of his P-47 to overspeed, a "runaway." With no hope of making it back to England, the lieutenant picked a spot near the coast that he hoped was inside the shallow American perimeter. Miller said he put down his P-47D "two hedgerows back from the beach."

His plane that day, named *Turnip Termite*, was a "razorback," an earlier version of the P-47D with the canopy blended smoothly rearward into the tall, high-profile fuselage. (Later Thunderbolts had a bubble canopy and a cut down aft fuselage, giving greater rearward visibility.) Miller, in fact, had crash-landed the plane usually flown by Capt. Arlo Henry. "Henry was a longtime Hell Hawk and one of the 'darlings' of the group," said Miller. "I think he never forgave me—a second lieutenant—for getting his 'personal' airplane shot down."

Climbing from the cockpit, he made contact with men of the 834th Engineer Aviation Battalion, who had been clearing a minefield atop the bluffs commanding Omaha Beach. Miller's skidding plane had swept more than a hundred yards clear of mines, and the appreciative engineers gave him some practical advice: "I grabbed my gear, backtracked as directed along the furrow left by my P-47, and they hustled me down to a foxhole overlooking the beach," he recalled. The young Hell Hawk was the first American pilot to land safely on liberated French soil.

Amid the tumult of beach traffic, with Allied naval gunfire ripping overhead, fighters rumbling into Normandy, and the sounds of battle just inland, Miller spent a memorable afternoon on shell-torn Omaha. The chaos left by the previous day's landing was still in evidence. "I wound up with a couple of navy signal guys working with the beachmaster, who was the busiest guy on that beach," said Miller.

By the time Miller returned to Beaulieu, more than two weeks later, Captain Henry had traded up to a new Thunderbolt, which, Miller thought, mollified his superior somewhat. Months later, in one of the war's strange coincidences, Arlo Henry's replacement, *Turnip Termite II*, was patched up in France using cowling parts salvaged from the original *Termite*, the very same P-47 Miller had skidded in above the beach.

☆

The Hell Hawks flew twelve missions over Normandy on D-Plus-One, with many of the pilots logging two or three sorties each. Late in the day, the Luftwaffe put in one of its rare appearances when seven Messerschmitt Bf 109s jumped the 387th Squadron as they worked over German road traffic.

One of the 387th pilots was 1st Lt. Russell E. Gardner, one of the founding Hell Hawks members who had trained in Richmond. "Like all fighter pilots, we thought we were good," said Gardner of his group, "but we didn't know beans." Gardner was the pilot of one of eight P-47s up that evening, led by Maj. (later Lt. Col.) Louis T. Houck. "We had been bombing and strafing targets of opportunity when I looked back and saw cannon winking behind me," Gardner said. Seven Bf 109s from the third squadron of JG (*Jagdgeschwader*, or "Fighter Wing") 3 streaked into the 387th, guns blazing. "I headed for the ground at full throttle," said Gardner, "yelling for Houck to come help me." Houck calmly told the twenty-two-year-old to "say your position."

"How the hell should *I* know where I am?!" shouted Gardner, who was flat-out on the deck, so low that he could see the bullets from the pursuing 109s kicking up dust on the ground ahead. The native of Stoneham, Massachussets, raced for the cover provided by the guns of the fleet offshore.

"I got going west to the beaches, and pulled up over the barrage balloons," said Gardner. His P-47 was hurt badly. A hydraulic line in the cockpit had been severed, and by the time he nursed the plane back to Beaulieu, his flight coveralls were drenched with the oily red fluid. Gardner got the wheels down and managed to get his Jug stopped without his brakes; he ran out of gas at the end of the runway.

It was well after 11:00 p.m. when the wheels of the group's last Thunderbolt touched down, with ground crews hustling in another all-night effort to ready them for the first dawn launch.

☆

The seventh of June had been a day of crisis for the Allied invasion, as the Wehrmacht desperately threw its armored reserves at the dirty, tired invaders seeking to widen their shallow foothold. Something of the urgency of the Hell Hawks' work came through in a message next morning from Maj. Gen. Lewis H. Brereton, Ninth Air Force commander:

> The situation on Omaha Beach, which was critical to the point of catastrophe yesterday, has materially improved. The rehabilitation of Omaha Beach was due [according to Field Marshal Bernard Law Montgomery, who had overall command of both the British and American landings] almost entirely to the continuing close support given by three fighter-bomber groups of IX Tactical Air Command: Lt. Col. Harold M. Holt's 366th, Col. Gil Meyers' 368th, and Col. Lance Call's 365th. [They] maintained continuous armed reconnaissance over the beach until dark yesterday with the specific mission of attacking enemy activity, particularly artillery, wherever seen. . . . The operation was long, slow, and exceedingly hazardous due to flak, and we incurred heavy losses.
>
> I sent the following commendation to General [Elwood R. "Pete"] Quesada: "On June 7, groups of your command furnished close and continuous support to the Omaha beachhead area. The situation was critical. The excellent attacks and continuous support by you restored a delicate situation."

Quesada added his own endorsement: "It is possible, if not probable, that your efforts were in a large part responsible for the attack on Omaha Beach continuing. History will show that you saved the day."

For their role in turning back German counterattacks on June 7, the Hell Hawks had paid a heavy price. Four pilots were killed in action, and three were missing or captured. Seven Thunderbolts were downed by flak, and an additional seven planes that did make it back to Beaulieu were badly damaged. If that rate of loss continued, the Hell Hawks would be out of business—combat ineffective—inside of ten days.

☆

The Luftwaffe tried again on June 8 to break the Allies' grip on air supremacy. Thirty-six Hell Hawks were cruising near Caen, just beyond the British front lines, when they spotted ten Messerschmitt Bf 109s. First Lieutenant Robert E. Young, from Winston-Salem, North Carolina, chased one enemy fighter in a dodging, turning fight down through several thin cloud layers, finally raking the 109 with .50-caliber fire from tail to cockpit. Young broke off the pursuit at two thousand feet in the face of intense flak, but the 109, its pilot wounded or dead, continued its steep dive toward the hedgerows. First Lieutenant Herndon Williams peeled off after another 109, and leading the Messerschmitt in its right-hand turn, scored heavily on his cockpit and engine. Whipping through successive cloud layers, Williams kept closing through a series of tight turns and climbs, registering strikes all over the Messerschmitt's nose. At two thousand feet the German bailed out of his stricken plane: two quick kills for the 365th.

The group's third mission of the day brought intense air-to-ground action forward of the beaches as the Wehrmacht attempted to stall the Allied advance inland. Late in the afternoon, Capt. Edward F. Boles, from Mineola, New York, led thirty-six Thunderbolts over Aunay-sur-Odon, southwest of Caen, and spotted more than forty enemy vehicles in an assembly area. Boles and his pilots worked over the target with repeated strafing passes, blowing up ten trucks and cutting down dozens of German soldiers despite a storm of 20mm flak and small-arms fire. Leaving a pillar of greasy black smoke spiraling up from the burning trucks, the group then caught a couple of half-tracks and two weapons carriers on the road, wrecking all four as each fighter pumped nearly fifty slugs per second into their targets.

John Malack, serving with the 899th Tank Destroyer Battalion, attached to the 9th Infantry Division, reported an incident when his outfit ran into trouble a few days after D-Day near Carentan, France:

> We received word that a couple of panzer units were headed our way. In fact, we could see them coming in the distance. The

Germans still had a few opportunities to throw us back into the English Channel with a little luck. We had some tank destroyers in the area but no heavy armor. I think at this point the only thing that was saving us was our air cover.

We were getting scared and nervous. Suddenly we heard the distinct sound of those P-47 engines. We picked up radio transmissions from the pilots telling us to stand firm and that they saw the targets. There were twelve of them in formation, and they began the deadliest strafing attack I ever saw in the war. The first plane would strafe, and if he saw a good target he'd let loose a 500-pound bomb. The second plane was coming right behind, and the third, and the fourth, and so on. By the time the twelfth plane finished, the first one was starting over again.

This went on for about twenty minutes. We could hear the concussion when the 500-pound bombs hit. They would actually go into the ground about five feet and then explode. We watched two tanks get flipped over when one of the pilots landed one square in the middle. They were very close to us. In fact the shell casings from the .50-calibers were landing in our area. We could hear the Germans firing on them, but not one of the planes ever got hit.

And then everything stopped. Everything became quiet, almost too quiet. After about a half hour of waiting, we started to approach the area with a lot of caution. The P-47s [had] plastered the whole area. I don't think any Germans survived, unless a few scrambled to retreat. But they sure had a lot of equipment there. Tanks, half-tracks, 170mm cannons scattered everywhere, all destroyed. Many of the Germans were not even hit. The concussion from the bombs was enough to kill many of them.

We would have never been able to repel such an attack, at least not at that time. I could go on and on about this great plane . . . .

The weight of fighter-bomber attacks struck fear into every German infantryman or panzer crew fighting in Normandy. One wrote in a letter to his parents, "The American fliers are chasing us like hares," and the commander of the Panzer Lehr Division later described the road from Vire to Villers-Bocage as a *Jabo Rennstrecke*—a "fighter-bomber racecourse." The cry of "Achtung, *Jabos!*" came with deadly frequency in the Wehrmacht fighting positions and marching columns in Normandy.

☆

Only the notoriously bad late-spring weather brought relief to the Germans. Low ceilings and poor visibility on June 9 grounded the Hell Hawks, and the Wehrmacht quickly took advantage of the gloomy skies. Back at Beaulieu, the exhausted ground crews knew the GIs were vulnerable without air cover, and they worked hard, hoping their Thunderbolts could get airborne if the weather broke, however briefly.

As they worked, two replacement P-47s approached Beaulieu simultaneously from the south and west. In the mist and haze, neither pilot, landing straight-in on intersecting runways, saw the other. Tragedy ensued: the heavy fighters collided at the center of the field. The whirling thirteen-foot prop of one P-47 hacked the other from cockpit to tail, hurling the pilot of the mangled plane onto the runway in plain view of dozens of stunned Hell Hawks. What had once been a vital young man stood up, ran a few steps, then crumpled in a bloody heap. His plane, prop still spinning, careened around a locked wheel brake until one of the ground crew ended the sad incident with a mercifully aimed machine-gun burst.

Combat resumed with the good weather on June 10, a day typical of the months of hard fighting to come. The group downed six enemy aircraft over Normandy: Capt. William H. Cornell downed a Bf 109, 1st Lt. Charles Ready Jr. got another, and 1st Lt. Charles L. Katzenmeyer knocked down a Messerschmitt over Le Havre.

In a wild melee over Caen, Capt. John R. Murphy, 2nd Lt. Raymond B. Porter, and 2nd Lt. Roscoe L. "Ross" Crownrich all scored, sending three Focke-Wulf 190s down in flames. The Fw 190, with a powerful BMW radial engine and heavy machine gun and cannon armament, was the Luftwaffe's most effective frontline fighter; in capable hands a match for the Thunderbolt. Luftwaffe pilots called their workhorse the Würger, or Butcher Bird. The Hell Hawks respected its maneuverability and speed in a dogfight.

"We had our whole squadron up that day," said Crownrich, a five-foot-six pilot in the 388th who'd grown up in Fort Worth, Texas. "We had put one flight at twenty thousand feet, another at twelve thousand feet, and one flight down low." Crownrich was in the low flight, circling beneath the overcast, when he heard radio traffic that the Germans were bouncing the top cover. "Debris started pouring down around us—drop tanks, pieces of aircraft. A few minutes after the high flight was attacked, the middle flight got bounced, too. We heard them shouting to each other," said Crownrich. Then came his flight's turn.

"Suddenly, right in front of me, here comes a Fw 190. He had been shooting at my flight leader, Capt. John R. Murphy." Crownrich got rid of his drop tanks and scrambled to clear Murphy's tail. "This 190 took a shot at me and went right by me; I went after him. We tangled with each other so low we were almost in the trees. I tried to maneuver with him." The German slammed several shots into Crownrich's P-47 as the pair twisted and turned for advantage. "I finally got behind him, now, maybe four hundred or five hundred feet above the ground, which was as high as we ever got." In this kind of fight, the terrain was as dangerous an enemy as German gunfire.

"I fired," Crownrich said. "I may have held the trigger down too long—a common thing—because I later learned my barrels were burned out. I hit him—I saw pieces fly off that Fw 190." The German pulled up, jettisoned his canopy, and bailed out. "His airplane went one way and he went another. I was surprised to see his chute open at such a low level."

During Cornell's tangle with the Bf 109s over Le Havre, 1st Lt. Donald R. Swinburne, one of the original 386th Squadron pilots, took evasive action and became separated from his flight. Swinburne radioed he was okay, but he and his Thunderbolt were never seen again. The same fate befell 1st Lt. Raymond N. Moraga, frequently Colonel Call's wingman, and known as "Eagle Eye" for his skill at spotting targets on the ground. Last seen entering a cloud bank while maneuvering against the Focke-Wulfs, Moraga vanished. He was listed as killed in action, but the passage of sixty-three years has produced no further clue as to his fate.

☆

Combat flying continued even as the Hell Hawks prepared to join the GIs across the Channel. Still operating from Beaulieu on June 25, the Hell Hawks launched just after 9:00 a.m. on an armed reconnaissance (AR) mission between Chartres and Dreux. Twelve Thunderbolts of the 386th Squadron carried two five-hundred-pound bombs each, while four planes with their fifties ready acted as "top cover" for protection against Luftwaffe fighters. From eleven thousand feet, Capt. William D. Ritchie's four flights (of four aircraft each) spotted about fifteen mottled grey Bf 109s with yellow wingtips heading east, three thousand feet below them. Ritchie ordered an attack.

His wingman, 2nd Lt. John B. Tweeten, chased a Bf 109 off the tail of another P-47 and ripped a burst into the German's engine and cockpit. The 109's propeller froze, and the aircraft spiraled downward to hit the ground in a fireball. White Flight's leader, Capt. George W. Porter, dove head-on into a gaggle of eight 109s, closed to within 250 yards of one Messerschmitt, and put two bursts into the cockpit area and engine. The fighter's Daimler-Benz engine spurted smoke, and the pilot, apparently hit by Porter's rain of .50-caliber bullets, did nothing to arrest the shallow dive. The fighter hit the ground near a small stream outside Évreux. Porter's wingman, 2nd Lt. Charles G. Young Jr., also dove on the enemy and got in a few short bursts at a 109 before the enemy pilot frantically rolled over into a gut-wrenching split-S. Young followed, ramming in aileron and yanking the stick back to his belly, the French countryside rapidly filling the windscreen. Blacking out in the high-g pullout, Young barely missed the treetops. His quarry wasn't so fortunate: 1st Lt. Lloyd Hutchins saw the diving Messerschmitt, attempting to pull out, slam into the ground.

In the ensuing minutes, 386th pilots shot half a dozen Messerschmitts out of the sky, but 2nd Lt. Marcel DuPont was separated from the squadron in the melee. The young Concord, New Hampshire, flier radioed that he was all right, but he and his P-47 were never seen again, probably jumped by a roving German.

The 387th Fighter Squadron, led by Maj. Donald E. Hillman, the deputy group commander, soon joined the action. Hillman's flight of Thunderbolts spotted two Messerschmitts on the deck near Chartres. The major, flying an olive drab P-47 razorback named *Ol' Jasper*, dove in pursuit. Hillman, another veteran pilot who'd been with the Hell Hawks since Richmond, was tall, steely, and viewed by some as aloof. He pulled out of his dive about five hundred yards behind a silver long-nosed Fw 190D, a very fast version of the workhorse Luftwaffe fighter which, with its liquid-cooled Junkers Jumo twelve-cylinder engine, could reach 430 miles per hour. The Hell Hawk snapped off several bursts at the German, but even with water injection and sixty inches of manifold pressure giving him 330 miles per hour, "it was obvious he was faster than I was," said Hillman.

The disappointed major was about to give up the chase when "someone called 'Keep your tail clear!' and I spotted three Bf 109s diving on me from my rear seven o'clock position."

Hillman racked *Ol' Jasper* around at full power into the three Messerschmitts. Soon, all four aircraft were locked in a tight Lufbery circle—each trying to draw a bead in a blood-draining turn. The lead 109 got in several bursts at Hillman, but no hits. Hillman, in turn, was closing steadily on the last of the German trio. The Messerschmitt was supposedly more maneuverable than the Thunderbolt, but the P-47's power and big wings produced surprising turn performance that doomed many an opponent. Hillman gained steadily and bored in on number three: "Why he [the last one] stayed in line I'll never know," said Hillman, but he finally got in a long burst that set the 109 on fire. As Hillman closed the range, still firing, the enemy pilot jettisoned his canopy to bail out, but from treetop level there was no chance. The German fighter smashed to earth, scattering burning fragments over the landscape.

He had the second 109 in range; Hillman snapped off short bursts as the pair howled over the Luftwaffe airfield at Chartres. In a three-minute-long turning chase, Hillman finally scored a fatal hit. The Messerschmitt smoked, dipped, and then dove abruptly into a clump of trees.

Several other Hell Hawks notched up victories during the morning's dogfight, some so low on fuel they had to recover at strip A-2 near Criqueville. The victors kept the intelligence officers at Beaulieu busy in the debrief long after their noon-hour return. Despite the loss of Lieutenant DuPont, the Hell Hawks had scored heavily: thirteen Luftwaffe fighters destroyed in the air, with one probable and seven more damaged. The Thunderbolt, eclipsed as an escort fighter by the P-51 Mustang, did more than hold its own with the Luftwaffe. The 365th also knocked out four other enemy aircraft on the ground and strafed and destroyed more than two dozen trucks and transports. The veterans marked June 25, 1944, as one of the most productive days in the group's distinguished history.

☆

The Hell Hawks, with the weight of their operations shifting to France, continued their daily, unrelenting air-to-ground campaign against the Wehrmacht. Major Arlo C. Henry and 1st Lt. Daniel Matusiewicz took off on one mission under an overcast so low that dive-bombing was impossible. Roaming low over hedgerow country, the pair spotted a large building at the edge of a prominent tract of forest. The major flipped on his gun switch and rolled in on the German-occupied compound. "In lieu of bombing, I told 'Matus' to close up and fire when I did," Henry said. "In the next five minutes we riddled every window and wall in that building. There was no flak, nor was there any activity on the ground. We finally completed what we considered target practice . . . and continued our armed reconnaissance . . . ." Next morning, group headquarters was surprised by a message from Maj. Gen. Terry Allen of the 104th Infantry Division, congratulating the Hell Hawks for their successful attack on the German headquarters. "Terrible Terry" reported that the enemy had abandoned the place in such haste that the Americans captured a number of vital plans and documents left behind.

For the Hell Hawks, Allen's message was rare and much-appreciated feedback, especially in light of the price they'd paid in June. Nineteen pilots from the 365th had been shot down—only three survived. The twenty-nine enemy planes destroyed seemed small compensation, even when adding the destruction they'd wrought on the increasingly desperate German army. But the Wehrmacht soldier knew all too well the toll taken by the Hell Hawks and the rest of the Ninth Air Force's fighter-bombers.

As Stephen Ambrose wrote in *Citizen Soldiers*, "from D-Day Plus One onward, whenever the weather was suitable for flying, the P-47s forced nighttime movement only on the Germans, at an incalculable cost to their logistical efficiency. . . . During the day, Germans caught in the open quickly paid. . . . 'The Jabos were a burden on our souls,' [German] Corp. Helmut Hesse said."

Ambrose continued: "German veterans still have awe in their voice . . . as they recall the terror of having [a Thunderbolt] come right at them, all guns blazing." Compounding the terror was the knowledge that their own air force was powerless to protect them. Said one prisoner, 'Ja, I saw the Luftwaffe. Seven of them, seven thousand Jabos.'"

Chapter Three

Who Were the Hell Hawks?

A FORTNIGHT AFTER D-DAY, as Allied armies battled to expand their foothold on Europe, Supreme Commander Gen. Dwight D. Eisenhower took his newly commissioned son John on a tour of the invasion beaches. Second Lieutenant John Eisenhower was astonished to see vehicles moving to the front, bumper-to-bumper, violating the textbook doctrine that called for dispersal to protect from air attack. "You would never get away with this if you didn't have air supremacy," John said to his father. The older Eisenhower retorted: "If I didn't have air supremacy, I wouldn't be here!"

Although the 365th Fighter Group didn't have Ike's "big picture," the young men of the Hell Hawks were part of the reason Ike *could* be there. For the pilots, the strategic overview didn't go much further than a bunk, a meal, a flight line, and a roundtrip in a P-47 Thunderbolt, with low-altitude fighting at the outward limit of the journey.

They didn't know what Eisenhower knew, but they were a part of a giant tactical air arm that provided Ike with indispensable cover while he moved his armies forward. Counting pilots, mechanics, armorers, cooks, drivers—everybody—the

Hell Hawks numbered about a thousand men: three squadrons, each with twenty-four P-47 Thunderbolts. But beyond their mere numbers, they were part of a much larger whole: The Ninth Air Force under Maj. Gen. Lewis H. Brereton consisted of 250,000 men with 3,500 warplanes in 1,500 units, including fighters, bombers, troop carriers, air defense, engineering, and service commands. The fighter component, IX Tactical Air Command under Maj. Gen. Elwood R. "Pete" Quesada, was responsible for eighteen fighter groups of P-38 Lightnings, P-51 Mustangs, and P-47 Thunderbolts, each the size of the Hell Hawks.

Quesada was a daring fighter pilot who would soon give Eisenhower a high-speed, low-level look at the Normandy fighting in a Mustang hastily modified with an extra seat. According to his biographer Thomas A. Hughes, Quesada's role in revolutionizing air-to-ground warfare in Europe was nicely summed up in a quote from another battle leader. "[Quesada] came into the war as a young and imaginative man unencumbered by the prejudices and theories of so many of his seniors on the employment of tactical air," said Gen. Omar Bradley. "To Quesada, the fighter was a little-known weapon with vast unexplored potentialities in support of ground troops. He conceived it his duty to learn what they were."

But Hughes and author Rebecca Grant also wrote that Quesada had a grating personality and was disliked, feared, and dubbed the "terrible-tempered Mr. Big." One pilot spoke of Quesada's "toothy grin, which always seemed to be contrived and phony."

What wasn't phony was Quesada's cutting brilliance. He imagined a world in which a foot soldier on the ground could talk on the radio to a fighter pilot in the air. He envisioned forward air control teams—airmen with cockpit experience—embedded with the GIs along the front lines to guide fighter-bombers to their targets. The Hollywood image of the fighter pilot had him fighting an air-to-air duel with the Red Baron up at thirty thousand feet. The Quesada image was a fighter pilot narrowly skimming the treetops, taking on the dug-in soldiers of the German Wehrmacht. The Eighth Air Force in England was going to fight an air-to-air war and produce aces and aerial victories. The Ninth Air Force on the European continent, with Quesada driving its tactics—his boss, Brereton, was largely a figurehead—was going to revolutionize air-to-ground fighting.

Quesada was the big boss to the 365th group's P-47 pilots, twenty-year-old lieutenants who would soon be waging their war not from the comfort of a base in England but from hastily constructed airstrips on the European continent. He was their boss, not their buddy. "Quesada didn't look me up to ask my opinion," one of those twenty-year-olds said later. The young men in Thunderbolt cockpits were rarely asked their opinions by anyone, not by Hell Hawks group commander Col. Lance Call, and not by their squadron commanders, Majors William D. Ritchie of the 386th Squadron, Louis T. Houck of the 387th, and John R. Murphy of the 388th. "Hitler and Roosevelt might have been wondering about my opinion," one of the lieutenants said. "As far as everybody else was concerned, my job was to listen to the briefing, know what kind of bombs we were carrying, and handle the stick and rudder."

So who were the Hell Hawks? Even the lowliest lieutenant of the lot had accomplished something at which tens of thousands had failed: he had completed flight training, had silver wings pinned on his chest, and was now officially qualified to pilot an aircraft. He had successfully made the transition to the mighty P-47 Thunderbolt, the "Jug," and survived to reach the combat theater. According to an official history of Air Training Command, fully 40 percent of student pilots were washed out without earning pilot's wings. Before reaching the war zone, fifteen thousand Americans died in aircraft crashes while training in the United States.

The most junior gold-bar lieutenant in the 365th Fighter Group had better eyesight, hand-eye coordination, and balance than 99 percent of humanity. They were perfect physical specimens, these young men who strapped into an eighteen-thousand-pound Thunderbolt, fired up a roaring, two-thousand-horsepower engine, and flew into battle lugging a veritable arsenal of bombs and ammunition. They had superb bodies and minds and the youthful confidence to believe they were unbeatable.

☆

They were inextricably linked, these Hell Hawks, to the P-47. To them, it was not only the most numerous fighter ever produced by American industry, but the best.

In the Republic P-47 Thunderbolt, American pilots had a rugged, reliable fighter, perfect for the mud and spartan repair facilities of their forward airfields. Its beefy construction and the efficient Republic design made it relatively simple to maintain under combat conditions.

Originally designed as a high-altitude interceptor, the P-47 first flew in May 1941. The blunt-nosed fuselage was married to a pair of graceful, semielliptical wings mounted with eight heavy .50-caliber machine guns. It derived its power from a 2,430-horsepower, eighteen-cylinder Pratt & Whitney R-2800 Double Wasp radial engine with a turbo-supercharger for high-altitude performance. With full tanks, ammunition, and two thousand-pound bombs, later models weighed in at a hefty 19,400 pounds, more than any other single-engine fighter of World War II.

The P-47D entered combat in March 1943. With Lockheed's P-38 Lightning needed in the Pacific and the superb North American P-51 Mustang still in development, the Thunderbolt filled the need for a long-range escort for the bomber offensive from England. Its big engine propelled the P-47 to a speed of 433 miles per hour at thirty thousand feet.

As the 1944 cross-Channel invasion approached, the Mustang arrived in the European Theater and proved both more agile and longer-legged than the fuel-thirsty Thunderbolt. The Ninth Air Force's Fighter Command, led by Quesada, needed a sturdy attack fighter to immobilize German reinforcements in Normandy and support the Allied ground forces after D-Day. The P-47's rugged design and powerful armament were perfect for those jobs.

Unlike the inline power plants of the Mustang and Lightning, the P-47's R-2800 radial engine was air-cooled. It dispensed with a radiator and liquid coolant system, which were so vulnerable to a lucky enemy shot. The Thunderbolt's Double Wasp could absorb shocking punishment and still keep running: more than one fighter returned to base with a cylinder blown away, its connecting rod protruding from the shattered crankcase.

The big engine up front, coupled with armor plate fore and aft of the cockpit, gave the pilot extensive protection from enemy fighters and ground fire. The turbocharger's ductwork, running the length of the lower fuselage, protected a pilot's legs from the jarring crunch of an emergency belly landing. Flight Chief Alvin E. Bradley of the 386th Fighter Squadron is adamant about the superiority of the aircraft he once maintained: "It was the safest, toughest plane to bring somebody back after it was damaged."

☆

Yet those who flew the P-47 believed their plane never received its due, nor did the war they fought receive the recognition it warranted. It was the war nobody told you about—the prolonged campaign in Europe in which pilots, maintainers, and support troops lived and fought under conditions that were only a little better than the life of a frontline infantryman.

Before it began, before they witnessed the spectacular armada assembled off Normandy, or slogged through the Battle of the Bulge, or helped force Germany's surrender, they had their eyes on the skies. "Ever since I was a little kid I dreamed of someday being a pilot," said Ed Lopez, who grew up in Los Angeles. "My brother Hugo and I would always wear our simulated leather flying helmets with goggles and chin straps. I suppose we looked kind of stupid, but we had a ball pretending we were pilots. I even remember the program we listened to on the radio. It was about a young pilot named Jimmy Allen. We never missed an episode."

Ed Lopez could probably have been Bob Hagan, or James "Mac" McWhorter, or Jim Wells, or any of the other Hell Hawk pilots, because they all had the same infatuation, and their descriptions of it often sounded identical.

Or he could have been William L. "Bill" Ward in Arkansas City, Kansas. "I went to Pershing Elementary School and had a fifth-grade teacher named Delbert Jones," said Ward. "In class one day, she canvassed the class: 'What do you want to be when you grow up?' The girls wanted to be nurses. The boys wanted to be firemen. Not me. Not for a moment. I never had any doubt. I admired airplanes, looked at pictures of them, and grabbed every aviation book I could find, although I didn't build models. I'll bet you a dollar to a doughnut that I'm the only one in that class who got to do what he wanted to do."

Or he could have been John H. Fetzer Jr., who grew up in Baton Rouge, Louisiana. With his twin brother, Cora, Fetzer made model airplanes and dreamed of flying. "I wanted to be the best," Fetzer said. "I wanted to make [ace Eddie] Rickenbacker take a back seat to me. We built beautiful models of real planes, like the famous German Fokker D.7 of the First World War. Later on, we learned to fly under the civilian pilot training program, or CPT, that the government sponsored before the war." The boys' mother had died giving birth to them. Fetzer's brother would die in a crash in navigator school at Ellington Field, Texas, in 1944—one of the fifteen thousand. "We didn't have instant communication then. I didn't even learn about it until a week later." Fighting in Europe with the Hell Hawks by then, Fetzer would decline an offer to travel home for Cora's funeral.

Though he'd grown up in Eureka, Kansas, on the eve of the U.S. entry into the war, Robert L. Saferite was in Burbank, California, working in the Lockheed factory as a riveter on P-38 Lightnings. "I had been building model airplanes since I was knee-high to a grasshopper," said Saferite. "I took my first airplane ride and my first flying lesson at Van Nuys. I soloed in a Piper Cub in 1941."

☆

For all of them, the journey to the P-47 cockpit began with the news that their nation had been attacked. Bill Ward was just out of high school working in a wholesale grocery company in Arkansas City. Someone told him that there was "big news" on the radio. "I ran across the street to a friend's restaurant. The owner, Mr. Resor, was standing next to his radio with his daughters. He was trembling. He was a World War I veteran and he said, 'Oh, my God! We're in it again!'" Ward quickly grasped the general idea, but not the details. "I knew it was a place in Hawaii but that's all I knew. I'm not sure I knew Hawaii was a possession of the United States."

John Fetzer was at Louisiana State University in Baton Rouge, an athlete and a student planner with the football team. He had just come from the dining room eating the midday meal with fellow college athletes. "I had an old radio," Fetzer said. "I turned that thing on. I heard them talking about an air attack on Pearl Harbor and I knew exactly what it meant."

Eugene A. "Gene" Wink, born and raised on the Mississippi Gulf Coast, was a cadet at the United States Military Academy at West Point, New York. "The excitement generated by the unprecedented sneak attack on Pearl Harbor caused the whole cadet corps to want to 'go get 'em' right away," Wink said. "We were told to bide our time, although they did accelerate our class." Like so many others, Wink had a love of flying. But in his case, his first priority was love of the military; he'd been a very young prewar National Guardsman before entering West Point in the summer of 1939. He didn't realize he had the flying bug, too, until he graduated with the Class of 1943 and began pilot training. "From the very first day, I fell in love with aviation."

Donald E. Hillman was already in uniform, on his way toward becoming one of the Hell Hawks' senior leaders. When Pearl Harbor was attacked, he was at Craig Field in Selma, Alabama, training pursuit pilots. "When I heard the news, I was eager to go overseas and get into the war," Hillman said.

Bob Saferite was off from his job at Lockheed on that Sunday afternoon in California. He and a friend were driving the friend's 1938 Ford south toward San Diego. "I heard about it on his car radio," said Saferite. He knew that Pearl Harbor was a U.S. naval base and that much of the U.S. fleet was there. "We saw a couple of sailors hitchhiking. We picked them up and took them to their base. Everybody in the military was supposed to get to their base. We returned to Los Angeles and there was a blackout that night because the authorities feared there might be Japanese battleships off the California coast." Within days, Saferite headed back to Eureka to sign up for the army.

Ed Lopez was still thinking of joining, "At this time [in 1941, just after Pearl Harbor]," Lopez wrote, "the German air force was making big headlines with their Stuka dive bomber and the Japanese with the Zero fighter. The air war was hot and heavy, especially over Britain. I was wondering when our air force would get into the battle. I did notice as I was going out to Redondo Beach, California, out in the meadow near the highway, there was a P-38 Lightning parked at the end of a grass strip. The pilot was evidently on alert: he had a small tent nearby to sleep in. In case of an air attack, his primary concern was the defense of Los Angeles."

Those who weren't already pilots (Hillman) or weren't already committed to the military (Wink) signed up in droves. One pilot already in uniform said, "Now we can throw away our neckties and concentrate on business." The Army Air Forces never completely discarded the necktie, but it did get rid of an insurmountable barrier to thousands of young men who wanted to fly. For a brief, shining moment it tossed out the requirement for a minimum of two years of college study as a prerequisite for pilot training.

Not every potential flier had the same motive. In his book *Masters of the Air,* Donald L. Miller described a mix of circumstances:

> Men volunteered for an endless range of reasons, from unsullied patriotism to a desire to escape the infantry. Young men who were still jobless and psychologically scarred by the Great Depression were lured by the prospect of steady work at decent pay. Freshly minted second lieutenants made $1,800 a year, plus a 50 percent supplement for flight pay, seemingly a pittance, but not at a time when the base salary of a four-star general was $8,000. But a remarkably large number of volunteers were attracted to the Air Force as a result of a youthful romance with flying. Growing up in the Golden Age of Aviation, they had whittled balsa wood into airplane models, followed the storied career of Charles Lindbergh, and thrilled to the aerial exploits of barnstorming stunt pilots who showed up at their local airports.

Between 1941 and 1943, there was a seemingly limitless need for new pilots. Despite their lack of a college education, by passing written and physical tests and persisting when recruiters sought to shunt them elsewhere, the young men who would be future Hell Hawks became aviation cadets. They now were addressed as "mister" and treated with a modicum of deference, even while being subjected to the rigors of military life. Miller described what happened to them before they ever strapped into a cockpit:

> For candidates who wanted to become flying officers, training usually began at an Air Force classification center staffed by Army doctors and psychologists. Its purpose was to determine if a man should be allowed in a combat plane and in what capacity. Recruits were given a battery of tests to check eyesight, mental aptitude, motor coordination, and psychological stability. Their scores, together with their personal preferences and the Air Force's needs, determined the training school to which they were assigned. . . .
> The tests were demanding. More than half the men failed. Most of these unfairly labeled "washouts" either volunteered for aerial gunner training or were shipped off to the infantry.

If they passed this first hurdle, and survived a brief introduction to aeronautics, they were off to primary flight training at a contract school operated by private companies for the army: the well-known Embry-Riddle, for example. The first plane the students saw in flight training was usually the Stearman PT-17, a fabric-covered, open-cockpit biplane that was deemed highly suitable for teaching basic aeronautics even though it was so loud that instructor and student communicated only before taking off and after landing.

If they could handle the PT-17, students advanced to basic flight training in the Vultee BT-13 Valiant (or "Vibrator," as they called it) and advanced flight training in the AT-6 Texan, both at army bases with army instructors. Until May 1, 1944, they might also be introduced to a fighter cockpit before completing training. After that date, the men were first recognized as pilots and then went into fighters.

After pinning on silver wings and second-lieutenant's bars, new pilots heading for the Hell Hawks had to undergo transition training to the P-47 Thunderbolt. They completed this form of graduate school—their last assignment before joining the Hell Hawks—at many locations around the United States. Wherever it happened, it was the way Eugene A. Wink (ahead of the newest men and already a first lieutenant) described it:

My first job was to learn to fly the airplane itself. This demanded much time devoted to the study of the airplane, taking exams on the systems, and taking and passing a blindfold check on the cockpit. Flying the airplane was relatively simple because it was so well-designed and put together. It was a gorgeous bird, and it made everything else I had flown look pale by comparison. Flying a P-47 as compared to the P-40 Warhawk [used in pilot training] was like driving a Rolls-Royce compared to a Model-T Ford. The R-2800 Pratt & Whitney engine purred like a kitten while putting out two thousand horses of power. The prop had a distinctive whistle and whine that I can hear to this day.

To be able to do something you had wanted to do all your life and be paid for doing it is something I would call a little piece of heaven. I must admit the job was time-consuming, but what a way to spend your time. We were told to keep the planes flying. The idea was to build up our time as much as possible and learn as much about the characteristics of the birds as possible. As I continued to build up my time in the Thunderbolt, I sought other pilots who wanted to practice combat tactics. We put the airplane in as many unusual situations as possible in order to learn its limitations as well as our own. Some of the maneuvers we practiced were spins, rolls, loops, uncoordinated turns, stalls, and high-speed stalls.

Upon completing transition to the P-47, the new fighter pilot proceeded next to his service assignment. Most went to a combat group. Dozens went to the Hell Hawks. For those who were present at the creation of the 365th Fighter Group, that entailed a journey to Richmond, Virginia.

The story of the 365th Fighter Group began in that city on May 15, 1943, when men began to assemble under an April 27 order from the War Department that established the unit, whose men came to call themselves the "Hell Hawks." The order also established the group's three fighter squadrons, the 386th, 387th, and 388th.

Other combat groups were forming all over the country as Americans built up their war machine, bolstered by the production prowess of the U.S. industrial heartland. The Army Air Forces (AAF), began the war with 152,115 men in uniform and would peak at 2,372,292 in 1944. At the start of the war, the AAF had ten effective combat groups; at the end, it had 218. The AAF would lose 53,007 men killed in action during the war, more than the total of 51,983 for the entire U.S. Navy and Marine Corps combined (34,607 and 17,376, respectively).

A second document, the 365th Fighter Group activation order, was dated May 15, 1943, and signed by 2nd Lt. Francis C. Robertson, who was acting group commander for a matter of days. The Hell Hawks would fight across Europe from well before D-Day until the surrender of Germany, and the saga of this particular combat group began when 2nd Lt. William L. Ward walked into the orderly room at headquarters in Richmond in May and began filling out papers to join the unit. He had come a long way from Arkansas. He had gone through pilot training in what the AAF called flying class 43-E, piloting biplanes at an airfield in Florida and advanced trainers at another base. He had transitioned to the high-performance P-47 Thunderbolt. Now, he would join an aerial band of brothers who would rehearse the craft of aerial warfare together before setting forth to fly and fight.

First, though, Ward was asked to which of the Hell Hawks' three squadrons he wanted to be assigned. "Let me see the names of the pilots in the different squadrons," said Ward. "I may know some of them."

"Can't do it, Lieutenant," replied the clerk. "There ain't no names." Ward learned that he was the very first pilot to report for duty with the new 365th Fighter Group.

Soon afterward, other pilots began trickling in. Second Lieutenant Neal E. Worley was from Kansas and was one of the first pilots on board. Others, too, were present at the creation, if slightly behind Ward in reporting for duty. Major Lance Call, soon to be a colonel, arrived in Richmond. Call was an old-timer: fifteen years earlier he had learned to fly as an enlisted navy pilot.

By the time the 365th group was formed, 1st Lt. Eugene A. Wink had graduated from West Point (because of the urgency of war, the Class of 1943 was graduated in January), completed pilot training, and been to Richmond for transition into the P-47. "It was a privilege to be assigned to the large airfield just outside the historic city of Richmond, the capital of Virginia," said Wink. "Richmond Army Air [Base], formerly known as Byrd Field, was a large piece of real estate that could accommodate a lot of military activity. It was being used to train pilots to fly the P-47, a top-of-the-line fighter that was taking the battle to the Germans and Japanese."

After two moves within Virginia, the 365th Fighter Group was at full strength—about 850 men—when its men and planes arrived at Dover Army Air Field, Delaware, on August 11, 1943. Although the airfield had been activated two years earlier, Hell Hawks remember it as a new air base with minimal facilities, perhaps a few open-bay barracks, and not enough billeting for all of the men.

John Fetzer lived "in a private home in Dover" and trained with his fellow P-47 pilots. "The first thing we did was learn how to fly formation," Fetzer said. "Until you catch onto it, it's kind of hard. . . . Then we started doing simulated combat, dogfighting. At one time we did a mock attack on Philadelphia."

The Hell Hawks were the only fighter group ever to train at Dover, employed in later years as a transport base. "The base was so new they didn't have anything built up," Fetzer recalled. "We worked in a tent, and the bathroom was outdoors and covered with canvas for privacy. I don't remember any buildings."

The group's mechanic-turned-historian, Charles Johnson, wrote that training greatly accelerated at the Delaware base: "There were practice flights for formation flying; there were dive-bombing missions [*sic*] at the Millville, New Jersey, bombing range; there were night flights to familiarize the pilots with instrument flying; and through all this the ground crews were expected to keep the planes flying no matter what. Colonel Lance Call, the group commander, issued the edict that 'No matter what the extent of damage to an aircraft, it must be flying within twenty-four hours of the time that it was called out.'"

☆

In fact, the Millville range was out over the water. Not one of the men would drop a bomb until reaching the war zone. The website for the Millville Army Airfield Museum, in extreme southern New Jersey, says that after months of P-40 operations, "in February 1943, the Millville Army Air Base opened as a P-47 gunnery school for the Philadelphia Fighter Wing, and airplanes became a part of daily life in Cumberland County." The Hell Hawks trained there in aerial gunnery with the Thunderbolt's eight .50-caliber Browning M2, or "Ma Deuce" machine guns. Backed with about 350 rounds apiece, the eight fifties were able to deliver a withering barrage of thirteen pounds of bullets per second.

"We would depart from Dover and fly up to Millville to remain for a day or two," said Gene Wink. "We all had to qualify in gunnery. We flew out over the ocean and fired at a sleeve drawn by a tow plane. They determined whether you were getting any hits by painting the front of the bullet. After we landed, we could look at the colors [bordering the holes] on the target to learn who'd gotten the most hits. I remember Millville as being quite comfortable, and my recollection is that they assigned eight or so P-47 pilots at a time to go up there."

Some stayed at Millville "for ten days or two weeks," said Wink. "I was there for a week. In Millville we lived in open-bay barracks. But there was never a moment to relax."

The training at Millville involved an average of six and sometimes ten flying hours per day. It was an intense, frenetic life, and it was not without risk. On October 18, 1943, 2nd Lt. John D. Rumbaugh of the Hell Hawks' 388th Squadron was piloting the target-tow aircraft for a gunnery mission. He called the flight leader and said he had to make an emergency landing, but never related the nature of the problem. Rumbaugh proceeded to Atlantic City Municipal Airport and attempted to land with the target still trailing behind his aircraft. As he descended toward the runway, the target was ripped off on a playground across the stream of water adjoining the field. Just over the runway, Rumbaugh's plane turned to the right and started to pull up sharply. The aircraft stalled, plunged into the ground, and exploded.

The second Hell Hawk killed during intense Millville gunnery training was 2nd Lt. James F. Thompson. The losses were a reminder that flying was always unforgiving. In 1943 alone, there were twenty thousand "Class A" accidents (the most serious category) at stateside bases that killed 5,603 men. Rumbaugh and Thompson joined the tragic ranks of those who lost their lives training for a war they never reached.

☆

Training at Dover and Millville continued until November 18, 1943, when the 365th Fighter Group returned to Richmond. Now, the men began final preparations for war. Supply clerks issued steel-pot helmets, M1 carbines, and medical kits. They left their aircraft behind for other trainees; the group would re-equip overseas with new Thunderbolts delivered by convoy to England.

On December 3, the Hell Hawks traveled to Camp Kilmer, New Jersey, their port of embarkation. After ten days of medical examinations and paperwork, a train took the men to New York's North River Terminal, Pier 90, where the ocean liner *Queen Elizabeth* awaited them. On December 14, crammed with fifteen thousand soldiers, the *Queen* put to sea for the thirty-two-knot dash to the British Isles.

Enduring all the experiences that come with an overcrowded, winter crossing on a luxury liner transformed into a drab troopship, the members of the 365th Fighter Group debarked in Scotland and were taken by train to Gosfield, Essex, England, their home for the next few weeks. They arrived on December 23, 1943, just a fortnight after a raid by German Dornier Do 217 bombers that killed eight Americans.

Preparations for combat intensified. The Hell Hawks would be part of the Ninth Air Force, which began air action over German-occupied Europe with a few small-scale missions in January 1944. Major General Lewis H. Brereton was the Ninth Air Force commander. He had already seen action in Java, India, and the Middle East, though he would soon be eclipsed by a subordinate, Brig. Gen. Elwood "Pete" Quesada, the head of IX Fighter Command. Quesada was by far the more dynamic and charismatic of the two leaders.

In contrast to the Eighth Air Force, which spent the entire war operating from England, Brereton and Quesada wanted Ninth Air Force to cooperate with and support the field armies that were preparing for the upcoming invasion of Europe. The Ninth was to be an air-to-ground strike force supporting the tactical aims of the ground commanders. It would range behind the front lines to destroy German reinforcements and communications. When needed, it would take direct action against enemy troops on the battlefield. The Eighth Air Force might earn glory with its far-reaching heavy bombers and long-range fighters, but the Ninth would be grappling at close quarters with the individual German soldier.

No one knew yet when the invasion would take place, but a plan on paper called for Brereton's command to have a strength of 197,000 by then. The Ninth would add a new combat group like the Hell Hawks once every couple of weeks in the new year of 1944 until it had dozens of groups ready for a very personal kind of air war.

☆

After growing up, after joining up, after training, after transition to the P-47, after Richmond, Langley, Dover, Millville, and the *Queen Elizabeth*, the Hell Hawks were poised at Gosfield. Already, they had suffered losses. On February 13, 1944, 1st Lt. Harold B. Johnston's P-47 crashed and burned on a test hop.

"I wasn't flying . . ." wrote 2nd Lt. Paul Van Cleef, "so Neal Worley and I jumped into [a jeep] and raced to the crash. Big mistake. We stood there and watched him burn, his brains boiling out of his head, something that haunts me to this day. That evening we had spaghetti for chow. Neither Neal nor I ate a thing." Johnston, an experienced fighter pilot, had died just nine days before the Hell Hawks' first combat mission.

At 5:00 a.m. on February 22, 1944, the charge-of-quarters—the enlisted men who watched over the silent barracks— blew their whistles to awaken the sleeping airmen wrapped in blankets inside their cold Nissen huts. Primed, ready, anxious but eager to finally get into battle, the pilots of twenty-four P-47s once again came up against the toughest characteristic of military life—hurry up and wait. They discovered that they would not be taking off in their fueled, armed-up "Jugs" until almost 11:00 a.m.

Finally, several flights lifted into the air. One was led by group commander Call and another by Maj. Rockford V. Gray, with Capt. Damon J. "Rocky" Gause as his wingman. Majors Donald E. Hillman and William D. Ritchie led other flights. For all the tension generated by the morning's delay, the first combat mission turned out to be a routine and eventless bomber escort run; the Hell Hawks did not even shepherd their charges all the way to their target in Holland. Unhappy airmen landed back at Gosfield. They had come a long way for this anticlimax. They had glimpsed flak only from a distance, and none had sighted a foe or pulled a trigger.

Chafing at delays, the Hell Hawks sat out a day of poor weather. On February 24, 1944, under Capt. Edward F. Boles, they escorted B-17 Flying Fortresses partway to the bombers' target. Boles witnessed a bomber exploding in midair, but the group saw no flak, no enemy fighters, no Germans. Were they ever going to see serious action? Fetzer, like many, wondered when he and his friends would come face-to-face with the enemy. Even the imagined terror of combat would be better than this waiting.

The Hell Hawks continued to fly relay escort missions, picking up bombers on their way home from their long runs over occupied Europe and Germany. This was not the action most had anticipated. Captain Ritchie began painting little white bottles on his airplane to signify these "milk runs." He would later stencil "likker jugs" below his cockpit to mark missions with a little more kick, but in the late winter and early spring of 1944 there were few of those.

The long combat drought ended on March 2, 1944, when twenty-nine Hell Hawks battled German Focke-Wulf Fw 190 fighters. Major Robert L. Coffey Jr. shot one down. Also falling from the sky that busy day was West Point's Gene Wink. For the rest of his life, Wink would never be sure whether it was mechanical trouble or a stray round of German gunfire that crippled his P-47. His wingmen remember him calling in: his engine had quit, he could not restart it, and he was going to have to bail out. Other Hell Hawks watched Wink's Thunderbolt glide into overcast at three thousand feet; no one knew if he had managed to get out. Wink wrote:

> Not until this very moment did it sink into my mind that this important phase of my life [as a combat pilot with the Hell Hawks] could very well be over. Gliding down with a dead engine, unable to fly back to England, and with high prospects of living the rest of the war in a German prison camp, my life with the 365th was all but over. It was enough to make a grown man cry, but crying was not something that I had time for at the moment.
>
> Decision time was ahead—bail out or crash land? Since the latter would provide the enemy with a flyable P-47, I elected to bail out. All I had to do now was decide how to go about it. Since the P-47 glides like a rock, my altitude advantage and time were rapidly vanishing. I scratched going over the side of the cockpit when I recalled hearing about fighter pilots whose parachutes caught on their tail sections. The only thing left for me to do was to turn the aircraft over and fall out.
>
> Having made the "exit" decision, I began to go through the detailed procedures required to make my bailout a resounding success. With my time rapidly expiring, I checked my parachute straps, disconnected my headset and throat mike, buckled my helmet chinstrap, put my goggles over my eyes, and opened the cockpit canopy. An important next step was to roll my elevator trim tabs forward. By doing this the aircraft would continue its forward movement rather than fly down toward me when I turned it over into an inverted position.
>
> The jolt of the air that hit my face as I left the cockpit almost took my breath away. I knew I was free of the aircraft, and I had a feeling of being completely motionless in the air as I looked the world over. I was experiencing an emotional joy because things were working the way they should, because I was safe thus far, and because although frightened a bit, I was enjoying this new and unique experience. There was no tumbling, only a good feeling,

and the question now on my mind was, "When do I pull my rip-cord?" To shorten my float time because of the possibility of enemy troops in the area, I delayed opening the parachute a few seconds.

The thing most indelible in my memory is that the descent was marked by complete silence. I had very little time to experiment with the feel of the risers, because I was mesmerized by the experience of floating down in silence. As I approached the ground, I was jolted back to reality by narrowly missing telephone wires, and I hit the ground with a solid thud. I tried to follow the procedures drilled into us by our parachute experts—feet close together, knees slightly bent, and rolling with the fall. The result was that the landing was safe and without injury but completely lacking in grace and style. Things seemed to be working well until a gust of wind ballooned my chute canopy and I was dragged across the ground. When I hit the quick release button, the canopy deflated and I was able to stand.

Wink was standing in German-held territory, the first West Pointer in the Ninth Air Force to be down behind enemy lines. Many Hell Hawks would follow, but Wink was luckier than most. The French resistance spirited him away from the Germans, and on April 14 he returned to the 365th at Beaulieu.

☆

As planning progressed for an Allied invasion of Nazi-held Europe, the Hell Hawks made a move to better support it. On March 5, 1944, the 365th Fighter Group moved to Beaulieu, Hants, England, close to the major Channel port of Southampton. Here, if a man could get off base into nearby Brockenhurst, he could enjoy a delightful pub called Mew's Ales and Stouts. Beaulieu offered the men better facilities, a more efficient fueling area, and a longer runway than Gosfield's. It was from this base that the Hell Hawks would learn the ropes of air-to-ground combat as a prelude to their D-Day mission.

The invasion was something Maj. Damon Gause would never see. He held a relatively senior rank because he had been captured during the Japanese invasion of the Philippines, escaped, and served for nearly two years fighting alongside Filipino irregulars. His participation in guerrilla operations was celebrated in some accounts, said to be exaggerated in others. Gause kept a Japanese flag beside his desk. Anyone called into his office for a dressing-down stood on the Rising Sun while enduring Gause's wrath.

Though he wore the silver wings of a pilot in addition to the gold oak leaves of a major, Gause had spent most of the war fighting from the jungle. Now, half a world away, he seemed slow to adapt to the P-47. His son would later write a hagiography that credited Gause with conducting test flights for the Hell Hawks to evaluate a new modification to the Thunderbolt's wings and flaps.

Gause had fewer hours in the P-47 than some second lieutenants. "Gause was not a test pilot and he was not performing a test flight. That was a figment of his son's imagination," said Maj. Donald E. Hillman. "He was a guy who couldn't fly. I found he couldn't fly. They didn't trust him to lead."

On March 9, 1944, Gause got into a steep dive near Beaulieu and crashed near the airdrome. There was little left of the Thunderbolt or its pilot. "He misjudged it," Hillman said. Gause paid with his life, becoming the highest-ranking Hell Hawk to perish thus far and underlining the grim fact that even in the war zone, about half of all aviation losses were attributable to non-combat causes. (Gause's admiring son learned none of those details. Ironically born Lance Gause after the Hell Hawks' group commander, he later changed his name to Damon L. Gause to honor his father.)

Between the end of March and the sixth of June, Hell Hawks pilots flew increasingly difficult combat missions into Nazi-occupied Europe. But Britain had its diversions: you could lose a bunkmate in combat one day and get a pass to visit London the next.

For a long time now, everyone in the British Isles had known that there would be an invasion. Everywhere in England, the wartime routine was being further disrupted by the arrival of men and materiel, training exercises, and preparations for the cross-Channel assault. Before long, the night lights of London, the swilling at the local pub, the bike rides in the English countryside, all would recede into the past for the Hell Hawks. When the Allied infantry stormed ashore on their five invasion beaches, the men of the 365th Fighter Group would follow close behind. For the Hell Hawks, the move to the Continent would mark the beginning of the most critical—and costly—chapters in their long combat saga.

Ninth Air Force
Fighter-Bomber Organization
August 1944

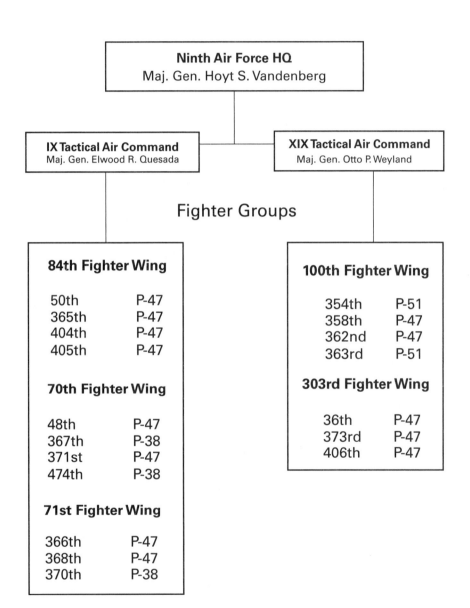

Ninth Air Force HQ
Maj. Gen. Hoyt S. Vandenberg

IX Tactical Air Command
Maj. Gen. Elwood R. Quesada

XIX Tactical Air Command
Maj. Gen. Otto P. Weyland

Fighter Groups

84th Fighter Wing

50th	P-47
365th	P-47
404th	P-47
405th	P-47

70th Fighter Wing

48th	P-47
367th	P-38
371st	P-47
474th	P-38

71st Fighter Wing

366th	P-47
368th	P-47
370th	P-38

100th Fighter Wing

354th	P-51
358th	P-47
362nd	P-47
363rd	P-51

303rd Fighter Wing

36th	P-47
373rd	P-47
406th	P-47

⭐ Chapter Four

Hedgerow Breakout

O N JUNE 26, 1944, NINTH AIR FORCE headquarters dropped a bomb-shell on the Hell Hawks: Col. Lance Call, the group commander, was relieved, effective immediately. Word raced down the flight line like a Thunderbolt at full throttle, shocking officers and enlisted men; Col. Call had led the group from its inception in May 1943 at Richmond Army Air Base through its first months in combat from England. Call was in his mid-thirties and, at six feet, five inches, too tall to sit erect in a P-47 cockpit atop his parachute pack (he flew instead with a chest chute). He had been a prewar naval aviator, later serving as an amphibian pilot with the Royal Canadian Air Force in England before transferring as a major to the Air Corps. His spit-and-polish enlisted background helped shape a reputation for uncompromising efficiency. Technical Sergeant Marion Hill, from Group Intelligence, said that "Colonel Call was an outstanding leader in my view, a no-nonsense career officer. He didn't pull any punches, but at the same time I knew he was sensitive to the needs of the enlisted men."

Hill remembered when the group arrived at Gosfield, England, on Christmas Eve, 1943, hungry and dead-tired from days of ocean, rail, and truck travel. The mess hall issued a meal of cold K-rations for the men. Call rounded up the base quartermaster and subjected him to one of his "super-professional ass-chewings."

"Get some real food down to those men!" Call roared, making it clear that there would be physical as well as disciplinary consequences if a hot meal didn't materialize, pronto. The Hell Hawks were doubly relieved: at their unexpected breakfast of powdered eggs, toast, hot coffee, and doughnuts; and that, for once, someone else was the target of their taskmaster's wrath.

Lieutenant Jimmy Wells didn't care for Call personally, but gave him grudging credit for running a tight organization. "He whipped the group into shape, I'll say that for him," Wells recalled. Call demanded synchronized watches and precise takeoff timing from the pilots. As inspectors watched during a crucial readiness drill at Richmond, "every propeller turned over at the same time," said Wells. Thanks to Call's emphasis on meticulous execution, each flight appeared overhead precisely on schedule. The senior examiner was impressed: "You can go ahead and buy your eagles, Call, because you'll be a colonel tomorrow." Said Wells, "That's what it took. We were on our toes, thanks to him."

As well-oiled a military organization as the 365th was, many resented Call's brusque, spit-and-polish demeanor. John Fetzer, a lieutenant and pilot in the 387th fighter squadron at the time, remembers that "Call was a pretty good guy. But he was something to see. He wore polished boots and carried a swagger stick, like Patton!"

Major David N. Harmon was the group's operations officer in late June 1944. Call had once publicly fired Harmon for leaving the base to visit a buddy in Cambridge, but the next morning Harmon found his boss waving him back to duty. "Just forget about it," said Call. Harmon had watched Call grant emergency leave to a staff pilot so he could see his newborn son before shipping out; just before that big move, Call then promoted to acting operations officer the relatively junior Harmon. "I enjoyed his confidence," said Harmon, who respected his leadership but acknowledged Call's limitations as a pilot.

Call's performance in the air worried the pilots. He "always wore Ray-Ban sunglasses," then-2nd Lt. Tom Stanton remembered, whether flight conditions demanded them or not. Stanton and others suspected instead that Call's dark glasses disguised prescription lenses. Says Stanton flatly: "We thought he couldn't see."

Call's "eyesight wasn't very good," Fetzer agreed, but more important, "Lance Call wasn't a very good pilot." Second Lieutenant Frank Luckman of the 388th said that Call "didn't lead flights in the air very well." The group commander often selected 2nd Lt. Raymond Moraga as his wingman. The men whispered that Call needed "Eagle Eye" Moraga to spot landmarks and identify the mission target. Even with Moraga on his wing, Call once led the group so far off course that he was far out over the Channel before getting his bearings; the wistful call of "There goes England!" made by an anonymous flier as the group headed further astray still gave veteran pilots a laugh sixty years later. Fuel-starved Thunderbolts were forced to land at bases all over southern England. On landing roll-out, Call turned into and clipped the wingtip of his wingman's Thunderbolt. Second Lieutenant Paul Van Cleef, from Salina, Kansas, got out, climbed up on Call's wing and shouted at him, "Colonel, you sure had your head up your ass."

"I sure did," Call answered, but the colonel, whose P-47 was too badly damaged to fly, didn't hesitate to take a fresh P-47 and head right off for Beaulieu. Wrote Van Cleef: "I had to fly *my* damaged plane . . . I never flew his wing again!!!"

There were also questions about Call's performance in combat. Said Fetzer, "Things were missing in terms of leadership." Ross Crownrich remembers that "every day that we went up he'd find something wrong with his airplane and abort the mission. . . . In the air, he'd say, 'Arm your babies' [bombs]." Crownrich relates that more than once, Call's bombs would then drop harmlessly into the Channel below. "Then, he would radio, 'Oops. My bombs fell off.'" Thus disarmed, Call would avoid having to dive with the other aircraft and run the gauntlet of flak. "We didn't have a very good impression of him," Crownrich said.

One Hell Hawk remembers the mission of April 20, 1944, when Call led what was an otherwise successful dive-bombing attack on a French marshalling yard. According to the pilot, during the climb-out from Beaulieu through a thick overcast, Call didn't carry enough power and let his airspeed decay, forcing the trailing planes dangerously near a stall. Hanging on their props, two pilots, 2nd Lts. James M. Allen and Daniel Matusiewicz of the 387th, ran out of airspeed and spun out of formation. The latter transitioned to instruments and pulled his shuddering Thunderbolt safely out of the dive beneath the cloud deck, but Lieutenant Allen couldn't recover. Plunging out of the overcast, he took to the silk at one hundred feet, too late for his chute to open. He died instantly as his body slammed into an English field.

Writing in the early 1970s, Staff Sgt. Charles R. Johnson took stock of his former boss: "Many disliked Call for his brusque manner, but he had a job to do in a short time with partially trained men. . . . He did it the only way he knew how, by the numbers. One wonders if a more liberal commanding officer could have completed the job in as short a time, and as well. . . ." Pilot Frank Luckman agreed: Call, despite his faults, "did a hell of a job getting the organization together." But ineptitude in the air and a seeming reluctance to close with the enemy, however anecdotal, were anathema to the young fighter pilots Call led. These were not the combat traits demanded by his pilots, nor expected by Call's boss, Pete Quesada.

There were rumors that some of the senior Hell Hawks were lobbying to have Call relieved and that General Quesada had a potential replacement waiting in the wings at Ninth Air Force headquarters. Harmon remembered what happened next:

> I was with Col. Call when General Quesada's P-47 landed at Beaulieu. As Quesada walked toward the operations building, he threw his arm over Call's shoulder, saying,"You're doing a hell of a job, here, Lance." A second's pause—"but you know I've gotta re-lieve you."
>
> Call didn't react, kept walking a step or two. Then he stopped [and] looked at Quesada. "What was that, sir?!"
>
> "I've got to relieve you, Lance. I've got another job for you."

It would fall to someone else to take the Hell Hawks to the Continent. The new commander was Col. Ray J. Stecker, a staff colleague of General Quesada's from the North African campaign, where both had helped create and implement the formative principles of effective air-ground cooperation. Stecker, a thirty-three-year-old West Pointer from Hazleton, Pennsylvania, was of medium height, with the easy smile and confidence of a top athlete; he'd been a football All-American at the Academy in 1932, his senior year.

His once-blond hair was now silver-gray, but his face remained full-cheeked and boyish, belying his experience. Resigning from the Air Corps just after pilot training, he'd run a felt manufacturing business near Boston during the 1930s, only to return to flying four months before Pearl Harbor. He'd experienced combat in Sicily and Italy with the IX Fighter Command, supporting Montgomery's British Eighth Army, before heading for England to join Quesada's nascent Ninth Air Force fighter organization.

Ross Crownrich recounted that the pilots "were glad to see the next group commander come along." Charles Johnson agreed: "Colonel Stecker proved to be an efficient, effective, and energetic commanding officer. . . . He was a taskmaster and a military man through-and-through, but the men respected his ability and his methods of getting a job done." Stecker ended the parades Call had held each Friday. Wrote Johnson, "The moral[e] of the entire group seemed to improve. . . ."

Lieutenant Colonel Don Hillman, deputy group commander, liked Stecker's unassuming style. "He had had no recent combat experience before joining us, so he took a flying refresher [course], and before he led a mission he would first follow one of our leaders" to sharpen his skills. "A top-notch leader," Hillman thought.

He would have to be, as the pace of combat over post–D-Day Normandy accelerated. By late June the Hell Hawks in the air each day knew their time at Beaulieu was short. Their dive-bombing and strafing missions were closely tied to the GIs grinding their way through Normandy's hedgerows. On each sortie, the flight to and from Beaulieu consumed an hour of flight time and fuel, limiting both the squadrons' bomb load and their loiter time over France. To meet the air-support needs of the Allied ground forces, the Ninth Air Force groups would have to operate near the battlefield in France.

☆

Combat engineers had been carving out new airstrips just inland from the beaches since D-Plus-One; Lt. Dick Miller had bellied in *Turnip Termite* near one being built just above Omaha Beach. The Hell Hawks' forward operating location on the Continent would be Air Landing Ground 7A (A-7 for short) at Fontenay-sur-Mer, a crude strip carved out of fields and apple orchards by the 819th Engineer Aviation Battalion. By late June, A-7 was well within the Allied beachhead, but combat raged just a few miles away in the direction of St.-Lô.

By June 21 each squadron's advance party was ready to ship out, its waterproofed trucks and vehicles carrying the immediate needs of the group for the days after landing. Delayed by the gales and high winds of the Channel storm that wrecked the Allies' Mulberry artificial harbor off Omaha, it was the evening of June 26 before the airmen boarded landing craft and joined a convoy headed for France.

Daylight on June 28 brought the French coast into view, along with the sobering sight of American bodies still drifting off the beaches. Sloshing ashore through waist-deep surf at Utah, the 365th men finally saw the devastation of war at firsthand. Crew chief Charles Johnson, setting out with full pack on his ten-mile trek to an assembly area, remembered the "long lines of German prisoners plodding towards the barbed wire stockades on the beach; the sunken ships; the hollow croaking of the frogs; the fitful flashes of the big guns lighting the sky to the west;

broken guns and burned-out tanks and trucks; bits of clothing and equipment; shell-scarred churches and damaged homes; and over all of this hung the lingering odor of decaying flesh."

The 386th Fighter Squadron ground crews made it to A-7 by the morning of the 29th, joining a rear-echelon contingent that had flown in on C-47 transports two days before. Then-2nd Lt. Ross Crownrich remembers not all the ground personnel made it to France courtesy of the U.S. Navy. "We cut holes in our compressed-paper drop tanks to carry supplies from England over to our new airfield. When we discovered that we needed a couple of crew chiefs very urgently, we flew them over inside those wing tanks. We cut a pretty big-sized hole in the side so they could breathe and see out. It was illegal as hell, but a few of them flew over that way."

According to Johnson, the newcomers were quickly caught up in a frenzied and determined search—for war souvenirs. "Soon the squadron area was littered with German rifles, bayonets, and other things." Hell Hawk 2nd Lt. Jimmy Wells of the 386th Squadron made his own grim discovery: "There were two German corpses right in a bush in the middle of where we were living, giving off a horrible odor." These frequent encounters with the dead dampened but did not halt the hunt for war booty.

☆

All the Ninth Air Force units moving into France were conducting flying operations in the grim backwash of the largest and bloodiest invasion the world had ever seen. Lieutenant Quentin Aanenson, a twenty-two-year-old Thunderbolt pilot with the newly arrived 366th Fighter Group based nearby between Omaha Beach and Pointe du Hoc, recalled that

> bodies of decomposing American soldiers who had been killed during the invasion continued to wash up on shore. We could look down from the bluffs overlooking the English Channel and see them. For the pilots who faced death on every mission, this was particularly upsetting.
>
> The graves registration people had moved on by that time—up closer to the front—so there was no one we could call on to retrieve the bodies. One evening our engineering officer—a solid, no-nonsense guy—decided something had to be done. He asked

several guys to help him, including some of the pilots. We carried five-gallon jerry cans filled with aviation gasoline, and several long poles with hooks attached to the ends, down the hill to the beach, then we carried everything to the area where the bodies were piling up. The mood was somber; there seemed to be a sense of unreality about what we were going to do.

It was a terrible, gruesome ordeal. Most of the bodies were badly decomposed and bloated, but some looked surprisingly normal. We hooked the bodies with the long poles, and pulled them together and piled them up as much as possible. We added as much driftwood to the pile as we could find. In a couple of instances we were able to get their dog tags for identification purposes, but for most of them, there was no way we could make any identification. Then we soaked the whole pile heavily with aviation gasoline.

The engineering officer had us back away, then he paused by the bodies for a minute as if in prayer; finally he ignited the pile. It burned furiously for a short time, then more slowly as the gasoline burned off. The driftwood kept the fire going for some time.

As I watched the fire consume the rotting bodies of these young American boys, I couldn't help but think about their families, and how it would drive them insane if they knew what really had happened to their sons. Better that they should picture their boys being instantly killed by a rifle bullet and then being given a proper military funeral, with a bugler playing "Taps" over the grave. But deaths in battle seldom involve dignity. They are horrible, brutal, degrading, and the fact that they died for a good cause cannot sanitize the reality of the circumstances of their deaths.

A few days later I again followed the mine-cleared path to the edge of the bluff and looked down to the water's edge. . . . More bodies were rolling in the surf, as the English Channel continued to give up its dead.

Ten miles west of Omaha, the Hell Hawks surrounded their new airfield with six-man tents and slit trenches, supply dumps, and crude latrines. The dirt strip at A-7 was 3,600 feet long by 120 feet wide, covered with waterproof tarpaper and overlain by a tough steel grid of wire mesh. The field had grass parking spots for seventy-five Thunderbolts.

For nearly ten days the three Hell Hawks squadrons had been landing, refueling and rearming at other frontline airfields. On June 28, they flew their first operational missions out of A-7. Finding German targets for their P-47s was no problem; Lt. Jimmy Wells reported "that I got shot at by rifle or machine gun fire right in the traffic pattern."

The last contingent of Hell Hawks would arrive at the new fighter strip by July 1, and with command tents up, maintenance gear in place, and fuel, bombs, and ammunition at hand, the 365th Fighter Group was ready for combat missions flown from French soil. On July 2, A-7 was declared fully operational.

☆

Three weeks after D-Day, Eisenhower's armies in Normandy were facing stiff opposition from German forces expertly using the hedgerow country to bottle up the Allied lodgment. The supreme commander's plans for a breakout depended on help from the air, and Pete Quesada's IX Tactical Air Command would play a key role as the "infantry's air force." His fighter-bombers would support the advance by dive-bombing enemy troops and supplies, defending against any interference by the Luftwaffe, and providing timely intelligence through aerial photography.

Despite the fighter-bombers' efforts, Wehrmacht reinforcements were finally reaching the Normandy front. Of greatest concern to the GIs was German armor, in the form of new and capable panzer models. Rommel's armored battalions were receiving the new, forty-five-ton Mark V Panther, armed with a lethal 75mm gun, and even a few Mark VI Tigers. Fifty-six-ton monsters nearly impervious to fire from American Shermans, the Tigers mounted 88mm, high-velocity cannon that out-gunned every Allied tank in the field. The eight hundred panzers Hitler had lurking among the hedgerows were outnumbered, but their technical superiority and expert handling made every Allied advance an exhausting and bloody hell.

☆

Amid the boom of heavy artillery, the Hell Hawks began their July flying amid low visibility and near-daily rain squalls. But there was plenty of action below the thick clouds. On July 2, Lt. Col. Bob Coffey was en route to Caen at the head of eight 388th Fighter Squadron planes to dive-bomb a bridge when his flight was bounced by a lone Bf 109 hurtling out of the overcast. Coffey and his wingman broke hard into the attacker and chased him down through broken clouds until Coffey, on the deck, had closed to within three hundred yards. His Thunderbolt's guns were sighted to converge at that distance, and Coffey raked the Messerschmitt as he closed to one hundred yards, practically point-blank range. Under the murderous hail of slugs, the German plane staggered, flipped over abruptly, and plunged into the Fôret-de-St.-Ercoult.

Second Lieutenant Donald E. Kraman in White Flight had his eyes glued to his leader, Capt. Norman V. Beaman, when twelve Messerschmitts hit their formation. Beaman broke up and into the enemy, and Kraman did what a wingman should, turning into and firing at a 109 already blazing away at his leader. The tactic worked: the enemy broke, pulled up and away to escape, and Kraman followed, closing steadily through an occasional cloud until his eight fifties had the range. His long and accurate burst tore into the Messerschmitt's cockpit; the plane wavered, rolled sluggishly, then descended, the German pilot apparently crippled. Kraman kept firing until his ammo was spent, while Beaman watched the 109's descent steepen into a dive that ended in a gout of flame on the Norman turf.

One of Coffey's 388th pilots was 2nd Lt. Ralph Kling, on his seventeenth combat mission, flying as White Four. Over the target, a railroad bridge, he spotted a gaggle of what he thought were British Spitfires down on the deck, strafing. Captain Beaman ordered Kling down to investigate.

Kling wanted to keep his bombs but preserve his options if the bogies were hostile. He dove at full throttle, "hit the deck going five hundred miles per hour, and zoomed over a plane that was just coming off a strafing pass." It was a Messerschmitt. "Man! Was I ever surprised," wrote Kling, "and the German pilot's eyes were as big as saucers as we passed within twenty-five feet of each other, he going from left to right under me."

The Bf 109 disappeared, with Kling, zooming for altitude, every bit as shaken as the German. Meanwhile a dozen more 109s had jumped Beaman and the rest of White Flight, so Kling dumped his bombs unarmed, then popped up through a thin cloud deck to see a 109, 450 yards ahead, shooting at a Thunderbolt. "I yelled for the P-47 to break right, and when he did I opened fire with the eight machine guns. Our shells met at 350 yards in front of the plane, and you were supposed to fire the guns for only six seconds at a time so the gun barrels could cool." By now Kling was inside 400 yards, and scoring. "By kicking in a little rudder I could see I was hitting him around the cockpit. He fishtailed a couple of times, turned over, and the canopy came off, but he didn't get out."

Kling kept closing, still shooting; his victim, shedding debris and smoking heavily, streaked earthward and struck very close to the Hell Hawk's target bridge at Bretteville-sur-Laize. The young lieutenant landed at A-7 with a victory, but his armorer soon let him know that his gunnery technique still needed work. "When the plane was inspected back at base, several of my gun barrels were burned out," said Kling.

☆

Victorious in the air, the Hell Hawks faced an ever-increasing threat from the ground: heavy and accurate German flak. On July 10, antiaircraft fire downed two planes from the 386th Squadron and heavily damaged three more. A 40mm shell burst near the cockpit of 1st Lt. Horace C. Lyons during a strike on a supply dump. He bailed out and was captured. First Lieutenant Valmore Beaudrault was luckier; after flak cut an oil line in his P-47, he made it to friendly territory and bellied in, sustaining a deep cut over one eye.

Next day, July 11, proved even more costly as the 386th Squadron continued its close-support missions under low ceilings, a near-perfect setup for the Wehrmacht's gunners. Lieutenant Colonel Bob Coffey, along with seven other Thunderbolt pilots, had attacked a railroad bridge near Château-sur-Loire, leaving cratered approaches, twisted tracks, and a damaged span. Sweeping the area near Angers, Coffey spotted a parked, camouflaged Fw 190 and opened up in a strafing attack, detonating the Focke-Wulf and flaming a nearby fuel truck. Pulling off the target, Coffey spied a twin-engine Junkers Ju 88 medium bomber and circled back to strafe. His eight fifties slammed into the grounded Junkers, finally setting it afire, but by now the flak gunners had the range. Coffey's Jug was bracketed by 20mm and 40mm shell bursts, blowing the ammo doors off the top of his right wing. Belts of .50-caliber ammo spilled from the gun bays, and his airspeed dropped from more than 300 to barely 160 miles per hour. Then the engine stopped.

No time to jump—Coffey locked his shoulder harness and glided in. *Coffey's Pot* slid to a stop, with its pilot only slightly banged up, and the downed Hell Hawk sprinted from the cockpit. For two days the lieutenant colonel played cat-and-mouse with the Wehrmacht, until on the third day he finally made contact with the underground. The resistance protected Coffey until they could smuggle him back through the lines in mid-August.

Coffey's comrades turned away from his burning plane, searching the surrounding countryside for Wehrmacht targets. The hedge-hopping Thunderbolts destroyed seven parked trucks and two German Kubelwagens, the equivalent of the American jeep, before turning for home. Cruising just under thousand-foot ceilings over Caumont, east of St.-Lô, they had A-7 in sight when the sky around them exploded.

A storm of light flak and automatic-weapons fire ripped the formation. Instinctively, the Hell Hawks pulled up into the sheltering overcast, but five planes were hit, among them the Thunderbolt of 1st Lt. Donald T. Newcombe. The twenty-three-year-old flier from Pontiac, Michigan, had already earned the Distinguished Flying Cross on March 24 for nursing his badly damaged Thunderbolt, one of its rudder cables severed by flak, back to Beaulieu. This time, his rugged P-47 was mortally wounded. Newcombe made a brief radio request for a heading back to base, but then there was silence. No Hell Hawk ever saw Don Newcombe again.

Fifty years later, Frenchman Remy Chuinard welcomed Newcombe's nephew, Canadian Rob Essery, and his family to Granville, on the Channel coast. Essery had discovered through Pentagon records that his uncle had crashed near Trois-Monts, southwest of Caen. Essery recalled his visit to the site, near the hamlet of Petit-Mesnil: "I saw a small, water-filled crater where metal tubing was visible. The mayor laid a small floral arrangement at the spot, and we observed a moment of silence to remember the young man who died there." In a Trois-Monts village hall, Essery saw two of the machine guns recovered from Newcombe's plane and learned from residents what had happened that cloudy July day.

"The villagers were just sitting down to lunch when they heard the scream of a diving plane and an explosion. They rushed to the scene along with German troops who were in the area." Newcombe's Thunderbolt had clipped trees and smashed into a small field, near a quiet brook.

The Germans found Newcombe's body thrown from the cockpit; he had died instantly. The soldiers left his body for the villagers to bury beside the sad remains of his Thunderbolt. Because Trois-Monts was in the British sector of the Normandy fighting, and no markings were discernible in the wreckage, they erected a small cross at the grave, inscribed "Fallen British Pilot, 11-7-44." The teenage daughter of the farm's owner tended the grave in the quiet pasture until a British grave registration unit recovered and identified Newcombe's body in 1946.

Donald T. Newcombe still rests in France, at the Normandy American Cemetery in Colleville-sur-Mer—Plot D, Row 6, Grave 4.

Shortly after Essery's visit, Remy Chuinard returned to Trois-Monts and directed the excavation of Newcombe's Thunderbolt. Its engine, propeller, and other remnants had marked the site of the young Hell Hawk's death for nearly six decades.

☆

Rain and low clouds kept the Hell Hawks on the ground on July 13 and 14, but they cleared enough on the next day for combat support missions to resume. Thirty-four P-47s took off early that evening on an armed reconnaissance mission, hunting for enemy airfields, planes, and troop movements. Ten Thunderbolts carried a single five-hundred-pound bomb each, meant for airfield installations and any vehicle or troop concentrations.

As John Fetzer discovered in his D-Day attack on a Tiger tank, the blast from an accurately dropped five-hundred-pounder was devastating. Another Thunderbolt pilot described the effects of his low-level bombing run on a Wehrmacht column: "I looked back and saw the blast pick a truck up . . . it actually came up in the air and rolled across the road. Pretty!" The danger from those low-altitude drops was that the attacker's P-47 would—if the fuse worked correctly—barely escape the blast.

General Quesada, visiting their field, asked the Hell Hawks in the briefing tent what they thought of the eight-to-ten-second delay fuses used on their bombs. "Here's what I think of your goddamned fuse!" yelled one angry pilot, hurling a mangled chunk of metal at the general. "Your bomb blew the damned thing right in the cockpit with me!"

After dive-bombing forward German airfields near Évreux on July 15, two squadrons went low, strafing everything that moved. The Thunderbolt's eight .50-caliber guns fired copper-jacketed lead bullets at a combined rate of nearly 2,800 rounds per minute. Each two-inch-long slug weighed about a tenth of a pound and left the barrel at about 2,800 feet per second. When he squeezed the trigger, a P-47 pilot could put nearly fifty bullets per second into a cone of fire that converged three hundred yards in front of his cockpit. A three-second burst put a fifteen-pound bolt of lead into the target at Mach three, the kinetic energy equivalent of a six-ton truck traveling at over eighty miles per hour. That tornado of metal would literally blow a 6x6 truck off the road, the cab and cargo already afire from the armor-piercing incendiary rounds comprising two of every five bullets in the ammo belts.

Scouring the countryside, the Hell Hawks demolished twenty-eight trucks and two railroad cars while enduring a storm of light flak. Captain George W. Porter landed back at A-7 in what onlookers called a "flying sieve." The pilot laughed it off, climbing from the cockpit while dismissing the accuracy of the German guns: "You should have seen the amount that missed me!" His crew chief mutely pointed to two holes on either side of the cockpit. A 20mm shell had ripped through the Thunderbolt an inch in front of Porter's belt buckle, barely an inch above his crotch. The captain had no more disparaging words for the flak gunners, at least for the rest of July 15.

One of the gunners that "missed" Porter also hit 1st Lt. James L. McWhorter, who wasn't so lucky. His engine was running so roughly that he put his Thunderbolt down at B-2, a Canadian fighter strip near Bayeux. A German bullet had made a neat hole in the intake manifold of his Pratt & Whitney's number-fourteen cylinder. "Mac" spent the night with the Canadian Spitfire pilots, but next morning patched the manifold by wrapping it with asbestos cloth and baling wire. His engine roaring like a volcano, McWhorter managed to take off and made a beeline for A-7. "The men at Fontenay-sur-Mer heard him from several miles away," wrote his crew chief, Charles Johnson. McWhorter told the staff sergeant why he risked taking to the air in a damaged P-47: "I had to get off that Limey base—all they had were English cigarettes."

☆

By mid-July the Allies' forward progress had slowed to a crawl, as the Americans fought to capture St.-Lô and the British struggled to take Caen from dug-in German defenders. Despite Eisenhower's air and materiel superiority, the Norman ridges, hedgerows, and compact fields were ideal defensive country for the Wehrmacht, which exacted a bloody toll for each mile it relinquished. The Allied tanks were bottled up by outnumbered but expertly sited Panthers, Tigers, and Mark IV panzers. Bradley and Montgomery, Eisenhower's ground commanders, sought a breakthrough stroke that would crack the German's taut defensive line and enable a war of armored maneuver in the open country beyond the hedgerows.

The operation was called "Cobra." Eisenhower would use his fleet of heavy and medium bombers, along with fighter-bombers, to pulverize a section of the German front southwest of St.-Lô, opening a route for the breakout. Once through the tough but thin crust of Wehrmacht resistance, Bradley's First and Third Armies, under Gen. Courtney H. Hodges and Gen. George S. Patton, respectively, could plunge south and west into Brittany, eventually turning east and unhinging the entire German defense in Normandy. The date for Cobra was set for July 24, 1944.

If the attack were to succeed, the Ninth Air Force would need to paralyze the Wehrmacht and prevent it from shifting forces to oppose the breakthrough. In the week leading up to Cobra, the 365th put its P-47s in the air to smother German movement. An armed reconnaissance mission on July 18, led by the 388th Squadron's Captain Norman V. Beaman, ran into more than just German troops and trucks; Beaman's eleven Thunderbolts found the Luftwaffe.

Vectored toward enemy aircraft near Vire by their radar controller, SWEEPSTAKES CHARLIE, the Hell Hawks joined in a wild dogfight involving twenty Messerschmitts and as many Mustangs. Beaman downed two Bf 109s before being shot up and forced to bail out. Another Thunderbolt went down in flames even as 1st Lt. Robert M. Fry caught another pair of Messerschmitts and sent them plunging to earth. In quick succession, 2nd Lt. Raymond B. Porter flamed two more. In these July 18 dogfights, the Hell Hawks downed six Messerschmitts, damaged four more, and caught another four in strafing attacks on the ground.

The Hell Hawks had helped turn back the Luftwaffe sweep at the price of four Thunderbolts. Captain Beaman evaded the Germans and returned through the lines in early August, but three other pilots were missing and presumed killed, a sobering toll. As Lieutenant Porter headed for A-7, he counted nine columns of black smoke swirling up through the summer haze, funeral pyres for young fliers of both sides.

☆

The rainy July weather, the worst in decades, did nearly as much as German resistance to slow the Allied push. On July 23, poor flying conditions and the absolute imperative to get into the air to support the GIs proved as deadly to the Hell Hawks as the German flak gunners.

Lieutenant Ralph F. Kling flew with every nerve tensed, fiercely gripping the control stick as he cleared the apple orchard at the end of A-7's muddy, 3,500-foot runway. With a five-hundred-pounder slung beneath each wing, the slick tarpaper field was barely long enough to get his Thunderbolt into the air. Kling used every foot of the bumpy strip, throwing spray up from the Jug's tires as he jockeyed for position on his 388th Squadron leader, Maj. John R. Murphy.

Fifteen seconds after takeoff the first ragged sheets of cloud whipped by his canopy as Kling climbed into the solid deck above, tucked in on Murphy's wing. In the murk, rain streaking back from his bulletproof windscreen and along his canopy, he could see his leader's wingtip light and vapor-wrapped fuselage, but little else. No other aircraft were visible, but he knew they were out there: dozens of Thunderbolts, Spitfires, and Lightnings, rising from airfields below. Closer to hand was the second element of the flight, White 3 and 4. Kling couldn't see them, but he could *feel* them. "It's not uncommon to be in a pool of sweat when you break clear," said Kling.

Kling squinted as Murphy broke into in brilliant sunshine. Other Thunderbolt pairs rose like ghosts from the dazzling white cloud deck, sliding nearer to join the formation. Looking to his left, the sun behind him, Kling saw White 3, 2nd Lt. Morris A. Weiner, emerge from the undercast, dipping a wing to rejoin Murphy. Weiner was still skirting the cloud tops, and as Kling watched his leader and Weiner's plane beyond, he noticed another P-47 lift from the murk close by. The sun directly in his eyes, 1st Lt. Allen Guest popped into the clear and rammed Weiner's Thunderbolt from below.

"Guest pulls right up under Weiner, who is immediately a great ball of flame," Kling wrote. He winced from the glare of the fireball and watched in horror as Weiner "rolled over and disappeared into the clouds. Guest's plane has all four propeller blades bent back, not turning, not on fire." Helpless, Kling could do nothing as Guest, too, slid down and instantly vanished into the undercast.

"Murphy and I are alone on top of the world, it seems; the other two flights have not yet broken through the clouds, and you can see forever in the bright clear sky," wrote Kling. The soft, pure white cloud deck below was marred only by an obscene black smudge marking Weiner's terrible demise.

The young Pennsylvanian had died instantly. Guest was luckier; somehow he kicked free of his shattered plane, but the Jug's horizontal tail struck his right leg even as he reached for his parachute ripcord.

Alone with Kling, Murphy seemed stunned as the pair continued to orbit. Finally he keyed the mike and told his wingman: "Let's go home." Kling can't even remember how they got back on the ground. Guest, pulled from the water by Royal Navy sailors, miraculously survived a severed artery and emergency amputation aboard LST 506 off Omaha Beach and lived until 1971.

☆

Cobra was set for the morning of July 24, but more bad weather rolled in, causing Air Marshal Sir Trafford Leigh-Mallory to postpone the saturation bombings kicking off the offensive. But 1,586 heavy bombers were already in the air, and some never received the recall order. Accidents and faulty tactics caused many of the 335 B-17 Flying Fortresses to drop short, raining down 685 tons of bombs on American troops poised at the jump-off line. More than one hundred GIs were killed, including General Lesley J. McNair, and more than five hundred were wounded in the tragedy.

The Hell Hawks' thirty-seven Thunderbolts had dropped their fragmentation bombs on target, but in the prevailing low visibility no one knew if they had damaged the waiting enemy, now forewarned. What was meant to be a shattering air onslaught had been a disaster for the attackers.

Leigh-Mallory tried again the next day, and with better weather the results were far different. Despite the disastrous attack of the 24th, the Germans had not moved their troops from the danger zone, and the armada of fighter-bombers and heavy B-17s roared in on schedule. At 9:41 a.m. on the 25th, thirty-five Hell Hawk Thunderbolts released seventy 260-pound fragmentation bombs on enemy troops fronting the Cobra attack corridor. Lieutenant Colonel Donald E. Hillman reported the strike went "as briefed," but the haze and smoke in the target area obscured the bombs' effects.

A better view of the P-47 delivery was had by famed war correspondent Ernie Pyle: "The dive bombers hit it just right. We stood in the barnyard of a French farm and watched them barrel nearly straight down out of the sky. They were bombing less than half-a-mile ahead of where we stood.

"They came in groups, diving from every direction, perfectly timed, one right after another. Everywhere you looked, separate groups of planes were on the way down, or on the way back up, or slanting over for a dive."

At 10:00 a.m. the Eighth Air Force's Flying Fortresses appeared overhead, releasing more than 3,300 tons of high explosives into the one-by-five-mile target box. German Gen. Fritz Bayerlein, commanding the Panzer Lehr Division, remembered the heavies just kept coming, "like a conveyor belt, seemingly without end." Again, some bombs went astray, killing and wounding more than six hundred GIs. But this time the effects on the enemy were devastating. The shattering concussion, whirling tree splinters, and steel fragments from the rain of detonating TNT destroyed the German front line. Touring his forward command posts immediately after the strike, Bayerlein surveyed a *Mondlandschaft*—a moonscape. "The shock effect on the troops was indescribable. Several men went mad, and rushed dementedly around in the open until they were cut down by splinters." Those soldiers who survived were combat-ineffective, stupefied by the bomb blasts. Four U.S. mobile divisions concentrated on a one-mile front broke through the shattered defenses and burst into the German rear. The great breakout had begun.

With a thick column of smoke and dust from the target zone visible from all over Normandy, the Hell Hawks flew a half-dozen missions through the rest of that day to expand the breach and freeze German reinforcements. The P-47s bombed truck columns, dropped bridges, cut road intersections, and strafed any military vehicles they spotted amid the streams of French refugees fleeing the battle zone. Earlier that month, General Quesada had ordered radios installed in the lead tanks of Bradley's columns, enabling the armor commanders to talk directly to the P-47s overhead. As American tanks spilled into the German rear area and raced southwest, each column of Shermans was covered by a flight of Thunderbolts, ready to demolish any strong points the Germans might desperately throw into their path.

☆

On July 27, 2nd Lt. John S. Vitz of the 386th Squadron was one of eight Jug pilots working over the area between Coutances and La-Haye-Pesnel, southwest of St.-Lô. Late in the day the squadron bombed several tanks and 88mm and 20mm flak positions, and strafed and set afire a column of ten vehicles. Attacking the panzers, Capt. George Porter and Vitz, his wingman, made two strafing runs trying to hit the tanks' treads or thinly armored belly. Vitz was "passing over the tank at about twenty feet . . . there was an explosion in my right wing root and flames poured into the cockpit. I zoomed for altitude and realized that there was no chance to fly back to base . . . ."

"At about 1,500 feet I was in the clouds with the plane really burning, so I unhitched my shoulder harness, opened the canopy, and dove over the side." The Minneapolis native popped his chute, drifted out of the low clouds, and landed in woods atop a small tree; "I was let down to the ground very gently." Vitz's P-47 had already exploded nearby, and the clouds were so low that the enemy didn't notice his descent.

Vitz hid in a cornfield until dark, his burned legs and face troubling him little at first. With the Wehrmacht crowding the roads during darkness, he cut through fields, working toward the American lines. "Near daybreak my legs were hurting so much that I almost asked for help in a farmhouse." But Vitz thought better of it (the farm looked too prosperous), and he hid in the woods overlooking the house. "At the crack of dawn, the door of the farmhouse opened and out came a squad of German soldiers. They walked out to one of the 88mm guns in the area, and it was then that I realized I was right in the middle of a battery of antiaircraft guns."

The wounded pilot got away that night and took cover in a marshy area near a stream, but was pinned down all the following day by Germans bicycling toward the front on an adjacent track. Now feverish from his infected burns, Vitz lay in the swamp until dark, too cautious and too weak to move.

German traffic on the path tailed off. Vitz thought he saw three soldiers approaching through a hedgerow. He thought they were Americans. He stood up and yelled.

He was nearly shot. "My lack of training showed," said Vitz. "Fortunately the point men . . . of the 2nd Armored Division were veterans and did not fire. They disarmed me and took me 'prisoner' and I was marched back to a major who interrogated me."

The GIs, satisfied with his story, gave Vitz a couple of belts of calvados, the local apple brandy. Evacuated to the beach for treatment, he wound up in a hospital in England; three months later, on November 1, he returned to the Hell Hawks and resumed combat flying until war's end. Vitz attributed his survival to "a little bit of training and a lot of dumb luck."

On July 27th the 386th lost three planes and pilots to German gunners, but both of Vitz's downed comrades soon returned to combat flying. One, Mac McWhorter, was peeved again at George Porter. Back from leading the mission, Porter reported the flak "only moderate, and only fairly accurate."

☆

As General Omar Bradley's armored breakout surged south and west from the shattered German front, the Hell Hawks could look back at the close of July with some satisfaction. In 127 combat missions flown on the twenty-one days of good July weather, the Thunderbolt pilots, with the essential support of their ground crews, had blasted bridges, road junctions, trucks, gun emplacements, staff cars, rolling stock, and Hitler's dwindling force of panzers. At least ten Luftwaffe fighters had fallen to the Hell Hawks' guns. But the group had lost six pilots killed in action, and scattered across the fields and hedgerows of Normandy were the wrecks of seventeen Hell Hawk P-47s, enough for an entire squadron.

Still, the Allies had broken the Normandy stalemate. First Army's tank spearheads were fifteen miles past their jump-off line, with little opposition to slow their thrust into Brittany and east toward Paris. The race to the Seine was on. Overhead, poised to knock apart any rallying Wehrmacht forces or slash at their retreat would be the five-hundred-pounders and buzz-saw fifties of the 365th Fighter Group's flashing Thunderbolts.

No one knew the effectiveness of the fighter-bombers' contribution in Normandy better than the Wehrmacht. Its foot soldiers noted bitterly that "if the aircraft above us were camouflaged, we knew they were British. If they were silver, we knew they were American. And if they weren't there at all, we knew they were German!"

Chapter Five

Falaise and the Race across France

THE 20MM SHELL EXPLODED just in front of his cockpit as 1st Lt. Carl Lindstrom pulled out of his dive-bombing run on a temporary bridge south of Tessy-sur-Vire, southwest of Caen. The burst ignited his razorback Thunderbolt's main fuel tank. Lindstrom, just twenty years old, rolled the P-47's canopy back for bailout and was instantly engulfed in flames. It was July 30, 1944.

Lindstrom had joined the 387th Squadron just a month before, flying into A-7 on a C-47 with his friend, 2nd Lt. Herbert L. "Herb" Prevost II. Now, on his twelfth mission, he was fighting for his life. "I knew I had to get out," Lindstrom said. Just fifteen hundred feet up, he rolled his plane inverted and fell through bright flames into the cool air. "I heard the roar of the engine for an instant, then quiet." Swinging under his parachute for just thirty seconds, the Calwa, California, native hit the ground already in shock.

"There was skin hanging off my hands," recalled Lindstrom, "but my shins and neck were burned the worst." In his first bit of luck that day, he landed next to a squad from the 30th Infantry Division, who hustled him to a field hospital.

Evacuated via Omaha Beach to England, he slowly recuperated in Oxford. Carl Lindstrom was awarded the Distinguished Flying Cross for his "heroism and superior airmanship," and he returned to flying duty with the Hell Hawks on October 15.

☆

Freed from the deadlocked hedgerow warfare by the success of the Cobra breakout, American and Allied mobile columns had an apparent chance to envelop the Germans east of the beachheads in the Falaise Pocket (or Falaise Gap), the area encompassed by the four towns of Trun, Argentan, Vimoutiers, and Chambois. Here, the Allies hoped to encircle and destroy the German Seventh Army and Fifth Panzer Army. If they succeeded, the P-47 Thunderbolts of the Hell Hawks and their Ninth Air Force counterparts would deserve much of the credit for impeding the German retreat. If they failed, the weather would be as much to blame as German resistance. It was always the weather. The Jug pilots of the Hell Hawks could be the winning card for the foot soldier, if not for the vagaries of weather.

The Hell Hawks were in a hellhole. The tar-paper and wire-mesh surface, uneven earth, and soggy conditions at the airfield known as A-7 at Fontenay-sur-Mer, their home since late June, hardly fit with the glorious image of the flyboy that many held before setting foot on Hitler's Europe. Mechanics and armorers worked outdoors, ate under a dripping mess tent—during one two-day period most of the group were down with food poisoning—and kept working, always, to keep the P-47s airborne. The overcast "crud" that seemed to hover over Fontenay too often refused to cooperate.

Lieutenant Lavern R. "Acorn" Alcorn of the 388th Squadron, a native of West Union, Iowa, remembered that while living in a six-man tent he would hear guns nearby. An American 105mm artillery battery had set up shop to slug it out with the Germans—and to disrupt the Hell Hawks' sleep. Alcorn slept anyway; he was a six-foot Iowa boy who had wanted to fly since seeing a movie about British fighter pilots. He hadn't envisioned conditions at A-7. For a time, pilots there were restricted to flying air-to-ground missions with lighter-than-usual fragmentation bombs, because the strip was initially just 3,200 feet long, too short for heavier bombloads.

By August 4 the German front facing the 12th Army Group under General Omar Bradley had largely collapsed. The Wehrmacht was pulling out, retreating east, trying to avoid being trapped on the southwest bank of the Seine River. The road network they used funneled through the Norman town of Falaise, and that modest but historic locale became the focus over the next two weeks of a desperate struggle between the Germans fighting to keep their escape route open and the Allies trying to snap shut the jaws of their mobile pincers.

On August 5, 1944, the third day of the Falaise fighting, "ground troops were on their own . . . because the weather was so bad that no combat mission could be flown," wrote the Hell Hawks' scribe, Charles Johnson. The 365th pilots were wet and uncomfortable as they waited out the rain. Hell Hawks armorers and mechanics were wet and chilled as they labored to keep the Jugs airworthy. But despite the low-hanging crud, General Bradley's 12th Army Group made significant advances. With Gen. George Patton's Third Army on their southern flank, the Germans were in danger of being cut off from the Seine bridges.

Patton was preparing for a dash across France that would be unparalleled in the history of armored warfare. It would become a feat so celebrated that the Hell Hawks and the rest of the American participants in the advance would wonder if their contributions would be entirely forgotten. On the ground, the GIs of Lt. Gen. Courtney H. Hodges' First Army, also advancing with P-47s overhead, often felt themselves overlooked while "old Blood and Guts" swept up the glory. In years to come, Hodges' men would be furious that historians often confused their own combat achievements with Patton's Third Army exploits. In days and weeks to come, flacks would write that Patton engineered the breakthrough at St.-Lô, took Paris, and made the initial crossing of the Rhine—when, in fact, with help from wide-ranging Thunderbolt pilots, all these achievements were the work of Hodges' First Army. Both Patton and Hodges launched serious offensive operations in early August, only to be stymied by foul weather and to collide, initially, with the German counter-effort that centered around Falaise.

When the weather improved on August 6, Capt. David L. Gross Jr. led a flight of Hell Hawks P-47s that strafed German supply trucks. Flying a new P-47 version that was several hundred pounds heavier than his customary Thunderbolt, Gross, having pumped machine gun fire into the German vehicles, apparently miscalculated when he began his pullout. He was too low. Gross perished as his Thunderbolt slammed into the ground, plowed through hedgerows, and exploded.

☆

The Germans launched a small but fierce counteroffensive on August 7 at Mortain. Hitler had ordered a desperate bid to cut off and isolate Patton's Third Army, but Typhoon fighter-bombers of the Royal Air Force cut the advancing panzers to pieces. The chief of staff of the German Seventh Army, Generalmajor Rudolf von Gersdorff, stated that "Towards noon, the attack by 1st SS Panzer Division was stopped . . . because the situation (due to losses of tanks caused by the tremendously strong low-level attacks) became untenable . . . the absolute air supremacy of the Allies made any further movement by the attack units impossible."

By the end of the day, Bradley's GIs were in Mortain once again. Hitler had unwisely thrown the cutting edge of his army westward at the very time when he should have retreated eastward.

The failed German thrust gave rise to the Allied opportunity around Falaise. Army group commanders Bradley and Field Marshal Bernard Montgomery moved to encircle the Germans. The initial plan was to send Canadian troops south through Falaise to link up with Patton's tanks attacking northwards to Argentan. As he would do so often in letters home, 2nd Lt. Grant Stout would write to his mother and father not about the Germans who stood against him, but about the British who fought beside him: "Naturally, the British took all the credit for repelling the counterattack the Germans made to recapture Argentan," Stout wrote. "Actually, the number of planes they used amounted to about 10 percent of ours."

Realizing that the Germans might escape, Montgomery modified the plan to close the gap between Trun and Chambois twelve miles farther to the east. The Germans were surrounded on three sides. With better weather on August 7, Thunderbolts were up while the Germans desperately tried to flee through the narrowing gap.

Second Lieutenant Roscoe Crownrich was attacking German tanks near Domfront that day when 88mm gunfire rushed up at him. "I should have gotten the hell out of there," Crownrich said. Instead, he dived to an altitude of two hundred feet and strafed German vehicles and troops. Crownrich's Thunderbolt was shaken by a direct hit just forward of the cockpit. The blast slammed the right rudder pedal into his leg and ankle with bone-breaking force. His canopy blew off. Fire erupted in his cockpit. Fortunately for Crownrich, the P-47 pitched up into a steep climb, taking him high enough to bail out.

"My right leg and ankle were shattered by the rudder pedal," said Crownrich. "My right foot was missing as I descended in my chute. My clothes were smoldering."

Twisting beneath the nylon canopy, Crownrich discovered that his foot was there, after all. "It's just that it was facing backwards." Small-arms fire swirled around him. He hit the ground hard and was immediately surrounded by German uniforms.

Thus began an incredible escape saga. Wehrmacht soldiers—the very ones he had been strafing—grabbed Crownrich and took him to a field hospital. "They kind of roughed me up a little when I landed," Crownrich said. A panzer captain interceded and stopped the beating. After a brief stay in a German tent hospital, Crownrich was taken to Nazi-occupied Paris. The Allies were approaching the French capital. Although Crownrich could not walk, Free French resistance fighters freed the young officer and stashed him in an attic until Allied soldiers arrived. He'd been shot down on his thirty-ninth mission.

☆

The 365th Fighter Group's Hell Hawks were only one of four combat groups supporting American and Allied troops in the fields of France. The Hell Hawks were part of a the 84th Fighter Wing, which also included the 50th, 404th, and 405th Fighter Groups. The wing, in turn, reported to Quesada's IX Tactical Air Command, which, in turn, fell under Ninth Air Force, where, on August 8, Lt. Gen. Hoyt S. Vandenberg replaced the lackluster Brereton.

☆

Also on August 8, Grant Stout was wounded. The big, athletic Stout was writing home regularly. He complained frequently about the British knack for claiming credit for achievements racked up by the Americans, and related his postwar plans to buy a camper and travel around the country promoting aviation at colleges and universities. He told his father that he had acquired a German machine gun they could "have fun with" after the war. He neglected to mention another prized possession: his pet duck.

Stout didn't hide from his parents the hard fact that making it home from this war was not a given. "Well, you can call me the 'Purple Heart Kid' now. On Aug. 8th, I got hit while strafing a tank. It didn't hurt me bad, though. The 20mm armor piercing [shell] came up through the floorboards and smashed the right rudder pedal out from under my foot. Then, [a] piece of the pedal tore through my shoe and cut my little toe. It is not bad though and I'll be flying again next week. I didn't have much trouble with the ship, however, and landed out of a left turn and cut the switches to coast to a stop as [the shell] knocked my brakes out."

Stout and other younger pilots looked to more experienced men to lead missions. Captain James E. Hill led numerous flights over the Falaise Pocket. On August 13, 1944, Hill led the Hell Hawks' fourth mission of the day, a strike mission by the 388th Squadron on some troublesome antiaircraft batteries. After taking off from their new home on the Continent, 2nd Lt. Lavern R. Alcorn's flight formed up over the English Channel and flew toward Caen.

Alcorn went after a flak emplacement. He thumbed the button on top of his stick to toggle his bombs, but one didn't release. He couldn't land at A-7 with a hung bomb, so Alcorn went down again and this time got a good drop. But German gunfire struck his Thunderbolt just behind the canopy. "My cockpit filled with smoke," Alcorn said. "I had no radio. I couldn't call for help."

With a cockpit fire imminent, Alcorn had no time to ponder options. "I set the rudder trim to skid the plane so I would miss the tail when I went out," Alcorn said. "I was using my knees to hold the stick, to prevent the plane from rolling, while I tried to climb out. But the plane rolled, too, and I was very low when I bailed out. I landed right after the chute opened and hit hard on my butt, bruising my tailbone badly."

It was about noon. In a small field amid hedgerows, Alcorn ditched his chute and had what he called "that 'all alone' feeling." He found his way to a wagon path and came upon four French civilians. Though they spoke no English, they hid him in double hedgerows and brought him clothing. The attire was for someone five feet four inches in height, and Alcorn, the robust Iowa boy, was six feet. He had to keep wearing his GI shoes.

Alcorn had no dog tags, having lost them in a volleyball game at A-7 earlier that day. He had to give up his pistol and equipment, while the French civilians tended to his bleeding chin and bruised tailbone. The thought struck Alcorn that without proper identity documents, he would be treated as a spy if captured.

Alcorn stayed in a trench all night. His escorts brought him cider and dinner. To Alcorn, it seemed the darkest night ever, but he slept and in the morning the civilians brought him breakfast.

The French bundled him onto a wagon cart piled high with furniture and personal goods, belonging to a family fleeing the battle area. Because his tailbone was so sore, Alcorn had to stand. German soldiers in the yard looked him over but did not suspect they were staring at an American fighter pilot. A sixteen-year-old interpreter told Alcorn he could join the fleeing French refugees, or he could try to evade by himself. He took his chances with the civilians streaming from Caen. His party consisted of two carts pulled by Belgian draft horses, carrying children and "an old lady right on top with me."

As the cart trundled along, Alcorn did his best to conceal his GI shoes and his very short trousers. He felt very conspicuous, and very much aware that none among his companions spoke a word of English. Hiding under the cart's load of timber, his party rolled right through a German army camp.

After five or six miles, they passed a German truck that had been strafed by Allied fighter-bombers. Alcorn noticed that the Wehrmacht vehicles going by all had a man on the back bumper to watch for prowling aircraft. Next day, a man in Alcorn's own refugee party was killed in a similar strafing attack.

On the night of August 14, Alcorn slept in an apple orchard. The next day, German soldiers were nearby but did not stumble upon the Thunderbolt pilot. The French moved Alcorn into an old house, and he slept on a mattress on the floor. One morning, he woke up startled to see a German soldier peering in at him through the window. He lay there, wearing his GI shoes, terrified. "I just lay still and kept silent," he said.

He holed up for a week, listening to the sounds of the German retreat. Then the fighting came to Alcorn. Advancing Canadian troops skirmished with Germans in the area, scattering mortar fire around Alcorn's hideout. Making contact at last with a Canadian soldier, he was turned over to a chaplain, who drove him to the rear as the ill-clad Alcorn held a pistol on two SS prisoners in the back seat.

Alcorn had made it halfway, but the British seemed in no rush to verify his identity and return him to his unit. He eventually "went over the wire" and made his way back to A-7 on his own. During his absence, the Hell Hawks had continued to fly as the Falaise battle unfolded.

☆

After the failure of their armored counterthrust at Mortain, the Germans had no choice but retreat, no goal save extricating themselves from encirclement. From August 7 to 14, the Wehrmacht headed for the rapidly closing escape route between Falaise and Argentan, the so-called Falaise Gap. Montgomery's British, Canadian, and Polish forces pressed down from the north, while Hodges and Patton under Bradley pressed northeast. German guns, tanks, trucks, fuel tankers, and horse-drawn wagons had only a few roads open to the east. As Allied artillery and fighter-bombers lashed at the enemy, the crowded roads became killing grounds. By August 13 the retreat had become a rout as the Wehrmacht tried desperately to hold open the gap even as its combat formations crumbled.

The British Second Tactical Air Force and the U.S. Ninth Air Force cut a wide swath of destruction across the pocket. In two days, August 13 and 14, the Ninth's pilots claimed sixty-three tanks, seventy-five armored vehicles, ten half-tracks, 1,081 motor transports, thirty-three trucks, twenty-nine artillery pieces, sixteen flak guns, seven staff cars, eight horse-drawn vehicles, nine rail cars, and eight ammunition dumps. For the Allied pilots, the Falaise Pocket was a shooting gallery.

The carnage made a deep impression on the pilots. During the second week of August, Lt. Quentin C. Aanenson of the 391st Fighter Squadron flew repeatedly over the pocket. Even from five thousand feet, he could detect "an odor of war to the place" as he searched for targets in those hot days of August. "We would shoot anything that moved in that pocket," said Aanenson. "On our armed recon missions, there were many fires visible amid the smoke, and it was difficult to stay within the 'bomb line' parameters and keep track of where friendly forces were."

Hans Eberbach, commanding the Fifth Panzer Army, was on the receiving end of the Thunderbolt and Typhoon attacks. "Enemy airplanes made any movement impossible . . . round about us smoke clouds were rising from burning cars." A planned counterattack proved impossible: "Most of the units were cut to pieces on the march because of traffic congestion during air raids. . . . The commanders, pursued by the fighter-bombers, tried to get their units together. . . . Many companies had not reached their march objectives, but on account of the incessant air attacks, had sought the nearest shelter." Road losses to the fighter-bombers reached 30 to 40 percent of combat strength.

As the gap narrowed on August 18 and 19, German troops headed for the narrow roads between Trun and Chambois. East of Moissy on the River Dives, one route choked with destroyed vehicles and corpses was grimly labeled the Corridor of Death. Generalmajor von Gersdorff recalled that "hundreds upon hundreds of vehicles that had been put out of action by enemy fire, untended wounded, and innumerable dead characterized a battlefield in a manner rarely seen throughout the entire war."

☆

Amid the fighting in and around the pocket, the Hell Hawks discovered the itinerant nature of the war they would wage on the European land mass. Just getting "comfortable" with the rude facilities at A-7 (they had flown out of Fontenay for just six weeks), the men began their move to their second Continental base. On August 14, 1944, an initial party from the group's 386th Squadron had begun arriving at Balleroy, ALG A-12, southwest of Bayeux a little over ten miles inland from Omaha Beach. While ground crews unloaded trucks, threw up tents, and dug latrines, the men heard the news of Allied landings in southern France. "Today we are moving to a new strip up nearer the lines," wrote Grant Stout in the same letter detailing his wounding six days earlier. "That's one of the nice things about this outfit. We will always be on the move. Because my foot is lame and I am still grounded, I'm driving the colonel's [Stecker's] auto to the new stop." As he did repeatedly, Stout bashed the British and praised the GIs on the ground: "Our tanks are sure doing a swell job over here. In fact, I don't see why the British don't withdraw their forces . . . and let us go on and finish the war. They haven't done anything yet except get in the way."

Stout's view of the British was shortsighted; their Typhoon and Spitfire fighter-bombers inflicted as heavy a toll in the pocket as did the American Jugs, Lightnings, and Mustangs. Spitfire pilot Ted Smith, a flight sergeant in 127 Squadron, described events in Normandy as the Falaise slaughter drew to a close:

> The Falaise Gap is reputed to be the aftermath of immense carnage. The German army, trapped in the closing of the gap, were slaughtered by the thousands. . . . The stench of rotting corpses of men, cows, horses, they say is unforgettable. The rumour that the Polish army is in charge of the cleanup is a *fact*. In practicality, they have turned a portion of the area into a used vehicle lot. Hundreds of vehicles, all incapacitated in one way or another, are passed in bargaining, for from 100 to 1,000 francs. . . .
>
> Dave Fyfe's sharp eye caught on an SS Mercedes Benz, looking, on cursory inspection, to be undamaged. He paid a Polish staff sergeant 500 crisp new francs, from his own and Asboe's escape pack. He was handed the keys, and got in the driver's seat. The others watched, as he leapt out immediately—threw himself on the ground—then choked, and vomited. He got up and staggered away,

retching. The headless cadaver of an SS major was on the rear seat. The head was on the floor."

The Hell Hawks were caught up in an air-to-ground battle that might decide the outcome of the war, but the Luftwaffe was still a threat, and every Jug pilot went into action knowing German fighters could bounce him. First Lieutenant Archie F. "Lin" Maltbie had experienced more air-to-air action than most: back on July 18, a Messerschmitt Bf 109 locked on his tail, refused to let go, and pumped bullets at him. First Lieutenant Jerry G. Mast spotted Maltbie in trouble, broke into the Bf 109, and fired into the German's cockpit. Maltbie was saved that day, but a month later on August 19—in another formation led by James Hill—he had another run-in with the Luftwaffe.

"The Falaise Pocket issue was still in doubt," Maltbie said. "The Germans were trying to get over the Seine. With Major James Hill leading my flight, we were patrolling the Seine trying to make things difficult for them. We were tearing up pontoon bridges. We shot up their motor transport. But just after we passed up a chance to shoot at an ambulance, the Messerschmitts bounced us."

Maltbie spotted three Bf 109s in the haze. It wasn't much of a fight. Before much of anything could happen, "a Bf 109 blew up in my face," Maltbie said. His Thunderbolt trembled and a wall of noise exploded around him, "My engine was burning. I had gas on the floor of my cockpit." There was little time to think. Maltbie pulled up his canopy handle and executed the technique for bail-out. As Maltbie left his airplane at six thousand feet, he saw its engine cowling wreathed in flames. Seconds later, the Thunderbolt blew up.

It was the beginning of another Hell Hawk saga of escape and evasion.* "I was too high when I popped my chute," Maltbie recounted. "Messerschmitt 109s circled me. I was descending at about 2,500 feet when I took ground fire that put four holes in my parachute canopy."

---

* The shootdown exploits of P-47 pilots like Crownrich, Alcorn, and Maltbie—especially when they came replete with tales of help from the resistance—would become a staple of men's pulp adventure magazines in the immediate postwar period. Although the real facts were plenty dramatic, articles in *Stag*, *Male*, and *Man's Magazine* (written by authors such as Mario Puzo, Bruce Jay Friedman, and Robert F. Dorr) transformed the resistance fighters into scantily-clad maidens, re-created the downed pilots as macho supermen, and, in turn, inspired movies and television dramas for years to come.

Maltbie landed in Fôret-de-la-Londe, Elbeuf, France, right on the Seine River. He came down in a clearing perhaps fifty yards in diameter, missing trees. It was about nine or ten in the morning—a good time to hide. Maltbie took off through forest until he found a spot where he could hole up in rocks off a trail. Four German soldiers passed by but did not see him.

Allied lines were fifty or sixty miles away, and Maltbie wanted to get there. He came into contact with a French woman who got him in touch with the Maquis, the resistance, and got him fake documents as a Basque. They hid him in a farmhouse.

Maltbie was terrified when a German soldier surprised him and came right into the farmhouse. He froze; the German ignored him and took salt, bread, and butter. Maltbie's scare was in fact a sign of the Germans' dire situation. The French told him that the Germans never took foodstuffs from civilians; their supply system must be breaking down. A series of adventures and close calls would eventually bring Maltbie back to friendly lines, but while he holed up in the farmhouse, he got a rare ground-level view of a Jug attack just three quarters of a mile away.

From August 18 to 21, as the Wehrmacht launched an armored counterattack to keep open the last escape route for their forces struggling to flee the Falaise Pocket, the Hell Hawks stayed close to the front and inflicted death from above. This was the job these men were here to do: not fighting Messerschmitts, not battling flak emplacements, and certainly not hitting the silk, but, rather, bombing and strafing the Germans' means of resisting the Allies. That might mean an armed reconnaissance mission, "an AR" in pilot shorthand. Plainly put, on an AR you went looking for a target of opportunity and did your best to pulverize it.

Much of the time, the target was motor transport, so the mission became "an MT" to pilots. Thunderbolt pilots became adept at flying very low and very fast, engaging utility vehicles, trucks, and even Tiger tanks. Unfortunately, however, the German logistics machine did not rely on motors. Horse-drawn supply convoys were common, and it was the destruction of just such a column of ammunition carriers that Maltbie witnessed.

From his hideout, the downed pilot heard the roar of engines and the thunderclap of explosions as the air-to-ground attack unfolded. Hours later, he investigated, cautiously looking over the killing field. "It was the saddest sight I ever saw," Maltbie said. What stuck in his mind was the sight of the dead, blackened, and bloated horses with dead German soldiers under and around them. Twenty to thirty ammunition carts had been destroyed along with three tanks; fifteen to twenty horses and twenty-five to thirty Germans lay dead amid the wreckage. "The German soldiers were scattered helter-skelter," Maltbie said. "There were pools of blood on the road. It was a mess. My heart went out to those horses. I didn't feel a darn thing for the men, but I felt for those horses."

One Thunderbolt pilot felt he could see the expression on the face of a German soldier when he began a strafing run at low level. Another touched off a cart full of ammunition, flew through the explosion, and returned to A-7 with part of his Jug blackened. Too often, there were tree branches or foliage caught in the cowling of a P-47. Too many times the men talked about the horses, always the horses. Part of their job was to kill men, and they themselves might die in the process, but why the horses?

The answer, as always, was that the Thunderbolt was a terribly efficient means of killing the enemy. As early as D-Day it was evident that Germany had more than enough weapons of war (planes, tanks, guns) and would continue to have more than enough—but did not have enough trained men, not in the air, not on the ground. The Germans' own numbers showed that if a Wehrmacht rifleman was wounded in ground combat, he had a 40 to 50 percent chance of returning to fight again. But if he was wounded in air-to-ground action of the kind being inflicted by the Hell Hawks, he stood only a 20 percent chance of ever again being a factor in the defense of the Reich.

☆

Men could not share the peril of this air-to-ground war without bonding. They did not all like each other. They were sometimes less than friends, often more. Only later, many years later, would some reflect on the notion that they were an aerial band of brothers. There was that famous quote from Shakespeare's *Henry V* that separated those who fought from those who lay abed back home, and it applied perfectly to the P-47 pilots of the 365th Fighter Group.

> From this day to the ending of the world,
> But we in it shall be remembered
> We few, we happy few, we band of brothers;
> For he today that sheds his blood with me
> Shall be my brother; be he ne'er so lowly,
> This day shall enoble his rank.
> And gentlemen in England, now abed,

Shall think themselves accursed they were not here;
And hold their manhoods cheap while any speaks
That fought with us upon Saint Crispin's day.

The English king's soliloquy applied to the Hell Hawks as surely as any band of men-at-arms. Shakespeare's Henry spoke not only of the bonding of strong men, but also their awareness of standing on the precipice of history.

Most of the Hell Hawks were younger men, like Crownrich, Maltbie and Alcorn. Others were in their early twenties, but maturing quickly: 2nd Lt. Robert L. Saferite, the Eureka, Kansas, youngster who was working for Lockheed on the west coast when the war started; 1st Lt. John H. Fetzer Jr., the athlete from Louisiana who lost a real-life brother in navigator training; and 2nd Lt. Grant Stout, husky, even more athletic than Fetzer, owner of the pet duck, Zeke, and plagued by a premonition. They were the ones who had been civilians at Pearl Harbor, like 1st Lt. Zell Smith, a 388th Squadron pilot, and 2nd Lt. Joseph R. "Dick" Miller, twenty-two, who had crashed his Jug near the beach on D-plus-1 and who, on August 14, was hit by flak and broke a leg on bailout.

There was 1st Lt. Allen V. Mundt, from Milwaukee, a flight-school classmate of Stout's who had attended the University of Michigan and lost a fraternity brother in the Pacific. There was 1st Lt. Andrew W. Smoak (Andy to some, Smoky to others), a South Carolina boy whose mother and father were hearing- and speech-impaired and who, like his father, faced a lifetime struggle with alcohol.

They were led by older men—most in their late twenties—who were good pilots, usually good leaders, and representatives of the most effective officer corps the world has ever produced. Contrary to myth, it was the American officer, not the German or Prussian or Russian, who came to his duty with the finest skills of leadership, flexibility, and initiative. Most were simply citizens who had chosen a military career.

☆

With Col. Ray Stecker on board as 365th Fighter Group commander, the happy few of the Hell Hawks at last had their own Henry V. "He was more easygoing than Call," said Lt. Col. Don Hillman, who shared a room with him in a liberated chalet at A-7. "He was closer in age to the pilots." Gene Wink recalled that Call was "an 'older generation' type leader, rather authoritative in his demeanor. To me he did not seem to relate well to the younger pilots except those he especially liked or would play cards with him. Stecker was different. Stecker was close enough in age to understand a first lieutenant."

But Stecker had a certain seasoning: In the December 1930 army-navy football match-up, the first between the archrivals in three years, *Time* magazine had reported that "Navy's Captain Blimp Bowstrom was punting perfectly and the big Navy line always held when it had to." But nobody was stopping halfback Stecker. The future all-American, future Hell Hawks leader advanced in an abrupt, swerving maneuver that confused Navy's defense, carried 56 yards to cross the goal line, and gave Army the 6-0 win.

A handsome six-footer with prematurely graying hair and a booming voice, the confident Stecker caught the eye of women and received more than occasional visits from journalists Clare Boothe Luce and Martha Gellhorn, wife of Ernest Hemingway. The Hell Hawks shook their heads in wonder, winked, and looked the other way. Stecker was a leader of men. Some would go through fire for him. One did. "He damn near got his butt shot off one day when a blast of fire enveloped his airplane, but he and I both flew through that fireball and survived," said 1st Lt. William L. Ward. The younger men in this brotherhood knew that Stecker was unlikely to develop engine trouble after takeoff or any of the other reasons for aborting that constantly plagued his predecessor, Call. Stecker, they knew, believed in leading from the front.

With Stecker up there at group headquarters was former 388th Squadron commander Lt. Col. Donald E. Hillman, now Stecker's deputy. "He had black, wavy hair," said Ward, "He was a kind of tall, thin fellow. Everybody got along with him but he wasn't the most popular. . . . He was a stiff and formal kind of guy." Hillman was the older generation writ large: his experience was invaluable when he led repeated missions in the Falaise Pocket. Yet more than a few described him as distant and aloof.

Stecker inherited the squadron commanders serving under Call: Major William D. Ritchie at the 386th (who painted "likker jugs" on his plane and played the cello), Louis T. Houck at the 387th (who was "quiet, introverted, respected," as one within the brotherhood put it, and piloted a P-47 called *Screemin' Weemie*), and Major John R. Murphy at the 388th ("Norwegian by descent," a wingman said, with a gap between his front teeth, "an airman's idea of a great guy"). Stecker benefited from other seasoned leaders, too, like Maj. Arlo Henry of the 387th Squadron ("a great guy, kind of laid back, who smoked a cigar on takeoff against the rules," one wingman recalled, but was stricken with "bad dreams at night").

☆

Near the end of August, 1st Lt. Robert M. Fry of the 388th Squadron surveyed the devastation of the Falaise Pocket from his Thunderbolt high above the battlefield. "I spotted a speck of dust on a road," Fry told his son after the war. "I'd expended all my ordnance but my .50-cal ammo. I saw this motorcyclist, an army courier, riding a straight-pipe BMW; he must have been going about a hundred miles per hour. I went to full throttle and came down on him from behind, firewalled and on the deck."

When Fry was close enough to see the dispatch rider's long, leather trench coat flapping in the wind, he "gave him a quick burst." He pulled the stick back and soared high above the road, dipping a wing and craning his gaze rearward. "When I looked back, there was motorcycle spread all over the French countryside. But he was the enemy, and he might have been hauling important communications."

For the Germans, the nightmare was looking over one's shoulder to see the blunt cowling and bristling wings of a P-47 head-on, a second or two from gun range—and oblivion.

Chapter Six

Bradley's Aerial Hammer: Tank-Busting across France

"**Y**OU HAVE BOMBED AND STRAFED all the roads, causing complete congestion and heavy traffic jams," one German told his captors. "You have also destroyed most of our gasoline and oil dumps, so there is no future in continuing the fight." Thomas A. Hughes recounted a letter from a German soldier to his wife: "It doesn't look very good. The most difficult thing has been and remains the enemy air force . . . it is there at dawn, all day, at night, dominating the roads."

Eisenhower, long afterwards, recalled his drive through the hell in which his airmen and artillerists had trapped the Wehrmacht: "The battlefield at Falaise was unquestionably one of the greatest 'killing grounds' of the war. I encountered scenes which could be described only by Dante. It was literally possible to walk for hundreds of yards at a time stepping on nothing but dead and decaying flesh."

Hughes described the scene: "Burnt-out vehicles blocked roads for miles around. In the hot summer sun, dead cattle and bloated German bodies crawled with maggots. In the most-bombed areas, fragments of bodies festooned the trees. Everywhere, there was very little dignity in death."

☆

The Allies closed the Falaise Pocket on August 20, and despite the successful escape of many German soldiers from the slow-moving pincers, the Wehrmacht in the West was nearly disarmed, having abandoned most of its combat gear. Twenty-first Panzer Division lost every one of its 127 tanks and forty assault guns. The seven panzer divisions collectively escaped across the Seine with just twenty-four tanks and sixty artillery tubes. Nearly every piece of heavy equipment—vehicles, guns, ammunition carriers, tanks, flak guns—was left on the west bank of the Seine. Many Allied generals were predicting the imminent end of the war in the West.

The Hell Hawks raced to keep up with their ground counterparts in General Courtney Hodges' First Army, who in early September were pressing northeast across the Seine and driving for the German frontier. Leaving Balleroy on the 27th of August, the 365th's recon party had moved out for a new field near Le Mans, but had just begun setting up when they were ordered to ALG A-48, at Brétigny-sur-Orge, twenty-one miles south of Paris. The recon team was joined by the A party of eighty Hell Hawks to set up an initial encampment. Back at Balleroy, near Caen, the B party kept the group's Thunderbolts in the air. Pilots began ending their missions at Brétigny; the flying tempo never slowed as the C party closed down Balleroy and brought in the remaining equipment. By September 3 the Hell Hawks were 135 miles closer to the front lines and dealing out destruction from A-48. They found plenty of targets.

On the 2nd, still flying out of Balleroy, twelve planes of the 386th Squadron led by Capt. George W. Porter found a German convoy of more than 150 motor transports on the road near Arras. As the light faded, Porter led the squadron down; four Thunderbolts carried a single five-hundred-pounder each, and they hit the front of the column and halted the rest. Then the slaughter began.

Wheeling into a strafing pattern, the dozen P-47s wrecked fully a third of the enemy column. When Porter's men drew off, they had destroyed forty-five trucks and heavily damaged nearly thirty more, leaving a ribbon of black smoke twisting up from the roadway and the acrid odor of burning gasoline hanging in the air.

The Hell Hawks had been fighting in the European theater since March 1944, but until now only a few of the pilots, those unfortunate enough to be forced down amid the Wehrmacht, had seen the devastating results of their aerial attacks at first hand. On September 3 the balance of the group moved up by truck convoy to their new base at A-48, traveling east over roads recently used by the retreating Germans. Charles Johnson was there: "The road south from Caen through Falaise to Argentan and east to Chartres was almost a solid line of burned-out trucks, tanks, and overturned horse-drawn artillery. The bodies of the many unburied dead German soldiers and the bloated remains of hundreds of horses and cows killed by mortar and machine gun fire filled the air with an unbearable odor." French refugees, some pushing wheelbarrows containing the pitiful remnants of their family's possessions, trudged wearily toward their ruined villages. A few managed to cheer the Hell Hawks as the airmen rolled onward toward Brétigny.

Armed reconnaissance missions continued even as the Hell Hawks shifted forward. On September 5, the 386th Squadron ranged to the Belgian-German border near Koblenz, bombing barges and railroad tracks and shooting up army vehicles along the Moselle River. Captain George Porter had just pulled up from torching a truck when he spotted a lone bogie on the deck, streaking northwestward. It looked like a Spitfire, but Porter couldn't be certain, so he rolled into a pass from above and behind.

Closing to within 1,500 feet, he recognized the chopped-wing silhouette of a Bf 109. But Porter had himself been spotted, and a puff of black smoke jetted from the exhaust stacks of the Messerschmitt as its pilot firewalled his throttle.

Porter shoved his own throttle wide open and thumbed the switch atop the lever for water injection—war emergency power. His Thunderbolt was soon closing fast on the enemy, nearing gun range at 500 yards. As his right index finger closed on the trigger, his prey did something Porter had never seen before. Yanking back on the stick, the German pilot zoomed skyward, popped his canopy, and rolled out of the Messerschmitt cockpit just eight hundred feet off the deck.

Porter watched, incredulous, as the enemy fighter arced over and plowed into the ground in a tumbling explosion. Circling, he flipped on his gun camera switch and collected a few dozen frames of wreckage, pilot, and the parachute below. Back at Brétigny, it took some coaxing by the intel officers to convince Porter to file a claim for this, his second kill.

☆

As the German army fled to the relative safety of their own frontier, scourged by flights of merciless Thunderbolts, Lightnings, and Typhoons, the Hell Hawks raced into the arms of newly liberated Paris. Trucked to the base of the Eiffel Tower, the first wave of men found the streets full of women eager to please Americans. Wrote Johnson, "It was impossible to go more than a block without being propositioned several times. Few of the men spent much time on their feet while in Paris."

A 386th intelligence officer later wrote of the experience: "Beautiful, friendly Paris, with its lovely and fascinating, and wicked women, was the downfall of practically the entire squadron, officers and men alike. Only by tremendous efforts of willpower were most of us able to drag our frayed and worn out bodies homeward long enough to make a half-hearted attempt to carry on the war—and to recuperate for yet another orgy."

Enough of the 386th survived the ordeal to mount a series of combat sorties on September 9, directly supporting the advancing First Army. The 386th had a dozen planes up over Belgium when Porter raised the forward air controller working with Combat Command B (CCB) of the 5th Armored Division. BURNER (the controller's call sign) was confronting German armor in the town of Arlons, Belgium, and Porter sent four Thunderbolts to the attack. Each had a pair of five-hundred-pound bombs; whistling down in a thirty-degree dive at over four hundred miles per hour, the pilots released a bare thousand feet above the target, pulling out in a face-sagging, high-g recovery just above treetop level.

The eight bombs burst in pairs amid the tanks, tossing them onto their sides and tumbling bricks and collapsed walls on top. Spotting more traffic, the Hell Hawks strafed and destroyed eight trucks and twenty-five horse-drawn transports. The hedge-hopping Thunderbolts next spotted a one-hundred-vehicle troop column near Mamer, Luxembourg. Eight Jugs roared down in line-abreast formation, spreading the flak tracers whipping up from the enemy column. Each pilot picked a target and at a range of under a thousand yards squeezed the control-stick trigger and began shooting. Troops jumped from the trucks, scattering like ants until the whirlwind of .50-caliber slugs caught them. Several passes over the burning column destroyed thirty-three trucks, probably claimed another fifteen, and damaged ten. Turning for Brétigny, the squadron wrecked a lone locomotive as the capstone to their afternoon's work.

Flying a silver P-47D emblazoned with the big red letters *Hot Fat II* that afternoon was Capt. George R. "Bob" Brooking, an experienced pilot with hundreds of hours in fighters, but all of it on uneventful Aleutian patrols in the Bell P-39 Airacobra. "I had just joined the 386th as a high-time captain, pretty senior for the group, but had never fired a gun in anger." Since his arrival, in fact, Brooking had only managed his obligatory three familiarization rides in the P-47.

Bob Brooking—a Bozeman, Montana, native—was the "new boy," one of the Hell Hawks' first replacement pilots, but he had nearly three years of flying under his belt in C-47s and P-39 fighters when he arrived in Normandy to join the Group. He had chosen P-47s instead of Mustangs because the P-51's five-hour-plus escort missions were longer than he cared for: the Thunderbolt had a more comfortable seat, said Brooking. "I had a skinny butt; I couldn't sit that long." Now over Belgium, Luxembourg, and the Reich frontier, he was seeing real combat for the first time.

On the 9th of September, Brooking was flying wing on Capt. Robert E. Young, the mission leader, as the squadron wheeled into a strafing run on a German train near the transportation hub of Trier, Germany. Young told Brooking to stay high, at eight thousand feet, out of trouble.

"I wasn't mad at anybody," said Brooking; he was just out to do a good job in front of the experienced Jug hands. From a mile and a half up he watched the squadron work over the train, but he grew impatient waiting, and dove to give strafing a try. On his first pass, he peppered the train with his fifties and came around again to finish the job.

The second pass was a mistake. The flak gunners watched his orbit and were ready. Screaming down on the train, Brooking was bracketed by heavy flak; *Hot Fat II* lurched, and his view forward instantly disappeared behind a spray of slick black oil. A shell burst had severed the quarter-inch oil supply line to his propeller controller. From the size of the leak spraying over his canopy, he knew he had only a few minutes before the eighteen-cylinder R-2800 melted its red-hot bearings and seized.

Turning west alone, Brooking tried to judge his position relative to the front lines, all the while pondering what he should do if the engine quit. There wouldn't be time to decide later: "The P-47 was not a good glider," he said. He knew German troops had been reported killing U.S. pilots as they parachuted to earth, so Brooking decided on a belly landing. Ten minutes after being hit, the Thunderbolt's engine shuddered to a halt.

Below him were piles of slag and the smokestacks of an industrial town, Esch-sur-Alzette, Luxembourg. Brooking managed to clear the steelworks in his path and belly into a grassy pasture, *Hot Fat II* crumpling under his seat but protecting him from anything worse than a good bruising from his harness.

The captain was down, having been shot out of the sky on his first combat sortie. Brooking jumped from the cockpit, waved at his squadron mates, and did a quick head swivel to clear his surroundings. No enemies were in view, but a civilian caught his attention, waving him over. "I knew there were Germans closing in, so I did the hundred yards to that guy in about nine seconds flat," said Brooking. The stranger hustled him to the loft of a nearby barn, gesturing for him to stay put.

"I heard Germans on the nearby road, and then gunfire. I found out later that the Germans had thrown a hand grenade into the cockpit of the plane," said Brooking. "When they questioned my rescuer, he pointed to some willows down by the creek." Having diverted the enemy squad, Brooking's host left, leaving the pilot's imagination beset by every worst-case scenario he could imagine. "I burrowed down into the hay and sweated it out for over two hours. But I still wasn't mad at anyone."

After dark his contact, Fred, returned with some friends and a coat, hat, and walking stick for Brooking. Dressed as a local, Brooking strode under escort to town, another man on a bicycle riding point to ensure the way was clear. "German soldiers were all over the place," Brooking said. Safely making it the two miles to Esch-sur-Alzette, he was escorted down steps into a large, dark cellar. When a candle lit the space, he was surprised to see thirty or forty townsmen gathered. "I was the first customer of the Luxembourg underground. The whole organization was there—and they were delighted to see me. Needless to say I was doubly delighted to see all of them." Brooking recalled.

Fred was the local butcher, and the pilot had landed in his pasture. The hospitality continued: the butcher's wife, Mrs. Keup, promptly fixed him a meal of steak and French-fried potatoes while her English-speaking daughter translated the candlelit conversation.

Next morning, Brooking ate breakfast while the locals watched—and applauded—through the kitchen windows. Brooking asked a World War I vet and resistance member named Joe why he merited all this attention. "He answered, 'Today you are the king.' It was my uniform and country they were thanking."

After another night with the Keups, Brooking woke to find the Germans were gone. He heard tanks in the distance—American, he hoped. The townspeople had hung white sheets and American flags from the windows in anticipation of the GIs' arrival, but the residents couldn't wait for the army. "The civilians carried me into the main square like a conquering hero, where *Hot Fat II*'s cowling was enshrined in the city hall," said Brooking. He spent the morning amid the throngs of happy Luxembourgers, singing "It's a Long Way to Tipperary" and enjoying gifts of wine and flowers. "All of the happy faces came close to bringing tears to my eyes. This was a picture of liberation that I wish everyone could have seen."

Soon a flower-filled jeep from the 5th Armored Division pulled into the square, and Brooking said good-bye amid a blizzard of kisses, handshakes, and good wishes. Riding shotgun with two Wehrmacht prisoners perched on the hood, Brooking thought about his good fortune on the ride out of Esch-sur-Alzette: "The faces of those people told me more about the war than anything I had heard or read before."

An L-5 Sentinel spotter pilot flew him out to the new Hell Hawks field at Juvincourt, France, where he found the base practically deserted. "I heard some commotion over a nearby rise and walked over the crest. Everyone was sitting on the hillside below watching Dinah Shore and her USO troupe put on a show." No one noticed his arrival.

In the crowd was the 386th commanding officer, Bill Ritchie, whom Brooking was due to replace eventually. "He'd thought my shoot-down meant his ticket stateside had just been cancelled," said Brooking, "and he'd be stuck for another tour. When Ritchie laid eyes on me, he grinned and hugged me like a long-lost brother!" After his interrogation by the intel boys, Brooking got a night off in Paris. Next day he was back on the flight schedule. "*That* got me mad," said the now-seasoned Jug pilot. His promotion to major came through just after his arrival, and "that went over big, as you might imagine," among some of the more cynical Hell Hawks, said Brooking.

☆

While Brooking had been gone, the Hell Hawks had been flying six or more missions a day in support of the rapidly advancing armored columns of the First Army. On September 11, a baker's dozen Thunderbolts of the 388th circled west of Bonn, Germany, shepherding Combat Command A of the 3rd Armored Division. First Lieutenant Zell Smith, leading, got the call from the CCA air controller, POODLE: "ELWOOD, POODLE. Target: Düren. Take out the gun position in a house blocking our advance, west side of town, red smoke on the target."

Smith gave the job to the two P-47s hefting a pair of five-hundred-pounders each. Capt. Robert M. Fry rolled in on the enemy position, reaching four hundred miles per hour in his dive before shallowing into his final run. The glowing white golf balls of 20mm flak reached up and whipped past Fry and his wingman, who followed in close trail.

Both planes released at treetop level, the four bombs hurtling into the strongpoint with pinpoint accuracy. Fry had barely cleared the rooftop when a split-second later the bombs erupted, the concussion rocking him in the cockpit. Straining to look back, he could see a roiling cloud of dust and smoke. The house was gone.

Fry pulled back into formation as POODLE called: "Excellent work, ELWOOD, right on target. Thanks to your two boys." Smith eyed the American column; as the tanks resumed their advance, he spotted a camouflaged panzer waiting in ambush ahead. POODLE cleared Smith in, and the lieutenant led the 388th down to strafe.

A German panzer's armor could shrug off .50-caliber fire, but in Normandy the Thunderbolt men had discovered that their copper-jacketed bullets, aimed to ricochet off the road surface, could sometimes penetrate the lower hull of the tank's engine compartment. Now Smith and his men poured bullets into the enemy tank, hoping to set it afire. The panzer commander twisted wildly to escape the concentrated gunnery. Flushed from ambush and desperate to escape, the tank blundered into the sights of the lead Sherman, which promptly knocked it out with a few well-placed shots. Over the radio came ecstatic praise from POODLE, joined a few days later by the words of Fry's Distinguished Flying Cross citation:

> Captain Fry executed an exceedingly dangerous attack against a strongly fortified artillery emplacement which was impeding the advance of friendly ground units. Captain Fry encountered an intense barrage of fire, but . . . he flew over the target at treetop level . . . resulting in the complete annihilation of the objective.

With the ground advance pushing steadily away from Paris, Quesada's headquarters ordered the Hell Hawks to leapfrog closer to the front. The 365th recon party left on the 10th of September for Juvincourt, twelve miles northwest of Reims, France. Juvincourt was set in the Champagne country of north-central France, much closer to the Belgian and German frontiers. The Hell Hawks shared the field's two five-thousand-foot concrete runways (captured from the Luftwaffe) with the 404th Fighter Group and a troop-carrier outfit.

Busy setting up tents and digging latrines, the recon party was subsisting on abandoned German rations: black coffee, sardines, and spinach. The strange diet, so different from field kitchen or even C-ration chow, gave the new latrines all the business they could handle. As the A and B parties arrived by truck, Thunderbolts began recovering at A-68 to continue operations. All the planes were at Juvincourt by the 15th; during the move, the group had missed just one day of combat flying.

Charles Johnson wrote that the men of the 365th spent off-duty hours exploring the maze of First World War trenches nearby, the exceptional cathedral in town, and the female population, "exploited by some in a very religious fashion also." It wasn't Paris, but it would have to do. *C'est la guerre.*

☆

The First Army met with increasingly stiff opposition as its armored spearheads approached the German frontier. The Wehrmacht, having tumbled back all the way across France while hardly making a stand, hoped to regroup behind the fixed defenses—dragon's teeth, concrete pillboxes, and antitank ditches—they called the West Wall. To the Allies, the fortifications were known as the Siegfried Line, and it would take the combined combat efforts of Eisenhower's tanks and artillery, along with the precisely aimed hammer of tactical airpower, to break through.

The Wehrmacht's withdrawal was mirrored by the Luftwaffe, which had evacuated its surviving tactical fighters from France and added them to the interceptor force opposing the strategic attacks of the Eighth Air Force and RAF's Bomber Command. Intelligence warned that the Luftwaffe would once more be seen in large, concentrated formations, employed both in high-altitude interception and against the fighter-bomber force. The prediction proved grimly accurate.

☆

With the kick-off of Montgomery's ill-fated Operation Market-Garden on September 17, the Hell Hawks were flying armed reconnaissance and "column cover" missions for the First Army's VII Corps. Late in the afternoon, Major William D. Ritchie, commander of the 386th Squadron, led a dozen of his planes over the historic city of Aachen, Germany. Searching the ground for targets, Ritchie's squadron, cruising at seven thousand feet, was bounced by thirty-six to forty Bf 109s and Fw 190s, diving from about fifteen thousand feet. The

Thunderbolt pilots broke up and into the attack, splitting the formation into elements of two planes each to grapple with the enemy. Ritchie's wingman was the newly minted major, Bob Brooking, still getting a feel for the P-47 in combat after his downing on September 9.

A lone Focke-Wulf peeled off and made a run at the pair, who turned into the attacker to disrupt his firing pass. The enemy fighter broke off his attack and dove past them; Ritchie checked the other enemy fighters, who weren't following, then banked sharply to follow the 190. "Watch this," Brooking heard Ritchie call, seeing his leader raise his seat slightly for a better view through his gunsight. From eight thousand feet, the duo raced after the Focke-Wulf with full throttle and water injection.

Nothing with a propeller could outrace a Thunderbolt in a dive, and Ritchie caught the enemy in the pullout at two thousand feet. Timing his rapid overtake, he fired a short burst from 150 yards, the tight concentration of the eight Brownings shredding the 190's fuselage. Spurting black smoke, the stricken fighter rolled crazily, out of control. Its pilot kicked free of the cockpit at five hundred feet, but before his chute could fully open, both pilot and plane slammed into the ground. Brooking, the student, had his best lesson yet on the air-to-air capabilities of the Thunderbolt.

First Lieutenant John E. Cave, from Ft. Lauderdale, Florida, was on his seventy-fifth mission as he pursued another diving 190. Racking his plane after the twisting Focke-Wulf, Cave turned inside his enemy and, leading him slightly, poured two effective bursts into him. The Luftwaffe pilot jettisoned his canopy and bailed out just before the Focke-Wulf careened into the ground. Cave pulled up from his victory, searching for his wingman, but found himself in the center of a storm of cannon and machine gun fire; another Fw 190 had slid in behind him. Cave's P-47, its cockpit area hit heavily, rolled over and crashed; he made no move to get out.

No one saw 2nd Lt. Jesse E. Rouintree meet a similar fate, but he became lost in the dogfight and never was seen again. Second Lieutenant Clarence E. Moreland was also shot up in the melee, reporting he had been hit in the right arm and leg, with oil and gas spilling into his cockpit. Turning toward ALG A-87 near Charleroi, Belgium, Moreland reported he was faint from loss of blood, and descending through a cloud deck he lost his P-47 escort. Ground observers saw his plane dive steeply into the ground three miles north of A-87.

Captain George Porter, seeing Moreland cut off and shot out of a circling "Lufbery" fight by a Focke-Wulf, turned inside Moreland's pursuer and squeezed off a burst. Porter's shots missed, but his tracers startled the 190 pilot, who broke out and down from the fight in a steep spiral. Porter's Thunderbolt overtook the Focke-Wulf in the dive; he pulled so hard leading his target that he was frequently "grayed-out" by the g-forces in the turn. The hammer of his guns blended with the roar of Porter's engine as the two planes raced earthward, bullets smacking into the Focke-Wulf's cockpit, fuselage, and tail. Passing through a thousand feet, the 190's pilot suddenly rolled out, and his canopy left the airplane. The damaged fighter snapped into a right-hand spin and impacted in a small field. Porter glimpsed an orange fireball roiling up to confirm his kill. His actions resulted in the award of a Distinguished Flying Cross.

It was small consolation to Porter, his intervention coming too late to save Moreland. The 386th had knocked down four Fw 190s, but lost four Thunderbolts in turn. Three of the four pilots were killed; only one returned to the Hell Hawks after he bellied in his crippled P-47.

Back in the air the next day, the group provided cover for the V Corps as they moved up to the German-Luxembourg border. Near Diekirch, Luxembourg, the 5th Armored Division controller, DIVEQUICK, called in the 388th Squadron for a strike on German armor. Twenty-four five-hundred-pound bombs rained down on the panzers, and the radio crackled with exuberant shouts from the American tankers below: "Well done, ELWOOD! Four tanks destroyed, the other five damaged."

Bomb racks empty, Capt. James E. Hill directed another attack on a Wehrmacht panzer unit: a half-dozen camouflaged tanks dug in on commanding heights to enfilade the American advance. The Thunderbolts engulfed each target in turn in a gale of armor-piercing slugs, disabling all six, then spotted and destroyed four half-tracks and four trucks, leaving the hillsides blazing and the way open for the 5th Armored.

When the 386th arrived forty-five minutes later with its dozen planes, Maj. David N. Harmon, the assistant group operations officer, got the call from the 5th Armored's CCB. BURNER, spotting targets from a lead Sherman in the column, called the Thunderbolts down on a tank concentration near Trier. Rolling in, Harmon's pilots quickly knocked out five panzers and damaged another three, with six trucks destroyed for good measure.

The Germans threw up a heavy curtain of antiaircraft fire against the 386th, everything from small-arms fire to deadly 40mm automatic cannon. One shot from this Swedish-designed Bofors cannon could blow apart a P-47, and the gunners were well-positioned on the heights surrounding the panzers. Harmon's men were jinking and weaving throughout each run to throw off the gunners' aim, but one 20mm shell blew through the canopy of Harmon's wingman, 2nd Lt. Roy W. Price. Price was struck by shell and plexiglass fragments and temporarily stunned, so Harmon stayed close while his young wingman tried to clear his head.

Radio knocked out, Price motioned that he was okay. Harmon had taken enough from the flak gunners: "[I picked out] a particularly troublesome battery that had already downed several of our planes; I could see their wreckage on the ground nearby. . . . I lined up on this bunch for a strafing run." Barreling in at more than four hundred miles per hour, skidding and weaving all the way down, Harmon closed to within three hundred yards before opening fire. His bullets lanced into the gunners even as the dirty white bursts of 20mm and 40mm rounds bucked and shook his P-47, *Elsie II,* named after his wife.

"I could see I'd already killed one man. He was hanging down, slumped over the firing bar." Yet the dead German's gun, a 20mm Flak 38, was still pumping out shells even as the unaimed barrel drifted skyward. Pulling out from his sixty-degree dive, "I got in too damn low," said Harmon, "and I went right over the top of that gun, and he got me in the belly."

The shell penetrated the main fuel tank, just beneath the cockpit. Its impact jolted the armor plate beneath Harmon and knocked his seat pan a few inches higher, but Harmon stayed glued to the deck and rammed in water injection to speed his escape from the gauntlet of antiaircraft bursts. "I had 20mm fire coming *down* on me from both sides of the valley, so I just stayed as low as I could and got the hell out of there." Hit but still at war emergency power, *Elsie II* roared on at treetop level for two or three miles. Harmon finally zoomed for altitude; "I caught up with Price and coached him back to base." The shot of bourbon proffered during the intel debrief was particularly welcome.

Back at Juvincourt, crew chief Harry Evans shook his head in disbelief at Harmon's plane. "I had that big hole in the belly, holes in the wings and fuselage, probably twenty-five or fifty in all," said the pilot. The 20mm round in the main tank should have blown him to pieces. "God was my copilot that day. The only thing I can figure is that I must have forgotten to switch to my main tank after takeoff [pilots took off using the auxiliary tank behind the cockpit] and so the main was still full. There was no oxygen in there for a fire."

Major Harmon's citation for his second award of the Distinguished Flying Cross reads: "Although an intense barrage of antiaircraft fire was thrown up by hostile artillery, Major Harmon descended to dangerously low altitude to plan his method of attack.... Now damaged by ground fire, he demonstrated gallant tenacity in leading his men on a highly effective attack of hostile vehicles and tanks."

Before scrapping the Thunderbolt, Staff Sgt. Evans fished around inside *Elsie II*'s main tank. He surprised Harmon by handing him the nose cap of the 20mm round that by rights should have killed him. Sixty-three years later, Harmon still adds this postscript beneath his signature: "The Luckiest Man Alive."

General Quesada cited the Hell Hawks the following day in a commendation: "Destruction of the tanks and support given in the V Corps area was directly responsible for the stopping of the counterattack taking place there which may have resulted in the loss of the complete armored combat team.... I wish to add my personal appreciation for the fine leadership and skill that was displayed during this attack. It is most gratifying to see that the fighting spirit of each and every boy in the 365th Fighter Group continues at the same level as in the past."

Quesada knew his men were making a difference on the ground, but they were daily paying a price. Some, like Dave Harmon, got back thanks to the ruggedness of their Thunderbolts. The plane could take tremendous punishment and somehow stay in the air. On a September 21 strafing attack near Blankenheim, Germany, a 386th pilot was attacking a vehicle column when he slammed into a telephone pole at close to four hundred miles per hour. The impact ripped skin from the lower left wing and tore up the left horizontal stabilizer and elevator. Despite the damage to his control surfaces, the pilot managed to stay airborne and return with the rest of the squadron to Juvincourt.

Colonel Ray Stecker led the 387th Squadron that afternoon in a dive-bombing attack on the highway bridge near Hillesheim, Germany. The dozen planes damaged the bridge and strafed a locomotive on the tracks near Morbach, leaving fifteen cars stalled behind the engine. Capt. Frederick H. S. Tate, from St. Augustine, Florida, split his flight into high and low pairs, then dove on the train with his wingman in tow.

As the pair of Thunderbolts roared down on their strafing pass, "all hell broke loose," wrote Charles Johnson. The train was a flak trap: panels dropped from the sides of the cars to reveal a battery of antiaircraft guns. Tate was hit several times in the dive but continued the run, strafing the gunners and then returning for another run. With his Jug hit and badly damaged, Tate steered for base despite his colleagues' urgings to bail out. His plane lost altitude steadily until it became clear he could not make it to Juvincourt. Just south of Verdun, Tate called that he was abandoning the P-47, then leaped from the cockpit. First Lieutenants Karl M. Kloeppel Jr. and Donald E. Kark watched in horror as Tate, parachute just opening, hurtled into the trees below. Next day they made a ground search for their friend's body, but couldn't locate the crash site. Tate was gone. American forces later recovered his remains near Vigneulles, France.

Nearby, the 388th Squadron attacked concrete gun emplacements holding up the GIs near Heinerscheid, Luxembourg. Their bombs destroyed two of the emplacements, and the squadron shifted targets to German guns dug in on a nearby hill.

First Lieutenant Ralph F. Kling, White 3, had been flying top cover in *Poppie*, a well-used olive drab razorback. Like the rest of his flight, Kling was not carrying bombs, but the target proved especially troublesome, and their flight leader directed a strafing run against the strongpoint, a building. The flight of four made their runs against the point target in single file, and the German ground troops under their flight path opened up with everything they had. A hail of small-arms and automatic-weapons fire met the diving Jugs. "Those guys with their burp guns just threw a bunch of lead right into the air ahead of us," Kling said. "They hit a fuel line on the left side of my cockpit, no thicker than my little finger." High-octane aviation gasoline flooded the floor of Kling's cockpit.

"We were just about through with the mission, I thought, and I'd dropped my oxygen mask to the side of my face so I could have a smoke on the way back. The fumes from the gas were just terrible, and I knew I had to get out. I zoomed the plane up into the vertical and dumped the canopy." Then the gasoline ignited.

Streaking upward at what he guessed was 350 miles per hour, Kling leaned out the left side of the cockpit to escape the flames. "My helmet tore off in the slipstream. I came back inside, released my lap belt, and dove out the right side." He almost jumped clear. But Kling's body jackknifed in the wind blast and his lower legs were pinned inside the cockpit, where the flames whipped to blowtorch intensity.

"It was only a few seconds, but it seemed like forever," Kling said. He had married his sweetheart, Irene, the previous February; now all he could do was ask God to free him, somehow, so he could return and care for her. "The instant I said that prayer I broke free," he said. "I got loose and was still going straight up. I was out and free; I knew I had to pull the ring. I must have pulled three or four different things before I found the D-ring. I think the chute opened under me while I was still going up. I took a long swing back under the chute, looked up to check the canopy, and then hit the ground." Kling was down, alive but terribly burned.

The fire had completely burned away his trousers from the knees down, and Kling had sustained severe burns on both calves. His face and hair were only slightly less scorched. "I didn't know I was burned. There was no sensation of pain," he recalled. The Hilmar, California, native hit the ground just a mile or two from the GIs he'd been supporting, but "I was in an open field with haystacks. There was no good place to hide. I took off my gauntlet flying gloves and the silk liners, and hid them under a haystack. Don't know why I did that. Downhill was some green grass and a little water. I thought there might be a good place to hide down there." It was late afternoon, 3:30 or 4:00 p.m., and Kling took out his handkerchief to wipe his face. He pulled it away sopping wet with the fluid oozing from his burns. "I got down the hill and there were two guys waist-deep in a foxhole, pointing their long rifles at me. I put up my hands and said 'Kamerad,' and that was that," Kling remembered. He had been captured by troops of the Waffen SS. Kling spent the next three weeks in a Koblenz hospital, face and legs swathed in bandages (see Chapter Thirteen). His long journey as a prisoner of war had begun.

☆

By late September the seemingly unstoppable Allied advance had run to the end of its logistical tether. Nearly all supplies for Eisenhower's armies were still being landed over the Normandy beaches. The liberated French ports had been wrecked by German demolitions, and Antwerp, while captured nearly intact on September 4, was still blocked by Wehrmacht units holding out on both banks of the Scheldt estuary. Without a working port, Eisenhower was forced to halt. His aim after the failure of the Market-Garden airborne offensive, where Montgomery had tried to vault "a bridge too far," was to bring his armies up to the Rhine on a broad front and capture the Ruhr, Hitler's industrial heartland. To prevent the Wehrmacht from holding defensive positions west of the Rhine, the Ninth Air Force ordered special attention paid to the German transportation and supply network. For the Hell Hawks, now hunting on and over the Rhine, the emphasis in their Armed Reconnaissance mission orders shifted from close support to attacks on railroads, locomotives, trains, and marshalling yards behind the front lines.

☆

On the Hell Hawks' fourth mission of September 27, the 388th, led by Major John R. Murphy, spotted through a break in thick cloud cover a fifteen-car train near Puderbach, Germany. Four of the dozen planes in Murphy's formation carried bombs, and their initial dive-bombing attack both destroyed the locomotive and revealed the train's cargo: ammunition. As each strafer swept in with concentrated .50-caliber fire, each car detonated in a spectacular explosion, hurling debris thousands of feet into the air. The 388th pilots ran a gauntlet of falling shards and burnt timber as they completed their attack runs and pounced on another train, wrecking two flat cars carrying tanks and sending a column of black smoke two thousand feet high.

Lieutenant Colonel Don Hillman and the 386th Squadron were in the air near Düsseldorf, Germany. They were pounding a rail marshalling yard with eight five-hundred-pounders when the top-cover flight—four Thunderbolts detailed high to provide protection to the diving pilots—called out unidentified aircraft, "Bogies!" The SWEEPSTAKES radar controller cautioned against mistaking friendly fighters for enemies, but Hillman saw three groups of oncoming planes, stacked high in line-abreast formation, directly over the city.

"I noticed they had flown over the hole in the [clouds] at Düsseldorf and had not received any flak. This seemed a bit unusual," Hillman wrote later. He throttled up and turned toward the bogies. "I realized we were closing fast on forty-plus enemy aircraft . . . Fw 190s and [Bf 109s]. I called for the squadron to drop . . . tanks and attack."

Hillman had a standing bet with Stecker in which downing a Luftwaffe fighter would win the victor a twenty-thousand-franc bounty. "Stecker's top-cover flight was several thousand feet above, and had not sighted the enemy. We apparently had not been seen by the enemy because they held formation until we were right on their tails."

The eight Hell Hawks tore into the Germans, scattering them "all over the sky above Düsseldorf," wrote Charles Johnson. Hillman overshot his first German, who turned inside and away, but he quickly latched onto a Focke-Wulf 190. The

Luftwaffe pilot racked into a steep left turn that Hillman had trouble matching in *Ol' Jasper*, forcing him to try a forty-five-degree deflection shot that would lead his target. Hillman missed.

Pulling to match the 190's turn, Hillman watched the enemy just disappear under his cowling; judging the necessary lead, he squeezed the trigger for a long burst. "Son of a gun if I didn't hit him," reported Hillman. The Focke-Wulf, smoking badly, tucked into a vertical dive, Hillman in pursuit. Seconds before impact with the ground, the enemy pilot dumped his canopy and bailed out, not far from the mushroom of orange flame marking the 190's grave.

"I called to Ray that he owed me twenty thousand francs," wrote Hillman. "Where are you, Red Leader," called Stecker, eager to try his hand. "North of Düsseldorf at twelve thousand feet," Hillman answered. Spotting another eight Bf 109s at fifteen thousand feet, just below the overcast, he kicked in water injection and climbed steeply, shepherded by his wingman, 2nd Lt. Lowell Freeman Jr. The pair cut behind the circling Messerschmitts, and Hillman fired from dead astern at "tail-end Charlie." The stricken 109 jetted smoke and rolled crazily over, heading straight down. Hillman's second victim burned, the pilot making no move to get out.

"Ray, make that forty thousand francs!"

"You dog! Where are you?" Stecker responded.

"South of the city at five thousand feet," Hillman had said, but "Ray never got in the scrap, because in a fight like this it can be over in less than five minutes. One minute you see fifty airplanes, and two or three minutes later, there is not one enemy plane in sight."

The Hell Hawks shot down five enemy fighters in the melee for the loss of one, Capt. Philip S. Isis, ambushed just above the overcast while climbing to meet the enemy. For his gallantry and initiative in turning back the superior enemy numbers on September 27, Don Hillman received the Silver Star, the third-highest award for valor given by the United States.

☆

On September 30, ordered from Juvincourt to get closer to the fighting front, the Hell Hawks began a shift north, their fourth move in three months. Their destination, reached this time by rail, was Chièvres, Belgium, southwest of Brussels, near Mons. The men had acquired a number of "permanent" possessions during their two months in France: bedsteads, desks, armchairs, rugs, mattresses, and footlockers stuffed with battlefield souvenirs and assorted booty. The string of French railcars looked more like a traveling circus than a fighter group enroute to the war.

Air Landing Ground A-84 had a pair of concrete runways, and by October 4 the last of the group's P-47s were spotted amid the field's hardstands, bomb dumps, and fuel depots. The Hell Hawks had proved indispensable to the Allies' September advance. Their ninety-three missions that month saw the group's Thunderbolts ranging far behind the shifting front to destroy Wehrmacht transportation, while delivering devastating direct support to the columns of Shermans, half-tracks, and trucks. The 365th destroyed sixteen Luftwaffe fighters in the air, but lost eight of their own pilots, only one of whom survived to become a prisoner. Only Juvincourt's plentiful champagne helped the fliers to forget the ever-present flak, the constant fear of a burning cockpit, and the ever-present prospect of sudden death in a dogfight.

From Chièvres the First Army's lines were directly east, a hundred miles away around the border city of Aachen, Germany. A rejuvenated Wehrmacht had blunted General Courtney Hodges' penetration of the Seigfried Line, and with ammunition and fuel in short supply, his troops were unable to mount sufficient strength for a powerful thrust through the German defenses. Eisenhower's armies were stalled along a six-hundred-mile front from the North Sea to Switzerland, his fifty-four divisions each spread over more than ten miles of front line. As autumn weather closed in, any gains would be incremental, the result of a slow battle of attrition. To support an eventual drive on the strategic Ruhr, the First Army would have to take Aachen, along with a dark and forbidding sector of hills and woods known as the Hürtgen Forest.

Chapter Seven

The War of the Regular Guys

A T JUVINCOURT, FRANCE, the war went on without letup, no matter the location of the battle lines. Fighting it would have been impossible without the noncommissioned officers and enlisted soldiers of the 365th Fighter Group. With names like Uhlrig, Piantino, and Johnson, they were a cross-section of America's citizen-soldier force. The men with stripes on their arms didn't pilot Jugs, but they made warfare in the Jug possible.

The Hell Hawks' P-47 Thunderbolt pilots would never have come ashore in Normandy, never advanced across Europe, never bombed a tank or bagged a Messerschmitt without the members of their team who cranked engines, loaded bombs, and kept the planes in the air. The enlisted members of the 365th Fighter Group were Hell Hawks, too, even if they were more like regular guys than those better-schooled officer fellows. They had warts and flaws, and once or twice they even had fights, but they, too, were part of a band of brothers in the profession of aerial arms. "They had spirit," said Capt. James E. Hill, who eventually wore four stars on his shoulder but never would have become a general without the advice and help of corporals and sergeants. Perhaps Master Sgt. Lewis "Moose" Uhlrig best symbolized the esprit of the enlisted men. His age is not a matter of record, but Moose, with almost thirty years in the army, would have been in his late forties. He was the old man among them: old by military standards long before Pearl Harbor, probably old enough to have sat out the war. In fact, he was ordered to sit it out, but refused to listen.

Before D-Day, before England, the men of the group were at Camp Kilmer, New Jersey, preparing to embark. Here, it was time again for the endless physical examinations the army seemed to have on tap for every occasion. "Bend over and spread your cheeks." First Sergeant Mitchell King remembered inoculations administered by army medics who seemed not to make any particular effort to insert the needle skillfully. Crew chief Sgt. Charles Johnson wrote that the doctors went over every inch of the men's bodies, and if they found any condition requiring attention, marked it with iodine. He may have meant merbromin, better known to most Americans by its trade name Mercurochrome, which was applied with a glass swab. "It was quite a sight to see this gaggle of GIs prancing around in the cold building," Johnson wrote, "some with iodine marks from head to toe."

None of the men bore more marks than Moose Uhlrig, the old man, the line chief of the 365th group's 386th Fighter Squadron. Uhlrig was an ordinary-looking fellow who wore a fleece-lined coat on the flight line, but he had more experience than almost anybody, including those who were examining him. He emerged from the medical exam fairly splattered with brownish red spots. "You ain't going overseas with these guys," somebody told the big sergeant. But Uhlrig knew that his experience as a seasoned noncommissioned officer would be needed by the younger men when they went into harm's way.

Moose telephoned Maj. Gen. Ralph Royce, an influential figure in the Army Air Forces for whom Uhlrig had been a crew chief back in the days of fabric-covered biplanes. Royce apparently intervened with higher-ups and got permission for Uhlrig to go overseas with the Hell Hawks, where he served throughout the war. Johnson later wrote that if Moose "were ever discharged from the army, he would starve to death on a street corner waiting for someone to yell, 'chow.'"

☆

Northwest of Rheims at Juvincourt, known in army talk as ALG A-68, Uhlrig, Piantino, Johnson, and the other enlisted Hell Hawks faced daily challenges, some familiar, some not. They were representative of the troops in eighteen fighter groups, fifty-four squadrons, and seventeen thousand pilots and maintainers who made up the fighter-bomber force on the Continent. To keep 'em flying, they had to prepare food, clean latrines, type up orders, stand guard, and repair and arm the mighty Thunderbolts. "This often meant we worked at night so pilots could fly during the day," said another of the sergeants, Glenn Smith.

This aerial army needed both bullets and beans. Enlisted troops at bases like A-68 did their best to carve out a comfortable life in circumstances little better than those for the GIs in the field. Before Col. Ray Stecker replaced Col. Lance Call as commander of the 365th Fighter Group, the authoritarian Call had "kicked some royal butt," as one man put it, when he discovered that the food reaching the troops wasn't good enough. At A-68, where the mess hall was run by the Hell Hawks, the enlisted man of the hour became Sgt. Herbert P. Allensbach, the mess sergeant who was honored by *Yank* magazine as the "chow champ" of the theater. The fare was straightforward; most of the officers and enlisted men had grown up on meat and potatoes. But there was plenty of it, served in a huge tent, and it was piping hot. There had been a brief incident of food poisoning for less than a day back at A-7, but at A-68 pilots and crew chiefs alike ate well.

Even with the enormous power of the American logistics machine behind him, it is unlikely that Allensbach fed his P-47 Thunderbolt fighter group using only "approved" GI-issue dietary items. After all, the Hell Hawks boasted among their ranks two regular guys who may have been the most formidable scroungers in an army that had many. Technical Sergeant Edward Cholewinski, boss of the medical section, and ambulance driver Pvt. James F. Jones were experts at living off the land. Cholewinski was renowned for "liberating" fresh eggs, chickens, mushrooms, rabbits, and even liquids known to contain alcohol. Uhlrig, Piantino, Johnson, King, Allensbach and the other enlisted Hell Hawks exhibited a studied indifference about where Cholewinski and Jones got the stuff. "It didn't occur to us to ask," said Glenn Smith.

☆

Turning around P-47s, loading ammunition belts, or stacking fuel containers was grubby work, all performed in the open, so the men prized bathing among all the other pleasures of field living. "A steel helmet does make a miserable bath tub," complained Major Arlo C. Henry Jr., the much-respected, cigar-puffing pilot of *Turnip Termite II*. The Ninth Air Force actually issued a press release about the role of scroungers Cholewinski and Jones in elevating the state of Hell Hawks hygiene:

> Shower baths in France are things which run the gauntlet [*sic*] of human ingenuity. Their general details of construction

and operation would even outdo the nightmarish devices of a Rube Goldberg cartoon. Being at an air base, the two medical "engineers" had plenty of tools handy with which to work, but equipment with which to construct a shower was a different story.

They set off on an expedition over the surrounding countryside. In a bombed-out German command headquarters they found a boiler that needed a great deal of welding, which it received; Sgt. Cholewinski swears that a grenade must have been tossed down its stack as it was so badly torn inside. Next a fifty-gallon drum of Jerry vintage was found, which was connected above the boiler. Above the fifty-gallon drum, slightly to the side, two auxiliary gas tanks from fighter airplanes were set up. Connections between tanks, drum, and boiler were made from salvaged oil and gas lines from fighter aircraft. Corrugated iron and wood also were secured at the German command headquarters, while from a nearby group of German gun emplacements that had been under construction came the cement for the flooring.

While scrounging for shower-house amenities, these regular guys unavoidably stumbled upon the wreckage of the war they were fighting. "While obtaining sand with which to mix the cement," continued the release, "Pvt. Jones came across a seventeen-year-old French boy with the lower portion of one leg blown away by a booby trap explosion. He administered first aid and hailed a passing American ambulance, and the lad was taken to an American field hospital."

Eventually Cholewinski and Jones dog-robbed enough material to construct a shower with two sections. "One section with two heads is used for officers," read the press release. "Another section with four heads is for enlisted personnel. Water can be brought to comfortable warmth in four minutes. The system at all times contains 365 gallons of water, which is replenished as used from a 500-gallon reserve in a German mobile water tank." Said Sgt. Cholewinski: "This shower bath sure cost the German taxpayers a pretty penny." The crude but ingenious rig eliminated the helmet-and-soap "whore's bath" so detested by the men.

Able to eat and bathe, the men of the fighter groups on the Continent naturally set forth to improve their living conditions. Frank Mangan, who was in a companion group to the Hell Hawks, described how the troops upgraded their GI accommodations: "After two weeks of living in tents, most of us began to collect stuff. We appreciated anything to help make life a little homier. I found a chair in a bombed-out house, brought it back to the tent, and used it to sit down and write letters home. We collected dozens of things, souvenirs, washstands, wooden shoes, you name it. So naturally, just when we got sort of comfortable, the word came to move up, since the infantry and artillery were moving so fast." When they moved in tandem with Patton's and Hodges' advancing armies, the men kept things that mattered to them but were merciless in disposing of stuff that didn't. "Some of the first things GIs dumped were their gas masks," Mangan wrote. "You could see hundreds of them all over Normandy. They're probably still there today under tons of horse manure."

If the dog-robbing talents of scrounger Cholewinski or the tent-furnishing touch of Mangan weren't enough to prove it, there was plenty of other evidence in the 365th Fighter Group demonstrating that American noncommissioned officers were men of initiative. From the late 1880s through the early 1940s, everyone versed in military affairs knew that the world's best soldier was the German. Rarely have so many believed in so inflated a myth. To be sure, the Wehrmacht troops who confronted the Hell Hawks were disciplined, capable, and courageous. They fought well even as the Third Reich disintegrated around them, and they were never less than formidable adversaries, even as the Allied advance thinned their ranks.

But corporals, sergeants, and for that matter junior officers in the American army had no peer. Germans were good at fighting, executing a plan, and adhering to orders. Americans were good at fighting, and when necessary, thumbing their noses at both the plan and the superiors who created it. Improvising their way to victory was their hallmark.

No other army gave so much authority to soldiers at such a junior level. On blood-soaked Omaha Beach, American corporals, sergeants, and junior officers transformed certain defeat into a hard-fought victory after every part of the plan went awry and ship-to-shore communications broke down. Similarly, it was initiative that enabled the striped-sleeve enlisted men of the Hell Hawks to keep the P-47 Thunderbolt in the air and make it an even deadlier weapon.

In later decades, the United States would field a professional army that prided itself on a warrior ethos. In 1944 at A-68 airfield, the nation still had an army of citizen-soldiers, making the achievements of the corporals and sergeants all the more remarkable. The army as a whole may have been technically less qualified than today's, but there is no arguing that they learned quickly and got the job done. The Hell Hawks' citizen-soldiers may have been mavericks, lax in military discipline at times, but they could think for themselves.

☆

Many of the young men climbing into P-47 cockpits at forward airstrips like A-68 may have never seen a military uniform before December 7, 1941, but the enlisted men who lay on the wing, grabbed a gun muzzle, and used hand signals to help the pilot taxi the nose-high Jug were mostly older and more experienced. They were not as ancient as Uhlrig, perhaps, nor as famous within the war zone as Allensbach, the "chow king." Older and more seasoned, they were also tremendously innovative.

All of twenty-five years of age in September 1944 when the Hell Hawks operated from A-68, Sgt. Joseph "Pete" Piantino was a model of maturity and industriousness. When the Japanese attacked Pearl Harbor, Piantino was a member of the Army Air Corps stationed at Albrook Field in the Panama Canal Zone. "I had trade-school training in aviation," said Piantino. "But I almost spent the war as an artilleryman."

When Piantino enlisted in the army in April 1939, he was immediately assigned to the coastal artillery, the ground forces' big-gun specialists who had the job of protecting friendly shores. In his first assignment he was a buck private at Fort Amador in the Canal Zone. "After I got there, I persuaded the commander to shift me to an air outfit at Albrook." When Piantino completed his Canal Zone assignment in January 1943, the Air Corps sent him to Richmond, Virginia, to become a charter member of the 365th Fighter Group. He demonstrated a particular knack for improving the tools used to load high explosives aboard the P-47 Thunderbolt—everything from the bomb service truck (BST, the troops called it) to the electrical wiring inside the Jug's three-hundred-square-foot wing. As the Hell Hawks went to England, landed in Normandy, and moved eventually to A-48, Piantino and his right-hand man, Tech. Sgt. William F. Rothery, kept devising new ways to handle bombs and bullets. If they didn't have the right equipment, they would scavenge it. Piantino may not have been as famous as the incomparable scrounger Cholewinski, but he made up in quality what he may have lacked in quantity.

Piantino notched his premier achievement even before the D-Day invasion, when the Hell Hawks initially made the switch from air-to-air to air-to-ground duties. It was clear that the Thunderbolt's dive-bombing performance needed improvement. The pilot simply confronted too many tasks at once: he had to hold position in the flight, keep an eye on the target, reach for the manual bomb release, and at the same time precisely control with stick and throttle his diving P-47. With the existing A2 release system, the pilot had to pull a handle that would in turn pull the supporting toggles on the wing shackle that held the bomb. The bombs would then separate and fall. But yanking the handle at the side of the seat was simply too big a coordination task for a single man in a single-seat Jug, and it became even more difficult when German flak and fighters were thrown into the equation. Until or unless some more efficient method could be found to release the P-47's bombs, dive-bombing results wouldn't meet the demands of combat.

Pilots and line personnel talked up the idea of some kind of an electrical release for the bombs. Piantino seized the initiative to replace the A2 manual release with an electrical/manual G4A bomb release. The purpose was to reduce the pilot's workload at the critical moment.

The new, modified G4A release offered what would be known to modern pilots as a HOTAS (hands on throttle and stick) capability: The pilot simply pressed the bomb-release button on top of the control stick. As Hell Hawks scribe Johnson described it, this activated a solenoid that pulled a system of wires that pulled the locking toggles back and released the bomb.

To test Piantino's invention, three Thunderbolts in the Hell Hawks' 387th Fighter Squadron were fitted with the G4A release. Captain James E. Hill and First Lieutenants Julius H. Almond and Andrew W. Smoak carried out a three-month test of the arrangement. Hill reported to his superiors that the new arrangement saved time, money, and hassle. In a second report to higher-ups, Almond wrote, "The effective increase in bombing accuracy and timing warrants investigation. Use of this release has not only proven worthy in bombardment of installations, but the time saved in its installation and its all-around maintenance is a constant improvement in operational efficiency."

Smoak's endorsement, though more formal, agreed: "Recent combat experience has proven the merits of this release. . . ." wrote Smoak. "The installation and maintenance of the G4A type release has tended to create accurate bombing and a simple, effective instrument for combat operations."

In addition to putting more bombs on the target, Piantino's handiwork earned him a Bronze Star, along with a citation signed personally by General Quesada. Of wider importance was Quesada's instruction to other P-47 groups to send armament officers and electricians to the Hell Hawks to learn how to rig the new releases.

☆

Piantino, the prewar veteran, was a rarity among the Hell Hawks. Most had been civilians when the war began. After Pearl Harbor, volunteers and inductees had streamed through the army's basic training and technical schools to fill the ranks of the air forces. Those with the right aptitude, perhaps aided by prewar experience as gas station attendants or factory workers, were trained as aircraft mechanics. Twenty-two-year-old Staff Sgt. Guy Bauman, for example, was a truck driver in Illinois when he was drafted in 1942. When the army sent him to engine school at the Republic factory in Farmingdale on Long Island, New York, he had never even seen an airplane before. He eventually joined the 365th as a P-47 crew chief.

A fighter group like the 365th had three squadrons, each with approximately twenty-five P-47s. Each airplane was maintained by a crew chief and his assistant, along with an armorer to load the .50-caliber machine gun ammunition, bombs, and rockets. A flight chief supervised the teams and looked after eight or nine aircraft. A squadron line chief—a senior noncommissioned officer—assigned cadres of propeller and radio personnel, sheet metal experts, and instrument techs to repair battle damage or broken systems, making sure each fighter was ready before dawn for that day's sorties.

☆

Each Jug bore the name of its pilot and a playful or caustic nickname, lettered on in bold colors, but as there were more pilots than planes, most pilots flew whatever aircraft was available at a particular time. It was not quite the same with those who maintained, repaired, and armed-up the Thunderbolts. A typical crew chief or armorer's job in the 365th Fighter Group boiled down to a single P-47 Thunderbolt, and thus to the pilot whose name was stenciled below the cockpit. Pilots and crew chiefs didn't socialize with each other when off-duty, but a pilot always knew when he taxied out that he entrusted his life to the skill and dedication of the enlisted men who tended his ship.

"My crew chief was more important to me than my mother," said 1st Lt. George Yoakum, a P-47 pilot with another fighter group on the Continent. "He was not a very sharp soldier and would not have made much of an impression on the parade ground. I don't think I ever saw his fatigues when they weren't streaked with stains of grease. He had a habit of forgetting to call officers 'sir.' But when that son of a gun got a wrench in his hands, I knew my airplane was going to purr like a pussycat. As a lot of pilots did, I kept my crew chief supplied with generous amounts of booze from my allotment, and he kept me in a P-47 Thunderbolt that never had a serious mechanical issue."

Captain Tom Glenn, also flying with another fighter group, actually negotiated with his squadron commander to get the crew chief he wanted, even though the man had a reputation for disciplinary problems. "I was getting the best crew chief in the squadron," Glenn wrote in a memoir. "True, he couldn't stay out of trouble. His last escapade was to get drunk, steal the engineering officer's Jeep, and wreck it; it cost him his stripes. But that didn't diminish his love for the airplane." Glenn, too, cemented the relationship with a fifth of whiskey and found that he and his crew chief enjoyed excellent rapport. Glenn piloted a finely tuned Thunderbolt, and his helper remained out of trouble for the rest of the war.

All these years later, Hell Hawks pilots can no longer remember why they and only they—not enlisted men, not non-rated officers—received a monthly ration of four bottles of liquor. First Lieutenant John H. Fetzer Jr., the athlete from Louisiana, didn't drink. So once a month, he walked out into a field behind the airstrip and had his crew chief, two armorers, and radioman draw straws. "The long straw got the bourbon," said Fetzer. "The next one got the Scotch. The short straws got whatever liquor was next. I gave it all to them. I never kept any."

Fetzer said he genuinely admired enlisted men like his crew chief, Tech. Sgt. Joseph F. Dimaio, and Cpl. Robert L. Sepulveda, who drove the 4x4 weapons carrier that transported 387th Squadron pilots to their planes. Dimaio was "about the most sincere person I ever knew," Fetzer said. "He was dedicated. He was honest. He tried his best to please me. He kept my plane immaculate, inside and out. You could turn my P-47 Thunderbolt upside-down and no dust would fall out. It didn't have a blemish. It didn't have a scratch."

A crew chief's typical day at war often began in frigid, pre-dawn darkness when he arrived at the parking revetment where *his* P-47 Thunderbolt waited. And it was his Thunderbolt, to be sure, and no one else's. At the A-48 Brétigny airfield, each P-47 crouched in a horseshoe-shaped parking spot with fifteen feet of sandbags protecting the aircraft; it had sufficient space for the pilot to taxi in, pivot the big aircraft on its wheel base, and aim the nose out the front. Except when he had been working all night on his Jug, as a crew chief often did, he typically came on duty around 3:00 a.m.

The daily routine was simple in concept but relentless in practice. "We'd get up early in the morning," said Sgt. Glenn Smith, who was crew chief for a Jug usually piloted by 1st Lt. Lloyd A. Hutchins. "You could feel the chill down to your bones on the flight line, even when you were inside the parking revetment. I was never so cold. It was never so dark."

It was Smith's job to bring the P-47 Thunderbolt alive. "The first thing I did, I pulled the propeller through. You had to turn the propeller manually because oil accumulated in the bottom of the engine while the plane was sitting still, and by turning the prop you could distribute the oil around the cylinders instead of having it in one big, cold lump."

Getting a new Thunderbolt to replace an older one wasn't always a pleasure for the crew chief. Smith remembered getting a new Jug with a defective cylinder. "It pumped oil out the exhaust pipe," Smith said. "We had to change that cylinder. Of course, we did all work like this outdoors. It was cold as hell."

While the pilot was still eating breakfast or sitting in a target briefing, the crew chief's next step was to open the canopy from outside the aircraft. "I got in the cockpit and pre-flighted it," said Smith. "I started up the engine and checked out the oil pressure, the manifold pressure, and all that stuff. I ran it up real fast, and almost opened it up all the way. I made sure the controls worked real good. I made sure the fuel and oil tanks were filled up."

Then came a complete check of the exterior of the plane, including the sheet metal, control surfaces, and windshield. Charles Johnson remembered that "when a 110-gallon tank of gas was attached to the belly, glass tubing was used to connect the two pieces of rubber fuel line," one from the tank, one from the airplane. The connection was a constant source of worry for crew chiefs, Johnson recalled. If a rough runway or turbulence broke the glass, the pilot could be forced to abort, or risk running short of fuel in the heat of a dogfight.

☆

Others, not the crew chief, worked on the radio, the guns, and the bombs. In Smith's case, Sgt. Sherman M. Pruitt Jr. was the radioman who kept the Thunderbolt's transmitter and receiver working. The armorer was in charge of weapons: guns and bombs. The practice was to keep the eight .50-caliber guns loaded all the time, so in early morning the ammunition was already aboard. If bombs were loaded, the fuse on the nose of each was checked to be sure the detonator safety wire was in place. Pilots aside, the armorers were most intimate with the P-47's ultimate purpose. "You didn't actually kill somebody face to face," wrote Frank Mangan in his 2003 memoir. "You merely helped from a distance."

Preflight complete, the ground crew waited for the pilots to arrive in a jeep or truck called the "fish wagon." One man would lug the parachute up to the cockpit while the crew chief helped the pilot climb onto the wing and lent him a hand with the parachute straps. The crew chief would get his pilot settled and ready for engine start. Often, bombs were slung under the wings only as the last step before a mission was launched.

The crew chief then helped the pilot taxi out. From the cockpit, the view forward while taxiing was blocked by the blunt cowling of the Pratt & Whitney radial. Pilots were taught to make continuous S-turns to clear the route ahead, but back in Richmond so many Thunderbolt tails had been clipped by the following airplane's prop that the crew chiefs had to take on a new job as "copilots." The crew chief lay prone on the top of the wing, hanging on for dear life with one hand wrapped around a .50-caliber barrel while using the other to signal the pilot. At the runway, the crew chief gave an informal salute and scrambled off the rear of the wing.

On one occasion, Smith was preparing to get down from the Thunderbolt moments before takeoff. For just an instant, he braced himself by reaching up and placing a hand on the canopy rail. His pilot chose that moment to close the canopy. Smith jerked his hand clear, narrowly avoiding a serious injury. More than six decades after the war, he could still see the permanent indentation the close call had left in his hand.

☆

The crew chiefs, armorers, and radiomen made a habit of watching their aircraft take off. No matter how many times they'd witnessed this sight before, they watched again. Like the pilots, most of them had been interested in aviation as youngsters. They never stopped watching, even as the Thunderbolts faded into the distance en route to fight the Nazis.

And then . . . nothing. "There was nothing to do," Smith said.

They stood around. They put their hands in their pockets. They waited.

The image of a crew chief waiting for his plane to come home has been overdone in every war drama. Yet the tension of that forced idleness was real. "It was nerve-wracking," Guy Bauman remembers. "You worried about that pilot all the time. They were just like a brother to you." If the aircraft parking spot was near the runway, the crew chief would wait there—and cheer enthusiastically when his pilot taxied in. Otherwise, he would join the other crew chiefs at runway's end, regular guys all of them, waiting, watching. They would count the returning Thunderbolts, and once in awhile, only once in awhile, there might be one airplane too few.

"You don't want to hear about that," said Smith.

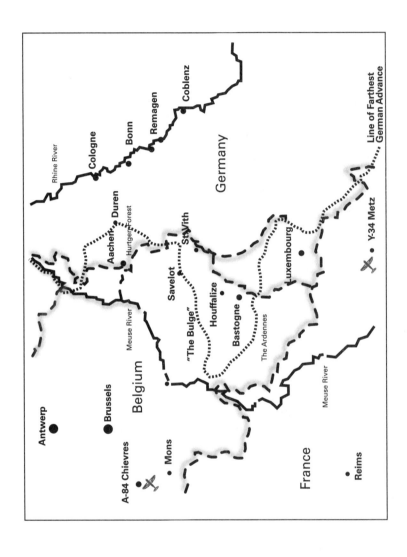

365th Fighter Group Area of Operations *December–January 1944*

Chapter Eight

Stalemate over the Hürtgen

F IRST LIEUTENANT SAMUEL B. LUTZ was unhappy. Returning from an armed reconnaissance mission in October 1944, the Chicago native and graduate of Beverly Hills High School was low on gas. "I wasn't sure I could make it home," he wrote later. His 387th mission commander, on his first sortie as leader, was busy on the radio getting a vector home from the radar controller. Lutz couldn't raise him to tell him about his fuel state, but worse, Lead's chosen course was straight over the Ruhr, Germany's industrial heartland. "This area was protected by more anti-aircraft guns per square foot than any other we flew over," wrote Lutz, and the leader "was taking us home at 3,000 feet in straight and level flight." A few anonymous Jug jockeys, knowing what was coming, keyed their microphones to issue low, anxious groans of disgust on the common frequency.

Tensed against the flak-lashing he was sure was coming, Lutz had one more problem. "I had to urinate something awful!" Exposed to enemy fire, low on fuel, and bladder near bursting, Lutz weighed the dangers and made a decision: "I began the task of trying to find my penis."

"The various accoutrements, such as seat and shoulder harnesses, oxygen hose and mask, drooping goggles, and finally gloves, made the task most difficult. The flight jacket, very long in front, didn't help. In addition, my coveralls, which were awkward to use while standing up had first to be unzipped. Once unzipped, I had to find the buttons on my OD [olive drab] pants. After unbuttoning the pants, a long shirttail had to be moved aside before the buttons in the usually unbuttonable woolen underwear could be reached. After what seemed minutes of fumbling with the underwear buttons, I reached my goal."

Lutz's joy was premature: "To make matters worse, my penis, which I considered quite normal in length, had shrunk to miniature dimensions." Flying with one hand, he struggled to align his reticent anatomy with the relief tube. "Finally everything was in place." His long struggle over, Lutz felt blessed relief as off-loading commenced.

"Almost immediately there was a tremendous explosion! I looked out the canopy at my wingmates, and it seemed they stood still while I raced backwards." Stunned, Lutz was momentarily certain he'd been slammed by a flak burst, but just as quickly realized the true source of the bang: his engine had quit with a tremendous backfire. He'd run his reserve fuel tank dry.

"Whirling madly in the cockpit, I switched to the main fuel tank, flipped the pressure boost switch, and adjusted the throttle before the engine coughed back to life. All the while my bladder kept pumping the pent-up urine. Few drops entered the relief tube," wrote Lutz, but he instead sprayed "everything from the canopy on down." The three pilots in his flight meanwhile took radical evasive action to avoid Lutz's "missing manhood" maneuvers.

Lutz landed, damp but intact, back at Chièvres, Belgium. At the hardstand, his crew chief, Staff Sgt. Patrick Tahaney, vaulted onto the wing and surveyed the dripping cockpit. In addition to the usual odor of burnt oil and sweaty leather, Tahaney detected a new aroma. Before he could speak, Lutz threw him a dirty look. "Sarge, that damn relief tube needs adjusting." Jumping hurriedly down from the Thunderbolt, Lutz brusquely called back over his shoulder, "See that it's taken care of."

Chièvres, occupied by the Hell Hawks on October 4, was to be their base for the autumn and winter Allied offensives, so the orders read. The group wasted no time in fitting up their pyramid tents to withstand the harsh weather to come. Using German materiel and scraps from destroyed buildings nearby, the men added wooden walls, plank floorboards and sidewalks, and even swinging doors and glass windows to their tent city. The improvements helped raise most of their daily existence a few inches above the churned-up sea of mud and standing water surrounding the concrete runways.

The autumn rains brought with them a North Sea chill, and good flying weather was seldom seen during October: the Hell Hawks were airborne only fifteen days of that month. The reduced air support made the Germans' defensive work that much easier as a brutal slugging match got underway in and around Aachen and the Hürtgen Forest, the latter a heavily wooded area southeast of the city, some fifty square miles in extent. Most of the fighting lay in a triangular area anchored by Aachen and the German towns of Düren and Monschau.

First Army under General Hodges wanted the Hürtgen, both to keep up pressure on the Wehrmacht in their front, and to obtain good jumping-off positions for the eventual attack on the Ruhr. But Hodges didn't realize at first that whoever controlled the forest would control the Roer River dams. The Germans were determined to keep them, for the dams could flood the river downstream and block an American advance eastward. Luckily for the Germans, the Hürtgen was near-perfect defensive ground. The thick stands of trees cloaking the hills gave the Wehrmacht excellent cover and protected fighting positions, while obscuring those defenses from U.S. air attack. The narrow, twisting, forest roads, made almost impassable by mud, negated the American advantage in armor. The GIs, advancing in the open, were exposed to terribly effective artillery fire, raining down shrapnel and flying splinters from the shattered trees. Without good observation points for their own guns, the American troops made liberal use of the P-47s, their own "flying artillery."

Sam Lutz, in his book *Just One of the Boys*, wrote about the Hell Hawks' mission over the Hürtgen: "Our job was to see that nothing reached the German troops on the front line. . . . The coordination between the fighter-bombers and the ground personnel was very good at that time, because, of course, we had so much practice. . . . Sometimes we would have one of our pilots in the forward tanks, very near the front. He could talk to us over the radio, and he could talk our language."

Near the front lines, Lutz looked down and saw

> what looked like hundreds of trucks advancing the supplies going
> to our front. We could see the artillery barrages, what looked

like a million men beneath us, and then suddenly we would hit the German lines and it was completely devoid of all movement, because, of course, we had absolute air superiority . . . .

They would tell us from the ground, 'Mortar shell on the way,' and we would start our dive. Sure enough, here would be red smoke coming up and we would bomb the red smoke. We . . . could see the antiaircraft fire, 20mm, coming toward us like flaming golf balls. We would fire our eight .50-caliber machine guns, and this should have kept their heads down.

What I didn't like was that as a wingman I was supposed to keep looking in the air for enemy aircraft. . . . We weren't supposed to take our eyes off the sky. . . . Of course we did look down. It was terribly fascinating, the heavy explosions and the tanks. It was just an amazing scene.

Lutz saw *his* side of the fight, and little enough of that; usually the best the Hell Hawks could hope for was a geyser of smoke and dirt rising from some obscure target, perhaps a secondary explosion, and best of all, a radioed pat-on-the-back from the forward air-control party. A Thunderbolt pilot was of necessity above the fray, no matter how many times he dove into the terrible flak. But 1st Lt. Donald E. Kraman of the 388th recorded the GIs' point of view in his two weeks of experience as a frontline air controller:

The Germans and the forest together were putting a high price on this little piece of real estate. . . . One company [about 120 men] of the 2nd Battalion, engaging the outpost west of the Weisser-Weh, ended the first day (October 6) with two officers and sixty men, little more than a platoon. Though not engaged during the day by small arms fire, another battalion lost one hundred men to shell bursts in the trees.

Advances . . . were painfully slow. Because each regimental sector contained only one trail heading east and because these and the firebreaks were blocked with mines and felled trees, tanks and other direct fire weapons could not assist. Fighting was reduced to . . . man against man, rifle against rifle, machine gun against machine gun. . . . So closely were the combatants locked that little of this fire [from artillery and fighter-bombers] could be directed against those positions posing the immediate problems. Relatively impervious to shelling themselves, the Germans in their bunkers could direct mortar and artillery fire to burst in the treetops that sprayed deadly ricochet fragments upon the floor of the forest that killed men who were lying in fox holes or in what they considered to be safe locations behind large trees. On the American side, the fight amid the firs was a plodding exercise in unsupported infantry maneuver.

Although frustrated by their inability to make a decisive difference by blasting the Germans out of their positions in the Hürtgen, the Hell Hawks did hear, from Kraman and others, what air power meant to the cold, muddy GIs struggling in the gloom of the forest below. As Max Hastings observed in *Armageddon*, the sight of German targets getting blasted by fighter-bombers was a huge morale boost for the soldiers on the ground. As one American infantryman wrote of a P-47 attack, "It was a beautiful sight to us. We could see the tracers bouncing off their targets, then they would dig down and let their bombs go. For a second or two, it would look as if they were duds; then a grey geyser of dirt and smoke would erupt." The air support may have enabled an advance of only a hundred meters, or taken out a single gun, strong point or observation post, but without the presence of the Thunderbolts, the GIs would have had no advantage over the Wehrmacht troops at all.

☆

On October 7, as the First Army fought to encircle the fortress city of Aachen and the 9th Division forced its way into the meat grinder of the Hürtgen (taking 4,500 casualties to advance three thousand yards), the 365th Fighter Group attacked Luftwaffe airfields just behind the battle zone, seeking to eliminate any air opposition in their sector. Thirty-six Thunderbolts bore down on an airfield in the Cologne-Bonn area; the first dive put six five-hundred-pounders into the airfield installations, wrecking one barracks and severely damaging three. A wave of strafers followed up the initial attack, while a curtain of German flak rose to knock down the Hell Hawks.

First Lieutenant John H. Fetzer Jr., the twenty-four-year-old veteran of D-Day and the breakout battles in Normandy, was at the controls of his P-47D, a razorback beauty he had called *The Madam* in honor of his wife. Fetzer, a native of Shreveport, Louisiana, had already lost his twin brother, an Army Air Forces navigator, killed the previous January in a stateside training crash. He was offered the chance to return home, but, as he put it, "I had a job to do."

On May 10, before the invasion, Fetzer had come close to sharing the fate of his brother during a low-level strike on the concrete railroad bridges over the Seine at Mantes-Gassicourt, France, thirty-five miles northwest of Paris. In that raid, Lt. Col. Robert L. Coffey, the deputy group commander, led thirty-two Thunderbolts from Beaulieu shortly after 9:00 a.m. The Hell Hawks had struck the bridge twice before in the previous three days, damaging but not cutting the vital span. The day before, they had pummeled the easternmost of the pair of rail bridges, which together straddled an island in the middle of the Seine. On this third attempt, the group hoped to finish the job.

Fetzer and his wingmates each carried a pair of thousand-pound bombs, one semi-armor-piercing, the other general-purpose, both fused for an eight- to eleven-second delay. Diving in pairs at thirty-second intervals, the bomb-laden Jugs would target the bridge while the top-cover would try to deal with any fighters or flak defenses. The pilots' fixed attack axis was sure to draw plenty of German fire.

Peeling off from ten thousand feet, the first Hell Hawks dove at a thirty-degree angle, pulling out to strike the bridge at deck level. Jinking to spoil the gunners' aim, they streaked in at full throttle, released their bombs at point-blank range, and pulled up just enough to clear the bridge abutments. The pilots took enough spacing from the plane ahead to ensure the previous pair of bombs had already detonated.

"Let's go, boy," then-Capt. Arlo Henry called quietly to Fetzer, his wingman. They were the third pair in, and halfway through the full-throttle dive Fetzer heard his leader exult, "We are *moving*!" Fifty yards behind and slightly wide of Henry, Fetzer's heavy Jug raced for the bridge at over four hundred miles per hour. Aiming at the point where the eastern span met the concrete abutment on the Seine's right bank, he squeezed the release button atop the stick.

"My right bomb came off, but the left one hung up," Fetzer said, "and that left wing dropped down almost to the water. I was fighting to get that wing up when somebody's bomb—I don't know whose—blew while I was still below bridge level," Fetzer recalled. "I didn't hear a 'boom'—this was a 'whang!' The blast blew me up over the bridge . . . there was a three-foot hole in my left wing and a basket-ball-sized hole in my right one." So much for the delay fuses.

"I was at 150 feet with no supercharger and no wingman," said Fetzer. Yet his Thunderbolt still seemed to be flying, so he manually released the hung bomb, twisted away from the searching gunners, and headed for England on the deck.

Bludgeoned by Fetzer's own and more than fifty other thousand-pounders from the group, the eastern terminus of the bridge disappeared in a maelstrom of fountaining water and debris. The Thunderbolts destroyed the rails atop the span and cratered the road approaches to the eastern abutment. Coffey's force pulled off the bridge, dodged some flak towers south of the town, and circled high to assess the results of their attack.

Orbiting overhead, the Thunderbolt men took a long, hard look at their target. Despite three successive raids and the heavy damage to the railbed and approaches they had just inflicted, the bridge remained standing. They sighted dozens of rail cars stacked up on temporary rails to the east by the bottleneck, but this was small consolation. In addition to Fetzer's, another P-47 had been hit—by blast debris from "friendly" bombs. Chagrined, the Hell Hawks withdrew.

Fetzer was in trouble: "My plane was hit bad." Unable to climb, he staggered back to base alone, the slipstream whistling through his perforated wings all the way to England. "They pulled chunks of the bridge concrete out of that plane and put on two new wings, a new tail, a new engine, and a new supercharger," he recalled. What stung the young Louisianan most was not his battered plane but the memory of a radio call from Coffey, the future politician. Just after Fetzer called in his damage, Coffey came up on the squadron frequency: "That's what you get for dragging." Laden with an extra helping of sarcasm, the rebuke implied that Fetzer had somehow mistimed his run and flew into the blast of Henry's bombs. Fetzer knew better. "Coffey really made me fume," he said. "I'm a straight shooter, and I knew I was a damn good wingman and formation flyer. I wanted to go work him over when I got back on the ground."

☆

Now it was October, and both Fetzer's temper and the weather had cooled. Over the German aerodrome, he and the other pilots of the 387th were caught in a vicious web of antiaircraft fire, lacing the sky with flak bursts and shrapnel.

"I was shooting up the field as Green Flight leader," said Fetzer. Dropping my nose to pick up speed, I looked back from my run and saw my wingman a mile behind, pulling streamers [wingtip contrails] to evade the heavy ground fire." Fetzer had just yelled at him to "get back in formation and stay there!" when an 88mm shell exploded close aboard, just forward of *The Madam*'s left wing. "The flak came in through the side of the cockpit where my name was stenciled; it slammed my left arm back," said Fetzer, known as "The Governor" in the squadron. "Oh, it hurt. It felt like taking a rap in the funnybone, times a thousand."

A shell fragment had torn into his upper arm at the base of the biceps, ripping its way toward his shoulder. Gritting his teeth against the pain, Fetzer released the stick long enough to reach over with his right hand and extract a chunk of aluminum—blown from the cockpit sheet metal—embedded in his left index finger and thumb. "It was so hot it was burning up the fingers on my left hand," recalled Fetzer. Another eighty-eight fragment, glowing white hot, "sat there sizzling on the floor." He called Capt. Neal E. Worley, Green Three: "I'm hit, Fox. Take me home."

Fetzer gave the flight lead to Worley and told his wingman to head 270 degrees, straight for Chièvres a half hour away. MUDGUARD, the sector radar controller, responded to Fetzer's urgent call with a steer back to base. Dodging more flak over Bonn, the pair finally spotted A-84. "I didn't know how I was going to switch to the main fuel tank and drop that belly tank," said Fetzer, but "I let the seat all the way down, and managed to barely reach over with my right hand [to my left side to pull the] switch and get rid of the belly." Approaching Chièvres, the crippled Fetzer reached cross-body again to retard the throttle and extend his gear and flaps. "It was the best landing I ever made," said *The Madam*'s pilot, who was met by the crash crew and medics at the end of the runway. Don Hillman was first up on the wing and helped lift him gently from the cockpit, saying "I never thought they'd get you, Fetz."

Fetzer, grimacing, managed to explain: "I couldn't let *The Madam* down." Capt. Howard H. Smead, the 386th's flight surgeon, and the other medics went to work on Fetzer's left arm in a field hospital tent, removing a jagged, one-by-three-inch splinter nearly an inch thick. His wounded arm would heal, but the flak left scars of another kind on Fetzer's wingman. The 387th Squadron commander, Major John W. Motzenbecker, later told Fetzer that after the mission, Fetzer's wingman walked in and declared firmly that he was through with combat flying. Motzenbecker found the shaken pilot a staff job, where he served out the rest of the war.

☆

Fetzer's crew chief was glad to have him—and *The Madam*—back, but fixing the badly damaged Thunderbolt meant more hard work for the ground crews.

All too often they saw their airplanes return with bent propellers, holes in wings and fuselage, and traces of the battlefield—dirt, stones, shrapnel, branches, leaves—embedded in the wings and cowling. But it was precisely the P-47's ability to limp back with seemingly fatal damage that made it the ideal aircraft for ground attack.

Pilots returned with their Jugs flayed by the withering antiaircraft fire, discouragingly accurate at medium and low altitudes. Carrol Joy, a staff sergeant from the 406th Fighter Group, reported that his Thunderbolt once returned with 105 holes in it. Warren Dronen, who flew eighty combat missions with the 362nd Fighter Group, once had his P-47 perforated by flak, bullets stitching his wing with "a sound like a sewing machine." He managed to get back safely. With the prop windmilling to a stop, his crew chief jumped up on the wing, took one look at the battered airplane, and said, "Jeez, Lieutenant! Why the hell did you bring that thing back here?"

But the ground crews turned to, and three hours after Fetzer's harrowing return, the group's three squadrons put up a dozen planes each for another series of airfield attacks surrounding Cologne and points south. The Luftwaffe decided to interfere.

Lieutenant Colonel Don Hillman was leading the 386th over Bonn, intent on pounding another German fighter base. "Colonel Stecker, the group commander, was off the base for the day. . . . Generally, while Ray was away, I didn't fly any missions but stayed on the ground to watch the store. This particular day was clear and warm and I was talking with Lt. Col. Clyde H. 'Fearless' Fuller, the group intelligence officer. We talked of the war in general and my part in particular. 'Fearless' observed that since I had already flown 145 missions, the odds of my continued survival were getting slimmer. My position . . . was that with every mission my odds were better, because of the additional experience I was continually gaining. In a few hours this discussion returned to haunt me."

When he heard the orders for a sweep over Luftwaffe airfields, Hillman decided to fly the mission personally. He dressed as he usually did, donning a cotton flying suit and leather jacket over his uniform. Hillman wore paratrooper boots and carefully folded his flight cap in a flight suit pocket, stuffing his escape kit in another. He didn't bother with a personal weapon. "I thought it was useless to try to fight my way out with a .45," he said. In the cockpit he strapped on his parachute harness, buckled his seat belt, pulled on his leather flying helmet, and snapped on his oxygen mask. He'd performed the same ritual on almost a hundred and fifty previous combat sorties.

Hillman took the 386th over Bonn, plastering an airfield near the city. "The Squadron experienced some minor flak damage but suffered no losses, so we went on in full strength east of the Rhine," Hillman wrote. One of the 386th pilots spotted a pair of Messerschmitts at low altitude, circling what appeared to be a farm field. "I told the squadron to stay at altitude, and my wingman and I went down to investigate. As we approached the enemy planes, it was apparent that they were circling to land on this innocent-looking field. The two of us began a pass to attack, but as we were lining up to fire, we were subjected to a barrage of flak from automatic weapons stationed all around the field."

First Lieutenant James L. "Mac" McWhorter was on Hillman's wing, and he remembered the flak: "Boy, it was horrible." In front, the lead Bf 109 pilot hurriedly tried to get his vulnerable fighter on the ground, but Hillman and Mac bored in. Hillman later wrote, "We both fired our guns and obtained strikes on the 109s, but because of the very intense enemy fire, we broke off our attack."

Hillman said with some understatement in a 2005 interview that it was "pretty exciting flak," and to evade the fire he dropped to the deck for several minutes before cautiously climbing for a rejoin. "While in the climb I smelled something electrical burning," he said, and after telling the squadron he was returning to base, he turned off the radio. "I continued climbing to about twelve thousand feet. . . . Just after crossing the Rhine, a fire erupted . . . an intense fire forward. I never knew whether this had been caused by flak or was the result of a mechanical failure. The fire was so intense that there was no alternative to bailing out, so I immediately blew the canopy, unfastened my safety belt, did a half-roll, and dropped out."

The twenty-three-year-old McWhorter, who had stayed low, remembered Hillman climbing into the overcast, then watched as his leader "came spinning out of the clouds, his plane on fire. He came down in his parachute."

Don Hillman, veteran of 145 combat missions and holder of the Distinguished Flying Cross and the Silver Star, would win no more bets with Ray J. Stecker. Shortly after Hillman's fellow Hell Hawks saw him bail out at nine thousand feet, his Thunderbolt blew up in a spectacular fireball near Bornheim. No one knew his fate, or that of three other Hell Hawks shot down in a swirling dogfight near Wahn, Germany. Second Lieutenant Clyde M. Shoup bailed out after being hit by enemy fighters, but his parachute never opened. In exchange for the four pilots, the group downed a pair of Focke-Wulfs and damaged two more, but on October 7, German flak and fighters had undeniably had the upper hand.

☆

The Germans used mobile flak guns to protect troop movements and communications and deny aerial reconnaissance of threatened portions of the front. The IX Tactical Air Command (IX TAC) noted, in fact, that the withdrawal of German flak batteries to the German frontier resulted in an antiaircraft concentration exceeding that seen in the Normandy fighting. The Wehrmacht routinely shifted gun positions overnight to prevent the Allies from targeting flak concentrations with follow-up raids. In this deadly game of cat-and-mouse, the Germans seemed always to stay one step ahead of the attackers.

One of the newest 386th pilots was 2nd Lt. James E. Murphy, who had just joined the Hell Hawks on September 30. The native of Wilmington, California, flew his first mission with Maj. George W. Porter, who in a dive-bombing run led the squadron through an incredible barrage of flak. Murphy had expected opposition, but the blizzard of tracers and bursting shells shook his newcomer's confidence. Amazingly, only a few planes were hit, none critically. At debriefing, he listened with interest to Porter's description of the antiaircraft fire. Would it be "intense"? "Extremely heavy"? "Impenetrable"?

To the intel officer's question about flak intensity, Porter considered a moment, then answered, "Light." Murphy was incredulous. That *any* Thunderbolts survived, let alone flew through unscathed, seemed a miracle to him.

The young Californian remembered reflecting that "if that was only light flak, this is going to be a long war." He quietly asked his flight leader for *his* assessment of the flak. He answered, "Aw, don't pay no attention to George Porter. He don't even see flak. He just said 'light' 'cause he knew there probably had to be *somebody* shooting at us. When he's after a target he's like a hog lookin' at an open gate."

The invulnerable Porter was in the air again on October 12, leading a dozen planes of the 386th to the aid of the 9th Infantry Division. Their controller, Seascout, had the Thunderbolts attack Wehrmacht troops and tanks near Roetgen, Germany, on the southwest edge of the Hürtgen. The GIs had marked the target with red smoke shells, and Porter had White Flight bomb and strafe the area until they had almost exhausted their ammo. Their radar controller, Marmite, then vectored the remaining eight planes northeast of Aachen. He had picked up unidentified aircraft and sent Porter and the 386th to intercept.

Southwest of Düsseldorf, Porter spotted two groups of twenty planes each; most were Messerschmitt Bf 109s, but a few Focke-Wulf 190s sprinkled the formations. Level with the enemy at twelve thousand feet, Porter broke hard left and came in behind a flight of four 109s.

Choosing the number-three fighter, the major gave it a couple of short bursts, hitting the wings and fuselage as the enemy dove for the overcast. Porter struck again in the dive, and the Messerschmitt fled smoking into the clouds. Porter zoomed to rejoin the fight, but oil streaming back from his propeller began coating his windscreen even as he opened up on a Focke-Wulf chasing another Jug. Peering through the side of the canopy, he turned for home; fifteen miles from Chièvres he was forced to belly-in at an old airfield near Diest, Belgium. For continuing the fight with a crippling engine malfunction, Captain Porter was awarded the Silver Star for gallantry, "brilliant leadership, and self-sacrificing devotion to duty."

"Mac" McWhorter, Red 3, with 1st Lt. Robert S. Maney flying his wing, heard Porter call out the bandits and direct the flight to "prepare to drop belly tanks in ten seconds." "The hell with waiting," thought Mac. "I dumped mine immediately . . . and looking up saw [my drop] was in last place!" Following Porter, he climbed through eleven thousand feet at three hundred miles per hour, chasing a flight of Messerschmitts, which scattered and fled. Bouncing one, McWhorter caught his enemy in a climbing right turn at about 270 to 300 miles per hour. He fired a burst that peppered the dark gray fighter's left wing and chopped loose its left main gear. As the 109 tightened the turn, Mac squeezed off a second burst that riddled the 109's fuselage and tail. Maney, concentrating on clearing McWhorter's tail, never saw the enemy but caught a glimpse of the shell casings and belt links pouring from his leader's wings. He thought for a terrible instant that Mac's Thunderbolt was disintegrating, hammered by strikes from a German coming head-on.

Instead it was McWhorter who had the range. He fired again just as the enemy pilot jettisoned his canopy. Too late: Mac's eight fifties blasted the enemy's cockpit and engine. The Messerschmitt's Daimler-Benz engine froze, and flames erupted from the 109's cramped cockpit. McWhorter saw his victim, spinning and aflame, hurtle down to spray a fireball across the landscape below. "In that forty-five seconds or a minute, I didn't have time to think about that pilot," said McWhorter. "That 109 was just a target." He pulled up and circled, looking for more, but by then the enemy was gone. He had a confirmed kill, and his courage and skill were recognized by the award of a Distinguished Flying Cross.

As the fight continued, Maj. George R. Brooking, leading Blue Flight, picked out a gaggle of six Messerschmitts climbing back toward Germany. The 109 at full throttle could outclimb a P-47, and the enemy flight evidently hoped to escape the swirling dogfight behind them by racing up and away. But Bob Brooking kicked in water injection and began to close, climbing at 2,500 feet per minute, about a thousand yards below and behind the enemy. Passing thirteen thousand feet, Brooking was within a thousand feet of the rearmost 109, which began a shallow bank to the left. "I cut inside and caught him in a climbing turn," said Brooking. Opening up at five hundred feet, Brooking's bullets slammed into the Messerschmitt's canopy. White smoke poured from the engine as the fighter snapped over into a violent roll, nosing earthward. "He bailed out in a vertical dive," said Brooking, who pulled up and over to clear his tail, then roared down after the enemy pilot, now hanging in his parachute. Hearing of American pilots machine-gunned after bailing out, Brooking had once asked his boss "if we shoot them [Luftwaffe pilots] in their parachutes." The answer was no, and on this diving pass Brooking merely turned on his gun camera and, squeezing the trigger, captured the enemy pilot on film. His DFC citation noted Brooking's "daring and accurate gunnery," and his courage and determination upheld "the finest traditions of the Army Air Forces."

☆

Throughout the rest of October, amid rain, low clouds, and fog, the Hell Hawks supported the GIs struggling to take Aachen and the bloody ridges of the Hürtgen Forest. The division controllers called in strike after strike on targets like tank concentrations, gun positions, flak batteries, mortar pits, barracks, and truck parks. Friendly artillery working with the air-control party marked the targets with red smoke, but seldom did the Hell Hawks have the satisfaction of seeing the results of their work. The pilots were lucky if, among the smoke and dust raised by their bombs, they received a verbal pat on the back from a forward air controller. Hidden in the forest depths, German defenders bent, but seldom broke.

On October 19, Hitler designated Aachen, the imperial seat of Charlemagne, as a fortress city, to be held to the last man. Two more days of hard fighting by the First Army led to the collapse of the surrounded Wehrmacht defenders, and at last the Americans owned the city, largely leveled by the house-to-house fighting.

The Hell Hawks had added their share of destruction to Aachen. Charles Johnson wrote of the chaos: "Burst sewers, broken gas mains, combined with the dead animals and men produced an almost overpowering odor. . . . The streets were littered with shattered glass; telephone, electric light, and trolley cables were dangling and netted together everywhere . . . wrecked cars, trucks, armored vehicles, and guns littered the streets." Johnson mocked Hitler's prewar boast: "Give me five years and you will not recognize Germany again!"

☆

The carnage gave the Hell Hawks little satisfaction. Their missions took a near-daily toll on pilots and planes, with little visible evidence that they were making a difference to the GIs. Bad weather wiped out flying for six days in the final week of October; not until the 28th did the Group fly combat again over the Hürtgen and Rhine valley, hitting factories, command posts, rail yards, and road convoys.

Bad weather limited the Hell Hawks to only forty-five missions during October 1944. With the First Army stalled in the Hürtgen and supplies still short, there was little prospect of a shift of fortune anytime soon. The group winterized their operations area at Chièvres, digging foxholes, laying gravel on paths through the mud, and keeping the planes battleworthy even as the rain poured down.

Charles Johnson wrote of October that "after living through a month of rain, night and day, all of the Hell Hawks now understood why their fathers talked so much about the mud of France during the First World War." Still, "they were all thankful that they were living in tents, and not in foxholes like the infantry."

Rain continued to fall, as did the Thunderbolts. "We figured our average life expectancy in combat was about seventy missions," said Sam Lutz. "And we knew something else: only the young and inexperienced died, not the mean S.O.B.s."

Both veterans and untested replacements like Lutz would soon find themselves pitted against the Luftwaffe's best fighters in one of the biggest air battles of their war. The date was October 21, 1944.

Chapter Nine

Air-To-Air

"**T**HEY WERE A THREAT TO BE RESPECTED," said 1st Lt. Eugene A. Wink Jr., the West Pointer who was already out of the war by the fall of 1944, shot down yet fortunately spirited to freedom by the French underground. Wink was referring to the "Abbeville Boys" of Jagdgeschwader (JG) 26, with their aggressive tactics and distinctive, yellow-nosed Fw 190s. But he might as well have been talking about the entire Luftwaffe. The German air force remained a threat right up to the final hour of the war, and its Focke-Wulfs and Messerschmitts constantly threatened to disrupt the Hell Hawks' mission of attacking Wehrmacht forces on the ground.

Minutes before his P-47 Thunderbolt fell from the sky (see Chapter Three), Wink met the Würger, or Butcher Bird, in a battle that included two of the Hell Hawks' most admired and aggressive leaders against the Luftwaffe. They were Majors Robert L. Coffey and William D. "Bill" Ritchie, who, respectively, commanded the 388th and 386th Squadrons of the 365th Fighter Group.

Coffey, who had seen combat over Normandy on D-Day and would be elected to Congress after the war, would become one of the handful of Hell Hawks to attain ace status by downing five enemy aircraft. The stocky, dark-haired Coffey would add a sixth for good measure.

Ritchie was "a tremendous leader," said another Hell Hawk pilot. "He was a six-foot-one or -two guy, very slender, very dedicated, well-liked. He was a good leader of a good squadron." Ritchie "liked to put up a front of not caring about anything," said Wink. "He was a little lax in his dress. He had to be the only fighter pilot who played the cello—quite well." Among the Hell Hawks, Ritchie became one of the few pilots consistently to rack up aerial victories against Luftwaffe pilots like those at Abbeville.

Wink witnessed one of Ritchie's early dogfights. His is a valuable, firsthand description of how it felt to take the Jug against the Würger:

> Suddenly, fourteen yellow-nosed Focke-Wulf 190s dove from twenty-seven thousand feet. Ritchie, who was flying top-cover with eight aircraft, made the initial call about the presence of the enemy. In addition, he tried to keep flights informed of specific locations of the German fighters. He called my leader, Lt. Col. [Oscar H.] Coen, and told him that an Fw 190 was below and in front of us. Our four-ship formation dove on the enemy at break-neck speed.
>
> When we spotted the enemy aircraft initially, the command was given to jettison belly tanks. I pulled my manual release, but I could not feel the tank drop. As Col. Coen dropped his nose and began accelerating in the dive, we were right with him in formation. As we continued in our descent and our speed increased, I continued to try to release my belly tank. Finally, it broke loose. It appeared that the German pilot had spotted us, because he began a high-speed dive to a lower altitude. The chase was on! The Fw 190 went through a cloud formation at about 9,000 feet, and we were rapidly closing on him. Shortly after reaching the deck, he broke left in an attempt to take evasive action. Our leader was unable to close on him for some reason, so his wingman, who was Major Coffey, began to close and fire. My wingman, 1st Lt. Paul Coffee, and I stayed with him. When the major broke left after seeing strikes on the enemy and parts come off the left wing, I continued firing and observed the Fw 190 cartwheel in flames into the trees.

Even though Wink put .50-caliber rounds into the Focke-Wulf, Major Coffey was credited with the aerial victory. Wink's firsthand description illustrates that it wasn't always clear who should receive credit. In these fast-paced air-to-air battles, the Hell Hawks often found that no one could even describe clearly what had happened.

The Fw 190 was the toughest piston-engined foe the Hell Hawks would encounter. But the opponent they met most often was the Messerschmitt Bf 109, a slightly earlier Luftwaffe design and the more numerous of the Reich's two principal fighters. It was built in larger numbers than any other fighter in history. The exact number built is hard to pin down, because the German air industry was widely dispersed during the war, but the total is at least thirty-three thousand. For comparison, there were twenty-two thousand British Spitfires. The U.S. fighter built in largest numbers was, as noted earlier, the P-47 at 15,683, closely followed by the P-51 Mustang with a total of 15,486. If it's hard to say how many 109s were built, it's harder still to agree on what to call it.

During the war, Americans called the plane the Me 109, a term sometimes rendered as ME 109 or ME-109. "It will always be the Me 109 to me," said retired Col. James L. "Mac" McWhorter, who came to the Hell Hawks as a new pilot in the spring of 1944. Some German documents also used the term.

Historians and writers today refer to the famous Messerschmitt as the Bf 109. That was the term by which the aircraft was known in the mid-1930s when Bayerisches Flugzeugwerke (Bf) manufactured it. In September 1938, the company reorganized, adopted aircraft designer Willi Messerschmitt's name, and became Messerschmitt Allgemeine Gesellschaft.

But although the company's later products were assigned an "Me" prefix, among them the Messerschmitt Me 262 jet fighter (Chapter Sixteen), historians today argue that the term Bf 109 applied to every aircraft in that series, all the way to war's end. German records seem to support that view. "By 1945, we were drowning in Bf 109 nameplates," said British aviation writer Bill Gunston, referring to the large number of German planes that had been shot down over England. "There is no excuse for not referring to the aircraft by its right name."

A typical Bf 109 was powered by a 1,475-horsepower Daimler-Benz engine, the DB 605A, an inverted V-12 with liquid cooling. The 109 had a maximum speed of about 360 miles per hour and was armed with one 20mm cannon and four 7.9mm machine guns.

At the time of its 1936 combat debut in the Spanish Civil War, the Bf 109 was one of the world's most advanced fighters. By 1944, the 109 was still formidable but had been eclipsed by newer designs. When U.S. experts evaluated captured German planes after the May 1945 surrender, they showed little interest in testing the Bf 109, a ubiquitous fighter with few secrets left to offer.

☆

The Messerschmitt Bf 109 was the Hell Hawks' opponent on June 7, 1944, when 1st Lt. Russell E. Gardner became separated from the rest of the 387th Squadron during a dive-bombing mission. Gardner told his side of the story in Chapter Two, but then-Capt. Arlo Henry, never at a loss for words, later described his view of the tangle with the 109s:

> It was a beautiful day. We had dropped all of our bombs on the target and were re-forming. There was no flak, and no enemy planes were in evidence. Suddenly, Russ Gardner was heard crying for help.
> "109s are after me!" yelled Russ.
> "What's your position?" I asked.
> "How the hell should I know?"

Henry determined that seven 109s had bounced Gardner, who was fleeing north. At full throttle, the 387th raced to find him, but had no luck. The enemy fighters perforated Gardner's plane, and he barely made it back to Beaulieu. Henry wrote:

> After landing I walked to Operations with Andy Smoak. During the walk, I asked him, "What the hell can you say to a guy in a spot like that?"
> He hesitated a moment, and then offered, "Don't let 'em get away!"
> At this point, we entered the Operations tent and saw Russ, who had returned before us. His plane had suffered battle damage.
> I said to Smoak, "Why not ask Russ why he let 'em get away?"
> "Like hell," answered Andy. "He's wearing his .45, and I'm not about to find out if he knows how to use it!"

In years to come, fighter pilots and historians would argue interminably which was the best fighter of World War II. These debates would usually leave out the German "wonder weapons," such as the Messerschmitt Me 262 jet fighter, which were not yet being used in large numbers in the fall of 1944.

The pilots' arguments almost always grew more intense as libations flowed, and they almost always invoked the standard bearers: the Fw 190, Bf 109, and the Mitsubishi A6M Zero. When the debate was about air-to-air combat, the American aircraft cited would almost always include the Lockheed P-38 Lightning, the North American P-51 Mustang, and the Grumman F6F Hellcat. If, like Wink, Coffey, Ritchie, Henry, Gardner, and Smoak, you happened to be a pilot of the Republic P-47 Thunderbolt with its powerful engine, eight guns, and cast-iron survivability, you could almost always be certain that no one would mention your aircraft at all. For decades, America's premier aviation museum did not even have a P-47 on display. A magazine article on "The War's Greatest Fighters" at the end of the twentieth century cited the Fw 190, P-51, and F6F Hellcat, but did not even mention the Thunderbolt.

As legend would have it, the Spitfire was still flying missions from England when the Hell Hawks became caught up in a spirited argument with one of their British counterparts. Variations of this tale have been related in the years since the war, but one version goes like this:

Brit: My Spitfire is the best fighter in the world, matey. I can defeat your Thunderbolt any time.

Hell Hawk: Not so. My Thunderbolt is the best fighter ever built. I can defeat your Spitfire anywhere.

Brit: Oh, yeah? I'll tell you what, matey. Let's just meet in the air and see who's got the better fighter.

Hell Hawk: Yeah. Let's do that, and I'll show you mine is the better fighter. Tell you what. I'll meet you at twenty thousand feet over Malta in three hours.

Brit: Malta? Are you out of your mind? You know my Spitfire can't fly that far.

Hell Hawk: You just proved my point, "matey."

Yes, the Thunderbolt had impressive range, even if it was surpassed in that department by the P-51 Mustang. Thunderbolt veterans knew their aircraft had served well in the Eighth Air Force's long-range operations over Europe, but this again was an accomplishment that nobody noticed. For the rest of the war, the Hell Hawks would be flying relatively short hops, often several a day if the always-troublesome weather permitted. The men bet their lives on the capabilities of their big Jugs, but wondered if anyone else respected the P-47.

The Germans did. They knew the Thunderbolt only too well. They went to great lengths to capture one—and did. They were impressed with its bomb load and ground-attack capability, but they also respected its effectiveness in downing far too many of their own fighters. Before the Hell Hawks even arrived in the European theater, the Eighth Air Force's famous 56th Fighter Group used the Thunderbolt to gain a three-to-one kill advantage over both the Fw 190 and Bf 109. Naturally, the Luftwaffe published a manual on how to combat Allied fighters. The P-47 Thunderbolt was chapter one.

After Normandy, the Luftwaffe continued to have very good fighters and enough of them. But the German pilots labored under serious handicaps. The man who later became the Luftwaffe's best-known fighter commander, Adolf Galland, reported some of the deficiencies to his bosses. As historian Donald L. Miller described it:

> Galland reported to the German high command that his fighter aircraft "had no instruments for blind flying, no de-icing of the cockpit, no safety arrangements for navigation or automatic pilots." And most of his pilots "had no knowledge of instrument flying or bad-weather methods of landing." Fighter leaders that did manage to break through the weather had to attempt to assemble their scattered formations above the clouds, a nearly impossible stratagem. The result: dispersed, less effective attacks. "Numerous German pilots were sitting in their completely iced-up cockpits, half-blinded, to become an easy prey for the Thunderbolts. The appalling losses of this period were plainly due to the weather," Galland wrote.

"The German aircraft and engine industry," wrote historian James S. Corum, "was poorly structure to fight a long, total war. Before the war, even the newest German aircraft factories were small compared with the British and American ones. Although a large number of small factories made the industry less vulnerable to grand strategic bombing, it also prevented the Luftwaffe from employing the most efficient methods of mass production."

In contrast, no one was bombing the factories at Farmingdale on Long Island, New York, or Evansville, Indiana, where the Republic Aviation Corporation turned out Thunderbolts at an impressive, ever-increasing rate. Dispensing with camouflage paint and rolling silvery, natural-aluminum-finish P-47s out the factory doors, Republic lined up the Thunderbolts so rapidly that there were never enough pilots to fly them away. One photo of the Farmingdale factory shows more than three hundred Jugs outside, waiting to be delivered. Women pilots did much of this ferry flying, just as women worked the rivet guns and harnesses on the factory floor. The endless ranks of newly built Thunderbolts were symbolic of an American industrial machine that turned out nearly one hundred thousand aircraft in calendar year 1944 alone.

The Germans never found it easy to destroy a Hell Hawks P-47. But even if they had, the factories in the U.S. heartland were pushing new planes out the front door faster than the enemy could chew up the old ones.

☆

Similarly, a mobilized America was able to turn out the pilots needed for a global conflict. During the last two years of the war, Army Air Forces Training Command produced 250,000 pilots. At the start of 1943, when many of the lieutenants in the Hell Hawks were earning their wings, the rapid expansion of flying training and a continuing shortage of facilities to process and house pilot trainees led to a huge backlog of men awaiting entry into preflight training. But by late 1944, when the Hell Hawks were flying from Belgium and no one yet knew how long the war would last—a few optimists believed Germany could be defeated that fall—the Army Air Forces had too many pilots. Training came to a standstill. Many highly qualified candidates, unable to get a pilot-training slot, ended up becoming aerial gunners instead. On April 1, 1945, five weeks before the end of fighting in Europe and months before the surrender of Japan, the AAF halted training of pilots, navigators, and bombardiers altogether.

Most AAF pilots, and all of the 365th's, were officers. The least experienced had had about sixteen months of preparation at a cost of over a hundred thousand dollars before first climbing into the cockpit of an operational warplane. They came from everywhere and represented every segment of the young, white male population of the United States (the AAF's black pilots served in segregated units). They shared the knowledge that they belonged to an officer corps that was the envy of the world. Of course, there were a few who did not rise to the standard set by most of them, but by any measure the American fighter pilot of late 1944 was a formidable adversary. It cannot be said too often: No other nation entrusted so much initiative to men of junior rank. The tall, stately, supremely experienced Lt. Col. Donald E. Hillman said that when a fresh new second lieutenant showed up to join the Hell Hawks, he (Hillman) could be certain that that young man had been trained properly. The newest, freshest lieutenant had been trained in navigation, bad-weather flying, formation flying, and the workings of his plane's big, complex engine.

Unlike their Luftwaffe adversaries, the Americans were in the war not for the duration, but for a finite tour of duty. Hillman and group commander Stecker did not worry much about burn-out, exhaustion, or low morale: the men knew that if they flew a certain number of missions and survived, they would have a free ticket home. One of the veteran Hell Hawks leaders, Lt. Col. Robert Coffey completed his tour of duty on the European continent on September 21, 1944. He did it in style, flying four combat missions that day. He did it after a four-week period on the run in France, evading capture, and with five aerial victories to his name, an ace. But when his time was up, Coffey packed his bags, said "So long," and went home. It would have been inconceivable for an officer, ace, and deputy wing commander with comparable experience to pack up and leave a Luftwaffe combat unit. Fighting a desperate struggle with powerful adversaries on two fronts, German pilots simply didn't go home.

In the summer of 1944, the Luftwaffe lost 18 percent of its fighter pilots in combat. Unlike the American air forces, the Luftwaffe had no vast reservoir of young men from whom to draw new recruits. Among veteran Luftwaffe pilots, fatalism outweighed talk of wonder weapons and last-ditch counterattacks. Many must have felt like the German pilot quoted by Donald L. Miller: "Every time I close the canopy before taking off, I feel that I am closing the lid of my own coffin."

Miller wrote that some Luftwaffe pilots "were fighting with patriotic ferocity." But unlike Stecker or Hillman, a leader like Germany's Adolf Galland could not count on new arrivals being of high caliber. Miller explained that "by mid-1943, the bone-grinding battle of attrition [over Europe] had begun to force the high command to strip its training schools of cadets with only 100 to 150 hours of flying time to fill the cockpits of its frontline fighters. And as a result of shortsighted [logistical] planning, these German flight schools were producing far fewer graduates than the mass-production training programs of Britain and the United States, which now required combat pilots to have between 325 and 400 hours in the air. By the spring of 1944, the Luftwaffe was running out of experienced fighter pilots, and their replacements, unable to handle engine and weather problems, or even land properly on rugged fields, were destroying more of their planes in accidents than the enemy was shooting down. In combat, these eighteen- and nineteen-year-old neophytes were hopelessly overmatched."

☆

We do not tend, naturally, to think of aerial engagements as battles. Unlike Yorktown, or Gettysburg, or the Battle of the Bulge, a fight between warplanes seems more an individual clash than a full-fledged battle. Moreover, an aerial engagement rarely receives publicity the way a ground battle might. Hell Hawk pilots explained simply that air battles last only minutes, sometimes seconds. Confusion and chaos are their hallmarks. The Hell Hawks would write their own chapter in the annals of air combat with a memorable fighter sweep on the afternoon of October 21, 1944.

Major John R. Murphy was in command as three dozen Hell Hawk Thunderbolts orbited over Bonn. It was just past 4:00 p.m., and the radar controllers kept calling Murphy, alerting the group to "bogies" to their east. So far, all the targets had turned out to be "friendlies"; he released four pilots with mechanical problems to head home to Chièvres.

Then SWEEPSTAKES called, "Heads up!" Murphy pushed up the power and charged east. He ordered the 386th Squadron up to twenty-two thousand feet, and spread his other two squadrons abreast, hoping to catch the enemy—if he was out there—between his high and low aircraft.

Two minutes later, as Murphy ordered full throttle and "Keep a sharp lookout," Maj. William H. Cornell, leading the 386th on top, called out bogies ahead, level at twenty-two thousand feet. At his suggestion, Murphy ordered belly tanks dropped, and the thirty-two remaining P-47s salvoed their centerline tanks in a shower of glinting silver.

The bogies Cornell had spotted turned out to be thirty Focke-Wulf 190As. The Focke-Wulf was highly maneuverable and heavily armed, mounting twin machine guns over the nose and a pair of 20mm cannon in each wing. Considered the top-line German propeller-driven fighter, in the hands of a skilled pilot the 190 was easily an equal to the Thunderbolt.

That day, however, the Americans had the better opening tactics. Murphy had set the enemy up perfectly, with the 386th five hundred feet above them and the 387th and 388th three thousand feet below. "We had a slight advantage in altitude, about five hundred feet, and the sun was at our back," said Murphy in a later interview. "The twelve planes flying top cover bounced twenty or thirty other 190s, which were taken completely by surprise and dived down to where they ran into eight P-47s from another one of our flights, at eighteen thousand feet." Closing head-on, the lead Focke-Wulf dove down and between Murphy's lower squadrons, the other enemy aircraft following. The Hell Hawks, up-sun and with altitude advantage, saw their opening and jumped them.

Cornell opened fire at extreme range and scored a few hits before his quarry broke down and away. Flying Red Three position with Cornell was 2nd Lt. Melvin W. "Tex" Miller, who caught up with a Focke-Wulf in a diving turn and hammered him with a long burst. The 190, on fire, whipped into a split-S that turned into an out-of-control spin. Miller followed as the cartwheeling fighter plummeted into the overcast at five thousand feet, then climbed back into the fight with his wingman, 1st Lt. Robert S. Maney, clearing his tail. Surging up through twelve thousand feet, Miller was greeted by a second group of twenty-five to thirty Fw 190s, tumbling down into the swirling fight. Turning into the attackers, Miller got behind one fighter, which again executed a split-S and dove for the deck. Miller's heavy Thunderbolt—unsurpassed in a dive—easily caught the enemy fighter, and Miller closed smartly to firing range as both pulled out on the deck. When the Hell Hawk opened fire, the P-47's eight fifties tore the Focke-Wulf apart: pieces of the left wing and tail departed first, and a second burst into the cockpit ignited the 190's fuel tanks. The Butcher Bird rolled off on its right wing and hit the ground in a smear of flame. His two quick kills earned Tex Miller the Distinguished Flying Cross.

Major Murphy was leading the 388th when the Germans broke down and between his lower squadrons. Chasing five diving Fw 190s to the deck, he picked one and was about to fire when the German peeled up in a tight chandelle to the left. Murphy followed inside the turn and opened fire just as the Luftwaffe pilot exited his cockpit. The German had made up his mind to leave even before Murphy opened fire, but his bailout cemented Murphy's victory.

Murphy pulled together about a dozen of the top-cover Thunderbolts and headed back into the fight against the second group of 190s. Choosing a target, he was closing from astern when the enemy pilot broke into him in a hard right turn. Murphy had the power and skill to stay with the 190, and in the turning chase he ripped off a long burst into the Focke-Wulf, whose pilot had had enough. Off came the canopy, and the 190 pilot dove earthward, abandoning his fighter.

In an attempt to capture more gun camera film of his latest victory, Murphy eased into a cloud layer chasing the pilotless fighter. Bad decision: before Murphy spotted him, another 190 closed to within one hundred yards astern, and Murphy reported that only violent snap-rolls to the left and a spinning descent into another cloud layer cleared his tail.

Murphy's escape probably had less to do with his maneuvering and more to do with his wingman, 2nd Lt. Jack L. Estepp, whose centerline drop tank would not release. The additional drag limited his top speed, a maddening and potentially fatal disadvantage. But intent on clearing Murphy's tail, Estepp doggedly stayed in the fight, spotting the Focke-Wulf pursuing Murphy and hammering it with a long burst. Estepp's .50-caliber slugs slammed into the 190's engine, and its pilot dove off in a steep right diving turn, trailing a thick stream of white smoke. Estepp fired at and diverted two more Focke-Wulfs from Murphy's tail before he again took position on his leader, now clear of pursuit. His courage and effective defense of Maj. Murphy were recognized with a Distinguished Flying Cross.

The second element in Murphy's Red Flight had their hands full of Focke-Wulfs, too. Red Three was 1st Lt. Joseph F. "Injun' Joe" Cordner, with 2nd Lt. Earl O. Walters as his wingman. As the first formation of enemy fighters dove for the deck, Cordner and Walters pursued, the pair winding up on the tail of five 190s heading east, deep into German territory. Cordner nevertheless opened fire, damaging one fighter and probably destroying a second, chipping away at the enemy until his guns jammed.

On the deck, he closed on a third Focke-Wulf, trying to bluff its pilot into fatally over-controlling right into the ground. Boring in, Cordner watched as the 190 pilot clipped a tree with his wingtip, but the German zoomed up, and suddenly the young North Dakotan found himself unarmed, facing three opponents.

"It was about time to get the hell out of there," wrote Charles Johnson of Cordner's situation, and so he yanked his Thunderbolt into a cheek-sagging climb into protective clouds, joining other Thunderbolts at twelve thousand feet. There he continued to make mock firing runs on the Luftwaffe, breaking up several attacks.

Cordner's wingman, Earl Walters, fell behind in their dive after the five 190s and was pursuing at one thousand feet when one of the Focke-Wulfs broke into him in a head-on pass. Closing at better than seven hundred miles per hour, both pilots missed, and as they rushed past each other the German pulled into a tight right turn. Walters whipped his Thunderbolt into a near-vertical bank and took a deflection shot at close range, slamming bullets into the Focke-Wulf's cockpit, wings, and fuselage. Fire flared behind the German's cockpit; the pilot bailed out just seconds before the enemy fighter hit the ground.

The 387th fighter squadron's White Flight leader, 1st Lt. Samuel E. Saunders, chased several enemy fighters in the initial tangle, but the flaming 190s he saw plummeting onto German soil were all victims of other Hell Hawks. "Sack" Saunders had just climbed back to fifteen thousand feet when the second swarm of Fw 190s dove into the Thunderbolts. The Kansan broke up and into one of the fighters, and his head-on firing forced one to twist down and away, running east for Germany. It took Saunders fifty miles to finally catch the Focke-Wulf, now down to five hundred feet. The enemy reacted by pulling into a tight evasive turn, but Saunders' powerful P-47 now had the edge. His shooting struck home, cooking off the 190's nose armament ammo just forward of the cockpit, and the German pulled up sharply and bailed out. On the deck, dodging flak all the way west, Saunders managed to escape damage and return to base.

Second Lieutenant William B. Thompson, from Charlotte, North Carolina, was flying White Three in Saunders' flight. He chased a Focke-Wulf on the tail of another Thunderbolt, forcing the enemy into a descending, tightening spiral. Thompson couldn't lead the enemy pilot enough to shoot effectively, but at about 1,500 feet, the German fighter shuddered into an accelerated stall. The 190 pilot nearly fell off into a spin before rolling upside down and attempting to escape by executing a split-S. This last move was a fatal one: the German ran out of altitude in the pullout and exploded in a fireball on impact.

Thompson wasn't through, returning to altitude and bouncing a second 190. In a tight, edge-of-controllability dogfight, the pair turned so sharply that vapor contrails continually streamed from the wingtips of both opponents. At five thousand feet, with Thompson shooting each time he gained in the turn, the Luftwaffe pilot flipped into a final split-S, dragging his fighter nose-down in a desperate at-

A P-47 Thunderbolt, or "Jug," of the 365th Fighter Group, the Hell Hawks, flies a combat mission behind German lines in Europe. *William L. Ward*

"My best friend" was the label Bill Ward, the Hell Hawks' first pilot, gave to this portrait of one of the four P-47 Thunderbolts he flew. *William L. Ward*

Second Lieutenant Joseph R. Miller's Thunderbolt gets a tow out of the mine field above Omaha Beach, where he bellied in Capt. Arlo Henry's *Turnip Termite* on June 7, 1944. *U.S. Army*

Colonel Lance Call was the 365th Fighter Group commander from May 1943 until late June 1944, just before the Hell Hawks shifted to Normandy. *Lance Call*

Major (later Lt. Col.) John R. Murphy was awarded the Distinguished Flying Cross for his actions in the May 3, 1944, strike against the V-1 buzz bomb sites in France. *P. Neville*

Colonel Ray J. Stecker (left) inspects a flak-damaged 365th Fighter Group Thunderbolt with Staff Sgt. Harry I. Greenwood at an airfield in France. *U.S. Army*

West Point alumnus 1st Lt. Eugene Wink poses on group commander Major Lance Call's P-47D Thunderbolt at Dover Army Air Field, Delaware, in August or September 1943. *U.S. Army*

First Lieutenant James L. McWhorter, seen with his crew chief in front of *Haulin' Ass II*, was shot down in Normandy on July 27 and returned to A-7 near Utah Beach a couple of days later. *James L. McWhorter*

Captain William D. Ritchie commanded the 386th Fighter Squadron on D-Day. Ritchie would fly 109 combat missions and wrote the book on fighter tactics for the Hell Hawks. *Richard Kiefer*

The Wehrmacht's Flakvierling 38 was a set of four 20mm antiaircraft cannon firing up to eight hundred explode-on-contact shells per minute. Its wide deployment made it the Thunderbolt pilot's nemesis. *U.S. Army*

Left: Flying low after he downed an Fw 190 over Belgium, Captain Arlo C. Henry Jr.'s propeller struck the ground and threw debris into his Thunderbolt's turbocharger, earning it the nickname *Turnip Termite*. *S. N. Rabinowitz*

Above: The carnage inflicted by fighter-bombers in the Falaise pocket stunned even hardened combat veterans. Here, a German crew lies sprawled around their self-propelled gun. *Rick Pitts*

Captain George R. Brooking was shot down on his first combat mission, on September 9, 1944, and evaded capture with help from the local resistance. After the Germans evacuated Esch-sur-Alzette, Brooking was caught up in the town's celebration. *George R. Brooking*

Major David N. Harmon receives his second Distinguished Flying Cross for leading a strike that destroyed five panzers near Trier on September 19, 1944. A 20mm shell (inset) penetrated Harmon's main fuel tank but failed to down his P-47. *George R. Brooking*

A German Tiger II abandoned in a dive-bombing crater near Wieden, Germany. Skilled Thunderbolt pilots could put their pair of five-hundred-pound bombs close enough to a panzer to overturn it or blow it off the road. *Allen V. Mundt*

Sergeant Joseph "Pete" Piantino, an expert Hell Hawks armorer, sits with bomb fusing schematics for the P-47 Thunderbolt. *U.S. Army*

Staff Sergeant Glenn Smith, a crew chief with the 365th Fighter Group, sits in the cockpit of a captured Messerschmitt Bf 109G at the Metz, France, airfield, overrun by the Allies in 1944. *Glenn Smith*

Left: Second Lieutenants Mahlon T. Stelle (left) and John H. Fetzer Jr. of the 387th Fighter Squadron in front of their tent at the Hell Hawks base in Beaulieu, England, sometime before D-Day, June 6, 1944. *John H. Fetzer Jr.*

Above: A self-propelled gun on a Panzer Mk IV chassis destroyed by dive-bombing near Dasburg, Germany. *U.S. Air Force*

Lieutenant Colonel Donald E. Hillman commanded the 386th and 388th Hell Hawks squadrons and was group operations officer when shot down and captured on October 7, 1944. He eventually made a remarkable escape. *Donald E. Hillman*

The Focke-Wulf Fw 190 was one of the two principal German fighters of the war, along with the Messerschmitt Bf 109. The Hell Hawks respected the Fw 190 as the more formidable of the two. *U.S. Air Force*

The canopy flies off a Luftwaffe Fw 190 caught in the sights of a XIX Tactical Air Command Thunderbolt. This fight is over; the pilot is preparing to bail out. *U.S. Air Force*

Ninth Air Force armorers load .50-caliber ammunition into the right wing gun bays of a P-47 Thunderbolt. The usual combat load for the guns was 2,500 rounds: nearly a minute of firing time. *U.S. Air Force*

Sergeant Robert Turcotte, left, and Cpl. Francis deGrand, both of the 387th Fighter Squadron, fit a five-hundred-pound bomb beneath the wing of a Hell Hawks Thunderbolt. *U.S. Army*

At Chièvres, Belgium, in late 1944, Capt. George W. King taxies a 386th Fighter Squadron Thunderbolt past an M45 quad-.50-caliber antiaircraft emplacement. *U.S. Army*

After a squadron-sized German attack on Y-34 Metz on January 1, 1945, a P-47 burns on the pierced-steel plank taxiway. Bf 109Gs used machine guns and explosive cannon shells to set the P-47s afire. *George R. Brooking*

"My entire squadron destroyed," wrote 386th Fighter Squadron commander George R. Brooking of this image of Metz after the Luftwaffe attack. A P-47 burns as an ambulance sits abandoned on the field. *George R. Brooking*

Luftwaffe pilot Oberfeldwebel Stefan Kohl, shot down by antiaircraft fire over Metz on January 1, 1945, was still in high spirits and insisted on combing his hair and polishing his boots before this photo was taken. *W. F. Rothery*

Miss Pussy IV, named for his girlfriend and later wife, Priscilla E. "Pussy" Pero, was the fourth P-47 flown by Capt. Valmore J. "Val" Beaudrault of the Hell Hawks' 386th Fighter Squadron. *Priscilla Beaudrault*

Cpl. Paul Markowitz of the Hell Hawks' 387th Fighter Squadron sits comfortably atop five-hundred-pound general-purpose bombs at A-7 Fontenay-sur-Mer Air Base, France, in July 1944. *Joseph Ornstein*

At A-7 near Utah Beach in July 1944, 365th Fighter Group commander Col. Ray Stecker flew a P-47D Thunderbolt with bubble canopy, a rear-view mirror, and the names of pilot, crew chief, and armorer stenciled on its side. *U.S. Air Force*

Capt. James G. Wells Jr. of the 386th shot down four Luftwaffe fighters and "wanted that fifth one so bad he could taste it." By spring 1945 the recipient of the Silver Star and DFC had risen to command the 386th Squadron.
M. T. Crouch

First Lieutenant Edward S. Szymanski and his dog Happy. After seventy-three combat missions, he was killed when he flew into an apartment building in bad weather while returning to Belgium from Paris.
W. F. Peters

Captain Neal Worley looked earnest and intent as he posed for a portrait wearing the Hap Arnold emblem on his left shoulder; it was the standard patch for Army Air Forces members.
Neal Worley

Colonel Ray J. Stecker prepares to lead a strike mission from airfield A-78, Florennes, Belgium, in February 1945. His personal P-47D, *Triple J,* waits with other Thunderbolts for the takeoff signal. *Allen V. Mundt*

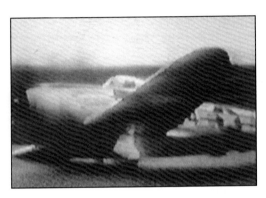

Captain Neal E. Worley makes a crash landing at Metz in February 1945 with only one main landing wheel down. This blurred sequence was later seen in the movie *Fighter Squadron* (1948) with Edmond O'Brien and Robert Stack. *Neal Worley*

When it first appeared in European skies, the Messerschmitt Me 262 was an unknown quantity to Allied pilots. This Me 262A-1 was brought to Wright Field, Ohio, where German jets were tested after the war. *U.S. Air Force via Robert F. Dorr*

At a pilots' briefing at Fritzlar, Germany, Capt. George E. Robinson, Maj. Gen. Elwood R. "Pete" Quesada (center), and Col. Ray J. Stecker discuss an upcoming mission. *U.S. Army*

At Chièvres, Belgium, in December 1944, three Hell Hawks stand amid their tent city: 1st Lt. Isaac G. "Gale" Phillips (left), 2nd Lt. Edward J. Lopez, and 1st Lt. Allen V. Mundt. *Allen V. Mundt*

At their new base in Fritzlar, Germany, 365th Fighter Group personnel work on P-47D Thunderbolts of the 386th and 387th squadrons. *U.S. Air Force*

First Lieutenant Grant G. Stout at a 365th Fighter Group base in Europe in late 1944 or early 1945. "Map in hand, poop in pocket, and raring to go," he wrote on the back of the original snapshot. *Lyla K. Stout*

This frame from a XIX Tactical Air Command Thunderbolt's gun camera shows a racing German locomotive gushing steam from its perforated boiler. *U.S. Air Force*

First Lieutenant Samuel B. Lutz was strafing an ammo dump near Zeithain, Germany, on April 20, 1945, when debris from an exploding bunker knocked him unconscious. After a harrowing pullout, he made it back to Fritzlar. *Samuel B. Lutz*

Second Lieutenant William L. Ward was the first pilot to report for duty when the 365th Fighter Group was formed. Ward would fly as a captain on the Hell Hawks' final combat mission and is seen here returning from that flight in *Sally Flat Foot 4th*, the last of several Jugs he flew. *William L. Ward*

A strafing fighter-bomber from the XIX Tactical Air Command detonates a tank car in a German rail yard. *U.S. Air Force*

A wrecked German locomotive and rolling stock at Dasburg, Germany, after fighter-bomber attacks in late January 1945 caught German forces retreating from the Ardennes. *U.S. Air Force*

tempt to pull through and escape. He was too low; Thompson watched as his overmatched opponent, twin streamers trailing from his wingtips, smashed into the earth.

Thompson, a "new boy" who had joined the Hell Hawks in July, damaged yet a third Focke-Wulf before it escaped into clouds. His gallantry and two victories in this action were recognized by the award of a Silver Star.

White Four was 1st Lt. Donald E. Kark. He lost Thompson, his leader, in the initial tangle with the Fw 190s, and instead picked up a 190 on his own tail. At full power, the two roared around the confines of a tight, descending spiral, each striving for advantage. "I latched onto a Focke-Wulf 190. The 190 could turn better than a Thunderbolt," Kark recalled, "but in a diving turn I could gain on him," cutting off the enemy by using power and speed to tighten his own turn radius. Kark steadily gained, pulling into firing position; the enemy pilot broke out of the turn to escape. The twenty-one-year-old Iowan rolled out and fired. To Kark, it appeared that he'd missed, but almost instantly the 190's canopy flew off and its pilot catapulted free of his aircraft. The lieutenant made a tight pass by the Luftwaffe pilot in his parachute, obtaining gun camera footage of his opponent, and then zoomed for altitude and home.

No one controlled this chaotic collision of two Luftwaffe gaggles and an entire Ninth Air Force fighter group. The Hell Hawks had nearly forty planes in the fight, while the Luftwaffe had half again as many, but at the point of collision it was every man, or two-ship element, for himself. Fighting swirled in every direction as each pilot sought any fleeting advantage and a chance at a shot.

One who dove into the melee following the second group of Focke-Wulfs was 1st Lt. Charles Ready Jr. of the 388th, who chose to pursue the last bandit in the formation. Ready cut in front of the diving 190 and turned head-on, trying to shake up the enemy pilot. When the Focke-Wulf was centered in the gunsight ring, Ready let go with a short burst from all eight fifties. As the German pilot passed wingtip-to-wingtip with his Thunderbolt, the Oklahoman was startled to see his opponent bail out.

Back on the tail of another 190 in a steep dive, Ready squeezed off one short burst, saw his bullets hit home, but found the earth rapidly filling his windscreen. He was below a thousand feet, and even with full back stick he barely managed to pull out. Ready chased another Focke-Wulf closing on a fellow Hell Hawk, lobbing an out-of-range burst at the enemy in an attempt to break up the attack. Ready's tracers so startled the German that he snapped his 190 into an unrecoverable spin, falling helplessly from six hundred feet to ground impact. For his gallantry, "determination, and devotion to his fellow pilots," Lt. Ready was awarded the Silver Star.

As Ready and the grateful recipient of his intervention climbed for altitude, they joined on Maj. Murphy, and the trio headed for base. From fourteen thousand feet, they looked back at the receding battle. "I never saw so many parachutes in my life," said Murphy, who had shot down two of the enemy. "It looked as though the paratroopers were landing."

First Lieutenant Franklin P. Luckman was very nearly forced to hit the silk himself. With the 388th Squadron's White Flight he dove after the enemy's initial force, chasing them from twenty thousand down to six thousand feet. "When the first group went through us, they didn't stop; they just kept right on going, right toward the deck. My plan was to not turn while there were still other enemy fighters behind me, because if I did, I was afraid I'd be giving them a free shot."

The Focke-Wulfs had scattered, so the twenty-one-year-old Philadelphian climbed for altitude, briefly joining Capt. James Hill en route to fifteen thousand feet. The pair arrived just in time to break into the diving attack of the second gaggle of 190s, and Luckman soon lost Hill in what Charles Johnson called a huge "skunk-pissin' contest."

"I swung around into a left diving turn," said Luckman. He didn't catch the first Focke-Wulf he opened on, but Luckman "spotted this 190; I was above and to his left, and I turned to follow." The tight turn required about a forty-degree deflection shot to lead the target. "It's about the toughest shooting you can do," said Luckman. "You're actually firing blind; once you start to pull much lead, your target is below your nose, so you actually don't see him when you fire." Luckman would fire a burst, then ease off the stick pressure, see where his tracers had gone, and try to correct his aim. "My shots, my tracers were going behind him, so I made a calculation as to how far, and then added additional lead. As soon as I finished firing, I pushed the nose forward to see what happened." Luckman had judged it perfectly: "I could see that it went right in the cockpit." The Focke-Wulf burst into flames.

He had no chance to savor his success, though. "At that instant I felt 'Whoomp, whoomp,'" because sitting dead astern was another Focke-Wulf, already firing. Two cannon rounds slammed into Luckman's Thunderbolt, one in the engine and another well back of the cockpit. He broke hard and whipped into a cloud, emerging moments later with his tail clear.

Coming nose-to-nose with him was yet another 190, "coming full-bore," said Luckman nearly sixty-three years later. "I spotted him and decided to take him head-on. I made a decision afterwards that it was bad news to make a head-on pass with a 190, because he had a 20mm cannon—he had a chance to fire on me and be accurate while I [was] still out of range."

There was no time to reconsider just then, though, because the closure rate was better than six hundred miles per hour. "By the time you're in range, you don't even get a chance to fire unless you just hold the trigger down." Luckman scored hits, but so did the German: "I felt him, but I didn't feel like I'd really been hit. But he put one shot in each wing, and damaged both my wing spars." In that last instant the enemy pilot appeared intent on ramming him; the American shoved the stick forward and ducked beneath the onrushing Focke-Wulf, barely clearing its dirty blue belly.

"I didn't see my gun camera film," recalled Luckman, "but the guys who did said that 190 flew right through my cockpit!"

Luckman popped out of the clouds and chased two more 190s, but they escaped into clouds just as his straining engine began running roughly. Worried now, the lieutenant sought cover in the clouds himself while calling for a steer home from the radar controller. "So many of our planes had left, and I was not in communication with them. The excitement and adrenaline are such that you can actually get a lump in your throat."

Thirty-five tense minutes later, he began a flat, straight-in approach to the field. "I thought that if I ever shot down an airplane, I'd come over the field and do a victory roll. Well, something told me, 'Don't do that.'" He touched down gently at Chièvres, taxied past the crash squad lining the runway, and cut his engine at the revetment, finally home.

"There were four holes in that airplane: one in the engine, one in the fuselage, and a hole in each wing's leading edge." Mechanics later discovered the cannon strikes in the wings had fractured both wing spars. A victory roll? "I could have torn both wings off," said Luckman six decades later, with more than a little grateful humility in his voice.

☆

One of Luckman's heroes in the 388th was Capt. Robert M. Fry, born in 1921 in Erie, Pennsylvania. "He was the best pilot of them all, deadly in dive bombing," remembered Luckman, "and as honest as the day was long." Fry, White Leader that day, dove with his four Thunderbolts after the first Luftwaffe group, roaring toward the deck at full power. His accelerating P-47 closed rapidly on the nearest Fw 190. Fry waited until within four hundred yards before opening, when his eight .50-calibers reached out with ball-and-tracer rounds and ignited the enemy fighter. The 190 tried to pull up, but instead fell uncontrollably earthward. Fry saw the pilot bail out just before impact.

So low he was forced to dodge German flak, Fry climbed back through twelve thousand feet, only to meet the second diving group of Focke-Wulfs. One of about fifteen Thunderbolts instantly engaged, Fry first snapped off a high-angle deflection shot that damaged one Butcher Bird, then slid swiftly in behind another, overtaking rapidly. Several short, accurate bursts set the 190 afire, and as Fry passed within a wing's length of the badly smoking enemy fighter, he caught the flash of its canopy flipping back into the slipstream. Breaking right, Fry looked back and was rewarded with the sight of the German going over the side.

☆

Before his near-fatal game of chicken with the 190, Frank Luckman had managed to force several Luftwaffe fighters to break off their pursuit of 2nd Lt. Robert P. Longley, who was in a bad way. In the initial melee he lost his leader and rejoined with some relief on what he thought were two Hell Hawks, only to find that he was flying wing on a pair of Fw 190s. He shook off his surprise in time to open fire at 150 yards, point-blank range, and his destructive fire took apart one of the enemy fighters, killing the 190's engine. Longley saw the canopy pop free as the cripple spun vertically toward the deck, but was forced to break away when more Germans closed on his tail.

Evading them, he had climbed to ten thousand feet to close on four 190s slightly above at ten o'clock. At three hundred yards he opened up on one of the quartet, damaging its engine, but the other three turned on Longley and he was soon under fire himself. Tracers whipped by his canopy, and one 20mm round slammed into his left wing. Another found and cut an oil line, spraying the black fluid all over his canopy, even oozing into the cockpit. Longley was in deep trouble, instruments damaged, flying nearly blind on an oil-starved engine that could seize at any moment.

Peering out the side of his canopy, Longley saw through the oil-streaked plexiglass the lovely sight of a Thunderbolt sliding into formation on his wing. It was Bob Fry, adrenaline still pumping from his two kills, calling in with an offer to escort Longley home. Fry led his crippled wingman, who couldn't see forward, to the Chièvres emergency strip. Slowing to just above touchdown speed, Longley watched Fry roar skyward just as his P-47's belly bounced onto the grass and slid to a safe stop. The young Marylander scrambled from his smoking Thunderbolt, covered head-to-foot in engine oil, his leather jacket shining like ebony. Only when he pulled off his helmet did the crash crew recognize Longley's familiar shock of blond hair.

☆

Another Hell Hawk who found trouble in the dogfight was 2nd Lt. Robert S. Hagan, but he couldn't blame his plight on a Focke-Wulf. Hagan, a twenty-year-old native of Kansas City, Missouri, with three months of combat under his belt, was the wingman of Maj. William H. Cornell, the 386th commander and leader of the Hell Hawks' high squadron that day. Diving after the first group of fighters, Hagan stuck with Cornell through the first several minutes of the melee, keeping enemy fighters off his boss's tail. Suddenly, Hagan's engine lost power, and smoke filled the cockpit. Instead of Focke-Wulf cannon shells, he'd apparently run into the stream of brass .50-caliber cartridge casings pouring through slots on the underside of Cornell's machine gun bays. Bad luck—that day the debris accomplished what the Luftwaffe could not and took down a Thunderbolt. Hagan dropped out of the action and turned toward Allied lines.

With his heavy Thunderbolt in a stable but steep glide, he knew the chances were slim that he'd make it to an emergency field. "There was oil all over the windscreen," Hagan recalled, "and I could only see a little bit out the side." It was just as well. Cornell, shepherding his wingman toward home, told Hagan later that the junior pilot had flown right through a dense concentration of 20mm flak bursts. "He said it was so thick he lost sight of me," recalled Hagan. Behind his oil-streaked windshield, the young lieutenant was unaware of his close call.

Hagan unbuckled his harness and squatted on the seat in preparation for bailout. "I was down to four or five thousand feet," he said. Hagan hesitated: he was almost certain to be captured if he abandoned his plane this far east. "I decided 'to hell with it.' I didn't want to jump." He sat back down, strapped in, and willed his P-47 toward the front line and safety.

With a sudden jolt, the Thunderbolt's big Pratt & Whitney finally seized. Beyond the motionless prop, Hagan could see hilly terrain with small woodlots below. Too low to bail out and with no sizable pastures at hand, his only option was a belly landing. Headed into a small clearing, he realized with alarm that his final glide would carry him into a clump of trees at the far end. At ninety to one hundred miles per hour, Hagan banked as much as he dared, trying to swing wide of the onrushing timber. "I tried to turn a little to the right."

It was too much to ask of the heavy Jug. The Thunderbolt's right wing dipped toward the racing earth and stalled. Catching a wingtip, the big fighter instantly cartwheeled across the pasture. As the P-47 tore itself apart, Hagan tumbled like a rag doll in a washing machine, protected only by the beefy cockpit structure and his seat harness. As the wreckage slid to a stop on the Belgian turf, the impact slammed his head against the instrument panel and cracked several ribs. "It was over pretty damned quick. . . . I landed right side up, with both wings, the tail, and the engine gone."

Shaken, Hagan was still clear-headed enough to crawl from the crumpled cockpit. "I climbed out of the airplane, and there was a jeep parked about a hundred yards away. He wouldn't come any closer, so I had to walk over to him."

Gasping, the battered pilot pulled up at the jeep, laboring between breaths to ask the soldier why he hadn't driven across to pick him up. "They told me after I got over there that they didn't want to come over 'cause it was a minefield.'"

Minefield or no, the clearing was four hundred yards inside American lines, and the lucky Hagan was hustled back to an aid station. Eight weeks later, in late December, he was back in combat, flying a new P-47.

☆

Hagan was one of just two Hell Hawks who failed to return to Chièvres after the fighter sweep, and neither pilot was downed by enemy action. In contrast, the three dozen Americans shot down twenty-one Luftwaffe fighters, probably destroyed another, and received credit for damaging eleven more. The 365th Fighter Group, on October 21, 1944, earned the first of its two Presidential Unit Citations for aggressiveness in aerial combat. Major General Hoyt S. Vandenberg, the Ninth Air Force commander, noted with satisfaction how the Hell Hawks "viciously attacked the enemy" and caught a second group of Focke-Wulfs using "the same devastating process as before." Vandenberg's citation recognized especially "the gallantry of the pilots and their exceptional flying ability" in "the brilliant execution of those two attacks against the numerically superior enemy aircraft."

☆

Frank Luckman never had any doubts about the P-47 he flew, or his fellow Hell Hawks' abilities to take on the Luftwaffe. "We were confident in what we could do from the beginning. My feeling—and it was always this way—was that I didn't feel it made any difference how many planes we tangled with." Luckman is angered even today by those who say that "the P-47 was not a good airplane for aerial combat. That's the farthest from the truth." On October 21, 1944, the Hell Hawks had proved him right.

Chapter Ten

Thunderbolts over the Bulge

N ear Lille, France, amid the dense fog of a gloomy November afternoon, local farmers heard the growl of a pair of Pratt & Whitney R-2800 engines. The planes were invisible in the mist, but they were two P-47 Thunderbolts of the 386th Fighter Squadron. At the controls were two of the squadron's top pilots: its commander, Maj. William H. Cornell, and Capt. William E. "Curly" Rodgers, his wingman. With the 386th and the Hell Hawks cut off from the battle front by low ceilings and terrible visibility, the duo were making a quick run for the comforts of England—a restaurant meal, a warm bed, and the receptive company of some English-speaking women.

But on that November 22, the weather was marginal to the west, toward the Channel and the fighter bases ringing London. Cornell and Rodgers were "scud-running," hugging the earth in the fog and mist, using compass and stopwatch to find their way. Swirling clouds forced them lower still, and forward visibility was marginal. Rodgers clung to Cornell's wing as they thundered over the rolling countryside at 250 miles per hour.

The rumble of radial engines surged suddenly to a scream, both power plants at full throttle. The locals heard an abrupt *car-rumph!*, followed by the note of a single engine, still at climb power, fading upward into the clouds. A bright splash of flame flickered through the fog on a gentle hillside outside Lille.

Cornell died instantly when his racing Thunderbolt slammed into the rising terrain he had failed to see in time. Rodgers, slightly astern, yanked the stick back reflexively as the hillside materialized out of the fog; his P-47 barely cleared the plowed earth as the glare from Cornell's fireball lit Rodgers' shocked visage. Chilled by his sweat-soaked uniform, Rodgers arrived in England, but his was an empty holiday, drained of any prospect of rest. Back at Chièvres the next day, he was still shaken by Cornell's sudden death and how close he had come to joining him.

☆

The loss of their commanding officer hit the men of the 386th hard. "Cornell was a good pilot and a nice guy," recalled Bob Hagan, who had been flying Cornell's wing during the big dogfight of October 21. "He broke off shooting at a 190 that day to help me out." Cornell's replacement was Maj. George R. Brooking, the liberator of Esch-sur-Alzette back in September. "Cornell was a soft-spoken Southern boy," recalled Brooking. "I didn't know him very well. He wasn't on any official orders that day, just headed for England for some time off. He shared a tent with his dog, a Scots terrier named McTavish. After the crash, I inherited both his briar pipe and the dog."

Colonel Stecker moved Bob Brooking up from his operations officer slot to take over the 386th. The new commanding officer spent his Thanksgiving Day, the day after Cornell went in, moving into his makeshift office near the flight line. The rest of the Hell Hawks chewed their chicken dinner (turkey showed up a day later) while digesting the news of Cornell's loss.

Brooking had eased into the ranks of the "old boy" Hell Hawks after his inauspicious combat debut in September, and after weeks as 386th operations officer, he was an experienced combat leader. "Brooking was a good-looking guy; did his job instead of giving pep talks," said Bob Hagan. Brooking would need all his talents in the coming weeks.

One of his first jobs was to counter one of Hitler's secret weapons: venereal disease. "My outfit [the 386th] had one of the best combat records in the Ninth," said Brooking, "but we also had the highest VD rate!" Stecker told him he was personally responsible for solving the problem. "I was catching hell from my superiors, so I stood up on the wing of a P-47, and told the whole squadron to get their act together." The solution was a "prophylactic station," staffed by the flight surgeons, that administered penicillin *en masse* to Brooking's troops. The squadron's enlisted men lined up in the mud outside the tent for a "short arms inspection" and a shot, if required, while those officers in need received a private consultation.

☆

One of Curly Rodgers' closest friends in the 386th was Capt. James G. Wells Jr., who on November 28 led fifteen P-47s over Lucherberg, Germany, twenty miles east of Aachen. Wells' men were about to attack some Tiger tanks when their radar controller, Marmite, diverted them to intercept some bogies near Cologne.

At five thousand feet the Jug pilots sighted six Bf 109s just above them, coming head on. As the two formations split into a tangle of pursued and pursuers, one enemy fighter shot up the P-47 of 2nd Lt. Carl O. Keagy, who was captured after a harrowing bailout from his burning fighter. Wells, too late to save Keagy, chased the Messerschmitt responsible, opened fire, and put a burst into its engine and cockpit. The smoking 109 flipped inverted, executed a split-S toward the Rhine below, and pulled out in a spine-crunching recovery at barely five hundred feet. Wells was right behind him.

"I got on his tail and out-turned him, something we were not supposed to be able to do," said Wells. "We were down to about a hundred and fifty feet when I got a good clear shot at him and knocked him down." Wells' last burst hit the 109's cockpit and engine, which burst into flames; the Luftwaffe fighter dove straight into the ground and exploded.

Back at six thousand feet, Wells ran into two Fw 190s coming straight for him, out of the clouds. The three opponents closed the range at a combined speed of over seven hundred miles per hour. "We went head-on at each other," said Wells, "and well, I just ducked my head down against my windshield, and I looked up and here his wing was actually going over mine, we were that close—staring at each other." Each pilot then broke hard to turn and gain a stern shot, but wound up coming head-on again. Two Focke-Wulfs, cannon flashing, raced at Wells, his eight .50-calibers spitting tracers out ahead. The three aircraft blew by each other, barely avoiding a collision. "He shot through my prop," said Wells, whose ammo was gone; he thought it a good idea that he be gone, too.

Wells made a beeline toward home, the pair of 190s in pursuit. "I'm heading west as fast as I can go, and I got [down low] with this guy behind me," he said. The Germans stayed on his tail for forty miles, all the way back to American lines. Both fighters took turns firing at Wells' damaged Thunderbolt. "About every time I'd look back, I'd hit the water injection and gain a little on him; I don't know just when it was that he finally quit tailing me," said a relieved Wells, who finally put his Jug back on the ground at Chièvres. "When we got back to the base was when I found out I had the hole through my propeller and had one magneto knocked out, I think. It was a hectic day." Wells remembered that he didn't think about the odds, outnumbered five or six to one. "I think we were all flying just to get victories."

☆

The Hell Hawks pilots and hard-working ground crews faced their biggest combat challenge during Hitler's last big offensive in the West. A furious attack by 250,000 German troops on December 16, 1944, surprised Allied troops in the Ardennes, a forested plateau on the Belgian-German border that had been the scene of earlier fighting in both world wars. The Germans opened the assault along a fifty-mile front, initially committing twenty-one infantry and armored divisions. They called the operation Wacht am Rhein (Watch on the Rhine); the Americans called it the Battle of the Bulge. It was the largest and most desperate battle U.S. forces would fight.

With the German attack in full swing on the 16th, the outnumbered GIs on the Ardennes front needed every plane in the air, putting bombs and bullets on the enemy. But the weather—low clouds, snow, and fog—was with Hitler, grounding every Allied aircraft and making air support impossible.

December 17 was little better, yet the Hell Hawks managed three missions over their sector, north of the Ardennes. Released by their ground controller from the Hürtgen Forest area, Blue Flight, under Maj. John W. Motzenbecker, commander of the 387th Squadron, was cruising at medium altitude over rugged country on the German-Belgian border. Tipped off by their controller of a possible counter-attack along the Prether River valley, Motzenbecker worked his way toward the breakthrough area. Nothing moved on the snow-covered landscape below as they followed the river between fir-covered ridges and fields.

Motzenbecker was a doctor's son, one of nine children, from Newark, New Jersey. He had already graduated from Georgetown University when he enlisted after Pearl

Harbor. "Motz" was a no-nonsense, strait-laced leader, but he knew how to fly: once he had flown inverted down the length of a cornfield, his P-47's propeller whipping the stalks, giving a subordinate in his back seat, who had needlessly abused Motz's crew chief on a previous orientation flight, a taste of his own medicine.

His wingman on December 17 was 2nd Lt. John D. McCarthy, who had just joined the squadron and was obviously anxious about the mission before take-off. Motzenbecker had already decided to radio in that he had engine trouble, an excuse to curtail the fruitless mission and get his green wingman back on the ground, when something below caught his attention.

"There's a main road down there," he radioed. "Give me some top cover and I'll go down and have a look."

Motzenbecker spiraled down and rolled wings level adjacent to the modest highway, and what he saw startled even this battle-hardened Hell Hawk. The road was jammed bumper-to-bumper with panzers, half-tracks, and trucks, heading south from Monschau directly toward the American lines. This was Kampfgruppe Peiper of the 1st SS Panzer Division; Motzenbecker guessed the four-and-a-half-mile-long column contained at least 150 vehicles; even the side roads feeding the highway were crammed with waiting trucks. He hadn't seen this many German vehicles in the open since the August shooting gallery in the Falaise Pocket. The convoy gunners saw him, too, and a burst of flak sent shrapnel tearing through his wing.

Motzenbecker pulled up and away to regroup the 387th for attack. He called the IX Tactical Air Command controller: "Send some reinforcements. We are going down on them." Most of the Wehrmacht convoy had scattered off the road for cover amid trees and brush, and light flak was already rising from the length of the column. But fifty of the largest trucks were still in the open. Motzenbecker split the squadron into four flights of four, and they attacked on the deck, spread into line-abreast formation. When the squadron opened, 128 .50-caliber guns tore into the German column.

Bob Hagan recalled his strafing tactics: "It wasn't like you see in the newsreels where the guys go in and strafe and they start shooting up the road, and they finally get to the convoy and shoot it up and keep shooting til they're past. You picked your targets and put a burst on them. You didn't need much—a second or so. If you were any good, you didn't need to run a line of bullets up to the target."

After three passes, the trucks were finished. Every vehicle on the road was burning fiercely or knocked sideways, blown into the ditch by the concentrated blast of the fifties.

Motzenbecker turned to targets on the side roads, finding a nest of tanks in the timber. Thirteen of the Thunderbolts carried a pair of five-hundred-pounders each, and the squadron dove at the panzers. Smoke from the bombs obscured the targets as the planes spread out, hunting. The pilots caught a glimpse of ruined tanks, burning, some turned turtle.

The flak was heavier now, lacing the sky in a deadly canopy. German gunners hit Motzenbecker's wingman, McCarthy, and his plane, streaming fire, crashed fifty yards off the roadway. McCarthy, whom Motzenbecker had tried to spare with an early return to Chièvres, had no chance to get out. As the vengeful Thunderbolts methodically strafed the woods, soldiers scrambled from their vehicles and sought cover in the burning brush. Nowhere did more than four or five vehicles escape the concentrated buzz-saw of the fifties.

☆

Back at Chièvres, the weather was still terrible. One of the pilots on the board for that morning's scheduled strike was Allen V. Mundt, who had flown his first combat mission just three days earlier. Though just a second lieutenant, he was proud of his new status, backing the silver wings on his blouse with the blue felt that unofficially denoted a combat flier. Yet Mundt wasn't anxious for his second foray into combat: "The fog seemed thicker than ever. My thoughts: they don't send good, young, all-American boys on suicide missions—do they?" The 9:00 a.m. briefing that morning was different: the pilots were all seated comfortably, waiting for the usual flight and intelligence information, when Col. Stecker strode in. The men jumped to their feet. Mundt remembered that "Stecker grimly told us what was at stake out there," how the GIs were desperate for air cover. Outside, Mundt couldn't see from one building to the next. But bad weather didn't deter Stecker, who told them in no uncertain terms, "This is gonna' go."

"I hadn't flown much over the last three months," said Mundt, "and I was rusty, like all the new boys." The pilots headed for the parachute tent. Mundt wrote later that "I resigned myself that this was going to be a one-way trip for me. . . . I have never been so afraid." He sat on the floor with the other Hell Hawks, all veterans, waiting for the weather to break. "I was convinced the only way I would get back on the ground was by parachute."

Sixty-two years later, Mundt was still emotional over what happened next. Captain Robert E. Robinson, one of the 387th's veteran pilots, came over and sat with Mundt, talking quietly to comfort him. "He alone made an attempt at reassurance. He sat by me and said a few quiet things; I'll be forever grateful." Mundt waited as the mission was delayed and delayed again, into the afternoon. "Finally," he said, "someone thought better of it and took my name off the mission." The new boys, in fact, didn't fly again until the worst of the Bulge fight was over. "Stecker scared me to death that day," said Mundt, who didn't take to the air until the group moved to Metz in late December. Spared on December 17, he went on to fly fifty-eight combat missions.

☆

Wherever the clouds parted, the Germans were naked to attack. By 11:30 a.m., Capt. Robert M. Fry's 388th Squadron arrived overhead to relieve Motzenbecker's men. Spotting six to eight tanks, Fry directed a diving attack that put twenty-six five-hundred-pound bombs on target. Two of the panzers were mangled. In a steep-walled valley, the squadron caught forty more trucks and horse-drawn transports and destroyed or damaged more than half.

As the first two squadrons headed for home, Bob Brooking arrived with a dozen P-47s of the 386th Squadron at about 1:30 p.m., on the hunt for more targets. On a secondary road a mile inside the German border between Monschau and Simmerath, Brooking spotted a column of 150 vehicles heading southwest, joining the northern flank of the Ardennes attack. Explosions flared on the snow once again as the squadron put twenty-four bombs into the clusters of armored vehicles and horse-drawn wagons, from both the 326th and 272nd Volksgrenadier Divisions. Then the terrible strafing began. Trapped in the road, the Germans threw everything they had into the air against the Hell Hawks. Automatic weapons fire and 20mm flak caught the Thunderbolt of 2nd Lt. Herbert A. Sting Jr. His twentieth combat mission—he had been with the group only since September—ended when his P-47 slammed into the ground and exploded near Monschau. When the planes pulled away, more than sixty vehicles were in flames, the black smoke roiling the air over the snow-covered hills. Before leaving for Chièvres at 2:30 p.m., Brooking's men strafed a column of towed artillery, hitting and damaging all the pieces, including several of the feared 88mm cannon.

Low clouds and fog soon blanketed the area, leaving the Germans to resume their advance during darkness. On the 17th, the official count credited the group with 107 Wehrmacht vehicles destroyed, 20 probably destroyed, and 45 damaged, and more than a dozen 88s wrecked.

☆

Morning on December 18, the third day of the Wacht am Rhein offensive, found the Hell Hawks in Belgium blanketed by an icy, opaque fog. In near zero-zero conditions, Maj. Bob Fry led seventeen planes off at midmorning, but all were forced to return; bad visibility obscured any possible target in the Stavelot, Belgium, area, where German tanks were reported moving up. Only flares lining the runway enabled the pilots to feel their way back to the ground at Chièvres.

According to a report of that day's action in *Yank* magazine, Col. Ray Stecker's phone rang about noon. On the line was Col. Gilbert L. "Gil" Meyers, the operations officer at IX Tactical Air Command, who knew of Stecker's long experience and success in conducting air-support operations in North Africa. No other IX TAC groups got the call that day, wrote the *Yank* correspondent, adding that Meyers had long regarded Stecker as a specialist at getting at the enemy under the worst conditions.

"That Jerry column you hit the other day," Meyers said, "has been reinforced and has broken through our lines to Stavelot [twenty-five miles south of Aachen]. In fact, there is now nothing between it and the English Channel but service troops and cooks and bakers."

"The weather—" said Stecker.

"I know," said Meyers, "the weather is down on the deck, and it probably will be suicide, but we've got to get something in there or the bastards will be in Liège. If you can just send a four-plane flight, it might help."

"I'll see what we can do," said Stecker. The group commander hung up and called in the 386th Squadron commander, Bob Brooking. His men had been standing by since daybreak. Stecker briefed him on what was at stake, and Brooking returned to brief his men.

"I heard Brooking say that the old man had just told him we had to get a four-man flight up, and we were the only four there!" recalled Capt. James G. Wells Jr. "That's how we happened to luck into the mission, if you want to call it luck. They told us the flight had to go, because we had to go look for these tanks."

Brooking finished briefing his flight, and the four boarded the beat-up pilots' truck, the *Weepin' Carrier*, to take them to the flight line. They arrived at their Thunderbolts around 12:30 p.m., the bone-chilling fog still swirling around the planes. Ceilings were less than a hundred feet, with visibility almost nil. "The weather was bad," said Brooking, "but when you're doing it every day you don't get intimidated." At 1:05 p.m. he led his flight—2nd Lt. Roy Wayne Price on his wing, with Wells leading 1st Lt. Robert C. Thoman—down the runway into an enveloping fog. "We just stuck close together" in the soup, said Wells. Each Thunderbolt carried two five-hundred-pound delayed-action bombs, one under each wing. Stecker ordered successive flights to launch at twenty-minute intervals.

Brooking, having fought in the area the day before, led his flight to the battle. A thick blanket of fog cloaked the countryside below, a solid white floor beneath their P-47s. Searching for a break in the undercast, Brooking orbited for half an hour without success. Two successive flights of Hell Hawks arrived, only to be sent back to Chièvres by Brooking. Frustrated, he keyed his mike button:

"I'm going down there to poke around by myself. There must be a break somewhere in these mountains."

"You're crazy," said Bob Thoman, who knew that some of the wooded ridgelines below topped two thousand feet above sea level. But Brooking circled lower, looking for an opening.

Finally, he spotted a hole in the undercast, with a bare minimum of flying room between the snow-covered forest and the clouds above. Brooking squeezed in, just above the tree tops, searching the valley floor beneath him. He found nothing; the valley roads were empty, and he managed a tight 180-degree turn and returned. Determined, Brooking tried another tactic.

Going low again, between the hilly terrain and the fog above, Brooking searched for an opening beneath the overcast that could lead him to the target. Ridge-hopping into the next valley, he nosed up into the overcast just long enough to clear the terrain, then dropped lower, tensing against an impact with the treetops just beneath this wings.

The *Yank* correspondent described what followed: "Suddenly he broke through the clouds! He wasn't more than twenty feet above a huge concentration of German tanks and armored vehicles. . . . The Germans looked at Major Brooking, and Major Brooking looked at the Germans," both parties so stunned at the appearance of the other that no one fired.

Brooking remembered, "It was hilly, rolling terrain, with a little village nearby. It looked like a mad scramble below, total confusion. I think they were completely surprised." He squeezed off one burst, then pulled back up and gathered his other three pilots in the clear. Finding the same hole, Brooking led the four in after the panzers together, hoping again to thread the needle to clear the adjoining ridge.

Wells remembered that "we finally got talking to [a ground] controller who could see the tanks, and could hear us, and he said that we were on the other side of this little mountain range from them. They kept trying to talk us in, and we tried to get there, but we kept running out of space. We were getting right into the treetops and we had to make a one-eighty to stay in contact [with each other]. Then, finally we found a spot where we could stay on top of the trees and get over."

The four Thunderbolts crested the ridge and whistled down into the adjoining valley, barely a hundred feet off the deck. Wells was astonished: "When we went over, we saw all these tanks lined up on the road."

The P-47s lined up for their attack runs. Brooking led, skimming the deck, just a few feet beneath the curtain of fog. The Hell Hawks chose targets in the column and opened up with their .50-calibers. Hurtling in on the line of armored vehicles, they were met with a tremendous concentration of flak thrown up by the now-alerted gunners. The tracers didn't stop the release of all eight bombs, which detonated up and down the road.

Wells recalled, "Well, when we found them, we did a three-sixty and went around, and each of us picked out a side of this tank column to hit. And we went in with delayed-action bombs [with an] eight- to eleven-second delay. So it was timed so that you could drop the bomb and you could look back. And I looked back and I saw that my bombs had hit right in this group of tanks."

Wells knew how to aim. "We were probably, I don't know, a hundred yards from them when we released . . . doing probably right around 350 or 400 [miles per hour]."

He put his bombs into a cluster of panzers cresting a small hill. The close-range blast effect was devastating, even to the seasoned Wells. "It just blew 'em apart," he said. "I just saw tank pieces flying everywhere. And where the tanks had been was a big gap in the road," blocked by his two bomb craters. Wells observed several tanks upended down the hillside, their 88mm main guns twisted at crazy angles. Soon, fires were burning amid the trapped vehicles, but the ground fire was undiminished in its ferocity.

Wells was asked if the Germans were trying to shoot back. "They were doing a pretty good job of it!" he answered, with the barest hint of a chuckle. "What you could see was the tracers coming, and they looked like they were coming right at you, and then they looked like they turned and went behind you, most of 'em. As soon as we got down from the run, that's when Brooking's wingman called and told us he was hit."

Lieutenant Price, from Sunnyvale, California, reported that his P-47 had been badly damaged. After radioing his intention to belly land, he disappeared, trailing flames, into the white fog bank over the battle. Price put the plane down gently enough to skid to a stop, shaken but unhurt. He stayed off the roads while heading generally west, and two days later met troops from the 30th Infantry Division near Stavelot. The GIs, wary of infiltrators, treated him with suspicion, especially after finding Price's sidearm: a German P-38 automatic. Fortunately, a first sergeant from Sunnyvale soon established Price's bona fides. He returned to the Hell Hawks just before Christmas, but not before his squadron mates had divided up his clothes, booze, and cigarettes.

As the flare from Price's P-47 disappeared into the white mist, Jim Wells noticed his own aircraft was trailing smoke. "Brook, I'm hit awful bad," called Wells. "Well, we passed a hospital a way back," Brooking answered. "I don't know whether it's American or German, but it had red crosses on it. Why don't you go and try to belly in close to it?

Wells wasn't keen on the suggestion. "I said, 'The hell with that. I'm taking this thing west as far as it'll go.'" Wells and Thoman popped up through the five-hundred-foot overcast and got a vector for Liège, where the weather was marginally better.

Wells' Thunderbolt, an all-aluminum-finish P-47D-25 named *Betty Girl*, streamed a thick trail of oily black smoke. "When I landed," Wells said, "I saw this crowd of guys standing out there, and it looked like they were changing money. I asked the mechanic what was going on, and he said 'Those guys was giving five-to-one odds that you would blow up before you got on the ground.'"

The 20mm hit had knocked out three or four cylinders on Wells' engine, yet the twin-row Pratt & Whitney had produced power all the way back to Liège. Wells couldn't stand the thought of abandoning that Thunderbolt; he waited a few days for repairs to D5-J, *Betty Girl*. Then, with her shrapnel holes patched and sporting a new engine, Wells flew her back to Chièvres.

Back in the target area, Brooking saw Thoman off with Wells, then orbited the enemy column, asking the IX TAC controller to send every available fighter-bomber. "When they get here," he said, "tell them to call me and I'll put them on the target. There's plenty for all." The 386th commander found other roads nearby packed with tanks and transports, and he repeatedly strafed and burned the lead vehicle, which in this hilly, snow-covered country effectively blocked the narrow lanes.

Other Thunderbolt squadrons arrived, the first from the 368th Fighter Group. Each flight checked in with Brooking, who led them to the proper hole in the shifting undercast. The Thunderbolts could now play hide-and-seek with the gunners, easing up into the mist to avoid flak and reappearing at will to snap into a sudden, devastating strafing run.

Brooking stayed as long as he dared, guiding each round of attackers in, only returning to Chièvres when his fuel was critically low. He turned his flak-scarred Thunderbolt off the runway two and a half hours after takeoff, running on fumes.

☆

The Hell Hawks launched ten strike missions into the fog over the Ardennes that day. Major Arlo C. Henry Jr. and Capt. Neal E. Worley both led missions from the 387th Squadron in midafternoon, following up on Brooking's initial strikes on the enemy column. Worley, just back from leave, recalled December 18 as "the hairiest and scariest of days for the Hell Hawks. The weather was snowy all over Belgium, with ceilings of 250 to 350 feet and nine-tenths cloud cover. In that fog, squadron-sized missions were impossible. We had to go with individual flights."

Worley, a flight leader, had been scouring his maps all morning for usable landmarks near the target. "We were antsy from the week or more of bad weather, anxious to get back into flying," he said. The Royal Air Force charts provided to the Hell Hawks were so detailed that even the shape of individual woodlots could be used as navigation checkpoints.

His flight, the seventh from the Hell Hawks to grapple with fog and German armor in the Ardennes that day, followed Arlo Henry's into the air at 2:55 p.m. Arriving near the battle area, Worley called his mentor ("I grew up flying on Arlo's wing," said Worley) to guide him in. "Arlo, where are you?" said Worley, and the reply was instant. "I'm working over the panzer division, over the mountain from where they told you," said Henry.

"I told my wingman and second element to come in close," said Worley, to keep from losing them in the clouds. The flight nosed up into the soup and climbed to clear the ridge tops hidden in the murk. "This is a hell of a way to fight a war," thought Worley, inching down now through the mist into what he hoped was the valley beneath them. "We broke out of the clouds so low that off my wing

I could see this big black raven sitting on a tree branch." Worley's flight hurtled down the slope beneath ragged gaps in the low clouds, exposing the smoke and flames still rising from the now-dispersed column. The four Thunderbolts picked their targets and dive-bombed deliberately.

"On my first run I spotted the biggest, tallest SS officer I ever saw, standing there in his black uniform, emptying his pistol at me," said Worley. "We stayed on them for fifteen minutes. One bombing pass, maybe four passes altogether. When we left, half-tracks and trucks were burning, and smoke was going up to about three thousand feet."

During their strafing runs, one of Worley's wingmen, 1st Lt. James F. McCabe, had his Thunderbolt bracketed by truck-mounted 20mm cannon. One pilot from another group wrote that "the flak tracers were like garden hoses with projectiles arcing lazily through the air towards me. I remember so violently slipping and skidding as streams of flak fire reached for me, sometimes within three feet of my wing surfaces." McCabe's DFC citation read: "Despite adverse weather and the hazards of intense and accurate enemy fire, Lt. McCabe fearlessly and skillfully dropped his bombs and completely destroyed three enemy tanks. . . . The explosion that followed caught his plane and seriously damaged it, but . . . he brought his plane to a safe landing."

Worley's flight claimed forty trucks upon debriefing back at Chièvres. Looking back, he was emphatic about his group's contribution to the fight in the Ardennes. "I got a lot of satisfaction from that mission. We were a tactical outfit. If you could pick one day to show what the Hell Hawks were all about—their value as a combat outfit—this was it. December 18 was one of our finest days in showing off our capabilities."

Late afternoon saw more Hell Hawks arrive over Stavelot, blasting tanks, half-tracks, and trucks. The combination of clear bombing conditions and determined attacks from these later missions destroyed nearly one hundred enemy vehicles. Pilots groped their way back to Chièvres through fog so thick that ground crewmen set burning flares along the runway to help them spot the base. By the close of the day's combat, the Hell Hawks claimed 15 panzers among a grand total of more than 125 armored vehicles and transports destroyed, with another 34 damaged. Given the tracer-filled skies over Stavelot that day, the toll from German gunners on December 18 was surprisingly light: two P-47s lost to crash landings and seven heavily damaged.

☆

Next day, a high-ranking First Army officer phoned Ninth Air Force commander, Maj. Gen. Hoyt Vandenberg, saying, "Thank God for your men yesterday."

Vandenberg's headquarters received a teletype on December 19, confirming that the air attacks on the enemy column forced it from its westward advance, diverting it south. Advancing First Army units, shoring up the northern flank of the Bulge on the 20th, discovered that the actual damage inflicted by the Hell Hawks and other fighter-bomber groups on the wrecked German column exceeded the pilots' claims. One who grudgingly recognized the effectiveness of the P-47s was Waffen-SS Gen. Sepp Dietrich, commander of the Sixth Panzer Army, who complained, "The worst of it is that those damned Jabos don't distinguish between generals and anyone else—it was terrible."

☆

Ray Stecker wrote commendations for both Motzenbecker and Brooking, but didn't hold out much hope for approval, noting that headquarters would dismiss the pair's heroism because "they didn't shoot down a single enemy aircraft." Of his boss, Brooking, Bob Hagan said simply, "He had a lot of guts, letting down in those clouds over the Bulge." For once, headquarters agreed with a lowly second lieutenant. The author of Brooking's citation noted how he led his four planes against the spearhead of the German attack: "Although weather conditions were extremely unfavorable and antiaircraft fire from the ground emplacements extremely heavy, Major Brooking remained alone . . . he fearlessly led and guided other flights to attack the tank column although his own aircraft was seriously damaged." For his gallantry, "skill, cool judgement, and courage," Brooking received the Silver Star.

☆

Bad weather played havoc with the Hell Hawks' efforts to repeat their performance of the 18th. For four days, snow and fog grounded the 365th, and although they got into the air on December 23, bad weather forced a mission recall. Wehrmacht advances during those five days, despite determined resistance by American GIs, created the westward-reaching "bulge" so obvious on the battle maps. The need for more air support on the southern flank of the Ardennes salient led Ninth Air Force on December 23 to shift the Hell Hawks south of the Bulge, to the battered former Luftwaffe base at Metz, France. There the group would operate under the commander of XIX Tactical Air Command, Maj. Gen. O. P.

"Opie" Weyland, Quesada's counterpart and the effective aerial partner to Lt. Gen. George S. Patton's Third Army.

The move to Metz would prove the most arduous of the Hell Hawks' eight moves on the Continent. The reconnaissance parties crossed west of the advancing German spearheads in unheated trucks, skidding down icy roads and holing up for the night in an ordnance depot near Verdun crammed with knocked-out Sherman tanks. Christmas Eve was marked by a dinner of cold K-rations, and Christmas Day's meal was a "festive" affair consisting of C-rations heated in an open field kitchen, the ground crews stamping their feet in the snow to keep warm. While the group mounted combat missions out of Chièvres, the forward parties dug latrines and wrestled up the frozen canvas of their tents, readying the flight line for the Thunderbolts' arrival.

☆

When the weather broke on Christmas Day, the Hell Hawks launched from Chièvres a trio of missions in support of the Third Army's efforts to break through to the surrounded defenders of Bastogne. Twenty-one-year-old 1st Lt. Oliven Cowan led one flight of the 388th Squadron's fifteen Thunderbolts, carrying five-hundred-pound bombs to hit a two-hundred-vehicle convoy near Beho, Belgium. "Our squadron immediately found plenty of targets to dive-bomb and strafe," recalled Cowan. "Flak was extremely heavy. It seemed that all antiaircraft guns, ground guns, and personal weapons were focused on our squadron. When I dive-bombed a convoy of vehicles, my left-wing bomb hung and almost caused me to flip upside down. After recovering, I made another run on a target and shook the bomb loose. Smith [1st Lt. Byron Smith, Jr.] covered me as I unloaded the bomb."

Cowan's Blue Flight was working over the convoy as medium and heavy bombers above struck targets in the surrounding towns; it made for a chaotic combat situation, especially when a gaggle of Fw 190s and Bf 109s attacked the bombers, then dove away right into the path of the Hell Hawks.

"As I was strafing a vehicle," Cowan wrote in 2001, "a [Bf] 109 crashed right in front of me and an Fw 190 came down through Blue Flight. Smith and I were evading enemy planes, dodging flak, and checking the bomb bay doors on the bombers while trying to strafe ground targets." Cowan radioed Smith, "Next one that comes through, we're going after him!"

He didn't have to wait long. During the next strafing pass, a 190 dipped in front of Cowan, who gave chase. "The German plane hit a treetop as I was closing in to shoot him down," wrote Cowan. Chasing the German, miraculously still in the air, Cowan checked Smith, his wingman, only to find him pursued by a bomber-escort P-51 that mistook Smith's P-47 for a Luftwaffe fighter. Unable to get Smith to break sharply by calling over the radio, Cowan "left the Fw 190 and broke hard left to get the P-51 off Smith's tail. When the pilot of the P-51 saw my big, elliptical wing, he left."

Cowan and Smith resumed strafing the convoy, adding to the squadron's total of fourteen motor transports, an ammo truck, one box car, a building, and sixteen horse-drawn vehicles. But the heavy flak scored on both of their Thunderbolts. "I got hit in both wings," wrote Cowan, "and Smith took a severe hit in his left landing gear well." Low on gas and ammo, he and Smith turned back for Chièvres, but their troubles were far from over.

"As we approached the field, I lowered my landing gear, and Smith said that I had a tire shot off. Smith tried to lower his landing gear, and only his right gear came down." Cowan touched down on "one good wheel and one rim," and the drag from the bad wheel pulled him off the runway and into the grass. Smith touched down on his right main gear, keeping the left wing up as long as possible. "When the wing came down, Smith's plane left the runway and came to a stop near my plane. Nothing less than a miracle can explain why Smith's plane didn't cartwheel." Cowan and Smith looked over the latter's damage: sixteen bullet holes, courtesy of that errant Mustang pilot. "Smith thanked me many times for saving his life," Cowan wrote, "but I have never felt that I deserved any recognition. I realize that if Smith had not stuck with me . . . that P-51 could have been putting bullets in my plane."

That Christmas night, Smith and Cowan walked with a few other pilots to a village church nearby. Inside, the Belgian congregation was singing a hymn. Cowan listened and joined in. "They were singing in French the song 'Silent Night,' originated in Germany. We were outside singing in English. . . . The song was peacefully penetrating, and all around us was war."

Christmas had a different mood for the Wehrmacht soldiers, whose confident advance had now turned, nine days later, into a bloody fiasco. With the advent of good weather, the Hell Hawks and the rest of the Ninth Air Force helped the beleaguered American GIs turn back the German advance. Although by Christmas night the fighting still raged and the outcome still seemed in doubt to many, the evidence of German defeat was growing. Historian Stanley Weintraub quoted Maj.

Gen. Ludwig Heilmann of the Wehrmacht 5th Paratroop Division, who described the scene at nightfall on December 24: "One could see, from Bastogne back to the West Wall, a single torchlight procession of burning vehicles."

☆

Another week of combat missions, both against the retreating German columns in the shrinking Bulge and the Luftwaffe overhead, brought 1944 to a close. The Group's pilots, planes, and ground crews finally reunited next to the frozen runway of Metz, but not before one officer was killed and several injured when their truck overturned en route to the new base.

A snowstorm closed out combat operations late on the afternoon of December 31. In the cold, unlit billets of a school they had commandeered near the airfield, the men of the Hell Hawks were not in the mood to celebrate New Year's Eve. The early onset of December twilight and an 8:00 p.m. curfew curbed those few intent on partying, and for the rest, there seemed little to do but sleep. The pilots, flying early the next morning, built small fires to heat rations and toast the coming German defeat, which, after their failure in the Bulge, seemed only a matter of time.

At 10:00 p.m., 1st Lt. Sam Lutz sipped a hot chocolate and thought, "Some celebration!" before turning in. Major Brooking, the 386th Squadron's commander, invited a few pilots into his chilly room and, by flashlight, shared a ration package from home. He didn't even have a glass of wine at hand to toast the new year. Cold, and tired from two weeks of constant fighting, the Hell Hawks slept.

Chapter Eleven

Death from Above

EW YEAR'S DAY, 1945, DAWNED COLD AND CLEAR for the men of
the Hell Hawks. Pilots and enlisted men shuffled out of their temporary
lodgings in the Alsatian city of Metz. The Luftwaffe had occupied the
cluster of commandeered brick buildings until just weeks before. None among the
chilled, sleepy-eyed airmen suspected the recently evicted tenants might still have
unfinished business at their old aerodrome.

The bumpy mile to the Hell Hawks' airfield, code-named Y-34, in a motley
collection of drafty, canvas-topped trucks and jeeps was mercifully brief. The airmen spilled out of the vehicles to their three squadron compounds surrounding
the five-thousand-foot pierced-steel-plank runway. On this first day of the seventh
year of World War II, Y-34 soon bustled with purposeful activity.

From the mess tent, pilots of the 387th Fighter Squadron headed for their
intelligence briefing and the day's first mission. Mechanics and armorers had been
on the job all night, working outdoors in the subfreezing air to ready the group's
four-dozen P-47 Thunderbolts for a full slate of ground-attack missions against
the German army in the Ardennes. The Battle of the Bulge had turned in the Allies'
favor, due in no small part to a vigorous application of firepower from these men
and their brothers-in-arms in the Ninth Air Force's fighter-bomber groups. Now,
with the British and Americans squeezing the Bulge from three sides, and the good

"victory weather" of the past week continuing to hold, the Hell Hawks would try to trap the Wehrmacht on the narrow roads of Belgium and Luxembourg. Their mission today was simple: put as many planes into the air as the group could muster, cut the Germans off from their homeland, destroy their weapons and transport, and kill as many enemy soldiers as possible.

☆

The rumble of Pratt & Whitney radial engines echoed across the field as the crew chiefs warmed up the squat fighter-bombers for the morning's first strike. From the ready tent on the 387th Squadron flight line, eleven pilots led by Maj. Arlo Henry emerged in winter flying gear and headed for their P-47s. Henry, from East Dearborn, Michigan, had been with the Hell Hawks since the group's formation in June 1943 and had destroyed a Focke-Wulf 190 in combat the previous spring. On the same mission, he'd flown so low avoiding a German flak tower that he'd clipped a Belgian field with his propeller and brought the evidence back in his turbocharger intake. The nose of his olive drab Thunderbolt, the second to be so named, bore the words *Turnip Termite II* (Henry was also inspired by the destructive insect pests of Al Capp's *L'il Abner* comic strip).

At 8:28 a.m., Henry led his squadron off in pairs, heading east from Metz into the bright morning sun. Each P-47 nestled two five-hundred-pound general-purpose bombs under its wings and packed more than two thousand rounds of ammo for its eight .50-caliber machine guns. The flight arrived in clear weather over Nohfelden, Germany, at the eastern base of the Bulge. On a rail siding etched black against the snow, one of Henry's pilots spotted twenty German railcars. The major ordered three planes down to attack, and less than a minute later the siding erupted in dirty clouds of smoke and debris. The flight regrouped and ranged eastward, leaving five cars destroyed and steel tracks twisted over the ugly edges of six bomb craters.

☆

Back at Metz, Capt. Jerry Mast, a Chicagoan and Hell Hawks veteran who'd won the Distinguished Flying Cross, gunned his P-47 down the runway at the head of thirteen Thunderbolts. The 388th Fighter Squadron trailed the 387th by about forty-five minutes, and Mast checked in with the Hell Hawks' divisional air controller, call sign MUDGUARD, for an update on their assigned target area. As the roar of the departing squadron faded into the high winter sky, the ground crews labored over last-minute checks on the planes for the third strike mission.

The 386th Squadron pilots had finished their intelligence and target briefings and were wrestling into their flying gear: parachutes, leather jackets, helmets and gloves, and .45-caliber pistols. Outside the ready tent, a string of shabby weapons carriers stood by, white exhaust wafting up in the frigid air, to take the young fliers to their waiting Jugs.

Unseen by the Hell Hawks' two airborne squadrons, another flight of fighters was aloft that morning, inbound for Metz. Oberstleutnant Helmut Bennemann, at twenty-nine one of the Luftwaffe's most decorated pilots, was at that moment hugging the low hills of Alsace-Lorraine at the head of Jagdgeschwader 53 (JG 53, the Luftwaffe's 53rd Fighter Wing, dubbed the *Pik As*, or Ace of Spades). Bennemann wore the Knight's Cross at the throat of his leather flight jacket, a tribute to the nearly ninety victories the veteran *gruppe* (group) leader had racked up in aerial combat. His two gruppen were flying Messerschmitt Bf 109Gs, "Gustavs." They scudded low over the German frontier, their mottled gray wings gleaming against the dark woodlots and snow-covered fields a hundred feet below. They were part of a bold gambit: a strike by hundreds of Luftwaffe fighters aimed at the frontline Allied airfields, a maximum effort aimed at destroying the Jabos on the ground and seizing control of the air over the Bulge.

Bennemann's two gruppen (a third had been scattered by patrolling P-47s and failed to make the rendezvous) had been briefed just before dawn. Lifting off from fields near Stuttgart with the rising sun, the Messerschmitts dropped to low altitude and took up a circuitous course for the target, just 130 miles away. Their objective: the Metz-Frescaty airfield, new home of the 365th Fighter Group.

The Luftwaffe's desperate lunge was aimed at the Allied fighters that had turned the Bulge into a living hell for the Wehrmacht units trying to preserve their gains of the last two weeks. Hermann Goering's weakened air force had marshaled 875 single-engine fighters for a hammer blow against the Allied fighter fields north and south of the Bulge. With Operation *Bodenplatte* (Baseplate), the Germans hoped to catch British and U.S. fighters on the ground just after dawn on January 1, while their pilots were still sleeping off the effects of New Year's Eve celebrations.

Unfortunately for the Luftwaffe, the Hell Hawks' New Year's Eve had been tame, a disappointment. Recently assigned to Metz, only a few miles behind the front lines, the Hell Hawks found there was little to do after dark in their frigid, unlit barracks but sleep. The 386th Fighter Squadron's commanding officer, Maj.

George R. Brooking, had huddled with a handful of pilots around a flashlight in his drafty, bare room. He shared a few treats mailed from home, but could only savor memories of the French champagnes they had enjoyed before moving to Metz. After a fitful night in his sleeping bag, Brooking rose before dawn and caught a ride to the field. Far from being hung over, he and his men were at work early, grateful for good weather and ready for a full slate of missions over the Ardennes.

As Brooking readied his squadron's strike, Oberstleutnant Bennemann's Bf 109G buzzed southwestward up the valley of the Moselle River, staying below the tops of the vine-covered ridges to avoid the Americans' early-warning radar. Upstream from Trier, the river's course took them gradually southward, approaching Metz from the north. He signaled the formation to drop belly tanks and arm cannon and machine guns. Stripped for combat, his two squadrons shook themselves into a wide line abreast, roaring low over the center of the battered city at more than 345 miles per hour.

Corporal Owen Monette stamped his feet on the frozen ground at the south end of Y-34's steel-plank runway. The twenty-four-year-old air-control specialist from Detroit held an Aldis lamp in a gloved hand, ready to coordinate the taxi and takeoff of the 386th Squadron's Thunderbolts, next up on the schedule. From his makeshift control tower, really nothing more than a jeep, portable radio, and a flimsy tent, he and the twelve men of Detachment B, 9th Flying Control Squadron kept one eye on the pale blue sky for the returning planes of Henry's flight. From the direction of Metz, just beyond the low hills to the north, a few black puffs appeared in the morning haze, followed by the delayed crackle of explosions. Monette and his buddies turned to stare at the unusual spectacle of antiaircraft bursts, their sound still muffled by distance.

Monette caught motion against the snow-covered hills to the north. What looked like a swarm of tiny black hornets emerged from the background haze and dropped low over the barren fields, growing larger by the second. The distant silhouettes numbered more than a dozen; what kind of aircraft were they? To Monette, who'd spent a year as a tower controller at Royal Air Force bases in southern England, the aircraft winging his way looked like a gaggle of British Spitfires, spread out in their typically loose formation. Maybe this RAF bunch was taking a rare chance this bright Monday morning to "beat up" the field and startle some hung-over airmen from their bunks.

Hauptmann Julius Meimberg, leading II Gruppe of JG 53, glanced left and right at the flanking fighters off his wingtips. The southern suburbs of Metz flashed under his plane, and the Knight's Cross wearer, an ace ten times over, eased back on the stick with thumb and forefinger to clear the low hills ahead. As Meimberg's fighters followed Bennemann across the snow-covered fields, he took one last glance at the Messerschmitts strung out to both sides as the gray smudge of an airstrip emerged from the flat landscape ahead. Sighting through the gunsight glass above the instrument panel, Meimberg lined up on a cluster of olive drab-camouflaged P-47s. Skimming low over the north end of the empty runway, his index finger squeezed the trigger button.

Monette changed his mind about the approaching formation. They weren't Spitfires, they were P-51 Mustangs, but what were those bright flashes winking from the noses of the fighters? The thump of cannon shells and whine of machine gun bullets snapped out an answer. Monette dove into a nearby foxhole.

Staff Sergeant George "Moocher" Wasson, a crew chief, was trying to dry a discarded cigarette butt, just retrieved from the frozen ground, when a friend, Staff Sgt. John Lehnert, noticed him fumbling with it. "Hell, George, have a Camel!" Lehnert called, and beckoned Wasson over with a fresh cigarette. The two stood smoking and talking for a couple of minutes. Just as Wasson resumed his walk to the hangar to retrieve a part for his P-47, he heard someone yell, "Look at those P-51s buzzing the field!" Lehnert and Wasson turned together and spotted the oncoming fighters—and muzzle flashes. "P-51s, my ass!" a nearby Hell Hawk shouted. "Those are Germans!"

Sixteen Bf 109s swept in on the deck, heading directly for the 386th's combat-loaded Thunderbolts clustered on steel-mat hardstands around the narrow taxiways. As dozens of startled men dashed for cover in nearby gun pits or handy depressions, the German fighters hammered the field with long bursts of machine gun and cannon fire. Tracers from the Gustavs' twin 13mm MG 131 machine guns ripped into one P-47 after another, caught like sitting ducks. Twenty-millimeter shells from the Messerschmitts' cannon, which fired through the center of the propeller hub, blew gaping holes in the stationary Thunderbolts. Explosions cracked across the open field as gas tanks caught fire, detonating bombs and ammunition.

With bullets smacking the ground nearby, Wasson leaped into a shell hole with a couple of other men, frantically using his bare hands to scratch his way deeper into the frozen ground. He shivered, but it wasn't from the cold. If Lehnert hadn't offered him that Camel, Moocher would have been on his way to the hangar, caught in the open by the strafers. Years later, Wasson would quit smoking, but he always believed that on that chilly morning, a cigarette had saved his life.

Near the 388th Squadron headquarters tent, the only projectiles flying around were made of ice. Sergeant John H. Hancock, of La Habra, California, had just arrived at Metz on New Year's Eve, part of the group headquarters contingent. He'd reported in that morning to the 388th for reassignment and soon was caught up in a snowball fight, pilots and enlisted men slipping and laughing in the drifted snow. Hancock saw a pilot freeze in midtoss and yell, "Bandits!" All eyes followed his outstretched arm as he pointed out the line of approaching fighters. "They're coming this way!"

Hancock dove for a shallow hole that had recently been used to store coal. Scrabbling at the frozen ground on hands and knees, he was flattened by the impact of another man landing atop him. Lifting his head, Hancock noticed blood dripping down from above. He was sure the man on his back had been hit and killed by the raiding Messerschmitts, now setting up a textbook gunnery pattern over the field. As he struggled to get out from under the "corpse," a surprised Hancock heard its owner speak up. The wounded man shouted through the din that the blood was just from a hand cut; racing to the hole, he had tripped over a tent peg. Despite the machine gun bullets whizzing just overhead, Hancock and his fellow fugitive laughed in relief.

Second Lieutenant Bob Hagan had just slung his parachute over his shoulder in the 386th Fighter Squadron ready tent. He was heading out to *Fran*, the Thunderbolt he'd named after the Baton Rouge girl he hoped to marry, when he heard the thud of explosions from the distant north end of the field. "Messerschmitts!" came the yell from a hundred men on the flight line. Hagan joined the general rush as pilots and ground crews alike searched desperately for cover.

Hagan, encumbered by his bulky winter flying gear, stumbled toward a shallow antiaircraft gun emplacement a few yards away. "We started hearing guns, and of course we scrambled out of the parachute tent and ran for some cover," he remembered. Diving atop the tangle of men already occupying the hole, the Missourian tried to flatten himself below ground level. "Get the hell off me!" came an angry shout from below. "I'll be more than happy to trade places!" Hagan yelled back, his shouts nearly inaudible amid machine gun bursts from the Messerschmitts. Now fully aroused, the army's antiaircraft gunners added the blasts of their heavy weapons to the thud of explosions from German cannon shells and blazing Thunderbolts.

☆

Fifty miles away from the chaos at Metz, Arlo Henry's 387th Squadron was efficiently wrecking another rail marshalling yard. Three miles north of Primstal, Germany, eight of his Thunderbolts dove on fifteen railcars and unloaded sixteen five-hundred-pound bombs, knocking out five and again severing the rail line. As Henry's flight wheeled homeward, they overheard a call from MUDGUARD on their group channel that the base was under air attack. Both Henry's and Mast's squadrons fire-walled throttles and pointed their Thunderbolts westward, anxious to intercept the Luftwaffe raid.

By now the German attack on Metz was in full swing. Technical Sergeant Marion Hill, then chief noncommissioned officer of the 365th's intelligence section, remembered diving for the foundation wall of a burned-out barracks. "That first pass was right overhead," Hill recalled. "They just missed us." His luck didn't hold. "I heard a whoosh." A shell fragment ricocheted off the foundation and hit him in the face. "I saw my gloves and lower left arm covered in blood." He was hastily bandaged under fire and evacuated on a stretcher.

Major George Brooking, the 386th commander, had been taking his ease in the officers' latrine, a canvas tent housing a wooden bench over a pit in the frozen earth. Hearing gunfire outside, Brooking pulled back the canvas tent flap to reveal an amazing sight: six Bf 109s coming head-on, their guns stitching fountains of dirty snow in a line headed right for him. The startled commander launched himself out of the tent and sprawled in the snow outside, heavy parka hood pulled over his head, bare buttocks exposed to the hot steel filling the air.

As the 109s pulled up into their next strafing pass, Brooking decided his parka didn't offer the desired protection; he jumped to his feet, pulled up his trousers, and dropped again into a rapid crawl for a gun pit about fifty feet away. The major tumbled into the emplacement, dignity retrieved, and joined the gunners who were blasting away with their four-barreled .50-caliber machine gun mount at the German fighters. Said Brooking, "They were shooting too low and behind the 109s. I started yelling over the gunfire, 'Lead 'em! Lead 'em a little more!'" His duck hunter's advice paid off: the quad-fifty crew put a burst into the cockpit of a Luftwaffe fighter, sending it smashing into the field just short of the gun pit that Hagan occupied.

The downed fighter tore itself apart, scattering wreckage in its wake and hurling its ill-fated pilot from the cockpit. Hagan watched the crumpled body tumble to a stop in a grisly heap a few feet from his hole. A couple of gunners scurried out under fire, grabbed the dead pilot's parachute as a souvenir, and sprinted back to safety. Flight chief Alvin E. Bradley of the 386th felt little sympathy for the dead German. "They got us into it, after all," he said. He'd been the last man to pile into one foxhole, and worried that his exposed "rear profile" would snag a German bullet. Another Hell Hawk grimly observed the enemy pilot's corpse: "I saw a ring on his finger. If I'd had something to cut that finger off, I would have probably got that ring off him." Somebody else beat him to it.

Second Lieutenant Carl Riggs, a preacher's son from Ames, Iowa, had joined the Hell Hawks as a replacement in November; his Thanksgiving dinner was a cold C-ration eaten on the train up from Paris to Brussels. Not scheduled for the 388th's morning mission, Riggs had been relaxing in the squadron area when the attack opened. Crouched behind the broken foundation and chimney of a demolished building near a hangar, Riggs remembered "being amazed that the Germans would mount such an audacious offensive."

With the Messerschmitts roaring in from every direction, the low foundation didn't furnish much protection, as Riggs discovered all too soon. The army gunners scored on a second 109, which dove out of control toward the hangar—and Riggs. "I didn't see it coming, as I was hugging the foundation wall," he recalled. The Nazi fighter clipped the roof of a radio trailer, burst into flame, and cartwheeled over his hideout. Instantly, Riggs was engulfed in a brilliant yellow orange fireball. "There was tremendous noise, a flash from the fire, then blackness," Riggs remembered. "I thought to myself, 'This is it. This is how I'm going to die.'" His leather flight jacket puckered in the heat of the fireball, and a hot fragment of the plane ripped into the back of his right shoulder. "The Messerschmitt bounced just high enough off the roof of the trailer to tumble over rather than through me," Riggs said. The smoking wreckage slid into the hangar just a few yards away, what was left of the pilot's body coming to rest nearby. Riggs took stock: "I remember being surprised I was not dead after all." He stayed put behind his wall as another 109 came screaming down the flight line.

By now, bombs cooking off in the burning P-47s were completing the destruction started by the Luftwaffe. Master Sergeant Joseph Piantino, chief armorer of the 387th Squadron, had been supervising bomb loading for his planes. Henry's Blue Flight was due back in about twenty minutes for refueling and rearming. Piantino had scrambled for cover with the rest of the Hell Hawks when Bennemann's planes made their first pass. Crouching inside the wall of a ruined hangar, he turned to look out the open doors just in time to see four 109s in line-abreast zoom down the field, guns chattering. Keeping his head down with a dozen or so other men, Piantino could distinguish the deep rhythmic stutter of the American fifties from the buzz-saw roar of the German machine guns. Whenever a Messerschmitt sprayed the hangar area with gunfire, he heard the bullets splattering the other side of the wall; an occasional 20mm shell smacked home to punctuate the crackle of flames and occasional thud of P-47 bombs going up.

Caught literally with his pants down by the attack was Staff Sgt. Donald J. Hutchins, from Fulton, New York: he'd been reading *Stars and Stripes* in the 388th latrine. When bullets rattled his way, he'd headed for the nearest shelter: straight down. He spent the rest of the raid huddled at the bottom of the latrine pit, cursing his hasty decision. Hutchins emerged after the attack, spectacularly fragrant but unhurt. Only his pride took a direct hit.

On a 386th Squadron hardstand at the extreme south end of the field, Staff Sgt. Robert A. Garbarine stood on the wing of his Thunderbolt, just beside the cockpit. Turning to look toward the sound of gunfire, the startled crew chief noticed a hole appear in one of the P-47's steel propeller blades. It was nearly the *last* thing Garbarine saw. Another 20mm shell creased his skull, throwing him unconscious onto the frozen ground. He woke up flat on his back a few minutes later, suffering only a superficial wound and a nasty headache.

Nearby, Staff Sgt. Kirby Garner heard the "ping-pinging" of German bullets on the steel mesh of the hardstand under the P-47 he'd been working on. Sprinting in his heavy sheepskin jacket and trousers away from the Jug, he glimpsed the snow spurting up in a line headed right for him. "I'm kilt! I'm kilt!" he shouted, running flat out toward a gun position. Bullets zipped past him, one searing his right arm as he hurled himself into the mass of bodies huddled in the gun pit.

In the alert-flight area at the south end of the runway, 1st Lt. Samuel B. Lutz tried to keep warm, squatting with a group of combat engineers around a scrapwood fire. Fellow pilot 1st Lt. Thomas Stanton was sitting in the cockpit of a P-47 standing alert duty nearby. With Lutz's own alert Thunderbolt down for maintenance, the young fighter pilot from Beverly Hills was without a plane when he spotted ten Messerschmitts headed right down the runway at him. Someone shouted, "It's a raid!" The men sprinted for any scrap of cover on the exposed ground next to the runway.

Lutz raced the engineers to their heavy steamroller as the enemy planes wheeled up from their initial pass and began systematically raking the field. The steamroller provided some protection, but with Messerschmitts strafing from every direction, the men had to constantly shift their position. Lutz had a ringside seat for the action.

By then the antiaircraft guns, the quad-mounted .50-calibers and both 37mm and 40mm rapid-fire cannon, were throwing up a tremendous amount of fire. Lutz was impressed by the noise, ack-ack guns adding their roar to the din of German cannon and machine guns.

To Lutz, crouching behind the steamroller, it seemed as if each of the Luftwaffe pilots was personally shooting directly at him. Anxious to fight back, Lutz stood up and began banging away with his Colt .45 automatic, but a weak recoil spring caused it to jam on every shot. He was scared, excited, and mad all at the same time. "I was especially mad about the beautiful P-47s burning and blowing up," he recalled years later, "and I was scared as many of the five-hundred-pounders started to go off nearby."

An incoming Messerschmitt streaked toward the group, guns blazing. It put a 20mm cannon shell directly into the now-vacant cockpit of Stanton's alert Thunderbolt, and as the onrushing fighter passed overhead, Lutz felt he could have touched the pilot at the controls. At that moment the 109 caught a burst in the cockpit from a quad-fifty, killing the pilot and instantly sending the Messerschmitt nose-first into the ground. The pilot's mangled body bounced and rolled clear of the wreckage, coming to a stop on the runway, where two gunners sprinted to the corpse and grabbed its prized flying boots.

A fourth 109 was shot down near the 387th Squadron headquarters, leaving a trail of smoking wreckage some eighty yards long across the flight line. The pilot was decapitated, both legs torn off just above the knees. The mangled corpse lay steaming in the frigid morning air, shreds of flesh suspended in the bare branches of surrounding bushes. Lutz watched in revulsion as a few Hell Hawks scavenged the dead pilot's remains, and silently hoped that if it was his fate to be scattered over the snowy countryside, the Germans wouldn't return the favor.

Some men seemed to lose all control in the excitement and frenzy of the attack. Brooking, helping direct the gunners' antiaircraft fire, watched as his crew downed another Messerschmitt. Once more the pilot's body was thrown clear, close enough to Brooking that he saw one of his own men run out to the dead German. "He was kicking the body and cussing the pilot as his body lay in the snow," recalls Brooking. "The guy was just taking out his frustration from the attack on this poor German."

Second Lieutenant James McWhorter of the 386th remembers huddling in an old German gun emplacement at the height of the attack with his fellow pilot, Capt. William E. "Curly" Rodgers. McWhorter said, "I was buried near the top of this pile of bodies, everybody yelling, 'Let me up, I'm smothering,' when I noticed Curly still had his pants down from where he'd run from the latrine. He was on top of the pile, firing at the -109s with his .45."

On a 388th Squadron hardstand, Cpl. Lee Weldon was trapped in the cockpit of a Thunderbolt, immobilized by a German bullet in his thigh. One of Weldon's buddies, Cpl. Emanuel Catanuto, spotted Weldon in the plane as it began to burn under repeated strafing passes. Ignoring the flames licking near the cockpit and the five-hundred-pound bomb slung under each wing, Catanuto reacted instinctively. Despite the imminent danger of an explosion from the bomb-laden Jug, he vaulted onto the wing and dashed toward the cockpit. Reaching through smoke and searing flames, Catanuto jerked Weldon free and tumbled backward off the wing with the wounded man. Grabbing Weldon's good leg, he dragged the blood-soaked mechanic unceremoniously over the frozen ground. Catanuto managed to put about thirty yards between them and the burning P-47 before its fuel tanks and bombs exploded, engulfing the pair in a whirlwind of shrapnel. Both miraculously escaped unharmed, and Catanuto's selfless actions won him the Soldier's Medal. It wouldn't be the last decoration for Catanuto; trained as an Army Air Forces mechanic, he would later serve in the infantry, earning a Silver Star for single-handedly knocking out a German antitank gun.

Sergeants John C. Lawless and Olin S. Holcomb were at work on their P-47 when the first pass by the Messerschmitts set it aflame. Lawless and Holcomb leaped clear, but just across the hardstand from their bombed-up plane was another loaded Thunderbolt. Realizing their plane's bombs would take out the other aircraft as well, the two grabbed fire extinguishers and smothered the flames, even as attacking fighters crisscrossed the field. "It was done on the spur of the moment," Lawless recounted. "I had no thought of the consequences. It wasn't until after the fire was out that I realized what could have happened, and it was then that I started to get a queasy feeling in my stomach." "Amen," said Holcomb. Both won the Soldier's Medal for their actions.

Crew chief Sgt. Gordon Hurt was nearby when the strafers hit a gas truck and set it afire. An orange red fireball rolled skyward, and burning gasoline spread across the ground toward Hurt's Thunderbolt. His Soldier's Medal citation reads, in part: "The spreading of the fire to the plane would have exploded the bombs and would have destroyed the aircraft. Disregarding his own personal safety, Sergeant Hurt and two other enlisted men rushed alongside the burning truck and up to the aircraft. At a great risk to themselves, they started the aircraft engine and taxied the aircraft to a safe distance from the blazing truck, thereby saving the aircraft."

One American pilot returned to Metz during the German attack. First Lieutenant Lavern Alcorn, from West Union, Iowa, had launched as the 388th Squadron's thirteenth, or spare, Thunderbolt in the second mission off that morning. He'd trailed Mast's formation south for about twenty minutes until they turned east and Mast gave him the all-clear to return to base. About 9:15 a.m., Alcorn sighted the Metz runway and began his routine letdown for the landing pattern. "All of a sudden I was bracketed by four black bursts of heavy flak. It really startled me."

Wondering what had gone wrong, Alcorn jinked violently to throw off the gunners' aim if they loosed a second salvo. "I couldn't figure out how I was going to get back if they were going to shoot at me." Alcorn was now close enough to Metz to see the black smoke columns and fires burning on the field. "I saw one German fighter low over the field, and about that time I heard a radio call from Metz telling me the field was under attack." The now-wary pilot quickly jettisoned his bombs unarmed into a French field, then turned in pursuit of the departing Germans. He raced east for five or ten minutes, "but I never caught up with them," said Alcorn.

As swiftly as they had come, the Messerschmitts suddenly departed, dodging away over the hills. The Luftwaffe lost eight of their number to the surprising accuracy of the airfield defenses, but their ten-minute attack had scored heavily on the Hell Hawks. Orange fireballs gave way to greasy clouds of black smoke, punctuated by occasional explosions as more bombs cooked off in the heat.

Carl Riggs, bleeding slightly from his shoulder wound and still wearing his singed jacket, went in search of the flight surgeon. "There was devastation everywhere," he recalls. "There were burning planes all over the place." Metz was a shambles. Twenty-two P-47s were burning on the field, and another eleven were badly damaged. The 386th Squadron was hit most heavily, with twelve fighters destroyed and seven knocked out of commission; those losses meant the unit was effectively out of action. At least eleven Hell Hawks had been wounded. The Germans destroyed ten more Thunderbolts from the other two squadrons and damaged another four.

Oberstleutnant Bennemann's JG 53 had surprised the 365th, but the attackers paid a heavy price: some two dozen Bf 109s were downed during the mission and fourteen pilots killed, wounded, or captured. McWhorter later saw a map taken from a dead Luftwaffe pilot, showing the Germans' home base near Stuttgart. Second Lieutenant Gordon Briggs of the 386th Squadron remembers thinking that the attackers couldn't have been very experienced: "They didn't know enough to turn away from the field after each pass. Instead they came right back over the runway, and a lot of them got shot down."

Bennemann's unit's losses were mirrored in Luftwaffe casualties all across the front. Despite local successes, like the havoc the Luftwaffe had wreaked on Y-34, Operation Bodenplatte was a failure: 40 percent of the 850 German fighters involved were destroyed or damaged, and 234 attacking pilots were killed, captured, or wounded. Those losses were irreplaceable.

The Allies never lost their grip on the air over the Bulge. Instead, Bodenplatte broke the back of the German fighter force. No less an expert than Generalleutnant Adolf Galland, commander of the Luftwaffe fighter arm, saw his service's epitaph written in the heavy losses suffered over the Bulge, capped by Bodenplatte's failure: "The Luftwaffe received its death blow at the Ardennes offensive. In unfamiliar conditions and with insufficient training and combat experience, our numerical strength had no effect. It was decimated while in transfer, on the ground, in large air battles, especially during Christmas, and was finally destroyed."

☆

For the Hell Hawks, the New Year's Day raid gave them a sobering taste of the war they had been bringing to the enemy. They had never imagined the Germans still had the daring to go on the offensive and strike them at their own bases. Many understood for the first time what it meant to be on the receiving end of an air raid.

After eight months of plying their deadly trade over the battlefield nearly every day, the pilots had become inured to close-in combat and the relentless pace of the war. After Metz, they saw their strafing and dive-bombing missions in a new light. Riggs remembers those long minutes under fire behind his sheltering chimney: "It was terrifying to be on the receiving end of those tactics." Up to that point, "going against the enemy in the P-47 was a thrilling way to fight the war." After Metz, "I had a gripping realization of what I was doing to the enemy. . . . It occurred to me that [my experience under attack] was just what I was doing to the enemy every time I flew." Seen through the crackling flames and smoking wreckage of Metz, final victory seemed to the Hell Hawks as remote a prospect as the end of the new year just begun.

Chapter Twelve

"That Is What Is Beating Us"

F OR A BRIEF, SHINING MOMENT, the Luftwaffe apparently believed the New Year's Day air attack had been a great success. Anyone would have agreed with the German fliers after seeing the twisted, smoldering wreckage of the Hell Hawks' Thunderbolts at Metz. But the story of a captured German pilot shows how wrong they were.

Oberfeldwebel (Master Sgt.) Stefan Kohl was confident the attack had succeeded. Never mind that his Messerschmitt Bf 109 fighter had been shot out of the sky as he approached Metz-Frescaty from the southeast. His New Year had begun with him parachuting into a cemetery near the Hell Hawks' airfield at Metz, where burning P-47s cast a greasy pall of smoke over the field.

Kohl was one of eight Luftwaffe pilots at Metz downed by the Army's antiaircraft defenses. Yet he obviously believed that his side had inflicted a major blow. Major Bob Brooking, commander of the 386th Squadron, encountered Kohl inside the Hell Hawks' headquarters shack. The youthful German jerked his thumb out the window at the smoking Thunderbolts and said in excellent English: "What do you think of that?"

Brooking stomped angrily out of the room; there was no denying the damage. But Kohl didn't know that American industry had turned out nearly one hundred thousand warplanes in the calendar year that had just ended. Within days, factory-fresh Thunderbolts brought from a marshalling center near Paris lined the ramp. Metz was in full operation again when Brooking went back to see the German pilot.

"I got him out of his little jail," he said, and pointed out to him a row of gleaming new P-47s outside. Brooking coolly addressed the POW: "What do you think of that?"

It was time for a little humility. Kohl took in the spanking-new aircraft, just arrived from a heartland that seemed capable of building an infinite number of them. "That is what is beating us," he admitted.

☆

After the wounded were taken care of, Mac McWhorter watched Doc Smead vigorously digging a foxhole. Eventually Smead was down seven or eight feet, dirt still flying from his shovel. Colonel Stecker noticed his work, and leaning over the hole, yelled: "Doc, if you go down another foot I'm going to put you down as AWOL!"

A sense of humor was a luxury Bob Brooking couldn't afford late in the morning of January 1. "It was pretty busy after the raid," he said. "The squadron was in a shambles, and we didn't even have any foxholes dug." The 365th ground crews, like those in other Ninth Air Force units hit that day, turned quickly to the business of salvaging and repairing their damaged aircraft. The maintenance crews dug slit trenches, dragged wrecked airplanes off the field, and patched those judged reparable. Cannibalizing the destroyed P-47s, the ground crews scrambled to turn around the survivors. By sharing aircraft from the two squadrons airborne at the time of the attack, pilots from even the burned-out 386th were back in the air that afternoon, dive-bombing and strafing railcars feeding supplies to the Germans in the Bulge.

Having miraculously escaped the Luftwaffe attack that morning without a fatality, the Hell Hawks were witness to tragedy that afternoon. Second Lieutenant James E. DuPuy, who had joined the 388th Squadron just five weeks earlier, pulled too hard in the traffic pattern while returning from a training mission. He stalled his Thunderbolt, the heavy fighter smashing into the dirty snow off the end of the runway, hurling DuPuy's body clear of the cockpit. Sergeant Andrew W. Stauder, driving his gas truck across the runway's approach end, was struck by the propeller hub from the disintegrating plane. Both men died shortly after in the hospital; at a combat airfield, death was never far away.

☆

After the fortuitous "Victory Weather" in the final week of December, flying conditions in early January were again bleak. Through January 9, snow and fog blanketed the area, curtailing air-support missions but granting the ground crews no respite. The crew chiefs and mechanics worked in the open in subfreezing weather, rigging blankets around the engines to cut the worst of the wind. Ground crews stood atop wooden boxes to keep their feet out of the snow. Mechanics doing intricate work on the engines couldn't wear gloves, and frostbite was a common affliction.

If not working on their Thunderbolts, the enlisted men tackled the drifting snow on the runways. They taxied P-47s to blow aside the biggest drifts and formed broom parties to sweep or plow away the rest.

Rumors of infiltrators and hostile civilians in this German border region made everyone jumpy. A French civilian tossed a grenade into an antiaircraft emplacement, killing both gunners. A bomb explosion, cause unknown, hurled bloody fragments of two ordnance men onto the snow outside the arsenal. On January 7, another Frenchman shot and killed a GI in a Metz café. Reacting to these incidents and the many Germans captured in American uniforms behind the lines during the Bulge fighting, the flight line Hell Hawks worked under arms, and everyone on base kept their rifles within easy reach.

Also on the 7th, the 388th Squadron held a memorial service for three of its fallen pilots. Many gathered in the chapel to remember Capt. Harry M. Hurd, who died in December in a plane crash in Paris; 1st Lt. Frederick W. O'Donnell, killed in combat the previous May; and Lt. DuPuy, lost three days earlier in his crashed Thunderbolt.

Such services for individuals were unusual in a combat fighter group. Most pilots didn't grant themselves the luxury of mourning comrades killed in combat. They deadened themselves to the frequent losses, trying to avoid the obvious conclusion that it was they who might be next. A formal service just reopened a painful wound.

E. A. W. Smith was a Royal Air Force ground-attack pilot based in Holland, engaged in the same brutal war of attrition the Hell Hawks were fighting. He recorded what one colleague experienced at a military funeral for a fellow pilot on January 1:

> They had to walk two hundred yards to the graves, and the path was narrow, and icy. He took the front end of a stretcher, and was dead scared he would slip and drop the body off. The body was

heavy, and he thought it was Pete's, because Pete was big when he was alive. When they got to the turn in the path the other bearers passed him, and he could see that they had Pete, because the legs in the blanket were all twisted, and it looked like there were no feet. Pete had died sitting in the cockpit, burnt to death because nobody was there to get him out.

They buried the soldier first. When it came to Pete's turn they could not get the body off the stretcher. When it did come free, there was a loud ripping noise, like when you tear a sheet in strips. As they pulled the body from the stretcher, he saw a great blob of congealed blood left behind. Then a little pile of black ashes fell from the end of the blanket. The Dutch civilians stepped back with gasps of horror. He couldn't listen to the chaplain anymore, he was crying too much. He told himself that fighter pilots didn't cry, but he couldn't stop till it was all over.

He did not make much noise, crying. When he got back to the airfield, he told the rest of the squadron pilots, and some of them had moist eyes, too. They thought that was a hell of a way to get buried, and said so.

Jan. 17, 1945, Woensdrecht: . . . Group Captain Morris has issued an order. No pilot from 132 Wing is to attend the funeral of any other pilot from here on.

By using P-47s to blow five thousand feet of the runway clear of snow, the Hell Hawks got into the air again on January 10. Captain Neal Worley followed up an earlier raid on the railyard at Cochem with an armed reconnaissance flight over German territory. He and the 387th's pilots spotted a barracks complex near Illingen and put fourteen five-hundred-pound bombs into the buildings, blowing them apart like matchsticks. As fires sprang up in the remaining structures, blue-coated German troops streamed into the open, "like flies out of a manure pile," wrote Charles Johnson. Running for any shelter, seventy-five to one hundred of the men were cut down by strafing. The 386th soon arrived to add to the carnage, bombing the remaining barracks, then repeatedly strafing and destroying thirty-three trucks and damaging ten tanks in the bargain. First Lieutenant Paul L. Van Cleef of the 387th, his plane perforated by flak and smoking badly, continued to lead his flight in those determined attacks. First Lieutenant James E. Murphy of the 386th helped destroy a locomotive and fifteen railcars; both men received Distinguished Flying Crosses for their aggressiveness and flying skill during this action.

Storms returned late that evening, snow drifting so deeply over the next two days that P-47s had barely enough room between piles of plowed snow to taxi clear of the Metz runway. The lull in combat operations gave the men of the 388th Squadron a chance to salute two of their commanders ordered stateside for a thirty-day furlough: Maj. James E. Hill, their commander, and Lt. Col. John R. Murphy, the deputy group commander and Hill's predecessor. Their going-away party featured tuna and lobster salad, sardines and crackers, and toasted sandwiches, washed down with White Horse Scotch. For the Hell Hawks in their unheated Metz barracks, this was high living.

☆

Jim Hill's successor as 388th commander was Capt. Robert M. Fry, an original Hell Hawk who had been Hill's operations officer for the preceding four months. Fry was a lifelong yachtsman and a midshipman in his junior year at Annapolis when the Japanese struck Pearl Harbor. Offered the choice of graduating with the class of 1943 or receiving an immediate commission and assignment to flying school, Fry opted for the Army Air Forces, and earned his wings in mid-1943, just in time to join the 365th at Richmond. By January 1945, Fry had racked up four aerial kills, but he told his son after the war that he never got used to combat: "We were fighting a war, and I lived day to day. Each time I flew I sweated through a T-shirt, Class-A uniform shirt, tie, a leather flying jacket, and into my parachute. Yes, I was scared to death. Anyone who tells you that he wasn't afraid up there is a goddamn liar. But we had a job to do."

Now Fry was taking the reins of the 388th as the Hell Hawks joined the rest of the Ninth Air Force campaign to cut off and destroy Wehrmacht forces trying to escape the Bulge. "It was a target-rich environment," said Fry. "Everywhere you looked there was a German tank or armored vehicle. When the weather cleared, we flew our butts off."

☆

On December 30, General Omar Bradley's 12th Army Group had attacked the Bulge from the south. Three days later, Montgomery launched a drive from the northern shoulder. Acceding to his generals' pleas, on January 7 Hitler ordered all German forces out of the Bulge to avoid encirclement. The U.S. First and Third

Armies closed the base of the Ardennes salient at Houffalize, Belgium, on January 16. Most of the surviving Wehrmacht soldiers had withdrawn ahead of the noose, abandoning their vehicles and equipment.

The Hell Hawks continued their efforts to cut rail transportation and thus hinder the Wehrmacht's ability to refit shattered divisions and resist an Allied drive to the Rhine. But the weather closed in again. On the 16th snow fell heavily, with winds gusting thirty to forty miles per hour amid temperatures falling to ten degrees Fahrenheit. The ground crews at Metz had great trouble starting the P-47s, with their weakened batteries and crankcases full of congealed oil. Nevertheless, they got their Thunderbolts in the air by 9:45 that morning, targeting marshalling yards and munitions trains inside Germany.

Instead of the usual dangers of ground attack, the six Hell Hawks missions of the 16th experienced a rare winter encounter with the Luftwaffe. Near Worms, Germany, a mixed force of two dozen Bf 109s and Fw 190s attacked the 388th Squadron. Its leader, Capt. Joseph Cordner, called for help from the 386th, led that day by Capt. James G. Wells Jr. "Injun' Joe" Cordner, who had barely outraced a trail of bursting flak shells over Falaise in August, had his men climb up-sun into the diving Germans, forcing them to fly directly into the eight-gun maws of their Thunderbolts. The two forces collided at about fourteen thousand feet in a swirling free-for-all.

Several Messerschmitts and Focke-Wulfs fell to the Hell Hawks' fifties before a 190 scored hits on 2nd Lt. James W. Burnett Jr., who had inexplicably failed to break when his leader called out an incoming fighter. The 388th's 1st Lt. Robert L. Dickinson looked back from his evasive turn to see his wingman's Thunderbolt tumbling earthward, with Burnett himself drifting under his parachute, headed for imminent captivity.

Another 388th pilot, 1st Lt. Donald E. Kraman, racked his Thunderbolt into a tight right turn after a Bf 109. Peering through the glowing ring on his gunsight glass, Kraman, from LaGrange, Illinois, saw the Messerschmitt roll out in a bid to escape. He snapped his wings level and caught the fleeing 109 with a long burst; the enemy fighter burst into flame as its pilot rolled left and bailed out.

Kraman, now five miles west of Worms, pointed his P-47 skyward toward more bandits. Passing ten thousand feet he spotted a lone Focke-Wulf on the deck, and Kraman dove, followed by his wingman, 2nd Lt. Henry Dahlen Jr. Another 190 chased and opened fire on Dahlen, who broke away, leaving Kraman, who didn't know his radio was out, in a one-on-one chase.

The German pilot ran flat-out low over Worms, threading the needle between a church steeple and tall brick smokestack. Narrow streets raced under the wings of Kraman's P-47 as he engaged the throttle button triggering emergency water injection. His Pratt & Whitney surged as Kraman squeezed off short bursts at his quarry, the enemy banking abruptly left and right to throw off the American's aim. Across the Rhine, farther into Germany, the pair raced east as Kraman's water injection died and his guns, one by one, exhausted their 350 rounds of ammo. Soon he was down to his number-three machine gun, deep in enemy territory—alone.

Noticing finally that he had lost his wingman, Kraman decided that discretion was the better part of valor. He was about to abandon the chase when the Fw 190 began a slow left turn. Kraman pounced. He curved within fifty yards and opened up with his lone machine gun. The bullets pounded the 190. First gray, then black smoke, then flames erupted from the Würger's engine. Struck just above the treetops, the Focke-Wulf careened across the landscape in "a comet of flame."

On the deck, dodging flak all the way, Kraman pushed his one-gun P-47 as low as he dared until he crossed the Rhine, at last spotting an American truck column below. He landed back at Metz to find that Dahlen, shot up but uninjured, had made a safe landing ahead of him.

☆

"When we get a chance to fight enemy airplanes it's like a holiday," Ray Stecker had told a journalist at a party in Metz. His newest squadron commander, Capt. Robert M. Fry, must have agreed as the swirling dogfight of January 16 continued.

Fry, leading the 388th's Blue Flight, engaged at fifteen thousand feet, turning after a diving Fw 190 and neatly catching him in a descending right turn. At thirty degrees deflection, Fry opened up, and his concentrated fire hit the enemy's wings and fuselage. That first burst hit the 190's pilot, and his aircraft spun out of control and crashed a few seconds later.

Turning from the mushroom of flame below, Fry zoomed back to twelve thousand feet and pursued a Messerschmitt Bf 109. In a twisting, diving chase the pair descended to two thousand feet, leveling in a right-hand turn, Fry closing. Twenty-millimeter flak was bursting around both planes when the 109 pilot broke for the deck, and Fry bored in from astern, his slugs shredding the enemy's fuselage. "The 109 stayed in a shallow dive as I fired and at about five hundred feet, I broke off to the right and watched this plane crash into some woods. I claim this Me 109 destroyed," wrote Fry in his after-action report.

Climbing back through five thousand feet with two quick victories, Fry spotted a Focke-Wulf to his right, headed east. The twenty-three-year-old squadron commander wrote, "I closed on him from behind and below with water injection on. He did not see me until I fired a short burst." The German pilot reacted to the tracers whipping by his canopy by rolling inverted into an abrupt split-S. Pulling his nose earthward, he exposed his wingspan and the length of his fuselage to Fry's guns. The American's long burst ripped pieces from the Würger as the enemy fighter arrowed downward. Fry kept firing, following as long as he dared; "we were dangerously low at this time, so I rolled out and zoomed to gain altitude." Fry looked back; a wrecked fighter was burning on the snow-covered landscape below. The 388th's commander claimed it as his third victory of the day. The ex-midshipman was now an Army Air Forces ace, joining Lt. Col. Robert L. Coffey Jr. as the second Hell Hawk to score five victories or more.

Blue Three in the 388th was piloted by a man who shouldn't even have been in the cockpit that day. First Lieutenant James F. Hensley, "The Voice," had been headed for two weeks' leave in England that day, but his air transport was delayed four hours. Hensley, his bags packed with fresh clothes and his carefully hoarded combat liquor ration, dropped by the 388th's briefing tent. "[I was] just in time to see that preparations were being made to make a fighter sweep into the old country," wrote Hensley later. "A fighter sweep! What a rare event! . . . it would be a good way to kill the time until 1400 [2:00 p.m.] and then off to England. One of the pilots overheard my desires, and he, having a 'hot item' in Metz to take care of, happily relinquished his Blue Three position to me. This was just perfect as far as I was concerned."

Hensley's squadron followed the Moselle River northeast to its junction with the Rhine, then turned south, where they sighted and attacked a covey of Fw 190s. Hensley, dressed that day in his sharply pressed Class A uniform, later related what followed:

> I attacked one of them, and after seeing hits going into the cockpit, I watched as the plane rolled over and from an almost vertical dive went into the ground and exploded.
>
> Pulling back up, I saw a P-47 in a Lufbery with one of the Fw 190s, so I pulled into position behind the enemy plane and fired a burst. Almost immediately all of the right-wing guns stopped

firing so I pressed the attack using only the left wing guns. The pilot of the Focke-Wulf dove for the deck, and I followed him like a lamb to the slaughter: right over the flak batteries on the ground. The flak looked like it was coming up at both of us, and it was sort of unnerving. In a hurry to get the hell out of there, I fired a long parting burst at the enemy plane. As I pulled up to the left to leave him, the Fw plowed into the ground and exploded.

Hensley climbed back to fourteen thousand feet, sighting a flight of northbound Bf 109s. Radioing their position to Joe Cordner, his mission leader, Hensley dove on the enemy fighters, the four-to-one odds against him apparently no deterrent: "I bounced from about fifteen thousand feet and got strikes on the number-four man, and then I pulled up again in a steep climb. . . . I decided to bounce them again. This time instead of climbing back up again, I sat on number-three, trying to have his ass. Number three tightened his turn to the left while numbers one and two split and came back to my rear position. The two of them then began to fire, and I had to break off number three's tail and go into a tighter left turn. All the time I was passionately calling Captain Cordner and explaining my predicament."

The two German fighters trapped Hensley between them, catching him in a tight turn with no room to maneuver:

> I could see the tracers passing over both wings when suddenly my left wing exploded and blew off and I went into a hell of a spin [the 109s had struck his ammunition bay]. Thinking of important things first, I reached into the map case and got out my new hat, a flighter [soft flight cap], and put it on and bailed out.
>
> As I floated toward the ground, I heard what turned out to be an attack by one of the Me 109s on me as I oscillated in the chute. . . . Luckily he missed me. I hit the frozen plowed ground hard and was almost immediately captured by the SS. . . .
>
> That night in the cell under heavy guard I kept thinking bitterly about what my quarters would have been in England that night had I not volunteered for the "rare event" as a means of killing some time. But the more I thought of it, the more I was sure I would have

done the same thing all over again with only one change; the next time I would shoot all four of those "bastids" down!

His two weeks' leave revoked by the Germans, Hensley spent the remaining three months of the war as their prisoner.

☆

By 4:30 p.m., both squadrons of P-47s had recovered at Metz, the crew chiefs looking for their own planes as each flight pulled up into the landing pattern. In the furious melee with the Luftwaffe, the Hell Hawks had downed thirteen fighters and damaged three more. Bob Fry was now an ace, and Lieutenants Dickinson, Dahlen, Frederick W. Marling, and Earl D. Schrank had each registered a kill. So had Hensley, but the group's celebration was tempered a bit by the knowledge that both he and Burnett were missing, probably captured.

When a mission returned, ground crews shifted into high gear. "The planes were in varying condition: broken windows, oily windshields, bullet holes or flak tears here and there," wrote Charles Johnson. If the pilots mishandled the throttle and water-injection system on takeoff or in combat, they'd bring back blown cylinders and broken connecting rods. When leaks developed in valve-cover gaskets, a fine film of oil sometimes sprayed back over the windscreen—a chronic cause of complaints among the pilots.

Crews had to fill fuel and oil tanks, install drop tanks, and top off the water-injection system next to the firewall, enough for about fifteen minutes of emergency power. The armorers reloaded the wing bays with fresh belts of .50-caliber ammunition, about 350 rounds per gun, and wrestled a pair of bombs into their underwing shackles. The crew chiefs and their assistants did most of the servicing, while flight and line chiefs assigned specialists to tackle battle damage or pilot squawks. The crews were lucky if they had an hour to get the P-47Ds back in the air.

As good as the big Pratt & Whitney engine was, maintaining it posed challenges. Staff Sergeant James C. Hagan of the 386th remembered that changing spark plugs was a knucklebuster: "You had to get your hand inside there, and there wasn't a whole lot of room." "You worked from the time it was light until you couldn't see anymore," said 386th Tech. Sgt. Alvin Bradley. Add guard duty and other work details to flight-line duties, and the ground crews were working almost around the clock. And yet they took it in stride. "I was never tired," said one. "There was just too much excitement."

☆

Added drama at Metz came on the 16th with the emergency landing of three B-24s and two B-17s. The damaged heavies, returning from a Berlin raid, arrived at about the same time as the group's "Christmas" dinner. The hard-working enlisted men came in from the snow long enough to devour turkey, potatoes, cranberry sauce, and stuffing; most quickly grabbed seconds. Charles Johnson wrote that by afternoon "it was difficult for the ground crews to climb on the wings of the planes, but all were happy." Thirteen victories and a full stomach: for the Hell Hawks, January 16 *had* to be Christmas.

Another winter storm moved in, grounding the Group until January 19, when they hit rail lines and a bridge inside Germany. Two more days of snow and low ceilings followed, even as the First and Third Armies fought their way up to the German frontier. The steady attrition from combat damage and bad-weather accidents forced Colonel Stecker to address the group on the 21st. The supply situation was not good: a shortage of P-47s and spare parts would reduce each squadron to twenty assigned aircraft, down from twenty-five, until further notice. But each squadron would still be expected to have sixteen planes operational at all times, Stecker emphasized. Malfunctioning parts would be fixed on the flight line or cannibalized from the wrecks destroyed in the New Year's raid. Johnson wrote that the "way Colonel Stecker was able to instill confidence in his men and to talk to them at their level" inspired each pilot and ground crewman to do anything to meet his challenge. The maintenance men soon built up a stash of scrounged spare parts from the "boneyard" that would be kept in reserve through the end of the war.

Despite foot-deep snow on the runway, the group was airborne again on January 22, supporting the 94th and 95th Infantry divisions near Orscholz, Germany. By the 23rd the Americans had retaken St.-Vith, a key road junction at the northeast corner of the Bulge; the fight to erase the German penetration was nearing its climax.

☆

Throughout the bloody campaign, air attacks by the Ninth Air Force's bombers and fighter-bombers had taken a terrible toll on the German forces. Clearer skies had enabled fighter-bomber strikes on German supply columns as well as enemy armor, and the P-47s had taken full advantage of the cold but sunny weather from December 23 to 27 to hit railways and marshalling yards. The Jabos were so devastating that by December 26, German Field Marshal Walter Model ordered an end to major road marches in daylight.

By late December, Ninth Air Force attacks on the railway lines leading to the salient had overwhelmed German repair efforts, delaying supplies at choke points for forty-eight hours or more. However, even these successes could not stop the German advance entirely. The return of bad weather on December 28, coupled with the inability of the Allied fighter-bombers to operate during the long winter nights, meant that the Battle of the Bulge had to be fought—and won—by the American GIs and their British and Canadian comrades.

Nevertheless, the fighter-bombers did accelerate the rapid collapse of resistance within the Bulge. German Gen. Fritz Bayerlein's Panzer Lehr division was forced to abandon fifty-three operable tanks, starved of fuel at the end of strangled supply lines. The Wehrmacht's weary survivors scrambled east for survival. By dusk on January 22, wrote historian Danny S. Parker, "the slaughter in the Dasburg area had reached Normandy proportions." Major General O. P. Weyland, boss of XIX Tactical Air Command, exulted in his diary, "Germans trying to evacuate the Bulge . . . worse than the Falaise Pocket . . . biggest day in TAC history of destructions." His four fighter groups, including the Hell Hawks, claimed 317 motor transports, six tanks, three armored vehicles, and twelve gun positions knocked out. The next day, the Panzer Lehr Division regrouped at the West Wall with just eighteen tanks and four hundred exhausted troopers; its commander estimated his losses at 80 percent.

☆

The Hell Hawks knew the crisis was over when they were ordered back to Belgium to resume work under Maj. Gen. Quesada's IX Tactical Air Command. The group's new base would be Florennes, Belgium, forty miles south of Brussels. Reconnaissance parties left to scout the move on January 26, while the men at Y-34 turned to packing with a will. Few would miss Metz's wind-drifted snow, cold barracks, and frosty inhabitants.

After three days of unforgiving weather, the group resumed combat operations from Metz on January 29. In early afternoon, a dozen planes of the 387th Squadron whipped the snow behind their whirling thirteen-foot propellers and lifted off for an armed reconnaissance of the rail lines along the Rhine.

Flying number four on the wing of Capt. Robert E. Robinson was 1st Lt. Paul Van Cleef. He had volunteered to join most of the veteran pilots of the 387th on this mission; the "old boys" would land at Florennes, thus avoiding the bone-chilling ride from Metz to Belgium in the back of a jolting truck.

Cruising south along the Rhine, Capt. Thomas E. Stanton, mission leader, located an inviting target: a runway and taxiways leading into the woods near Bingen, Germany. The taxiways led to revetments harboring a number of Junkers Ju 88 medium bombers.

Stanton's pilots peeled off into dives and plastered the airfield's installations with twenty-four five-hundred-pound bombs, then wheeled back to strafe the bombers. Robinson and Van Cleef made their first firing passes and spotted several well-camouflaged Ju 88s near the field's perimeter. Screaming across the runway at treetop level, the pair yanked their Thunderbolts around in a 270-degree turn to line up on the new targets. The flak gunners, fully aroused by now, sent glowing golf balls of 20mm fire whipping past Van Cleef's canopy as he bored in, raking one of the Ju 88s with his eight machine guns. Wham! A tremendous jolt shook his P-47, filling the cockpit with smoke and fumes. "I couldn't see a thing in there," said Van Cleef. Already too low, he jerked the stick back and zoomed for bailout altitude, jettisoning his canopy and unstrapping in the climb.

His P-47 soared into the overcast at two thousand feet. As he popped out above into sunlight, the double-row Pratt & Whitney was still roaring, and the smoke in the cockpit had vanished. He wasn't on fire, but circling above the clouds, he could spot no one from the squadron, and his radio was out. Van Cleef headed for Metz.

Hunching down against the two-hundred-mile-per-hour wind blast—"It was so damn cold!"—the Kansan began to shiver, both from the frigid slipstream and the fading adrenaline rush of combat. Flying west, he descended through the overcast, trying to spot a familiar landmark. The Moselle River would do, but the unfamiliar countryside below gave him no clue as to where Metz might be.

Facing empty fuel tanks, Van Cleef decided to belly in. He lined up on a nice-looking field and made a perfect wheels-up touchdown in three feet of snow. His battered Jug skidded safely to a stop, and the relieved but near-frozen Hell Hawk reached behind his seat to don his heavy parka. Turning to leave the cockpit, he froze at the sight of a Frenchman, forty yards away, aiming at him a "double-barreled twelve-guage shotgun with the largest-looking bores I had ever seen." Van Cleef hurriedly shouted "Americanische!" to establish his nationality; to his relief, the Frenchman lowered the gun, and the pair walked a few miles to the nearest village, whose chief of police welcomed him to dinner in his own home.

Van Cleef had come down near Nancy, France, just thirty miles south of Metz, and a couple of days of hitchhiking brought him back to Y-34 just in time to catch one of the last trucks leaving for Florennes. It was the last time, Van Cleef vowed to himself, that he would ever volunteer for a mission.

☆

In the airfield attack, the 387th had destroyed seven Ju 88s and damaged another two, while the 386th had jumped an armored convoy and wrecked nineteen vehicles. The 388th finished its day by blowing up a pontoon bridge over the Saar River. Earlier missions that day had claimed more motor transports and damaged a railroad bridge.

The Hell Hawks' missions on the 29th were a microcosm of the Ninth Air Force's efforts against the Wehrmacht during January 1945. During the month, the pilots of the three tactical air commands claimed 7,706 motor transports, 550 tanks and armored vehicles, 101 locomotives, 3,094 rail cars, 1,125 buildings, 234 gun emplacements, ten bridges, 556 rail cuts, and 207 road cuts. After the battle, sample counts of German tanks and armored vehicles wrecked by air attack showed that the pilot claims against panzers were about a factor of ten too high, but strikes against trucks and railways were unquestionably effective. Rail traffic west of the Rhine had been paralyzed, bringing on a German supply crisis that doomed their Ardennes assault to an early failure.

Over six hundred thousand Americans had fought to halt Hitler's counteroffensive. In the Battle of the Bulge, the United States lost over eighty thousand men killed, wounded, or captured, while Hitler's failed gamble cost the Wehrmacht at least one hundred thousand soldiers. Worse, its reserves of men and materiel that might have resisted the Allies in their coming spring offensive were destroyed. Albert Speer, Hitler's reichminister for armaments and war production, later wrote tellingly that "the failure of the Ardennes offensive meant that the war was over."

Chapter Thirteen

Getting Shot Down

T HE CRUCIBLE OF THE ARDENNES CAMPAIGN was still several months in the future when 1st Lt. James "Mac" McWhorter pivoted into his parking revetment and cut his Thunderbolt's engine after a mission on October 7, 1944. Hell Hawks gathered around. They told McWhorter that one Jug had failed to return— then suddenly everyone was shaking his hand. "I didn't get it at first," McWhorter said. "Then somebody said, 'Thank you, Mac! You got rid of Hillman for us.'"

Obviously, not everyone was a member of Lt. Col. Donald E. Hillman's fan club, not even in an aerial band of brothers. The stately, aloof Hillman "wasn't the most liked man in our outfit," McWhorter said. "I was flying his wing when he was shot down while strafing a plane landing on a German field. Hillman went into clouds against procedure and got hit while in the clouds."

If anyone should have known what it meant to be shot down, it was McWhorter. It had happened to him already, on one of his first missions as a "new boy" Hell Hawk. But he had been one of the lucky ones, landing amid friendlies and getting a free ride home. He would be forced down again, too (as described in Chapter Eight). Getting shot down happened to far too many Hell Hawks. However, few experienced anything quite like what happened to Hillman, who at that juncture was not yet at the midpoint of a long and distinguished career.

Hillman would later fly jets, appear on the cover of *Life* magazine, and command a combat group. But the day he became a symbol of all the Hell Hawks who were shot down, he was just another P-47 pilot. His story and those of other captured Hell Hawks illustrate how the lot of the prisoner of war, or POW, changed in those final months between Normandy and V-E Day.

☆

Before the Allied advance reached the Reich's frontiers, the Germans treated most American prisoners reasonably well. Early in the conflict, a pilot who parachuted into the midst of civilians could expect to be turned over to the German military and imprisoned under relatively comfortable circumstances. At war's end, he was as likely to be killed by those civilians or even by German military personnel. Early on, some, especially some who were Jews, found themselves not in POW but in concentration camps. Nonetheless, in October 1944 most prisoners were being held in accordance with the Geneva Convention. They were held in camps and allowed a command structure within. Their military ranks were respected. All of that went very well for months on end, but all of it changed during Don Hillman's period in captivity.

Every pilot told himself that getting shot down and captured was an event that could only happen to someone else. Among the dozens of Hell Hawks who were shot down, each had a different approach to thinking about the unthinkable. Before he was shot down, badly wounded, and repatriated (see Chapter Five), 2nd Lt. Roscoe "Ross" Crownrich said he "never gave the slightest thought to what might happen" if his plane was blown out of the sky. When he made a battle-damaged belly landing in Belgium in his Thunderbolt, 1st Lt. Russell E. Gardner couldn't remember ever having contemplated what the experience might be like and was relieved to walk away from his plane. Captain Grant Stout, on the other hand, returned safely from mission after mission, yet shared with others a premonition that something might go terribly wrong. Some pilots carried good luck charms. Some prayed before taking off.

They all had photos taken in civilian attire that were supposed to help them escape and evade. But they had no real training for bailing out, hitting the ground, attempting to escape, or for what to do if captured. "At the briefing, the squadron commander told us that if we were hit and had to bail out and were captured, we should tell the Germans only our rank, name and serial number," said 1st Lt. Edward Lopez. "This was all we were required to give and no more." It was almost all they were told, too. "I don't remember any training for what to do if shot down," said 1st Lt. Ralph Kling. "I had an escape kit in the inside pocket of my A2 jacket. It was maybe four inches square and an inch and a half thick, plastic, with scotch tape around it. The only content I remember was a cloth map of France. Most of the stuff in that kit eventually proved totally useless to me."

☆

Although he seemed aloof and preachy to some, no one ever accused Don Hillman of not leading from the front. He simply saw flying as part of his military duty and always assumed that skill and experience would see him through. On October 7, pulling away from the vicious flak over the enemy airfield, he had headed up into the overcast when he caught the ozone-like smell of burning electrical insulation. A minor but worrisome sign like that was sometimes a pilot's only hint that his luck was about to run out. In contrast, when Lieutenant Crownrich was shot down, his P-47 was jolted with a sudden, slamming impact that left not even a split-second's doubt that the damage was mortal.

The Hell Hawks who were shot down, who evaded, escaped, or became prisoners of war each coped differently with those first seconds, or sometimes minutes, when they knew they were going down. If time permitted, a key decision was whether to bail out or ride the aircraft down. The P-47 wasn't an easy plane to climb out of. "I knew you had to go out the right side of the aircraft so the prop wash wouldn't slam you into the tail," said 1st Lt. Ralph Kling.

When time permitted, most pilots thought the Thunderbolt was a safe aircraft to belly land, wheels up. First Lieutenant Neal E. Worley managed to crash five P-47s ("If a German had done that, he'd be an ace.") during his tour with the Hell Hawks, but was never captured. Worley said the big radial up front acted as a kind of battering ram, knocking down any tree, bush—or person—that stood in the path of a Jug making a belly landing. "You could stall it out twenty feet above a plowed field and you'd know you would be okay," said Worley. "There isn't a P-47 pilot alive who wouldn't elect to belly one in rather than bail out." But it depended on circumstances, and sometimes there wasn't much choice.

Another pilot who trusted the Thunderbolt's protective qualities was Mac McWhorter, who, long before he witnessed Hillman's downing, had survived a forced landing in occupied France. Mac recalled the P-47's honest if unspectacular gliding performance and its ability to absorb crash forces: "A lot of people said it landed better on its belly than it did on its wheels. It was an ideal belly-landing plane. They told us, 'If you see trees, try to go through the trees and shear off the wings.' I've heard of an incident where a P-47 cartwheeled across a field before coming to a stop, only to have the pilot step out and walk away [Bob Hagan on October 21, 1944] but usually the plane stayed intact. That's what happened on July 27, 1944, when I bellied in."

It was nine o'clock on an evening when daylight lasted until well past ten. Mac was one of eight Jug pilots working over the area between Coutances and La-Haye-Pesnel, southwest of St.-Lô. He had a five-hundred-pound bomb under his belly. The squadron bombed several tanks, 88mm and 20mm flak positions, and strafed and set afire a column of ten vehicles. McWhorter had just pulled off his strafing run when a string of 20mm shells exploded in his engine. He racked his plane into a tight turn for A-7, simultaneously calling out to his element leader, 1st Lt. Lloyd Hutchins: "They hit me, Hutch—I'm headed home!"

"That's tough shit, Mac. They missed me," Hutchins answered. "How's your oil pressure?" It looked fine, said Mac, but Hutchins responded, "It won't be for long—look behind you." McWhorter saw "the entire sky was black from oil smoke" trailing his Jug. "It was the hydraulics. I had a black cloud behind my aircraft, and there was a grinding sound, like something happening in your intestine." The crippled Pratt & Whitney gave him about two minutes of running time before seizing.

"What'll I do, Hutch, bail out or belly in?" asked McWhorter.

"Suit yourself," Hutchins answered, "but you'd better make up your mind in a hell of a hurry."

With only a thousand feet of altitude, McWhorter elected to belly in. "There was one apple tree in the center of this field," said McWhorter. "I came in. I hit the ground and slid toward that tree. I hit the tree. I jumped out, ran across the wing, and headed for a hedgerow trying to get away from my plane." He had skidded to a stop about a mile southwest of Coutances, still carrying that five-hundred-pounder. It was about 9:30 p.m. and the light was fading.

With his flight overhead providing cover, the twenty-three-year-old sprinted from his Jug through a pasture dotted with the rotting carcasses of cattle killed in the Operation Cobra bombings. Mac passed several log-covered German trenches in the center of the field, but "the stench was so bad that I chose the most obvious dugout instead," next to a road.

Sure enough, a German patrol out looking for him stopped—right outside McWhorter's hiding place. "They didn't bother searching the dugout, but fired several rounds from a pistol into it. I was dug in on the dirt wall under the log roof so that with only a casual look, they wouldn't discover me." Deterred by the stench, the soldiers instead lobbed grenades into the pasture trenches and moved off down the road.

McWhorter remembered that the P-47 carried an "identification, friend or foe" (IFF) unit that he'd been told was vital to destroy if the Jug went down behind enemy lines. Other pilots do not remember being told this, but McWhorter took it seriously.

Lying low until after midnight, McWhorter crept back to his Thunderbolt, tore up his handkerchief to make a fuse, then lit off the gas tank. "It touched off my airplane and the plane's ammunition started cooking off and sent rounds flying over my head. That's when the bomb detonated."

The fireball threw nightmarish shadows from the stiff limbs of the bloated cattle as he sprinted clear. Reaching Coutances, McWhorter holed up for nearly forty-eight hours in a garden. He was not wearing a flying suit; he'd gone aloft wearing his regular uniform. Grubby, hungry, and disheveled, he peered out between rows of climbing beans for some sign of friendly residents. No one came.

On the 29th, tired of waiting, he decided to make his way to the Allied lines on his own. Just after he moved out around 9:30 a.m., pistol and machine-gun fire erupted in the town. McWhorter imagined the Germans, searching for him, "were shooting [the French] to make them reveal my hiding place. As I listened, however, the shots had that 'flat pop' characteristic of the .45-caliber, but I wasn't about to investigate!

"About forty-five minutes later I heard tanks coming down the dirt road 150 yards behind me. I peered between the bean vines and thought I saw a Sherman," but Mac wasn't yet willing to reveal his position. "Then the second tank appeared with a big white star on the side of it; I jumped up and started running towards the road, yelling 'Stop that son of a bitch!'"

The column halted, all right—the young pilot found himself looking down the barrels of four 75mm cannon and the rifles of about a dozen GIs. "I stopped real quick and put my hands up so high over my head that you would have thought they were out of joint."

The column was from the 3rd Armored Division. "They yelled at me to toss some ID in front of me." The American soldiers, it turned out, had seen McWhorter's P-47 go down behind German lines but had not expected the pilot to be alive. Once identified, McWhorter settled in with some K-rations and a half-track crew to await the arrival of the headquarters company.

In the waning daylight, a flight of four Thunderbolts roared overhead, the voice of the leader crackling in over the radio of the half-track: "WHITESAIL, this is PLASTIC [the 386th Fighter Squadron call sign] Leader, do you have any targets for me?"

McWhorter knew that voice; it was that of fellow Hell Hawk, Capt. William E. "Curly" Rodgers. "I grabbed the mike and yelled, 'Curly, I'll be home tonight, so put my cigarettes, whiskey, and clothes back!'" McWhorter was trying to head off the implementation of an unwritten pilots' agreement: if a friend went missing, his buddies would send home only one complete uniform, plus any personal items that wouldn't embarrass the missing pilot's family. The balance of his possessions was fair game for division among his fellow Hell Hawks. An especially valuable item was clean underwear, always in short supply.

Overhead, Rodgers had bad news: "Hey Mac, sure glad to hear you and know you weren't captured. I'll see what I can do about your clothing, but your whiskey and cigarettes are long gone."

Mac was soon back at A-7. "That afternoon, everyone was there to meet me, and true to his word, Curly had some of my clothes. But my whiskey and cigarettes were gone, and it took me about a week to get all of my underwear back."

For McWhorter, the shootdown, evasion, and rescue had all happened quickly. When his aircraft was hit, there was no doubt he was going down—and he had few choices about how to react. On the other hand, when Don Hillman smelled burning wiring in his P-47 on October 7, he had a little more time, but his P-47 was no less doomed. The lieutenant colonel soon found himself swinging under his parachute. "My first reaction was the amazing contrast between the excitement and action and noise of the combat mission I had just been on and the very quiet, peaceful sensation of gliding down in the parachute," said Hillman. "I also felt a great relaxation as if I had been relieved of a very heavy burden. I recognized that this feeling resulted from the realization that for me, the war was over."

Hillman apparently had not thought, until that moment, that Germans facing the growing specter of defeat might not behave civilly toward a Jug pilot descending beneath a nylon canopy. He was promptly brought up to speed. "[My] peaceful feeling was short-lived," said Hillman. "I heard small arms fire and realized that people on the ground were shooting at me."

Hillman observed civilians running toward his projected landing spot from one direction and Luftwaffe gunners running toward him from a flak installation in the other. He slipped his parachute to glide toward the Luftwaffe antiaircraft troops, hoping that they would protect him from the angry rural population. "As I landed and got out of my parachute harness, the troops fortunately surrounded me. The farmers looked as though they would have dismembered me if they had a chance. One farmer did break through the ring of soldiers and hit me in the back with a pitchfork handle, but he was immediately stopped by the troops. This began my career as a 'kriegsgefangeneng,' or prisoner of war." Many Hell Hawks used the short version of the term: "Kriegie."

The Luftwaffe troops marched Hillman back to their flak installation, which was nothing more than open pits with 40mm guns in them. He spent the afternoon watching the batteries "take pot shots" at American fighters. He observed no hits. "At sundown a truck came along and picked me up and drove me about fifteen miles to the Cologne airdrome that we had dive-bombed that day," Hillman said. "I was taken immediately to the officers' mess of the Junkers Ju 88 fighter squadron that was stationed there. There, the German pilots and I proceeded to do what fighter pilots the world over do when they get together—talk airplanes."

Hillman discovered that several of the German pilots spoke English fluently. The first question they asked went like this: "We have been shooting down your airplanes, fighters, and bombers for three years now, and every day we see more and more of them. Where the hell do you get all the airplanes?" The Republic plants at Farmingdale and Evansville and the Curtiss factory in Buffalo were, indeed, continuing to churn out P-47 Thunderbolts faster than pilots could fly them away. The Luftwaffe pilot captured at Metz had learned a lesson about the prowess of American industry, and Hillman's captors were similarly impressed.

The Germans told Hillman they were developing secret weapons that would drive the Allies off the Continent. The Luftwaffe squadron commander confiscated Hillman's leather flight jacket and put his own insignia on the shoulder tabs. They talked airplanes a little more and then threw Hillman into a cell.

"The next day, two guards took me into Cologne. I was put on a train for Frankfurt where the Luftwaffe interrogation center was located. I recall feeling very uncomfortable, as I was obviously an enemy airman in the midst of an angry civilian population. But fortunately I received only mean looks and pointed remarks from the civilians that I came in contact with during the ride."

Continued Hillman, "At the interrogation center I spent four weeks, all in solitary confinement. I was taken out once a day for interrogation, after which I was put right back in my cell. Second Lieutenant Ulrich Haussmann was the interrogator assigned to my case. We became well acquainted during the four-week period. Several times, he took me to the radio listening center where I could follow the progress of the air battles, listening first to the Allied communication channels and then to the German channels. The Germans had lengthy dossiers on all of the Allied aircraft units with extensive information on the individuals assigned to them."

Hillman believed the purpose of visiting the communication center was so the Germans could impress him with how much they knew about the Allies' air operations, including those of the Hell Hawks. Hillman felt that since he was a lieutenant colonel, he possessed a great deal more information than some other prisoners. That was why, he believed, he was kept in solitary confinement longer than others.

In early November 1944, Hillman was uprooted and placed aboard a train. He ended up at Sagan in eastern Germany at the South Camp of Stalag Luft 3. This was the place where, earlier, prisoners built three famous escape tunnels, Tom, Dick, and Harry, that were later portrayed in the movie *The Great Escape*. Hillman felt relieved to rejoin his "comrades-without-arms," as he called them, and without much difficulty he settled into prison life.

☆

Most Kriegies felt that life in a prisoner of war camp operated by the Luftwaffe was about as tolerable as imprisonment can get: "Not too bad," as Hillman put it. In another view of prison life, Lieutenant Kling said, "We had friendly guards and unfriendly ones. We had good days and bad days." But late in the war, the SS took over many camps, and some were broken up as the Nazis' situation deteriorated. For Hillman, the routine of prison life changed radically on January 31, 1945. At about 8:00 p.m., the Germans told prisoners that because of Soviet advances on the Eastern Front and the Red Army's proximity to the Stalag, the prisoners would have to be evacuated. Two hours later, the Germans marched 1,500 prisoners out of the South Camp. The temperature was ten degrees below zero Fahrenheit.

As Hillman said later, much has been written about this winter march and the many casualties resulting from the freezing temperatures and weakened condition of the prisoners. After a week on the road, with little sleep and meager food rations, the men were loaded on freight cars. The Kriegies spent the next five miserable days crammed inside the cars en route to Munich. There they were taken to a place that Hillman remembers as being named Stalag 17, a huge camp of fifteen thousand prisoners from other Allied nations.

"After observing the routine at Stalag 17 for a few days, Major Hank Mills of the 4th Fighter Group and I felt there was a reasonable escape possibility by way of the daily work details that went to Munich," said Hillman. "The Geneva Convention, which the Germans closely adhered to, allowed enlisted men to work but not officers or noncommissioned officers. As the American enlisted men were in a compound effectively isolated from outside, it took several days of negotiations, conniving, and diversion for Hank and me to effect an exchange of persons and identities with two U.S. privates first class."

Hillman and Mills went out on the work gang for several days to determine the best escape procedure. They escaped by preparing a hiding place in the rail yard where they were working. One night, when the work gang left by train to return to the Stalag, they holed up in their hideout.

"We were dressed to appear as the French 'displaced persons' who did farm labor in Germany," said Hillman. "But our escape philosophy was to avoid being seen whenever possible. To accomplish this we traveled at night, resting out of sight during the day. We had accumulated as [many] rations as we could in a prison environment where food was scarce. When the small amount we had was gone, we scrounged food from farm fields or stole some whenever the opportunity presented itself."

After five days of slow travel, Hillman and Mills, trying to get water from a farm well, were caught by members of the Volkssturm, a German peoples' militia made up of those most qualified for active duty. "Because escapees were currently being shot," said Hillman, "we told our captors we had just been shot down and were trying to evade capture. We were taken to the nearest prison camp, a small one in a village a short drive away. As we entered the room of the chief interrogator, I was utterly dismayed to see Lieutenant Haussmann, whom I had gotten to know so well in Frankfurt!"

The German interrogator immediately recognized the P-47 pilot and said, "What in the hell are you trying to pull, Hillman?" With no other approach he could take, Hillman tried the obvious. "Ulrich," he said, "you know that Germany is losing the war. You'd better look ahead to what's coming when Germany surrenders. You'd better start making your plans."

Haussmann responded by throwing the two Americans into solitary confinement. "The next morning," said Hillman, "the cell door opened and in came Ulrich, locking the door behind him. 'Just what did you have in mind yesterday, Don?' he asked. I explained that we wanted help to continue our escape and in turn I would see that he would be rewarded in terms of considerate treatment for himself and his family after the war.

"After days of clandestine discussions, Ulrich arranged for our transfer to another camp farther to the south. Four of us departed on foot: Hank, Ulrich, Luftwaffe Sergeant Haneman, and me.

"Traveling this time was much simpler than before, when Hank and I were going it alone. When we needed food or shelter, Lieutenant Haussmann would go to the closest farmhouse, show his official orders, and get what he needed. Hank and I slept in the barn at each farmhouse, while Haussmann and Haneman slept in the farmhouse. After any children of the farmer had gone to bed (they would have informed on their parents), Haussman would talk the farmer into listening to the British Broadcasting Corporation on the radio. That kept us informed of the location and direction of the Allied spearhead thrusts into Germany, and this information determined our travel route."

Hillman continued his account: "With the transfer orders, we were able to pass the scrutiny of the SS troops who became increasingly inquisitive as we approached the front lines. On the last night behind enemy lines we ate with a squad of young infantry troops, armed only with rifles and bazookas. They expected to encounter our tank columns the next day. Their orders were 'Hold your positions regardless of the price.' I felt sorry for them.

"Early the next morning, just after dawn, we were awakened by gunfire. An American tank column had approached the village nearby. The Americans had encountered enemy resistance. The four of us mobilized and ran into the shelter of a large forest."

Seeing the armored column a half-mile away, Hillman led the group through tall grass on hands and knees. "This was the most critical of many critical moments of our escape. Would we be recognized as friendly—or what?"

About three hundred yards out, Hillman and Mills stood up. "[We] put on our U.S. Air Corps flight caps with our rank insignia, put our hands over our heads, and called out to the tank column. It worked!"

The end of Hillman's ordeal was swift. As friendly troops approached, Haussmann and Haneman handed over their pistols and became prisoners of the Americans. The tankers gave Hillman a jeep, and he and Mills escorted the two Germans to the rear. Eventually, said Hillman, "I got a flight to Ninth Air Force headquarters. There I got permission from Maj. Gen. Hoyt S. Vandenberg to fly a P-47 up for a great reunion with the 365th Fighter Group in West Germany."

The fate of interrogator Haussman makes an interesting footnote. Hillman made sure that he and Haneman were released as soon as possible at war's end. The Hell Hawk sent CARE packages to Haussman, his wife, and children for several years, even visiting them at their home near Innsbruck, Austria. Acting as their sponsor, Hillman helped them settle in the Seattle area, where Haussman became successful in industry, his two children graduating from the University of Washington. The unlucky Hillman, forced to hit the silk, eventually provided his redoubtable German benefactor a golden parachute ride to America.

365th Fighter Group Operations Area

January–May 1945

Chapter Fourteen

Moving Up

EIGHT MILES NORTHEAST OF COLOGNE, Germany, a dozen Thunderbolts on armed reconnaissance, looking for rail traffic along the Rhine, received a vector toward a possible target. It was February 8, 1945. Captain James G. Wells Jr. turned his three flights of P-47s and soon spotted a locomotive and ten passenger cars heading southeastward toward the battered city, its medieval cathedral looming starkly over a central district reduced to rubble by Allied bombing. Wells shook out one of his flights, left another as top cover, and ordered a dive-bombing attack.

One after the other, four Thunderbolts dove steeply toward the train's engine. Eight bombs bracketed the train and detonated with devastating effect, while a second flight of the 386th Squadron chose individual cars for strafing. As the Hell Hawks bored in, German troops in blue-gray uniforms poured from the coaches and ran. Thirty-two .50-caliber guns opened on the men. There was nowhere to hide.

Some idea of what happened next was related by American fighter ace Hubert "Hub" Zemke, famed commander of the 56th Fighter Group. Zemke, a fellow Jug pilot, had been a prisoner of war since being downed and captured in late October. On December 11, 1944, en route to another interrogation, he sat under guard in a German passenger coach:

> I was seated beside a young German girl. At first the child, who
> was about ten years old, showed fear at the presence of the enemy
> prisoner and was amazed when I started to talk to her in her own
> language. After a while quite a rapport was established.
>
> The pleasant scene suddenly erupted into carnage. Bullets
> smashed into the carriage, killing one of the guards sitting opposite
> and nearly decapitating the small girl, whose body fell across my lap.
> As the train came to an abrupt halt, the side of the carriage was blasted
> by an explosion. Instantly realizing Allied fighters were at work, I
> made a dash for the door to take shelter behind some rail-side rocks.
> . . . Between the fighters' strafing runs, I made trips into the carriages
> to help out the wounded. The hysterical mother of the little girl and
> another small sister were brought to safety. Having exhausted their
> ammunition and ordnance, the attacking fighters departed.

Just so, the Hell Hawks' guns chewed into the cars, blew up the locomotive, and
cut swaths through the fleeing troops. Second Lieutenant Bob Hagan looked back
after his strafing run and saw bodies flung in grotesque heaps along the railbed,
later reporting laconically to the intelligence men, "I know we killed a lot of them."
Hagan's squadron made but a single pass on the train near Cologne, as Wells was
intent on saving ammunition for other targets; his squadron blew up two more
locomotives and a switch engine before returning to Florennes in early afternoon.

Back at the base, A-78, the Hell Hawks received belated recognition for their
role in blunting the late German offensive. Lieutenant General George S. Patton
wrote to his tactical air commander, asking Maj. Gen. Weyland to "pass on . . . the
sincere appreciation of myself, and the officers and men of the Third Army, for
your magnificent cooperation in the reduction of the Ardennes salient." Weyland,
who had operational control over the Hell Hawks during the Bulge fighting, in
turn wrote to his XIX TAC fighter groups: "Your ability to rapidly switch from the
Saar basin to the Ardennes salient in coordinated attack with a determined army
defeated a cunning and desperate enemy. All this accomplished under the adverse
conditions of a severe and bitter winter.

"It is the slashing flexibility of the air power of this command integrated with the might of the attacking Third Army that will lead us to bigger and better victories."

The 365th Fighter Group had transferred back to IX Tactical Air Command, under Maj. Gen. Pete Quesada, on January 31, but the praise from Patton and Weyland was still welcome, for hard work lay ahead. In early February, winter combat flying continued with armed reconnaissance missions against the German rail net along the Rhine. Allied intelligence reported that the Wehrmacht was so desperate for troops and equipment in the West that it risked running military trains even in daylight.

The gamble played right into the hands of the Hell Hawks. On February 9, one of their top scorers against locomotives was in the air. He was a Brooklyn, New York, native, 1st Lt. Edward S. Szymanski of the 386th Squadron. The veteran of over seventy combat missions made train attacks his specialty.

One of Szymanski's squadron mates was 1st Lt. James E. Murphy, who had joined the unit in late September 1944. He described the pilots preparing for a typical morning strike as

> ... sleepy, cold and restless in the bitter early-morning Belgian winter, standing and shuffling to keep warm even though they were bundled [up]. They wait for the transportation to the flight line. It is early and dark, the 386th is scheduled for a daylight takeoff, and down the road comes the 'fish wagon,' a one-and-one-half-ton truck with a boxlike enclosure hand-built on its bed.
>
> Off to one side, standing alone is Szymanski with his hands jammed down into his pants pockets, hunched over slightly, and gritting his teeth against the cold. All that he usually wore were his "pinks," shirt and pants, and this was his usual uniform no matter how bad the weather. It seemed as though he did not want to be encumbered with a lot of clothes. This might also explain why he often did not wear a parachute on a mission.
>
> After being briefed, the aircraft would take off and clobber the target and return; all except Szymanski. He seldom returned with the Squadron, and when the flight leader for the mission asked, "Szymanski, what the hell happened to you?" He would smile and shrug and say, "I got lost."

What he actually was doing was conducting his own private war against the Wehrmacht. He wasn't satisfied until he had fired every bullet in his guns at the Germans, so he managed to detach himself from the squadron to fly his own armed reconnaissance mission every time he got the urge. He got the urge often enough to raise real hob with the German transportation system. It was because of this quirk that he shot up so many trains, and he didn't pass up ambulances either, as he used to say that they blew up worse than the ammunition-carrying trucks that he hit.

On February 9, when his squadron caught a convoy of northbound trains along the east bank of the Rhine near Andernach, Szymanski was everywhere. Two planes dive-bombed the tracks to halt the trains' forward progress. Then the squadron spread low, line abreast, to pick out individual cars as strafing targets. Szymanski personally destroyed four locomotives and derailed two of the flatbed cars carrying panzers. The 386th fliers called him "Loco."

Rail targets were heavily defended by both fixed gun emplacements protecting marshalling yards, and flak batteries mounted on each train. On the 9th, 2nd Lt. James D. Simpson, a late-November replacement in the 386th with just seven combat missions, was hit after one of his strafing runs. He zoomed into the overcast but failed to return to A-78. Simpson's plane was reported to have crashed and burned near Düren; the young pilot's body was found in the wreckage.

Rail transportation stayed high on the target list during mid-February. Second Lieutenant Bob Hagan of the 386th described the tactics his fellow Hell Hawks used when attacking a train: "If it was running down a track, we'd shoot the locomotive up broadside. If we were dive bombing, we'd dive bomb parallel with the track. . . . According to the book, the dive angle was fifty to seventy-five degrees or so. We would mostly dive bomb marshalling yards and train tracks. . . . If we hit, more than likely we'd hit the track instead of the train, and derail them. . . . one time I was dive bombing a train, and the guy coming in behind me said, 'That was a hell of a shot! Made a big hole for him to run into.'

"In marshalling yards, we'd set up a pattern and just go round and round. Each guy would pick out a locomotive, or a car that he wanted to hit, and shoot at those."

Hagan would enter a dive-bomb run from a typical altitude of nine thousand feet or so, then release and start the pull out at about a thousand feet. Asked by one of his new pilots how he knew when to release his bombs, the 386th's Capt. Jimmy Wells told him to hit the button "when that red light goes on. 'Red light?' asked the new boy. 'What red light?' Well, the one in your head that comes on when you've dropped a few hundred bombs."

On the 12th, the 388th had already attacked and destroyed two locomotives when the squadron bounced another northwest-bound train of twenty cars. First Lieutenant Frank E. Sejtka led one of the elements in the attacking flight. Instead of releasing at normal height, the Chicagoan roared down to treetop level and flung his bombs at the locomotive, destroying it and setting fire to the ammunition cars. Sejtka returned to strafe the burning cars, which exploded violently, flinging debris high into the air. The squadron left four cars destroyed and five derailed, and Sejtka won the Distinguished Flying Cross for his determined attacks.

A day later, Jimmy Wells was in the air leading a flight of four to the vicinity of Düren, where the Americans were preparing to cross the Roer River valley and meeting heavy resistance. Near Pulheim that morning, Wells and the 386th attacked a southbound locomotive pulling twenty-five cars. In the dive, German gunners hit his plane, a silver bubble top marked with the letters D5-J, in the engine. While his flight dropped accurately and damaged the locomotive, Wells rocketed out of the target area, bombs still slung under his wings, blinded by the film of oil coating his windscreen.

Sweepstakes, the IX TAC radar controller, gave Wells a steer for Florennes; using only his compass and wristwatch, he dead-reckoned his way back across the snowy landscape. Frosty, the airfield controller, vectored him onto final approach, and Wells landed his Thunderbolt gently using instinct and "the seat of his pants." His crew chief shook his head at the ravaged Thunderbolt: under the perforated cowling, three pushrod covers were blown off the engine, and the left magneto was completely shot away.

The twelfth of sixteen missions flown on February 13 by the Hell Hawks consisted of a single flight of four, recognition that the Luftwaffe threat over the battlefront was minimal. The 386th's planes picked out one lucrative rail target after another, and at the center of the action again was Lieutenant Szymanski, who personally claimed credit for most of the dozen locomotives destroyed. Loco's tactics were to ignore the railcars and just concentrate on wrecking the locomotive: He dryly noted that without the engine, the train was just not going to run.

His seemingly fearless brand of flying came with considerable risk. "I called him 'Schamoile'; some called him 'Loco,'" remembered 2nd Lt. Joseph G. Preston, who often flew with the train buster. "He was a wild man! Very strong, physically . . . he used to work on the Brooklyn docks." At night, Szymanski often drank. And he often talked about how as a Pole, he was determined to get back at the Germans. "He loved to go where there was a lot of flak," said Preston. "He'd tell me over the radio that 'We're going to go get 'em.'"

And so he did. During one of Szymanski's many runs on the trains that day, flak struck Preston, his wingman. One of his oil coolers was hit, coating the bubble top and spraying hot oil into his eyes when he opened the canopy to see out. He radioed from his cripple that he was headed for a nearby Belgian emergency field, but at low altitude he struck power lines. "I mushed in just beyond and crashed," said Preston. Downed near Wesel, Germany, he was captured immediately and taken to a German command post in a farmhouse. "They treated me well enough. My eyes were burning, but they washed the oil out of them." No one saw him go down, and he was lost to the Hell Hawks and his family until the Allies liberated his POW camp at war's end.

☆

Strikes on German rail and road transportation reached a climax at the end of the following week. On the morning of February 23, the U.S. Ninth Army began its crossing of the Roer River, just to the west of the industrial town of Düren. The 365th had been supporting preparations for the river assault by attacking gun positions, artillery observation posts, troop concentrations, and command centers across the Roer. After the 104th Infantry Division made its assault crossing, the Hell Hawks continued to conduct air strikes directed by forward air controllers in and over the front lines. One army observer, Maj. Harry A. Franck, a travel writer before the war, witnessed several days of air-to-ground operations in which the Hell Hawks were at center stage. An air operations lieutenant colonel described to Franck how, on the previous day, one squadron of the group "plunked all but two of their bombs on a factory just across the river. The Germans came running out as the walls began to topple, and the anti-flak barrage cut them to bits. [The army laid on suppressing artillery fire during a strike to kill the exposed flak gunners.] That was one strong point the 104th overran without too much difficulty in the early hours that morning."

A little before 8:30 a.m. Franck watched as the 387th Squadron arrived over-head, directed by a spotter plane working through the division air controller, THIN-BOY. The target, marked by artillery smoke shells, was in the town of Arnoldsweiler, just northeast of Düren.

Franck described the scene: "The first squadron started its bomb run. The smoke was on the target and the anti-flak barrage had begun. We could hear BLUE-BIRD Leader instructing his men to 'break out of the clouds following me, release on the red smoke, then zoom back into the clouds before they can hit you.' . . . The report came in from the Cub observer and White said, 'Thank you, BLUEBIRD. The bombing was damned good . . . all of 'em right in there. You may proceed on your recce. Over and out.'"

Franck climbed an observation tower overlooking Düren across the Roer: "Suddenly eight P-47s appeared from the west and started chasing one another in a ragged circle, just below the overcast. . . . The leader flipped over on one wing into a dive and like magic two blobs of red smoke appeared on the white haze, like candied cherries on whipped cream. One by one the planes swooped and dropped their bombs, little flickers from their guns showing that they were strafing, and fountains of light flak tracers reached up, sometimes going beyond them as they dipped to the bomb-release nadir. As they pulled off, black puffs appeared near them and they began to weave. . . . The five-hundred-pound bombs made much more of an explosion than any of the artillery shells I had been watching erupt here and there for miles and miles along the front. . . . I counted seven Cubs [prob-ably L-4 Grasshoppers] darting hither and yon about the skies, one of them im-pudently floating over Düren itself, which was spattered with a dozen explosions every minute and belching smoke and clouds in a hundred places.

". . . we watched an eight-plane squadron arc down into the artificial fog, then up again, like small boys diving for coins, chased by what appeared to be little orange dots. Of all the battle noises we could hear . . . by far the most constant was the angry buzz of the Thunderbolts overhead, sometimes out of sight in the lowering clouds. Time and again we saw them chase each other's tails, then line up at wide intervals and swoop, one at a time, to drop their bombs and perhaps strafe where the red smoke indicated, then zoom up and break to one side or the other, often speeded on by streams of light flak or punched at viciously by black blobs of heavy anti-aircraft fire. . . . I did see at least three Thunderbolts execute a full ninety-degree dive. They started from plenty of altitude, went straight down like Newton's apple, and were able to pull out all right in every case—but it was a heart-stopping maneuver to watch."

Major Franck, commissioned to write about the day-to-day work of the Ninth Air Force, next visited A-78, Florennes, where he was introduced to the 365th's commanding officer:

> Tall, slender Colonel Ray J. Stecker has prematurely gray hair but not so long ago . . . he was an All-American football player at West Point—and for two years was on the All-American basketball team. . . .
>
> "A fighter bomber pilot is a unique individual," the colonel said when we told him that we would like to meet the pilot he considered most representative of those we had watched wheeling around in the skies near Düren and diving into the smoke and flak. "To a great extent he is dependent upon himself alone, which means he must be navigator, bombardier, gunner and engineer as well as pilot. It's a big job. A difficult one. I'd suggest you have a talk with Major Fry—he's as good as they come."
>
> Major Robert M. Fry, commander of one of the group's three squadrons, twenty-three years old, comes from Erie, Pennsylvania, and had shot down seven German planes in more than a year's combat.
>
> "Nothing much has happened to me," he told us, with no pretense of coy modesty, though his statement hardly seemed true, because he had the Silver Star, the Distinguished Flying Cross, a much-clustered Air Medal, and a Soldier's Medal—this last, so Colonel Stecker informed us before he left us with Major Fry, for pulling a dazed pilot out of the cockpit of his burning plane just after it crashed on the group's landing strip in Normandy.

Fry, asked to describe the emotional impact of combat, explained, "When the Jerries are shooting at you and you point the nose of your ship down into the bursting shells to make the bomb run, you feel yourself drawing together in as tight a mass of flesh as possible, and you imagine that your plane is hardly moving . . . even though your airspeed indicator registers 400 mph."

Fry said that his squadron's pilots had made a special effort that morning to get airborne and thus over the Roer early, despite the heightened risk of a take-off accident in the hazy dawn. The 388th's new commander, promoted from first lieutenant to major in less than three months and now in charge of forty pilots and more than 250 enlisted men, spoke with satisfaction of one particular air-to-ground incident from the previous autumn:

> An American tank column was held up southeast of Aachen . . . by a heavy German tank hidden in a woods and an 88-millimeter gun planted in a farmhouse on a hill overlooking our troops. We bombed the house and destroyed the gun and then chased the tank out of the woods by strafing. The tank scurried across a field till it came to a road; then, when we strafed it again, it moved toward a sharp bend around which our tanks were deployed.
>
> I could see what was going to happen, so I radioed our tanks that the Jerry tank would come around the corner in fifteen seconds. It did, all right, and our tanks were ready for him, hitting him with shell after shell till he started burning, went off the road, and rammed a barn, which burned up, too. Then the American tanks returned to the road and we felt damned good about clearing the way for them.

At mid-afternoon on February 23, while the GIs threw bridges across the Roer under fire and the 386th Squadron was off dive-bombing a factory and rail targets near Frechen, the 386th crew chiefs waited at the end of the runway for their planes to return. Warming themselves around a small fire, they watched a flight of Lockheed P-38s, also stationed at A-78, wing off on their own ground-attack mission. One of the twin-engined Lightnings lost power soon after takeoff, and its pilot wheeled wide around the field to make his single-engine approach. As the men watched the P-38 flare for landing, one spotted a flicker of flame from its nose—gunfire! "Hit the deck!" yelled one.

The men threw themselves on the ground, but Sgt. Norman V. Condreit jumped up instead of out from the box he was sitting on. A 20mm shell from the P-38's cannon took him below the right arm, the impact hurling his body ten feet backward. Charles Johnson wrote that Condreit died "before he hit the ground." The young sergeant was just twenty-one. He left behind a wife of nineteen.

The Lightning pilot, who had forgotten to flip off his gun switches in the pattern and inadvertently touched the trigger, taxied to the end of the strip and noticed the commotion among the ground crews. He cut his remaining engine and clambered down from the cockpit. Seeing Condreit sprawled in death, the young man broke down. Inconsolable, he was in no shape to even taxi his plane clear of the runway; he swore he would never fly again. The arriving medics had their hands full quieting the emotionally devastated pilot and getting him away from the scene.

☆

Just before 1:00 p.m. on the 23rd, the Hell Hawks launched the eleventh mission in their maximum effort to assist the attacking 104th Infantry Division: eight planes of the 386th Squadron. The Thunderbolts reconnoitered the area near Brühl, just south of Cologne, and attacked a fifteen-car train headed toward Bonn. Four bombs quickly cut the track and damaged the locomotive, and the pilots went on to destroy a nearby factory.

Second Lieutenant Kenneth C. McHugh was leading White Flight, with 2nd Lt. John S. Vitz as his wingman, during the initial strafing run on the train. Climbing back to provide top cover for Blue Flight in their turn, McHugh started a gentle left turn to enable his flight to join up at ten thousand feet. He held the turn a little too long—and alert enemy gunners below took notice. McHugh wound up in the crosshairs of a German heavy flak battery, whose gunners calculated the lead perfectly and put one of their 88mm shells just in front of the spinner on his Thunderbolt's propeller.

Instantly, McHugh found himself *inside* the black smoke and red flame of a shell-burst. The Nebraska native had so much smoke in the cockpit he thought he was on fire; smoke belched, too, from the engine's torn cowl flaps just forward of the cockpit. His Thunderbolt shuddered and shook, as if on the verge of a stall, and McHugh dove to keep his airspeed up. The altimeter unwound as he pushed past seventy degrees in the dive, but the drag from his slowly turning prop seemed to hold the plane back. Abruptly, his engine quit. What next?

Passing through six thousand feet, he got his answer. The Jug's thirteen-foot, four-bladed Hamilton Standard prop snapped off at the shaft and departed the airplane. Amazed, McHugh watched it whip over his right wing and begin spinning to earth like a pinwheel. Back to flying—the vibration had left with the propeller, and he eased back to a thirty-five-degree dive to maintain one hundred miles per hour.

"Mayday! Mayday!" called McHugh, and Sweepstakes answered with a vector—to Liège, some 150 miles away. *Without a propeller, I'll be lucky to get fifteen miles*, he thought. He headed west, trying for the nearest American lines, all the while trailing heavy smoke and a string of pursuing flak bursts. McHugh stretched his descent as much as he dared; he would have enjoyed the glider ride if only the gunners would have given up on him.

A cloud deck waited below at about 2,500 feet, and McHugh planned to bail out at 2,000 or when he broke out of the clouds. Engulfed in the soft white mist, the lieutenant was preparing for bailout when he suddenly broke into the clear, directly over Düren, Germany, ground zero for the battle of the Roer crossings.

Light, medium, and heavy flak explosions engulfed McHugh's P-47. One 40mm shell tore off most of the right flap. White tracers of 20mm shells filled the sky around his cockpit. *The hell with bailing out*, McHugh thought; he hunched down and sailed silently over the city, sans propeller. He finally dumped his Thunderbolt into a field, too short by half, taking out two fences, an irrigation berm, and a row of small trees before shuddering to a stop, barely within American lines. McHugh, like so many other veterans of a Jug's forced landing, was unhurt. *Stars and Stripes* reported on his strange arrival: "A squad of GIs and a chaplain had been watching the plane come down—and the chaplain went over to meet McHugh as he walked from the wreckage. 'Is this a jet-propelled craft you were flying?' he wanted to know. The Pawnee City, Nebraska, pilot told him flak had shot off his prop and canopy. 'That's all right, my son,' said the chaplain, 'you're a good soldier—trying to keep a secret.'"

Three days later, McHugh swapped his A-2 jacket for a ride back to Florennes in an L-5 liaison plane. Thirty years later he mused it was still possible that somewhere out there was an elderly Ninth Army chaplain convinced he had seen the first combat use of a jet fighter by the Army Air Forces.

Fellow 386th flier Bob Hagan was well acquainted with the consequences of a moment's inattention in a combat zone. Aware he was always being watched, he never flew straight and level for more than a few seconds. "They were really chasing you, and you were taking evasive action. You could look back and see where you'd been because of the 88 bursts." When asked which type of German antiaircraft was most dangerous, Hagan answered, "They were all effective. I don't see why they didn't shoot down more bombers. In one instance, I was flying at about eighteen thousand feet. I had an 88 [millimeter shell] go off right below the nose of the airplane. The engine stopped because of the concussion for just a second and then started again. Scared the hell out of me! It went 'boom!' and the smoke was there. But I didn't have a scratch on the airplane."

☆

The Hell Hawks flew eighteen missions to support the Roer assault on the 23rd, and Ninth Air Force put 661 sorties into the air that day to aid the crossings, the highest total since the previous summer. On February 25, 1945, VII Corps captured Düren, two days after the Marines raised the flag on Iwo Jima's Suribachi, half a world away. Soon the GIs had a bridgehead over the Elft River, and U.S. patrols would reach the Rhine just south of Cologne by March 4. The Allied advance into Germany had resumed, and the Hell Hawks would range far ahead of the battle lines to isolate and cut off opposing Wehrmacht forces.

Intelligence distributed a captured German circular, issued in early February by Field Marshal Walther von Model. In part, it read:

> The Anglo-American ground-attack aircraft are the modern highwaymen. They are searching not only for columns of traffic, they are hunting down every gasoline truck, every truck of ammunition. . . . Our fighters and antiaircraft have had considerable success during the days of the great winter battle . . . but cannot be everywhere.
>
> EVERY SOLDIER CAN AND MUST JOIN IN THE FIGHT AGAINST GROUND ATTACKS . . . EACH SOLDIER WHO KNOCKS DOWN AN ENEMY STRAFER WITH HIS INFANTRY WEAPON RECEIVES 10 DAYS SPECIAL FURLOUGH; UNITS WHICH HAVE PARTICULARLY SUCCESSFUL SCORES . . . WILL RECEIVE SPECIAL RATION ALLOTMENTS.
>
> Therefore, SEEK COVER FIRST; THEN FIRE AWAY!

At the risk of granting Wehrmacht units special ration allotments, the Hell Hawks kept flying. On the 25th, the eighth and last mission of the day saw eight P-47s of the 388th Squadron airborne at midmorning, heading for the shell-ravaged town of Düren. In the lead was 1st Lt. Robert P. Longley, who coordinated his strike with THINBOY of the 104th Infantry and dove on a red smoke shell marking artillery positions in nearby Buir. The planes carried a dozen five-hundred-pound bombs, and a weapon relatively new to the Hell Hawks.

Napalm was a jelly-like substance added to gasoline, causing it to stick to the target and burn with fierce intensity. A drop-tank full of napalm exploded in a mushrooming fireball that not only ignited enemy soldiers and buildings, but also consumed all available oxygen, suffocating even those escaping the flames. It was a terrifying weapon; even fanatical defenders would abandon their positions when faced with a napalm-charged flamethrower.

Longley's flights hit their target with all twelve bombs and four 108-gallon tanks of napalm, engulfing the enemy position. THINBOY then asked for a strike against some nearby panzers, and Longley told his squadron mates to orbit while he scouted the enemy. Diving on a wooded tract, he streaked low over the position and immediately drew intense flak.

On October 21, Bud Longley, drenched head-to-toe in oil, had made it back to Chièvres after being hit by enemy fighters. One had blown a hole in his left wing big enough that Longley could later stand straight up through the gaping cavity. Bob Fry had shepherded him home then, telling Longley to crack his oil-covered canopy open an inch so he could see enough to fly Fry's wing to a safe landing.

This time was different. As Red Flight watched in horror from above, Longley's Thunderbolt burst into flames. Failing to raise him on the radio, Capt. Charles Ready Jr. dove after Longley, pulling out on the deck amid flak bursts to spot the burning wreckage of a P-47. When the advancing 104th Infantry captured the area, they located the crash site. Bud Longley was dead.

☆

Jimmy Wells was enjoying his dinner. Seated at the officers' mess table at Florennes with the young captain were Stecker and Quesada. The liquor was flowing, the cigar smoke was thick in the room, and Wells, a combat veteran closing in on a hundred missions, listened to the banter between Quesada, commander of the IX Tactical Air Command, and the 365th's boss.

"[Quesada] said he and our group commander, Stecker, were getting in a B-17 and flying back to the states for R&R," Wells recalled. He considered the combat situation over the past few weeks. As the Germans gave ground grudgingly eastward, they pulled their antiaircraft guns along with them; the flak became more concentrated, the gunners more desperate. The pilot knew that with this frantic flying pace, it was just a matter of time before some 20mm crew got his number. Considering his lengthy stint on the Continent and the well-lubricated state of the head table, Wells took a chance. He had nothing to lose.

"I said, 'General, that's sure nice, but what does it take for a GI pilot to get back to the States?'"

Quesada stared hard at Wells through the cigar smoke, but smiled as he spoke: "Well, Captain, how long have you been over here?"

"About a year and a half, General."

"And how many missions have you flown?"

"Over ninety, General," Wells answered.

Quesada spoke coolly. "Well, Jimmy, you should be getting close to being eligible for a trip back to the States. You didn't by any chance get one of those thirty-day leaves back home, did you?"

Wells replied that he had.

Quesada looked down at his coffee and brandy. "Oh, well, I wouldn't think about going home. The reason we have those furloughs is to get experienced personnel home, then back over here to stay until this thing is finished." The general wanted his pilots to enjoy some time off, but then return fresh and rested to share their experience with the younger men.

"You'll still be here in a year," smiled the general. He took a big sip of his cognac and coffee, and then fixed the war-wizened captain with a hard gaze. "That is, if you're alive."

☆

Edward "Loco" Szymanski, the train-buster, had been called to Paris on the 26th for an Armed Forces Radio appearance, with Loco as the star. The public affairs types wanted to show off this aggressive young first lieutenant by broadcasting a live interview with Szymanski. He hated the idea; it had taken a direct order to make him fly back for the session. Late that afternoon after the broadcast, in steady rain that had closed down combat operations back at Florennes, Szymanski took off and ducked below ragged clouds, headed for A-78. It was a routine hop, far less hazardous than any of his seventy-three combat missions. He didn't see the French apartment building looming out of the mist until it was too late.

Chapter Fifteen

Into the Reich

THE ROER HAD BEEN FORCED less than a week earlier, and American troops were pushing forward from Düren toward the Rhine. On March 1, the Hell Hawks flew a dozen support missions for the 3rd Armored Division, part of the First Army's VII Corps, which had advanced through the Roer bridgeheads and was now striking toward Cologne.

One of the air controllers guiding the Hell Hawks during the 3rd Armored's advance was Capt. Quentin C. Aanenson, who had been flying a P-47 in combat with the 366th Fighter Group since before D-Day. Aanenson wrote vividly about his experiences on the ground for his award-winning 1993 film, *A Fighter Pilot's Story*:

> Having fought my war up to this time from the air, it was a major change to now be on the ground directing the close-air support in front of the VII Army Corps. I worked with a radio man, a driver, forward observers on the ground to locate targets, and a small observation plane, which operated over the front lines. When a target—or several targets—would be located, they would telephone the target descriptions and map coordinates to me.
>
> Throughout the day, fighter squadrons would check in with me to see if I had targets for them. I usually did.

Some days I was kept very busy, handling one squadron after another. Sometimes a plane in a squadron I had ordered to attack a particular target would be shot down. It bothered me to know I had given the order that led to that pilot's death, but I gradually got used to it. It was part of war.

Several times I operated from frontline tanks, using my high-frequency radio to direct fighters against targets right in front of us. When the attacking fighters would come right over our heads with guns and rockets blazing, it was an impressive, and at times, frightening sight. I can imagine what it must have been like for the Germans.

Often Aanenson, who knew just how good these fliers were, had them hit targets just a hundred yards from his own position. "The sound—it blows you away," he said. "This monster is coming at you at three hundred to four hundred miles per hour with engines screaming in the dive, all guns roaring. You could hear the ground impact of those bullets, about a hundred shells a second." Yet he felt little pity for the enemy being flailed by those guns. Aanenson recalled his comrades shot in their parachutes or killed by mobs after bailout; "at those moments I hated the Germans."

And the battle was hardly one-sided:

> I had several close calls while doing this job. One day a German 88 blew up the tank in front of us, and all the men were killed. The commander of the tank I was in tried desperately to back off the road into a more protected area, but as he was turning, an 88 shell hit our left tread and knocked us out of action.
>
> We scrambled out and rolled into the ditch just seconds before the Germans hit us again, and our tank exploded. The impact of the first shell . . . reverberated throughout the tank with such intensity that it was two or three days before my hearing returned to normal.

From a castle on the west bank of the Roer, Aanenson had witnessed the forty-five-minute preparatory bombardment ("the light was so bright, you could read a newspaper") and the infantry's February 23 assault crossing into Düren. At dawn, he returned to his radio and maps to direct the arriving Thunderbolt strikes:

> As soon as it was daylight, I started calling in my fighter squadrons. Except for three or four fifteen-minute breaks, I didn't leave my radio until it got dark. I handled twenty-four squadrons that day. . . .
>
> Shortly before noon a German artillery shell came through an opening in the castle wall, and exploded about fifty feet from me. I was partially shielded from the explosion by a stone support column, but an enlisted man, who was standing about fifteen feet from me, had the top of his head blown off by a piece of shrapnel. Brain tissue and blood were thrown all over me and my maps.
>
> I was handling two fighter squadrons when the shell hit—one squadron was in the middle of its attack, and the other was waiting for my command to dive. As soon as I found out my equipment was still functioning, I got back to work. A couple of medics carried the dead man away, and treated the wounded. They cleaned the blood and brain tissue off my leather flight jacket and out of my hair. As they wiped off my maps and equipment, I remember being surprised at how pink and fluffy brain tissue looked. It seemed to float in the air.
>
> I thought the day would never end. When things finally got quiet, I crawled into my cot, which was in a corner just a few yards away, and even with the roar of the guns continuing throughout the night, I slept the sleep of the dead.

With supplies restocked and the Roer barrier breached, the U.S. First Army was closing in on the transportation hub and Rhine River port of Cologne, while farther south, Patton's Third Army was preparing a rush to the Rhine north of its junction with the Moselle River. The northern advance by the British and Canadians had established a tight bridgehead at Wesel, northwest of Essen.

Hell Hawks pilots also were detailed to serve as forward air controllers. Second Lieutenant Edward J. Lopez, twenty-one, of the 387th Squadron was summoned to his commander's office just after the Roer crossing. Major John

W. Motzenbecker gave "Lopey" the news that he would be spending two weeks up front with the 3rd Armored.

On his first night on the line near Düren, Lopez was asleep, dead tired, when he heard a loud thud. None of the GIs in the makeshift barracks reacted, so he went back to getting some shuteye. Next morning, the men discovered a German shell—a dud—had penetrated the roof and smacked into a wall where the sleeping men lay. "We all would have been killed," Lopez wrote later.

After a C-ration breakfast, Lopez met the 3rd Armored sergeant commanding the tank housing his ground-to-air radios, and they were off. Crossing into Düren, "for the first time I got to see the devastating results of our air attacks, and I knew the many missions I flew had an impact on the war. As my tank commander maneuvered our tank around rubble and destroyed buildings, he would pick out pockets of German soldiers and fire his 76mm cannon. When he did, the whole tank shook; it was a teeth-rattling experience."

The Wehrmacht was entrenched in a strong position outside Düren, so Lopez called in his flying artillery. Using maps the pilots had in their cockpits, he coordinated a strike and had the tank men mark the target with red, green, and yellow smoke (a sequence designed to thwart German attempts to misdirect the bombing using their own colored smoke shells). After the P-47s delivered their concentrated attack, "it was much easier for us to proceed. As we were fighting our way forward we passed many dead Germans; the lucky ones were captured by our infantry. One German officer we captured gave me his Luger . . . he was glad to be out of the war.

"After some harrowing experiences of being shot at by the [88mm] gun mounted on Tiger tanks and seeing how our fighting GIs outfought the Germans, I came to realize how tough it was to fight on the ground. Oh, sure, we had our tough missions in the air and we lost a few pilots, but at least between missions we had time to enjoy ourselves away from combat and danger. The men I was with were constantly on alert or in a fierce battle . . ."

Lopez felt particularly vulnerable when the Sherman he rode in engaged a Tiger or Panther, whose high-velocity guns could knife through American armor with ease. When a Luftwaffe strike hit his tank column, "I got on the radio and asked for help from our air cover. At least I did until my own tank was hit and I had to scramble out or get burned to death. I did manage to save the radio, which I later put into another tank and continued my communication . . . ."

After helping capture Cologne, the 3rd Armored took a well-deserved break from combat. Lopez returned to the 387th, but not before procuring a few souvenirs—a fine shotgun, a Nazi ceremonial dagger, and a huge swastika banner—taken from abandoned houses in the bombed city. Lopez reflected on his brief stint with the frontline troops: "On my arrival I was the envy of the rest of the pilots, for not only had I experienced what our ground troops go through, but also had the opportunity to see the damage we had done to the German war effort, the burned out gun emplacements, destroyed Tiger tanks, gutted buildings, etc. . . . and how grateful the GIs were that we were there to help them."

☆

While Lopez was forward with the 3rd Armored, the Hell Hawks worked closely with other controllers accompanying the tank columns, the pilots both attacking designated targets and warning the GIs of opposition ahead. In midafternoon of March 2, Major Arlo C. Henry was leading another pair of Thunderbolts, each lugging a pair of five-hundred-pound bombs. The 3rd Armored Division controller, FORMROOM, directed Henry to a suspected tank concentration near the small Cologne suburb of Stommeln. His information was accurate: Henry picked out three panzers traveling at five-hundred-yard intervals into town. Henry wrote later:

> We were asked to seek out a tank or a mobile 88mm gun in or around the town of Stommeln that was holding up the column. From the air we could see the complete problem. Most of the column was behind the northwest/southeast railroad embankment which ran about one-half mile south of the town. About four or five [American] tanks had ventured through the underpass to head north towards town. They were either stalled or burning after being hit by enemy fire.
>
> We circled the town two or three times at low altitude without spotting a gun or a tank of any size. Further, we received no ground fire. Suddenly, one of my flight members called out, "Three tanks coming south towards town!!" I immediately called FORMROOM to confirm that no friendly troops were north or northwest of the town.
>
> "Negative. Identify and destroy!"
> "Roger!"

We made a fast in-trail pass to look at the tanks and saw the muzzle brakes and crosses on the turrets. "Tigers! They're closing up—let's try to get them before they split up!"

By this time I was coming around for a low pass with bombs. The tanks had pulled up and stopped bumper-to-bumper at the east-west street. We had to get those bombs in broadside before they split up! I punched the button to release the bombs and pulled up sharply to miss the power lines strung across the street. I then made a low tight turn to the left to see how we had done.

The intersection was clouded over with dust and smoke as Red Two and Red Three dropped their bombs very close to mine. As the wind cleared the scene, I could see that one of the tanks was down in a ditch on the opposite side of the north/south road with its 88mm gun turned down and to the side. The second tank was pulling around the corner heading east on the main street.

"Get him with your guns!" I yelled. "Make a steep angle of attack and aim for the ventilator grates. Set his engine on fire! He's on hard surface," I continued, "ricochet them up into his belly— front and rear!"

A Tiger I's hull armor was impervious to nearly all American tank fire, and even the 25mm armor on the turret top and rear decking would defeat a .50-caliber round. On paper, .50-caliber machine gun fire would do nothing but rattle the Tiger crew's eardrums. But there were cooling fan gratings and air intakes on the rear deck, and thin armor on the underside, that might allow a P-47's sheer volume of fire to score a lucky hit and disable a Tiger's engine.

Henry continued:

A glance back to the intersection showed the third tank backing to the north about a hundred yards into an orchard. He could wait his turn, I thought.

The second tank pulled off the main street into a dirt lot between some buildings. When we kept hitting his ventilator grates with our bullets, he pulled out and to the east. He then parked between two buildings on the north side of the street. We continued to work on his grates until he pulled out and turned back to the west on the main street. That was one harassed Tiger!

As the Tiger continued west past the intersection, we continued to ricochet .50-caliber bullets into its belly and pounded its grates as before. Finally the tank stopped in the middle of the street and remained there despite our attacks. It was now time to worry the third tank. We made one high-angle attack on the grates of the third Tiger. This forced it to move out of the orchard on to the secondary road from whence it had come.

By this time, one or more of us was either out of ammunition or extremely low, so we advised FORMROOM of the tank's status and took off for home.

Next morning we received a wire from the tank force commander expressing appreciation for the attack. His forces took the town without further casualties. They found one Tiger destroyed, the second was incapacitated and it was captured, while the third had gotten away. From this we learned that our guns could cripple a Tiger tank despite its supposed impenetrable armor.

The character of the war in March resembled the previous summer's campaign in Normandy. The Allies were gathering strength for a winning breakout. To assist the Rhine crossing, the P-47s would work to keep reinforcements from reaching the front. "There was a lot of activity reported in the area between Siegburg and Cologne, so our group was given the task of patrolling that corridor," wrote Lopez. "To go on and mention the various marshalling yards and trains we strafed, many of them blowing up and indicating that they were loaded with munitions, would be repetitive. Suffice to say that we were kept busy wrecking the German army."

The men's living conditions had improved. "At Florennes we were billeted in a beautiful old chateau which must have belonged to a very wealthy Belgian family," wrote Lopez. "It had many rooms and was well decorated.

"The squadron commander [Maj. John W. Motzenbecker] made a deal with the local baker. He would furnish the ingredients if the baker would bake pastries for the pilots, a delicacy we did not enjoy before."

The quality mess fare and the welcoming disposition of the female population of Florennes would soon be nothing more than pleasant memories for Lopez and the Hell Hawks. Their time in Belgium was drawing to a close. To better support the ground troops and cut the transit time for the fighter-bombers between base and front lines, combat engineers had laid out a new airfield at Aachen, Germany, the ancient capital of Charlemagne's Holy Roman Empire. Over the next nine days, the Hell Hawks moved rapidly to make their new home at Y-46 operational.

Unlike some of the captured Luftwaffe bases they had flown from in the past, Y-46 was carved by the 818th Engineer Aviation Battalion from farmland on the city's outskirts. Without serious civil engineering, the soft loam, soaked by late winter rains, would have swallowed P-47s whole. Road-building, drainage ditches, and a serviceable steel-mat runway were first priorities.

By demolishing old German barracks and trucking thousands of board-feet of salvaged lumber to the field, the Hell Hawks built wooden walkways to lift them reasonably clear of the mud. A "liberated" depot nearby supplied coal, electric cable, wire-mesh matting, and chairs and tables for the mess hall. The 388th's Tech. Sgt. William N. MacNeil led crews that laid roads and spun a web of walkways through the muck. Technical Sergeant John E. Jones built a serviceable bridge over a lake and added a road between Operations and the living area. Staff Sergeant Peter E. Krupinski supervised the building of a J-8 hut for the kitchen and officers' mess. Other details dug foxholes, laid floorboards, erected tents, and established the operations and maintenance work areas. All this had to done before a single sortie could be mounted from Y-46.

☆

Amid bad weather that kept the Hell Hawks grounded on March 7, the American 9th Armored Division captured intact the Ludendorff rail bridge over the Rhine at Remagen. Ironically, P-47s of the 36th Fighter Group had been scheduled to attack and destroy the bridge that morning, but bad weather cancelled the strike. The Wehrmacht failed in desperate attempts to blow the bridge's demolition charges. U.S. infantry and tank units rushed to the eastern bank and established a precarious bridgehead.

To cover the Remagen bridgehead, IX TAC fighters were to protect the crossing against Luftwaffe attacks and fly armed reconnaissance behind the lines to prevent the Wehrmacht from moving up reinforcements. As in Normandy, the

Hell Hawks were to help isolate the battlefield, enabling the GIs in the bridgehead to overwhelm the German defenders.

The weather finally cleared enough on March 9 to permit wide-ranging interdiction missions. The Hell Hawks bombed under radar control through the overcast—"pickle barrel" missions—and attacked rail targets anytime a hole could be found in the undercast.

On the day's seventh mission, eight Thunderbolts of the 388th Squadron found a trio of locomotives and about 150 rail cars in the marshalling yard at Remscheid, Germany. Anything on the rails was considered a legitimate military target. Even when a train carried civilian passengers, soldiers rode as well, and most of a train's cargo was bound for the fighting fronts. One of the most experienced of the train busters was the 388th's Maj. Robert M. Fry, who knew both his own limitations and the dangers of attacking box cars laden with God-knew-how-many tons of high explosives: "I was a better flier than I was a marksman. I had to get close to make sure I hit what I was shooting at."

The 365th's usual tactic was to dive-bomb the railbed just ahead of the locomotive, derailing it or forcing the train to halt. Then each flight would spread wide and come in line abreast to pick out individual rail cars for bombing or strafing. Wiping out the train's defenses in the initial passes, the planes would continue their assault and destroy as much cargo and rolling stock as possible. The pilots took a fatalistic attitude toward the work, which was gritty, dangerous, and frequently terrifying.

Fry recalled another encounter that nearly killed him: "I dove on a train, balls-to-the-wall, and I hit that guy with a burst. The train was hauling troops or ordnance—the damn thing exploded and all of a sudden I wasn't flying anymore. I thought I was done for. I had 'no air.'"

It was Fry's way of explaining how, when the powerful blast wave hit his P-47, the scorched and roiling air robbed his plane's wings of lift. His nine-ton P-47 was instantly wallowing on the edge of a stall, staggering through the turbulent fireball until his wings bit into the cool air on the far side of the train. Fry hauled his Thunderbolt out of its death dance and returned to Florennes—and what must have seemed like an endless future of train-busting missions.

As the 388th pulled off the yard at Remscheid, 2nd Lt. Marvin Gregg called in that he'd been hit and would head back toward the Allied lines. The desperate pilot radioed again saying he was at three thousand feet, just west of the Rhine near

Cologne, and that he was losing control; he'd have to bail out. His squadron mates saw him next in a forty-five-degree dive, passing through two thousand feet. No one saw a chute. Ground troops with the First Army reported later that they had found Gregg's body in the wreckage of his P-47 in Cologne's western suburbs.

On the day that Gregg went down, trucks bearing the A parties of the 387th and 388th made the four-to-five-hour journey from Florennes to Y-46. When the men crossed the German frontier below Aachen, wrote Charles Johnson, "the hatred that they saw in the faces of the young Germans, seven to ten years old, standing along the road was hard to believe." Expecting a hand grenade to come sailing into the trucks at any moment, the men rode with helmets on and loaded carbines at the ready. On other rides across the Continent the Hell Hawks had been met with flowers and cheering. Now only silence and the hostile stares of the "Master Race" greeted the conquerors.

In the bombed-out town of Eschweiler, the Hell Hawks looked upon the surreal. Beneath a church steeple decapitated by bombing was a black, horse-drawn hearse, parked beside hundreds of wooden crosses used to mark the temporary graves of those pulled from the rubble. Amid the shattered buildings and debris-filled streets, the men again reflected upon the devastation that the Nazis had invited and the Allies had delivered with industrial efficiency.

Back at Florennes, two veteran Hell Hawks received welcome news. Bob Fry and Capt. Charles Ready Jr. heard on March 10 that they both were headed for thirty-day furloughs stateside. Fry had been flying in harm's way since February 22, 1944, racking up 318 combat hours in over 130 missions. Having shipped overseas with the Hell Hawks as a second lieutenant in late 1943, he had seven confirmed air-to-air kills, making him the group's top scorer.

Ready had joined the 388th Squadron at A-7 near Utah Beach the previous June, and had been in combat ever since. He had shot down two enemy fighters and amassed 247 hours of combat time through 108 missions. Within a week of the pair's departure, Maj. James E. Hill, on his own furlough since the group left Metz, returned to 388th Squadron command, replacing Fry. Four days later, 387th Squadron commander Lt. Col. John W. Motzenbecker departed on his own thirty-day operational leave.

The Hell Hawks said good-bye to Motzenbecker, Fry, and Ready while the group was still shifting forward to their new base, their eighth since arriving on the Continent. Amid relentless work on the ground and an uninterrupted series

234

of interdiction missions in the air, the 365th completed its move to Merzbruck, a northeastern suburb of Aachen, by mid-March. Construction was in high gear: engineers labored in mud up to four feet deep, filling in trenches and pillboxes, working twenty-four hours a day under floodlights to complete the runway. On the 16th, the first squadron-sized combat mission to take off from German soil was airborne from Y-46 at 1:07 p.m. General Quesada was at the field to mark the occasion, and stated that "the Group could well be used as an example of what could be done to make an open field livable."

But to some Aachen was hardly a move up. First Lieutenant Paul L. Van Cleef, who in one streak of twenty-four missions in January and February had been struck by flak seven times, was appalled at the field conditions:

> The engineers had put the PSP [pierced steel planking] down while the ground was still frozen—the only way they could. We operated from there about a month, and the tie-downs along the edge of the runway started pulling loose. We could only take off one ship at a time down the middle because the sides of the runway [rose] up and were as high as ten or twelve feet above ground on the edges. Twin-engine planes couldn't use the field at all because their wingtips hit the edges of the runway!
>
> When the ground thawed, the runway (and everything else) turned into a sea of mud covered by steel matting which soon became like a washboard. Taking off was difficult, but landing was even worse. The engineers worked constantly filling in the holes, which were washed away by the little rivers of water that were everywhere.

Throughout March, Y-46 was a marginal fighter strip, and living conditions were little better. Van Cleef recalled how the pilots lived in the little town of Weiden—Aachen itself was just rubble—camping out in bomb-damaged buildings with blown-out windows and no stairways. "About six of us lived on the second floor because the first floor wasn't fit to live in," he said. Even their digs upstairs had four inches of dirt on the floors; "but we just ignored it. The weather was terrible—lots of rain—but we flew anyway."

☆

Ed Lopez was back in the air before noon on March 13, still sobered by his tour up front as a forward air controller. Instead of the usual close-support or train-busting mission, the 387th was to conduct a fighter sweep east of the Rhine bridgehead at Remagen. Colonel Ray Stecker led a dozen planes, working with Marmite's radar, searching for enemy fighters at fifteen thousand feet. Over Ahrweiler, Lopez and the squadron spotted three Arado Ar 234 jet bombers, flying in a wide Vee, ten thousand feet below. With the advantage of altitude, Stecker rolled into a dive, followed by the rest of the Thunderbolts, straining for a chance at the usually untouchable jets.

"We were doing at least five hundred miles per hour and closing in on them very fast," wrote Lopez, "but the German pilots knew what they were doing. They let us get near but not in range. . . . When it looked like we were going to get some easy targets, the German pilots gave their planes full power and took off at a forty-five-degree angle and left us like we were standing still." Lopez was grateful that thanks to Hitler's mismanagement, the German jets never appeared in significant numbers; they were "far superior to anything we could put in the air," he wrote.

Another witness to the jets' potential was prominent CBS journalist Edward R. Murrow, who visited the 365th in mid-March. Murrow later broadcast two reports from Europe about the combat exploits of the Hell Hawks. The first came a week after the seizure of the Remagen bridge:

> This is Edward R. Murrow in Paris. And this is going to be mostly about Captain William E. "Curly" Rodgers, a short, smiling fighter pilot who flies with the 365th Fighter Group, and who thinks that train-busting is the most fun ever invented by anyone. He flies a P-47 Thunderbolt, has about 250 combat hours, comes from Hartselle, Alabama, thinks the Ninth Air Force is doing a great job, and that his outfit is the sharpest one over here. As fighter pilots go, he's old: twenty-three.
>
> Yesterday afternoon he folded me into a little seat behind him in a piggy-back Thunderbolt and took off for the Rhine. . . . We were going upstream, and soon Bonn and its broken bridges was

below us. Suddenly Curly pointed and said, "Look at that Junkers!" [probably an Arado 234 Blitz]. It was a German jet plane coasting in, just level with us. Its bomb dropped away, and Curly turned into the attacking plane saying, "You never want to show your tail to one of those babies!"* With this, the German pilot veered off and poured on the coal and disappeared in the haze. Then we were bounced! Four red-nosed Mustangs (P-51s) were coming down on us, and Curly rolled up on one wing so they could identify us, and at the last minute they veered off.

We were almost to the bridge. . . . We could see our artillery shells bursting white across the Rhine River, and then we were over the bridge. The vehicles crossing looked like brown bedbugs crawling along a black string. A few German shells were landing on our side of the river. . . .

We were over the bridgehead when a "bandit" came down the Rhine . . . probably a lone German fighter-bomber, although we couldn't see him clearly. And then, the whole sky was filled with light flak and tracers. It was like thousands of sparks flying upward from a huge furnace, all converging in one spot. I saw a glint of metal a few thousand feet above the cone of flame and realized that a Thunderbolt was peeling off, going down through the flak to make sure of the kill, and then another peeled off, and another! They must have been in a ninety-degree dive. Curly Rodgers said, "Look at those boys go!" For one horrible moment I thought that we were going with them.

. . . the boys who fly the fighter-bombers are doing their share. The 365th Hell Hawks have received a Presidential Citation. They have moved bases nine times without missing a day's operations, and there are little blue squares on the big charts to indicate the men who didn't come back . . . ."

---

* The Blitz actually had no forward-firing guns, but this was not known to the Allies at the time.

Murrow talked about the Hell Hawks again from London on March 18, summarizing the Allied efforts to cross the Rhine and the successful establishment of the Remagen bridgehead:

> The American Air Corps [*sic*] has developed air-ground cooperation to the point where the hyphen should be removed from the two words. The ground forces now talk to the air forces just as though they were in the same room. The communications system is vastly better than it was during the Normandy campaign, and the whole thing works with the precision of an adding machine. . . .
>
> The other day, Col. Ray J. Stecker, who commands the 365th Fighter Group . . . was leading a flight, when the ground controller pulled him down to bomb a column of tanks. Those German armored columns carry plenty of 20mm flak guns [mounted on half-tracks or trucks] . . . the courage required to go down through that flak is, if anything, greater than that demanded of the bomber boys when they must fly straight and level on a bomb run. . . .
>
> There's a curious kind of discipline in these fighter-bomber groups. At briefing, the commanding officer at interrogation will say: "Now I don't want any of you guys to go down so eager that you go down too low after tanks or a railway train and don't give yourself enough room to pull out, and you go and mush into the ground."

Leading a flight on one of those rail-cutting missions across the Rhine was 1st. Lt. Archie F. Maltbie, "Lin" to his buddies. Maltbie had been with the 388th since April 1944, and had survived a bail-out the previous August when a Bf 109 blew up in his face over the Seine. Maltbie and his fifteen fellow fliers first attacked a marshalling yard near Dillenburg. "We would peel off from eight thousand to ten thousand feet," Maltbie said, "diving at a steep forty-five- to fifty-degree angle. I'd release at about a thousand feet, then pull hard so as to bottom out three or four hundred feet above the target. You didn't want to pull out too low and mush into the ground." Aiming at a string of cars or a place where the tracks converged, four planes planted eight five-hundred-pounders among the hundred-plus railcars there, knocking out twenty cars, wrecking two buildings, and cutting the tracks in four places. Maltbie's men then gave the yard at Haiger the same treatment.

Just east of Remagen, the flight caught sight of a black and green Junkers Ju 88 twin-engine fighter-bomber, one of the war's most versatile attack planes, headed for the crucial Ludendorff Bridge. Maltbie's combat report says the Ju 88 was at slightly above his flight, over the Rhine, inbound for the crossing. "At the time there was a no-fly zone around the bridge, meaning anyone flying in that area was fair game for the army's gunners," said Maltbie. "By this stage of the war we were scrounging for targets [in the air] . . . things were getting mighty lean. Guns or no guns, we decided to go in and get him."

Maltbie and Blue Flight jettisoned their bombs at twelve thousand feet and pursued, but he had trouble closing the range. "I was surprised at the speed of this sucker. We had to go flat out to catch him." About six hundred yards out, Maltbie squeezed off his first burst. His first few shots were aimed at making the 88 maneuver, so he could cut inside his turn, but the enemy's abrupt evasive tactics stymied the pursuing Thunderbolts. Finally, headed east "back into the Fatherland," Maltbie cut off the Junkers in a climbing right turn. "His forward fuselage looked like it was made of corrugated metal, almost 'jerry-built', and I guess it was," said Maltbie. At two hundred yards, his series of three-second bursts knocked pieces off the bomber's right side, torching the right engine.

The German pilot popped the left-side crew hatch and bailed out just as the Junkers exploded in a brilliant puff of orange flame. The flaming wreckage, the remaining three crew members presumably still inside, tumbled end over end toward the German town of Ewersbach.

"We sensed we were on the downhill side of the war," said Maltbie, who was awarded the Distinguished Flying Cross for his actions. "Things were tough on the ground for the Germans. If we could push a little harder to get this thing won, we were eager to do it." The Hell Hawks' "push" would come at a fearful price.

Chapter Sixteen

Fighting the Jets

I T TOOK A SPECIAL KIND OF GRIT to step out of a wrecked aircraft, climb into another, and take off again. There had to be men who couldn't do this: At least one pilot turned in his wings to Col. Ray Stecker and said he couldn't fly any more. But most kept flying when buddies died, when bullets struck their aircraft, and even when they survived a crash. One of these was Capt. Andrew W. Smoak, a poker player, a drinker, a man who seemed to love life and perhaps loved it even more each time he almost lost it. By early 1945, as the Bulge fighting ended and German jets began appearing in large numbers, Smoak was piloting his third Thunderbolt.

He apparently flew into battle carrying a French pistol that wasn't issued by the U.S. taxpayer. The pistol exists today. "I have the French revolver my dad brought home from the war," said retired Brig. Gen. Andrew W. Smoak, the P-47 Thunderbolt pilot's son. "He said he got it one day when he walked into the village near his airfield and saw a GI with a load of swords, daggers and sidearms. It seems when the army moved through an area, they disarmed everyone and locked the arms in a cellar. When follow-up forces arrived, they would break in and take souvenirs. This one individual was a little overly ambitious and dropping stuff as he walked by my dad. My father picked up the gun and offered it back to the guy, but he said to keep it because he had too much to carry."

Smoak, the Hell Hawk, could be serious. He could be funny. He could even be mellow, a trait not defined in the fighter pilot's handbook. After the war, his crew chief related a story about Smoak landing in a shot-up P-47. The crew chief was excited to learn what had happened. Smoak said he had shot down a German aircraft. Crew chiefs took much pride in their aircraft when a pilot scored a victory. Smoak's chief ran off to get the gun camera film developed. To his shock he found that the armorer had forgotten to load it. He reported this to Smoak, who scratched his head for a moment and then said, "Well, if you're going to forget something, I'd rather it be the film than the bullets."

Something of a teaser and a prankster, according to a sister, Smoak responded to his first air-to-air sighting of a Messerschmitt Me 262 jet fighter not with awe or dread but by doing an imitation of the German pilot's difficulties coping with not having a propeller. "He loved to make faces," said Molly Smoak Jesse. "He was a great teaser."

But Smoak's wit was overwhelmed at times by the carnage that was part and parcel of the Hell Hawks' mission. His sister said that every day, Smoak kept flying combat, strafing Germans and confronting the deadly flak, but never finding a way to turn that into an object of his humor. "What he did in the war bothered him a lot," said Jesse. "Strafing people bothered him a lot. Strafing horse-drawn vehicles bothered him a lot. It was always on his mind. He felt badly about it. That bothered him and influenced his drinking."

Like many of the Hell Hawks who kept going back into the crucible, Smoak had many close brushes with fate and death. The first time he lost a Jug was on one of those mass takeoffs when the whole 365th Fighter Group was going into the fray. As his son remembers Smoak's telling of it, "The plane next to his was slightly ahead and lost a bomb, which tore my father's undercarriage out." Smoak lost his second P-47 during landing when suddenly his plane began taking shellfire. He did not immediately see where it was coming from. Smoak made a rough belly landing near his airfield, and members of an American antiaircraft crew came to pull him from the wreckage. They told Smoak he had been shot down by an aircraft with no propeller. Smoak had never seen the German jet. He initially thought the American gunners were making something up, but reported what they said to intelligence officers during his debriefing. They confirmed the Germans had jet fighters and that the jets had been operating nearby.

When German jets began to appear in the skies of Europe, no one on the Allied side had a good plan for coping with them. The Hell Hawks' Maj. John W. Motzenbecker, the commander of the 387th Squadron who flew 113 missions and earned a Silver Star, didn't have any secret knowledge or special insights. Everybody knew the Messerschmitt Me 262 was a lot faster than the P-47 Thunderbolt, the portly Jug. Nobody knew much else.

Decades later, when Motzenbecker was no longer around to reminisce about encountering Hitler's new "wonder weapon," his son Peter Motzenbecker reconstructed an early encounter with the Me 262:

> I once asked my dad if he had ever been in a dogfight with a German jet. He told me no, that the Thunderbolt was not built for that kind of fighting, but rather for bombing and strafing. But, he did tell me a story about an encounter with a German squadron of much faster, more nimble enemy aircraft [Me 262s].
>
> He and his squadron came upon this group of German jets. He said [the Hell Hawks pilots] were outnumbered, as well as out of their league for air-to-air combat. My dad made the decision to bluff them by taking the offensive, rather than attempting to flee a faster, more nimble German fighter. The Germans turned tail and fled. My father thought later that perhaps they were inexperienced; they did not realize that they would have had a distinct advantage. Dad's decision may have saved them.

In the fall of 1944, the Hell Hawks' 1st Lt. Grant Stout wrote home about seeing a Messerschmitt Me 262 jet in the distance. The United States did not have a jet-powered fighter. Stout had heard about the German jets, and the first time he saw one, he "admired it," he wrote.

Stout was hardly the only Jug pilot to encounter the vaunted German jet. First Lieutenant Archie F. Maltbie of the Hell Hawks' 388th Squadron observed a formation of Me 262s very late in the war, on March 2, 1945. Maltbie, a Kansas boy who took naturally to fighter cockpits, was not afraid to fight—two weeks later, he would shoot down a twin-prop Junkers Ju 88—but for whatever reason, he did not engage the jets. He did not know that the Third Reich, or at least its Führer, was placing high hopes in the new aircraft. By the time of Maltbie's sighting, the Hell

Hawks were also spotting Arado Ar 234 Blitz jet bombers; group commander Col. Ray Stecker sighted one on March 13.

That day, there was an Me 262 encounter that made it into the pages of historian Charles Johnson's tale of the Hell Hawks:

"2nd Lt. Frederick W. Marling, flying Blue Three, with 2nd Lt. Henry Dahlen his wingman, joined a chase of Me 262s by the entire [388th] squadron. Soon they were outdistanced. Maltbie then called the squadron to re-form. Marling and Dahlen broke right and climbed back to 17,000 feet to rejoin the squadron. They came in from the rear and it was then that Marling saw an Me 262 barrel-assing eastward at 7,000 feet.

"Marling and Dahlen did a partial split-S coming in out of the sun right on the tail of the Me 262. The enemy pilot was unaware of their approach until Marling began firing from 300 to 400 yards. He continued to close rapidly until he was within 600 feet, firing all the time. He was getting strikes all over the enemy plane." Marling kept shooting until he saw an explosion from the 262's fuselage; the jet, trailing smoke, dove steeply into the clouds and disappeared. Marling, arguing that the pilot had too little height to pull out of the dive, claimed a kill.

Some Allied pilots may have dreaded the German jets. Some may have felt that they were being sent up against a foe that could not be defeated. Some almost certainly attributed super powers to the Messerschmitt Me 262. They were unaware that the Luftwaffe was in turmoil, Germany's leaders were divided on how to use the new plane, and the Me 262 was, in any event, flawed.

☆

The Messerschmitt Me 262, which made its first flight on April 18, 1941, was the world's first jet fighter to enter service. It could have been fielded at least a year earlier, and might have been available in greater numbers to stalk the B-17 Flying Fortresses and B-24 Liberators of the U.S. Eighth Air Force—to say nothing of the Hell Hawks' Thunderbolts. Total production of Me 262s was about 1,430, but because of a series of foul-ups, only about 60 were operational at any one time.

Hitler believed Germany's so-called "wonder weapons" would prove the salvation of the Reich. Over the years, historians have debated whether he hastened his own defeat by ordering Me 262s converted into "blitz bombers" to strike advancing Allied troops when the planes were more effective as fighters, intercepting bomber formations. As described in the biography *Hitler 1936–*

1945: Nemesis, by Ian Kershaw, Hitler's concern over the Messerschmitt's fuel consumption led to a lowering of the plane's top priority for production. Hitler changed his mind when he saw the plane demonstrated in December 1943 at Insterburg air base in East Prussia. Kershaw wrote that on January 7, 1944, with "British testing of jet planes almost complete, Hitler demanded production on the Me 262 be stepped up immediately so that as many jets as possible could be put into service without delay."

In May 1944, following up on remarks he'd made at Insterburg, Hitler ordered the Me 262 fleet converted into bombers. Today, some historians argue that the Luftwaffe essentially ignored the order. Belatedly, the first Me 262s entered Luftwaffe service in July 1944.

A typical Me 262 was powered by two 1,984-pound-thrust Junkers Jumo-004B axial-flow turbojet engines. The jet was armed with four 30mm nose cannons and reached a speed of 540 miles per hour.

Of course, the Hell Hawks knew none of this. They knew only that the Me 262 was faster than their P-47. Eventually, once intelligence started to become available, they would start to hear about ways they might be able to defeat the jet.

To the Hell Hawks, the jets were only a rumor when, in April 1944, a unit dubbed Erprobungskommando 262 (roughly, "262 proving group") was formed at Lechfeld, Bavaria, to begin Me 262 operations and train pilots to fly it in combat. When Major Walter Nowotny took charge three months later, the group was redesignated Kommando Nowotny. Though its primary function was developmental work and initial trials, Kommando Nowotny held the distinction of being the world's first jet fighter group. By contrast, no U.S. jet fighter group ever reached Europe in time for combat.

Nowotny began attacking Allied aircraft formations in August 1944. A high-value target for the Luftwaffe was the Royal Air Force's fast, high-flying Mosquito reconnaissance aircraft. The German unit claimed its first aerial victory against a Mosquito on July 26, 1944—the first kill of an aircraft in combat by a jet—although British records indicate the Mosquito was merely damaged and recovered in Italy. The Me 262 scored its first real aerial victory on August 8 when it bagged another Mosquito. An Me 262 downed its first Allied heavy bomber, a B-17 Flying Fortress, near Stuttgart on August 15.

In late September Hitler finally recognized the failure of the Me 262 as a bomber and ordered the emphasis of production be changed to fighters. Later, on November 4, he would order all Me 262 production shifted to fighters. While this flip-flopping was going on, there was an internal dispute within the Luftwaffe that temporarily denied top leaders the counsel of one of their most experienced combat pilots and leaders, Generalleutnant Adolf Galland. By the time Hitler endorsed the use of the jet as a fighter, the potential of the Me 262 had been seriously undermined.

☆

Accounts of 1st Lt. Grant Stout's encounters with the Me 262 come from several members of the 365th Fighter Group. It's unclear whether they remember the same incident, or whether there was more than one; their dates do not seem to have been recorded.

"We encountered the Me 262 after we'd been covering an army unit all day long," said 1st Lt. Allen Mundt of the Hell Hawks' 387th Squadron. "We had been launching four-ship formations at twenty-minute intervals all day long. We were pulling up from a strafing run preparing to go home when Stout saw a 262 on our right, in a dive.

"Stout saved my butt when that Me 262 came in on us," said Mundt, who frequently flew on Stout's wing. "All four of us turned into him, confronting him with our thirty-two .50-caliber machine guns. The Me 262 broke off and we followed." 1st Lt. Donald Kark, who was leading the four-ship flight, apparently tried to catch the German jet but could not close the range.

Stout seems to have tried the same tactic as Motzenbecker—bluffing. Apparently Stout succeeded in scaring off an Me 262 without firing a shot.

☆

Becoming more proficient in the Me 262 each day, Nowotny's outfit claimed nineteen Allied aircraft for six Me 262s lost. There is little evidence the Luftwaffe pilots were deterred by some of the early problems associated with the new technology—the slow acceleration of the Me 262's Jumo engine, the brakes that almost never worked and made the Messerschmitt nearly impossible to handle on the ground, or its poor handling qualities at low speed around the airfield. However, the German fliers fared poorly in early air battles with Royal Air Force Hawker Tempests—the rough equivalent of the Hell Hawks' Thunderbolts—and soon Allied intelligence began to glean facts from the wrecks of Me 262s that had crashed in friendly territory.

Hell Hawks intelligence officers apparently gained access to a British report on the Me 262, which was prepared after examination of crashed German jets. The British took captured Jumo engines to Farnborough and showed them to the experts who were developing Britain's own jet program, including Group Capt. Frank Whittle (inventor of the British turbine engine). Two British officers at Farnborough prepared a report which for months thereafter was the Allies' gold standard on the jet's characteristics. The report summarized:

> The outstanding advantages of the Me 262 are its high-level speeds, very high diving speeds, and probably high ceiling. [These] give it a good performance at 35,000 feet. Its disadvantages are due chiefly to its high wing loading—namely a high takeoff speed requiring a long takeoff run, a high stalling speed, and poor maneuvering qualities. It will also tend to overshoot its target at high speed, like any jet-propelled fighter.
>
> The Me 262 will have the usual poor performance of a jet fighter at low speed. Thus, it can be attacked most easily by fighters now in service when it is cruising or climbing. In maneuvers, the Me 262 should be forced into tight turns or into a zoom, unless the altitude at which it is encountered is near the ceiling of the attacking aircraft.
>
> When conventionally-engined aircraft are avoiding the Me 262 they should not dive, since the Me 262's acceleration in a dive will be larger than that of a conventional fighter, enabling it to escape the attack, or to press home an attack on its opponent. If jet-propelled aircraft are used against the Me 262 [something that never happened], diving tactics may of course be employed. In fact, both aircraft can carry out the same maneuvers. British jet-propelled fighters now in service [Gloster Meteors] have a lower wing loading than the Me 262, and thus better turning qualities. They should be able to out-maneuver the Me 262.

The Allies were also worried about the Messerschmitt Me 163 rocket-powered fighter, which was little more than a piloted projectile with plenty of thrust. The Hell Hawks, however, rarely saw an Me 163, which were fewer in number and intended for attacks on bomber formations.

One American who faced the jet threat was Capt. Valmore J. "Val" Beaudrault of the Hell Hawks' 386th Fighter Squadron. Beaudrault had made a long journey to the war and to the showdown with German jets. He was another of the Hell Hawks who walked away from his share of wrecked Jugs. While the 365th group was still forming stateside, he apparently crashed a P-47D at Langley Field and escaped unharmed. After the group began flying combat from the Continent, Beaudrault was hit by flak on July 10, 1944, bellied in, and survived with just a cut. On at least one additional occasion, he stepped out of a crashed, mangled Thunderbolt and resumed his war.

There may have been a war going on, but the United States Army never forgot about its property. After he'd survived the July 10 crack-up, Beaudrault realized he didn't know where his sidearm was. The brass demanded that he account for one "pistol, automatic, caliber .45, model M1911A," valued to the U.S. taxpayer at $26.97, plus one "holster, shoulder," which even the government said was of "unknown value." Beaudrault took such matters seriously and was disturbed at having to prepare a statement saying, "I crash landed the plane and [was] knocked unconscious. Medical aid men picked me up and transported me to the hospital. I have no knowledge as to what happened to the pistol carried on my person. I questioned the medical men at the hospital and it proved fruitless." Fifteen days after the crash, the army determined that the handgun "was lost in combat as a result of enemy action not involving negligence or culpability." The 4th Convalescent Hospital handed Beaudrault this message absolving him, along with a Purple Heart.

Although born in Gardner, Massachusetts, Beaudrault hailed from Weare, New Hampshire, belonged to the Congregational church there, and talked about flying before he ever drove a car. He kept his sense of humor under wraps, and he often seemed a little too intent, too earnest. He graduated from Milford High School in Weare only six months before the Japanese attack on Pearl Harbor.

On October 2, 1944, when he was just twenty-one years old, Beaudrault was flying a mission led by Capt. George W. Porter. It was the sixty-fourth of Beaudrault's eighty-three missions, during which he would log 217 combat hours. Near Düsseldorf, Germany, Beaudrault spotted a "bogie," an unidentified aircraft. He and Porter eyeballed a course to intercept the apparent foe and turned their Thunderbolts to engage. Afterward, the October 1944 *Yank* magazine would call Beaudrault "one of those large, rugged citizens the sports writers like to describe as 'indestructible.'" Beaudrault told friends he was "simply a fighter pilot," but as superbly trained as the typical American fighter pilot was, nothing in Beaudrault's training had prepared him to fly a prop-driven Jug against a swept-wing jet. In *The History of the Hell Hawks*, crew chief and author Charles R. Johnson described Beaudrault's jet encounter:

"After the unidentified aircraft passed in front of him, the captain bore down on its tail, at which time the [German] pilot made a sharp 360-degree turn. Beaudrault had no trouble turning inside of him with his P-47D28. During these maneuvers, Capt. Beaudrault still failed to definitely identify the aircraft, so he held his fire. The plane then rolled over out of the turn and applied full throttle and started to pull away even though the P-47's throttle was to the firewall."

Beaudrault took pictures of the plane, saw German insignia on the wing, and satisfied himself that it was an Me 262. Nearby, 1st Lt. William F. Peters engaged a second 262 but was soon left behind as the jet outdistanced him in a climb.

Beaudrault's initial adversary, however, was unable to take advantage of his one-hundred-mile-per-hour speed advantage over the Thunderbolt. The Me 262 emitted white puffs of smoke from its exhausts. Its engines stopped. In midair, far from any runway, the German jet apparently had run out of fuel.

Beaudrault pounced on the Me 262 in a three-hundred-mile-per-hour dive. He prepared to fire his Thunderbolt's eight .50-caliber machine guns. Before he could squeeze the trigger, however, the 262 veered abruptly, its wing struck the ground, and the German jet disappeared in a tremendous explosion. Johnson wrote that "there was nothing left but fire and shiny pieces of metal scattered over three acres."

Beaudrault was awarded the Silver Star for downing the Me 262. According to the citation that accompanied the award, Beaudrault "exhibited calm presence of mind and conspicuous aerial proficiency in an attack against a formation of hostile planes. . . . Since by their design the attacking aircraft did not prove to be any currently recognized type of German plane, Beaudrault withheld his fire and, by employing extreme tenacity and flying skill, he was able to close within short range. After taking several photographs, he forced a high speed jet-propelled aircraft to crash to the earth." In addition to downing the jet, Beaudrault "obtained recognition data vital to the prosecution of the Allied war effort," the citation said.

Beaudrault, who was also credited with shooting down a prop-driven Messerschmitt Bf 109 on June 25, 1944, was publicly recognized as the first Ninth Air

Force pilot to destroy an Me 262. The Air Force recognizes maneuvering an adversary into the ground as equivalent to downing him with gunfire, but for reasons unknown, the destruction of the German jet does not appear today on the service's official aerial victory list. (A month later on December 5, 1944, Beaudrault claimed a Heinkel He 111K twin-engined bomber; Headquarters IX Tactical Air Command found "insufficient evidence to confirm destruction" and gave him credit for an enemy aircraft damaged.)

The shootdown of the German jet made it into the *Stars & Stripes* newspaper and brought Beaudrault a handwritten letter from Capt. (Dr.) George B. Hood, the physician who had treated him after the Hell Hawk's earlier shootdown (though there is no indication Hood lifted Beaudrault's .45). "I was the first one to reach you that July 10 and with Maj. Brown and Maj. Lyman [both medical officers], got you on your way to a hospital. You don't remember much of what happened out there that day, probably because of shock and morphine, but your first question was whether you were behind the lines and your second whether you would fly again. The way your eye looked then I wasn't so sure, but I see by the papers that you have your wish and are getting a chance to pin their ears back. You did a swell job of getting that P-47 down that day. Apparently, you are doing all right. Now, we here [at the military hospital] wish you continued successes."

☆

The Hell Hawks never got a shot at the German officer who introduced the Messerschmitt Me 262 to air combat, but other Americans did. On November 8, 1944, two pilots shared credit for shooting down and killing Major Walter Nowotny. The victors were Capt. Ernest "Feeb" Fiebelkorn of the 20th Fighter Group, and 1st Lt. Edward "Buddy" Haydon of the 357th Fighter Group. Still coping with the Me 262's handling difficulties, the Germans withdrew Kommando Nowotny to revise combat tactics and conduct more extensive jet training.

In January 1945, the Germans formed Jagdgeschwader 7, or JG 7 (roughly, their 7th Fighter Wing) as a pure jet fighter unit to fill in behind Kommando Nowotny. It took weeks for JG 7 to become operational. In the meantime, a bomber unit, I Gruppe, Kampfgeschwader 54, or KG 54, was equipped with the Me 262 for use in a ground-attack and fighter role. The unit met with little success: it lost twelve aircraft in combat in a couple of weeks and had little impact on the Allies.

"By the time the German jets went into production, it was too late, and nothing was going to change the outcome of the war," said British aviation historian

Jon Lake. Messerschmitt Me 262s shot down about a hundred Allied aircraft by war's end—not enough to make a difference.

Some members of the Hell Hawks would distinguish themselves as jet pilots after the war, but none ever sat in a jet cockpit while the fighting was going on. The Allies had only two practical jets. Britain's Gloster Meteor was powered by centrifugal-flow turbojet engines (deemed more reliable than the axial-flow engines of the Me 262) and joined the Royal Air Force in 1944. The first practical U.S. jet fighter, the P-80 Shooting Star, reached Europe by May 1945, but saw no combat.

☆

The Hell Hawks had been grappling occasionally with the German jets for months when the 388th Squadron spotted an Me 262 strafing American troops near Düren on February 22, 1945. The pilots had responded to a call from a ground controller: "Any P-47s in the air south of Aachen, we need some help!" Two Red Flight Thunderbolts were aggressively but vainly pursuing the Me 262 as it headed back into Germany. White Flight leader, 1st Lt. Oliven T. Cowan in *Touch Me Not*, angled to intercept, but the German pilot sighted the pursuit and fled east at high speed, just above the tree tops.

Cowan and his wingman rolled in on the jet from eleven thousand feet. "I pushed everything forward," wrote Cowan. His howling Pratt & Whitney R-2800 using water injection soon had him indicating 530 miles per hour in the dive.

The jet's pilot apparently never saw Cowan, coming in with the sun at his back. Cowan shallowed his dive, lined up the target, and fired. At his first burst, the 262 disappeared beneath Cowan's nose, just three hundred feet off the deck. The pilot from Lowell, North Carolina, instantly eased his stick forward for another shot. As the jet popped into view above the Thunderbolt's cowling, Cowan saw the Messerschmitt slam into the ground.

A puff of black smoke—no flame—and scattered bits and pieces of wreckage were all that remained of the Messerschmitt. Cowan had used altitude and the Thunderbolt's superb diving ability to catch the speedy enemy. His downing of the jet was the 175th aerial victory for the Hell Hawks, and it came exactly a year after the group had flown its first combat mission in the European Theater. Flying jet or prop, the Luftwaffe had yet to find a way to best consistently a Thunderbolt in the hands of a Hell Hawk.

Chapter Seventeen

The Price of Victory

HE OUTCOME OF THE WAR had to be obvious by March 1945, yet the Hell Hawks could see no end to it, even as a few finished their tours of duty and rotated home—something their Luftwaffe adversaries would never do. Many years later, no one in the 365th Fighter Group could remember that anybody suffered from "last-man syndrome." Somebody was going to be the last man to die in this war, but if anybody thought about it, no one dwelled on it. Each day brought heavy fighting. The down-low, up-close, and very personal war between the P-47 Thunderbolt and German ground forces continued.

The conflict was now entering a starker, more brutal final phase. As the Third Reich began to collapse, the niceties of the Geneva Convention and the rules of warfare began to crumble with it. In March and April 1945, an American downed over German territory had at least as much chance of being murdered as of being taken prisoner. Those who already were captives faced upheaval, forced marches, and sometimes violence and even death.

No Hell Hawk wanted to be hit by enemy gunfire, but it happened. When it did, it was loud. It was violent. Gunfire ripped into 1st Lt. Grant G. Stout's P-47D Thunderbolt high over Dortmund, Germany, near midday on March 19, 1945, and his Thunderbolt trembled and shook. Other pilots saw the P-47 shedding pieces. Grant Stout's final journey had begun.

Stout's story is the saga of a citizen-soldier—in his sister's words, "a young farm boy who wanted to fly and who ended up doing exactly what he wanted to do"—and of a big, burly warplane that was tough as a tank and built in greater numbers than any other fighter in the United States.

Grant Stout was born in Pike, New York, in 1922. His parents owned a 181-acre dairy farm that also produced potatoes and grain. Following high school graduation in 1941, he worked in a munitions plant, where he earned money for private flying lessons. "Our mother was not aware of this until he flew over the farm and waved to her," Stout's sister recalled. "It was a thrill for both of them, although of some concern to our mother."

Stout cut a strapping, athletic figure. A member of Army Air Forces flying class 43-J (along with 1st Lt. Donald E. Kark, who would later be close by over Dortmund in the final minutes of Stout's life), Stout was one of thousands of AAF aviation cadets who underwent primary training in the Stearman PT-17, basic training in the Vultee BT-13 "Vibrator," and advanced training in the North American AT-6 Texan. After seven hours of instruction, he made his first solo flight in the PT-17 at Avon Park, Florida, on May 15, 1943. "I was the second in our group of 200 men to solo," he wrote home. In one of several pessimistic comments that today seem prescient, he wrote of how eagerly he wanted to succeed as a pilot, but, "There will be a lot of hard work and . . . the 'law of averages' is against me."

While in basic flight training at Gunter Field, Alabama, Stout wrote home with unconcealed enthusiasm about a new fighter he'd seen. "Last Saturday afternoon we had a P-47 Thunderbolt show," he wrote. "They brought four of them over from a nearby field and they showed off to us, doing loops and other acrobatics in a very tight formation. Our instructors were all sore because the big shots made us take time off to watch them."

The Hell Hawks uniformly considered their P-47 Thunderbolt to be the war's greatest fighter. By March 1945, the overall contribution of that warplane was better understood. Stout's perspective on the fighter is instructive, even if his account does repeat some characteristics already voiced by others. Stout's biggest thrill, simply, was becoming a Thunderbolt pilot. The aircraft evoked fierce loyalty from those who flew it, but that sentiment wasn't felt by Stout immediately.

From Spence Field, Moultrie, Georgia, still in training, Stout wrote home on October 22, 1943, that he had now accumulated six hours in the P-40F Warhawk. On November 3 he sent a telegram to his parents with the happy news that he'd pinned on pilot wings and second lieutenant's bars. Soon afterward, at Richmond, Virginia—finally—he was introduced to the P-47 Thunderbolt. He wrote home: "Imagine landing at 130 miles per hour!" A few days later, he wrote: "This Thunderbolt is more like a rocket ship than an airplane. You have no idea how powerful those eighteen cylinders are until you get hold of the throttle, and then she really goes places."

Stout's reaction was much like that of squadron mate 2nd Lt. Paul L. Van Cleef, who wrote:

> Our first impression of the P-47 was—'Wow!!!' That's BIG! Does it fly? It had a massive body, a 2,300 hp engine with 18 cylinders, and a huge 4-blade propeller. There were four .50-caliber guns on each wing. It weighed 13,900 pound empty and carried 370 gallons of fuel internally plus 150 gallons main [center] line or 108 gallon wing tanks. At normal cruise speed it used 100 gallons per hour—or about three hours of flying time. It could climb rapidly at full bore to a scheduled altitude of 42,000 feet. The highest I ever got was 41,000 feet when I was on a solo flight and decided to see how high I could go!
>
> It had very strong armor behind the pilot with good protection, and the thick wings would take a beating without giving out. The cockpit was amply sized and comfortable. It was easy to fly, and we all took to it immediately. The landing gears were wide apart, so it was stable and easy to land. We had been well-briefed on its size and abilities, but still the first impression was—that's a BIG airplane!

Similarly impressed was Stout's wingman on March 19, Allen Mundt. During Mundt's initial training in the P-47, his instructor took him down to the boneyard to look over the sad wrecks of a dozen or more Thunderbolts. "That pilot was killed," he told Mundt, pointing out a shattered hulk. "But in this one, this one, and that one," said his instructor, "the pilot walked away." Mundt remembered the lesson: "All the survivors locked their shoulder harnesses before impact." Mundt, Stout, and their fellow pilots knew that in combat or a crash landing, the Jug was the bird you wanted to be flying.

P-51 Mustang pilots on high-altitude escort missions may have found moments to savor the joy of flying that had prompted most to join the air force. But for Grant Stout and other pilots in the 365th Fighter Group, the Hell Hawks, the job meant living in infantry-like conditions at snow-covered, mud airstrips on the Continent (soggy Aachen was a typical example) and flying low-level strafing and bombing runs. "Not clean, not comfortable, and certainly not glamorous," said another 365th pilot, "but necessary. . . ." In Stout's outfit, the 387th, one P-47 returned to its base with body parts from a German soldier embedded in its engine cowling. Another landed safely, but riddled with 138 holes from bullets and shrapnel.

In France shortly after D-Day, Stout, in his P-47 with one working machine gun, had chased a Wehrmacht soldier down a Norman lane, "the bullets clipping the wall about two feet above the German's head as he ran." When his fighter group came ashore after the Normandy invasion, Stout was observed to retain his usual sense of humor—he had a pet duck named Zeke—but he also spoke, occasionally, as if something bad lay ahead.

On an August 8, 1944, mission led by Lt. Col. Donald Hillman, the Hell Hawks had bombed ammunition bunkers at Pré-en-Pail, France. Hillman then led the men on a strafing attack in the area and destroyed four trucks in two attacks near Putanges. During the attack on the trucks, Stout's Thunderbolt was struck by flak and Stout himself was hit. He was able to fly his plane back to Fontenay-sur-Mer, where he landed. He got the P-47 stopped without working brakes, and limped out of the fighter with a serious laceration on his foot. Because of the wound, Stout was briefly assigned a half-track and a driver to enable him to act as a forward ground observer, but he eventually returned to flying. By March 1945, Stout had seen every kind of combat action the Hell Hawks had encountered, including a run-in with the Me 262, a jet fighter the young pilot openly admired.

☆

Now it was March 19, 1945. "The day Grant was shot down was bright and sunny," 1st Lt. Allen Mundt later wrote. "It was a morning mission for the purpose of attacking ground transport of all sorts. There were a lot of trains out that day. They proved very vulnerable up to the time Grant and I saw this last one just before we regrouped to go home. He didn't know until it was too late that the train was heavily armed with flak guns. I was far enough behind on the initial run to be able to pull up, but Grant's plane flew right through a cloud of flak. He pulled up then, too, and seemed to have good control for a minute, but then the ship rolled over and went down. I saw his chute open a split second after the ship crashed."

Stout's mission leader, Arlo Henry, wrote later that his parachute "was seen to open and land safely." First Lt. Donald E. Kark saw Stout's chute on the ground a few minutes later. He remembers thinking that Stout was now a prisoner of war. In fact, Stout was in the final minutes of his life, a situation he almost seemed to have foreseen.

A few days earlier, Stout had allowed a buddy to take a snapshot of him standing in front of a P-47, "map in hand, poop in pocket, and raring to go," as he wrote to his sister, Lyla. "The boys gave me that old 'song' about having your picture taken before a mission," wrote Stout, alluding to the old pilots' tale that posing for a photo was inviting bad luck. "I needed to go out and explode that superstition."

Luck had turned against Stout, but the Hell Hawks were at least certain that he was on the ground and alive. Even if captured, their friend would be liberated within months, if not mere weeks.

The Hell Hawks were wrong. Two years passed before word came of Stout's fate. In 1947, the War Department informed his family that the pilot's remains had been recovered from an isolated grave near Dortmund. Stout had been reburied, the Pentagon reported, at the Neuville-en-Condroz U.S. military cemetery, near Liège, Belgium. In 1949 the family had his body returned to his hometown of Pike. His mother was still not convinced the remains were indeed those of her son.

Someone told members of the family that Stout had been mortally injured in the bailout. The family didn't believe that could have happened. And if a pilot bailed out successfully and was captured, as they believed Stout had been, wasn't he supposed to be accorded humane treatment as a prisoner of war? His mother, his sister, and others in the family all wondered: What happened to Grant Stout?

Even while reeling under bombing and strafing attacks, most Germans treated downed Allied pilots with respect and humanity. Captured aircrew simply became prisoners of war and lived under spartan but tolerable conditions until the end of hostilities. On the very rare occasions when Germans violated the law of war by killing a downed pilot, the perpetrators were usually civilians rather than uniformed members of the Wehrmacht or Luftwaffe.

Stout's case was different. Even long after V-E Day, the Stout family never understood how seriously conditions had deteriorated inside Germany in the final weeks of history's most brutal conflict. In the 1990s, a Canadian doctor, Robert Reid of London, Ontario, was researching a related topic when he learned about one of hundreds of low-level war crimes trials held by U.S. authorities after the war. Reid uncovered documents from a U.S. war crimes tribunal held in Dachau in July 1947. An official summary of that trial says that 1st Sgt. Georg Mayer, commander of the German antiaircraft battery at Brackel (a suburb of Dortmund), paraded Stout in front of townspeople and "incited the crowd to beat and kill the flier." According to the summary, three other Germans, described as "miners" with "unknown" military status, went along with Mayer and used clubs, stones, and a shovel to brutally attack the P-47 pilot. The summary says Mayer finished off Stout with a pistol. All four Germans were convicted; Mayer was sentenced to life imprisonment for the killing and is thought to have died while imprisoned by U.S. occupation forces.

Reid contacted the Stout family with his discovery. "We learned the truth only in 1997," said Stout's sister, Lyla K. Stout, of Rochester, New York

But additional research into the events surrounding Stout's death show the U.S. Army's official version may be incomplete or incorrect. Reid, who visited Dortmund and has worked in collaboration with a German researcher, believes the war crimes panel convicted the wrong culprits. It was unusual for a German soldier, acting on his own, to execute a downed airman. Reid and the German researcher concluded that a mob of enraged civilians—not Mayer or his three accomplices—killed Stout, beating him to death with a shovel.

But if Mayer wasn't involved, what incited these other townspeople to murder a surrendering pilot? While all Americans who participated in the mission say Stout was strafing a train, the two researchers say American fighters strafed civilians that day, including a funeral procession for a small child. No proof is forthcoming after sixty-two years, and the proposition is questionable at best.

No matter what the Thunderbolts were firing at, no matter how great the suffering of people on the ground, international law requires captors to protect a downed airman who is unarmed and has surrendered. On that day, on the ground in Nazi Germany, the laws of war and society utterly failed Stout, who in death joined the countless victims of Hitler's Reich.

There may never be a wholly satisfactory explanation of what happened to Stout after he landed near Dortmund. Along with Army soldier Theodore Hunt, Stout is one of only two residents of Pike, New York, to have lost his life in World War II. Today, the Hunt-Stout Post of the American Legion in Castile, New York, near Pike, honors the service of these two young men.

☆

As Stout's tragic story unfolded on March 19, the Hell Hawks' war ground on without him. The men had a job to do. The good weather on that March day enabled the group to put twenty-two armed reconnaissance missions into the air. Each eight-plane mission carried a full load of five-hundred-pound bombs. As usual, the pilots' rules of engagement were to pounce on anything that moved.

Captain Archie F. Maltbie led eight P-47s from the 388th on one of those missions, bombing a marshalling yard near Marienheide, wrecking fifteen cars and setting six buildings afire. Northeast of Bensberg the pilots jumped a truck convoy and strafed one of the vehicles into a flaming pile of junk. However, 2nd Lt. William S. Lukas carried his run too low and slammed into a hill coming off the target; he died instantly. The pilots viewed the loss of Stout and Lukas with regret, but the war moved on, and there wasn't a damn thing they could do about their loss except get back in the air and go at the Germans again. The IX Tactical Air Command flew 807 sorties on March 19, more than on any other day of its operations against the Wehrmacht.

Just after 7:00 a.m. on March 21, Capt. William E. "Curly" Rodgers led fifteen planes off from Aachen, heading for the railroad bridge at Marsberg. To cut the rail traffic across this vital link, Rodgers' men dove to put all thirty of their bombs onto the span. Explosions rocked the bridge and pockmarked the southwest end and rail bed with craters, but the smoking structure still stood. With the tracks cut, the 386th men strafed the stalled trains in the town, destroying or damaging two locomotives, then moving down the tracks to wreck another half-dozen locomotives. Next the Hell Hawks attacked a truck convoy near Arnsberg, northeast of Aachen, destroying five transports and an armored vehicle and killing two horses pulling a trailer. As Wehrmacht soldiers jumped from the trucks, the pilots caught more than fifty in a concentrated crossfire of .50-caliber bullets, leaving dozens sprawled across the road by their burning vehicles.

Rodgers led his men on to damage another three locomotives before returning to Aachen. Waiting at the end of the soggy runway was his crew chief, Staff Sgt. Guy

Bauman. The twenty-four-year-old from Urbana, Illinois, had been with Rodgers since the beginning. He'd once kept Rodgers' olive drab Thunderbolt, *Pizzed Off*, in the air for a string of 105 consecutive missions before another pilot lost it to ground fire. The emotional bond between crew chief and pilot was genuine: "When you're waiting there at that runway," Bauman said, "it was kind of nerve wracking. You worried about that pilot all the time. They were just like a brother to us." The crew chiefs knew their aircraft's appearance and their pilot's place in the returning formation well enough to register the loss instantly if "you see that one plane is missing."

This time Rodgers came back, only one plane of the squadron slightly damaged. His relentless determination to attack the bridge, trains, and road traffic earned him a Distinguished Flying Cross. It took eight missions to the Marsberg bridge that day for the Hell Hawks to finally topple the southwestern span into the river. Returning from one strike, 1st Lt. Melvin W. Miller of the 386th completed his one-hundredth combat mission. In the past, such a milestone would have resulted in rotation home, but a new Ninth Air Force policy balancing frontline pilot needs against the supposedly lessened risk of combat flying against a weakened Germany kept the Texan from San Angelo in the cockpit.

☆

In late March 1945, as the Allied armies prepared for a breakout from the Remagen bridgehead and readied assault crossings of the Rhine to the south and north, the 365th was assigned strikes well behind the front lines to prevent German reinforcements from moving up. On the eighteenth of twenty-one missions flown by the Hell Hawks on March 22, the 386th arrived over Inger to attack a panzer concentration. The pilots found no tanks, but plenty of flak from a pair each of 40mm and 88mm guns. The Thunderbolts dive-bombed their tormentors, silencing the battery with the blast from sixteen general-purpose bombs. Melvin Miller was there, on his 102nd mission; a bullet slashed through his canopy and damaged the goggles sitting atop his flying helmet. He landed back at Aachen unhurt, pointing at the bullet hole and joking that he was living on borrowed time.

The 22nd of March also saw the Hell Hawks destroy 294 rail cars, one locomotive, thirty-eight trucks, eight armored vehicles, twelve buildings or factories, and one horse-drawn cart, and they damaged a nearly equal number of targets. Patton's forces crossed the Rhine that night just south of Mainz, and Montgomery's armies pushed across in the north the following day.

March 23 saw the Hell Hawks intensify their assaults on the Wehrmacht's transportation web. Major Bob Brooking led one of the fourteen missions flown that day, dropping 260-pound fragmentation bombs on troops spotted in the woods at Hachenburg, and unloading five-hundred-pounders on airfield installations. During the airfield attack, Brooking dove on a target, released his bombs, and broke hard left to avoid the intense flak. "I hit [the blast from] my own bomb in the turn; it really messed up my left aileron," said Brooking. "I had quite a time trying to control the roll," to say nothing of the trouble he had recovering from the dive. The 386th Squadron's commander struggled to make it back to Aachen in a P-47 that could only turn in one direction. With careful planning and a long, straight-in approach to Y-46, Brooking managed to get his Thunderbolt—and himself—back on the ground in one piece.

On the eleventh strike mission of the day, Brooking's 386th wasn't so lucky. Over the town of Much, 1st Lt. Robert C. Thoman spotted through the haze a concentration of trucks, armored vehicles, and light tanks heading east. "The pilots smelled a flak trap," wrote Charles Johnson, but they winged over into their attack runs anyway. Instantly the German gunners opened up on the string of Thunderbolts, hitting 1st Lt. John H. Wallace Jr., whose diving plane tumbled out of control.

Wallace had a few days earlier struck a German command post and defensive position holding up an American attack. His napalm bombs had obliterated the target in a sea of flame, burning the vehicles parked nearby and incinerating the defenders. Wallace won the Distinguished Flying Cross for that mission, and wryly told his crew chief before takeoff on the 23rd that he was out to add an oak leaf cluster (a second DFC), even if he had to get it posthumously.

Struggling in the dive, Wallace wrenched the stick back. Pulling his hurtling P-47 out of its plunge, he nearly made it, but his right wingtip struck a slight rise, and the massive Jug cartwheeled. The napalm load ripped free and ignited, and his fellow fliers prayed the Massachusetts native had died before the flames reached their friend.

The German gunners caught a second P-47 in their web of cannon shells. Second Lieutenant Matthew P. Smiles, of Detroit, Michigan, got his damaged Jug away from Much and stayed airborne until he reached friendly territory near Erkelenz, Germany. There Smiles bailed out rather than risk a forced landing. Leaping from the cockpit, he was swept back by the slipstream and slammed into the vertical stabilizer. Somehow he reached and pulled his parachute D-ring; GIs on the ground hustled him to a field hospital, but Smiles died enroute. Matthew Smiles and John Wallace—roommates—died the same day.

☆

March 25 saw the 386th roving down the east bank of the Rhine, searching for motor or rail traffic opposing the breakout from the Remagen bridgehead. Major Bob Brooking's two flights of four Jugs each found trucks and armored vehicles near Weyerbusch. Dive-bombing and strafing runs left tanks, trucks, and gun positions in flames, but one of the Thunderbolts was raked by the accurate Wehrmacht gunners defending the area. "Tex" Miller from San Angelo, flying his 105th combat mission, had run out of borrowed time. No one saw his P-47 go down.

The 387th Squadron visited that same area on the very next mission. One of the pilots was 1st Lt. Samuel B. Lutz, flying his fifty-third mission. Lutz was Red Three in an eight-plane squadron, six of the Thunderbolts carrying bombs and two, including Lutz, carrying two seventy-five-gallon napalm bombs, one under each wing.

The squadron cruised south from Cologne along the Rhine, scrutinizing the east bank for any activity. Near Weyerbusch east of Bonn, Lutz spotted a truck racing north, intent on making it into some concealing woods, so he asked for permission to leave the formation for a strafing pass. Permission duly given by Capt. Neal E. Worley, he smoothly nudged the stick to the right, fed in coordinating rudder, executed a beautiful wing-over, and dove on his target.

"As usual, I was going too fast and too low, and the instrument panel blacked out as I pulled from my dive. I heard one of the pilots say, 'My God, look at all those tanks down there!'"

Lutz and the squadron made another run on the panzers: "On my second pass I hit a German tank with my napalm bombs, blocking the single road through the forest so no one could escape." Seven tanks were trapped and destroyed as the five-hundred-pounders tore into their hideout.

En route to the target, 2nd Lt. Morris H. Miller Jr. went missing. Lutz wrote later, "With all the activity in the area, we lost five P-47 aircraft that day. . . Two were from our group. Both pilots were named Miller (Melvin W. and Morris H.), both were over six feet tall, and both were from Texas."

Lutz and the other 387th pilots recalled Morris Miller's habit of turning with a vengeance on any flak position that opened on him. Such "balls-out" aggressiveness on this mission might have cost him his life, but no one knows for sure how he died.

The two Millers went down a few miles from each other. It took five years for Morris Miller's father, after much correspondence with army and local German authorities, to discover his son's remains. Even with a map drawn by Capt. Herb Prevost, "Tex" Miller's leader that day, the crash sites were difficult to track down. Mix-ups over the correct identity of the two missing pilots with identical surnames took months to resolve. Finally, the German mayor of Ansbach wrote to Miller's father that a P-47 had crashed in marshy terrain near Mehren, Germany. The wreckage was buried deeply upon impact. The mayor wrote that only in early 1950 did American search teams definitively link the plane's engine and machine guns to Morris Miller's aircraft. His body had been buried nearby, and local residents helped the authorities locate the grave site. Morris H. Miller Jr. now rests in Galveston Memorial Cemetery, near his boyhood home.

☆

To the Hell Hawks in March 1945, the Allies' triumph seemed tantalizingly close. These men would never see it:

2nd Lt. Marvin Gregg	Killed in Action	March 9, 1945
1st Lt. Grant G. Stout	Killed in Action	March 19, 1945
2nd Lt. William S. Lukas	Killed in Action	March 19, 1945
1st Lt. John H. Wallace Jr.	Killed in Action	March 23, 1945
2nd Lt. Matthew P. Smiles	Killed in Action	March 23, 1945
1st Lt. Melvin W. Miller	Killed in Action	March 25, 1945
2nd Lt. Morris H. Miller Jr.	Killed in Action	March 25, 1945

Chapter Eighteen

The New Boys

THE NOOSE WAS CLOSING on the Wehrmacht in the West. A quarter of a million German army troops and another one hundred thousand men of the Luftwaffe's flak regiments were caught in the industrialized Ruhr Valley, the heart of the German war industry. The American First and Ninth armies were rolling forward to complete a vast encirclement of German forces in the Ruhr, and the Hell Hawks were in the air to help blast the opposition out of the way.

On one of the final missions of March 1945, eight planes of the 387th Squadron roared aloft from Aachen to support Maj. Gen. Maurice Rose's 3rd Armored Division. The tankers were engaged in a vicious fight with fanatical cadets, instructors, and armor specialists defending the panzer training school at Paderborn, Germany. Called out by their controller and armed with napalm and fragmentation bombs, the Hell Hawks attacked an enemy column in the town of Hovelhof. Their bombs turned more than a dozen trucks into flaming hulks and set the town afire. The Thunderbolts returned to strafe the remaining vehicles.

"Although we were giving the Germans hell, they were not sitting still—they were giving as much as they were receiving," wrote 2nd Lt. Ed Lopez, flying his silver P-47D, "We were getting shot up pretty bad. On one of my runs I got a direct hit on the canopy." The bullet penetrated his bubble-top, hurled shards of Plexiglas into

Lopez' eyes, creased his skull, and then exited the cockpit opposite. "Although it was not a deep wound, it caused me to bleed excessively. I had blood streaming all over my face, but I had spotted where the guns were that got me."

Lopez wasn't beaten. He grimly stayed focused on the half-track-mounted Flakvierling 38 as he circled for another run. "Wiping my eyes clear of blood so I could see my target clearly, I came around and got them in my gun sight." He did not miss. "I obliterated him," said Lopez; he also destroyed two other guns that day. Lopez made it back to Aachen, where he was stitched up before receiving the Purple Heart. For his "skill, courage, and leadership," the Los Angeles native received the Distinguished Flying Cross.

☆

Lopez was one of dozens of Hell Hawks who joined the group as replacements, well after the outfit crossed to France. The charter members of the 365th were present at the group's organization in Richmond, or were assigned stateside before the Atlantic crossing on the Queen Elizabeth. These were the "old boys," second lieutenants in 1943, who by early 1945, through attrition or recognition, had risen to become flight leaders, operations officers, even squadron commanders.

Major George R. "Bob" Brooking was one of those replacements, joining the Hell Hawks in September of 1944. He had a lot of stick time but no real combat experience when he arrived in France; his reception by an unimpressed old guard was distinctly chilly. They were further irritated by Brooking's promotion to major, word of which caught up with him just after he reported in. Gold oak leaves or no, this new boy would have to demonstrate his stuff. The new major promptly got himself shot down on his first combat mission, a feat only partially expunged by his single-handed liberation of Esch, Luxembourg. But within two months Brooking was the 386th Squadron commander. Cornell's death on a French hillside was the official cause, but Bob Brooking's flying and leadership abilities would have elevated him eventually. Given their losses over the next few months, the group was fortunate to have many such leaders.

Another replacement in the fall of 1944 was 2nd Lt. Isaac G. "Gale" Phillips, who joined the 387th Squadron in November and racked up fifty-two combat missions. The new man was assigned to Capt. Julius "Jug" Almond's flight and introduced to the real world of ground attack. On one early mission, Phillips was ordered to make a low pass over a wooded area suspected of harboring a battery of formidable 88mm flak guns. He hurtled down, the guns opened up, and Phillips found himself bracketed by angry bursts of black smoke. He was six feet, six inches in height, and his helmet grazed the inner surface of the canopy when he flew, so he felt the concussion rattling his plane with each burst. "I hit the water injection and pulled out of there," said Phillips, but not before his P-47 was riddled with twenty-seven jagged shrapnel holes. One of the flight's old boys came up on the radio: "Hey, Phillips, those must have been instructors shooting at you!"

Second Lieutenant Dick R. Schlegel took a circuitous route to the Hell Hawks. Born in Bloomfield, Iowa, he was working in Washington, D.C. when the news of Pearl Harbor being bombed interrupted a movie he was watching at the Capitol Theater. The first recruiting office he encountered walking down G Street was for the U.S. Army Air Forces, so he signed up there. Assigned to P-47s at Richmond after pilot training in April 1944, he took a teaching slot at Bradley Field, Connecticut, partly at his wife's request. He did so well in the Thunderbolt that his commander kept him on for more than six months. The twenty-three-year-old finally requested combat duty and arrived at Aachen and joined the 387th in early March, 1945.

He reported in to the deputy operations officer, Capt. Paul Van Cleef, late at night. Van Cleef, an original Hell Hawk, looked over his flight records. "Hell, you've got more time in the -47 than the CO has! How are you at leading a flight?" Schlegel modestly admitted he'd had a lot of experience leading students at Bradley; he hoped he would be able to get right into the air, flying formation, if possible. But Van Cleef dismissed him with orders to get a few familiarization missions in the area first. The conversation was over.

Van Cleef mentioned to Arlo Henry, the 387th operations officer, that "we got our new replacement in."

"What do you think of him, Paul?"

"Well, he thinks he's a pretty hot type. Thinks he can lead a formation in combat." Word quickly spread that this new boy was pretty sure of himself.

Schlegel was soon flying combat, but he noticed that many of the outfit's old boys treated him with suspicion or outright distrust in the couple of months of combat flying left. He couldn't figure out why. It was years later at a Hell Hawks reunion that Schlegel finally heard the story from Van Cleef of why he'd been given the cold shoulder. "You mean you don't know?" asked the veteran pilot in surprise. Van Cleef considered the mix-up a joke, but Schlegel, who had questioned himself for years over his reception, was livid when he found out.

☆

Not every replacement had the bulging logbook that Brooking or Schlegel had when they reported to the 365th. The original pilots in the group had received extensive gunnery training stateside, and several picked up time at the Royal Air Force dive-bombing school in England as the Hell Hawks switched from escort to attack flying. Several months of training before D-Day had honed the unit to a sharp fighting edge. The new boys arrived with perhaps a hundred hours in the P-47 and uneven exposure to formation and instrument flying, and realistic combat tactics. Most had been taught by or flown with returning combat veterans, but European weather and determined flak gunners were a world away from stateside training. Second Lieutenant Joseph G. Preston of the 386th remembered arriving at A-7 in Normandy with about ninety hours in the Thunderbolt; the old boys crossed the Channel with 240 hours under their belts. His element leader briefed him before his first familiarization, or "fam" flight. Preston recalled the dialogue: "'OK, you'll take off on my wing,' he told me. 'I'll what?' I answered. He wanted a formation takeoff, wingtip to wingtip. I had to admit I'd never done one." His leader just shook his head in amazement.

Captain Jimmy Wells was the operations officer of the 386th as replacements arrived in the winter of 1944-45. The new boys had adequate training but needed someone to show them the ropes. "We'd take the new pilots out and fly with them and dogfight and try to show them some German examples, and we'd get 'em prepared to be combat pilots and show them how to dive-bomb. . . . Then during a mission you'd see how they acted, how they flew. Some of them were kind of timid, others were very aggressive, and it was pretty easy to judge which one was a good pilot."

Wells knew there was a fine line between aggressiveness and foolhardiness, but admitted, "I was not one that was cautious—I was one that was gung-ho. I used to take all my pilots out and dogfight 'em and see how they did. If I had one that I couldn't whip, that would've been the day." Asked on the sixty-second anniversary of D-Day if he got whipped very often, Wells' reflexes were still sharp: "No, it didn't happen at all."

There was no manual for how to be a successful combat pilot in the 365th Fighter Group, but one Hell Hawk took a stab at passing on hard-earned experience that could save a new pilot's life. Before moving up as Stecker's deputy at Group in October 1944, the 386th commander, Maj. William D. Ritchie, wrote a treatise called "Hints on Combat Flying in the ETO [European Theater of Operations]." A few paraphrased samples of Ritchie's pithy advice follow:

- A change in altitude is the best [flak] evasion, since gunners must re-fuse their shells, which not only takes time but gives the maximum possibility of error.
- Attacking airfields: *Never* make a second pass, whether any or all targets are destroyed on the first pass.
- Strafing: Give a short, accurate burst and break violently up either to the left or right. Climb back as high as possible while coming in position to make a pass at another vehicle.
- Attacking trains: Begin the pass around five thousand feet in a thirty-degree dive, with the flight leader aiming at the locomotive and the other three in line abreast aiming at flak cars or tank cars.
- Begin shooting as soon as possible to determine if there are any explosives on the train.
- Aerial combat: Break with a climbing turn into the enemy and reduce the effect of his initial advantage with a head-on attack with your maximum firepower.
- Use your diving advantage and catch him before he reaches safety.
- The best fighting team is a pair.
- Stay well up in formation when attacking, because it is difficult to catch the squadron after initial acceleration and impossible if full throttle is used. You will find yourself late, unhappy, and most important, alone in a dogfight.
- If the enemy is on your tail, begin a diving, tight turn to the left, letting the airspeed build to about 350 miles per hour. At this speed, it may be possible to outturn him.
- Continue into an overcast or to the deck and, with water injection, outrun him.
- While outrunning him, slip, skid, duck behind trees, pump the stick violently to gain or lose fifty feet, and turn down valleys to prevent him from hitting you until you get out of range.
- *Never* try to turn with an Me 109 or Fw 190 below 250 miles per hour, because the more speed you have, the more aileron control you have over him.

- Listed below are some of the dos [that have gotten pilots home] and don'ts that have in the past caused fatalities:
- DO:
  o Keep clearing your tail and watch the sun.
  o Know your ground elevations before dive bombing.
  o Learn aircraft recognition.
  o Bypass towers and towns while on the deck.
  o Always know the course for home.
- DON'T:
  o Let a train blow up in front of you.
  o Concentrate on a ground target and forget to pull out.
  o Fly straight when anticipating flak.
  o Stooge around below four thousand feet overcast in a flak area.
  o Buzz-bomb concrete—even with delayed fuse.
  o Fly straight ahead or in valleys while on the deck.
  o Fly in trail of someone firing their guns [or you'll run into their shell casings].
  o Feel free from attack until on the ground.

Sometime in February, 1st Lt. William B. Thompson joined a group of pilots for a drink in one of their rooms at Florennes. With the Hell Hawks since July, but still regarded by the old heads as a new boy, he had something to celebrate: he was finally getting assigned a personal plane, a Thunderbolt with his name on it. The group, delighted at his good fortune, asked Thompson what he was going to call his first Jug. "Well, I was thinking of calling it *New Boy*—but I'm afraid they'll take it away from me."

☆

During early April, new and old boys alike were helping complete the American encirclement of the Ruhr Pocket. The Ninth Air Force was sealing the roof over the Wehrmacht, eliminating strong points and any daytime movement. His scalp wound mending, Ed Lopez was up with the 387th Squadron on April 3 when the Jabos caught nearly a dozen panzers near Bödefeld moving to ambush a U.S. column. "The American tankers were unaware of the trap," wrote Lopez. "Before the Tiger tanks could engage the Americans, we attacked them with sixteen five-hundred-pound bombs from our eight P-47s." The fountains of earth and crack of explosions wrecked three of the panzers, scattering the rest, "making them easy targets" for the advancing Shermans.

Bad weather kept the Hell Hawks from most serious flying over the next four days, but ground activity intensified, with orders to move up to a new airfield. The American advance had seized an intact Luftwaffe training base at Fritzlar, about twenty miles southwest of Kassel, Germany. Recon parties set out on the 186-mile leapfrog forward from Aachen, crossing the Rhine on a pontoon bridge and passing long lines of refugees and captured German soldiers, all trudging west. Charles Johnson wrote of the "burned-out vehicles, dead horses, dead German soldiers and dead civilians, shattered houses, wrecked marshalling yards, ruined bridges," and homeless Germans living amid the rubble of Hitler's "Thousand-Year Reich."

Fritzlar was the antithesis of the Hell Hawks' months of hard living amid mud and cold. The German base included concrete parking areas, hangars, barracks for the men and officers, and even hot and cold running water. Fritzlar, Y-86, was just too good to be true.

On April 8, 1st Lt. James L. McWhorter was leading eight P-47s northeast of Kassel on an armed reconnaissance when he sighted hundreds of five-gallon jerry cans under cover amid a cluster of houses and sheds and scattered in the adjoining fields. White trucks with red crosses—ambulances—were moving to and from the suspected fuel dump. "Our orders were that if we saw ambulances, we were to strafe them," said McWhorter. "I hated to do that." But the pilots knew from experience that the Germans used ambulances to haul vital munitions and fuel. "Somebody asked, 'Should we shoot one of 'em?'" said McWhorter. Mac gave the order: one of the planes peeled off and down to strafe.

"It blew sky high!" said McWhorter. "It was full of gas or ammo. There must have been ten or twelve ambulances. We hit 'em all." The two flights put sixteen bombs into the cluster of vehicles. Amid the bomb blasts and roiling smoke came tremendous secondary explosions, rocketing debris five hundred feet or more into the air. Heavy black and gray smoke poured from the raging fires as the squadron hunted down the road toward Echte. They found more than forty more white trucks with red cross markings, and strafed thirty-one into flaming wreckage. The P-47s, flashing through the smoke at low level, jumped another convoy nearby and took out eleven more trucks with their fifties.

Strafing ambulances—it was that kind of war. Little surprised the Hell Hawks by April 1945, and the German deception did little to change their businesslike attitude toward combat. Few hated the Germans they strafed, but few felt sympathy, either. As Jimmy Wells put it, "No, I wasn't mad at them, I just figured we're gonna have to kill all we can. Kill them or they kill us."

The killing intensified over the Ruhr Pocket and east of Fritzlar as the Wehrmacht recoiled toward Berlin. American troops had moved ahead so rapidly that the Thunderbolts frequently identified "panzers" that turned out to be Shermans. On April 8 the Hell Hawks had been directed to hit a tank column that turned out to be American, and they tossed ten five-hundred-pounders into the Shermans before the controller and pilots caught the error. The fliers took some solace in the fact that six of their bombs clearly missed, and the results from the other four were unclear. Friendly fire was inevitable in a war where you opened fire at 450 miles per hour.

Late on April 10, Capt. William E. "Curly" Rodgers swept over the IX Tactical Air Command's assigned area near Leipzig, leading seven planes of the 386th. The men came upon a camouflaged airfield with at least two dozen aircraft parked under cover around a runway on the valley floor. Rodgers led the dive-bombing attack, but as he hurtled through 4,500 feet, green and red flares soared up toward him from the field. Every gun on the aerodrome opened up at once, creating a flak umbrella so intense that he ordered all bombs dropped from medium altitude. The drops were accurate enough, though, wrecking a hangar, a barracks, and several aircraft revetments.

Rodgers then spread the squadron and came in low for a strafing pass, hoping the gunners couldn't track multiple aircraft coming in on the deck. The pilots pressed so low over the runway that their props flattened the grass. Fifty-caliber bullets ripped into the bombers and reconnaissance planes sheltered around the field, destroying three and damaging another eight.

One Thunderbolt zipping through the blizzard of shells thrown up by the German gunners was flown by 1st Lt. Robert S. Hagan, who had cartwheeled into a Belgian field on October 21 and survived the Metz strafing by flattening himself atop a mound of fellow pilots. "We formed up and came back to strafe," said Hagan. "You get right low to the ground. It depends on what your target is. On this one we got off to the side of the airfield and got low to the ground, and came in. I was right over the flight line . . . close to the hangars. I think it was a Ju 88, I'm not sure, parked next to a building. I probably hit it, but it didn't burst into flames or anything. I started on down the field and they were shooting at us from the side of the airfield. You could see the tracers."

And the gunners could see him—only too well. Hagan's Thunderbolt was hit. "It was kind of 'Oh, shit!' I didn't hear anything. Evidently it clipped something, and while I was still down low to the ground [the engine] started smoking. I just had to keep going until they quit firing at me. Then I pulled up and began heading back to the field, back to our lines."

Hagan made it up to eight thousand feet, gingerly nursing his stricken plane westward. Prepared to bail out, he located an emergency field still being laid out by the engineers. The pasture next door looked more inviting, so he eased in for a successful belly landing. On the ground, he waved to his squadron mates to indicate he was okay. Trucked back to Aachen the next day, he went right back into combat. In 2003 he was still a bit chagrined at his tactics, admitting, "We did a dumb thing. We dive-bombed the dang field *before* we strafed it. Not too smart to do things like that. . . . You'd think we knew better. It was toward the end of the war; we were maybe a little over-confident."

☆

As the elements of the 365th Fighter Group moved up to Fritzlar, the pilots continued flying from Aachen, supporting the 3rd Armored Division's advance. On April 11, the 386th had eight planes in the air over Nordhausen (site of the underground V-2 rocket factory) when they were attacked by more than twenty-five Bf 109s. The Luftwaffe had been so scarce that dogfighting was one of the last things on a P-47 pilot's mind during March and early April. Thus, when the 109s bounced them, the Hell Hawks were at a disadvantage. Their P-47s were carrying bombs, and the diving enemy was piling in from nearly twice their eight thousand-foot altitude.

White Flight was under command of 1st Lt. Robert C. Thoman, who quickly ordered bombs jettisoned to meet four 109s streaking in from eight o'clock high. Thoman broke up and into his attackers, only to find another four Messerschmitts joining the fight. The odds against them were now two-to-one, and three of the four Thunderbolts were tailed by unusually aggressive German pilots.

Circling to the left to stay inside the 109s wasn't working; three Thunderbolts broke down and away to escape. Thoman himself noticed 20mm tracer fire streaking past his wings; he rolled over and executed a split-S from ten thousand feet, pulling out just 1,500 feet above the deck.

The Rochester native's P-47 pulled away from his two pursuers, and he lost them in low-altitude haze. Swiveling his gaze for more bandits, he spotted a lone

109 on the deck and dove after it. Thoman misjudged his closing rate and couldn't fire before skidding right by the enemy pilot, who broke left and headed east for home. But the veteran Jug pilot, who had attacked the panzers with Bob Brooking on December 18, pulled in behind and closed the range. From 300 yards down to 150 yards, Thoman fired short bursts, then cut loose with a long blast that tore up the enemy's tail section. The Messerschmitt did a slow half-roll from a thousand feet and slammed into the ground.

Thoman's battle wasn't over. His engine was running rough, his oil pressure was dangerously low, and U.S. Army gunners on the ground fired a salvo at him that matched the best of the German flak for accuracy. One particularly close burst blasted his right-side aileron, rudder, elevator, and ammo door, and his four right-side Brownings opened up on their own in one long, continuous burst, shaking the plane badly. Trying to evade the flak, Thoman turned southwest, but his P-47 caught fire, and he knew it was time to get out. Hauling himself out of the cockpit, he pulled the ripcord and his parachute opened just in time for him to watch his Thunderbolt detonate in mid-air. A friendly infantry patrol picked him up soon after.

☆

By April 13 the Hell Hawks were flying combat missions out of Aachen and landing at Fritzlar, where the last of the overland parties were arriving to complete the transfer operations. The trucks from Aachen were laden with so much captured furniture and booty, accumulated in their seven moves since Normandy, that Bob Brooking likened the Hell Hawks convoys to "the Okie invasion of California during the Depression." New arrivals found local depots stuffed with supplies and potential loot. Captain Paul Van Cleef landed at Fritzlar on April 12, and soon he and 1st Lt. James F. McCabe were roaming the unfriendly countryside in search of valuables. A burning warehouse attracted their attention; upstairs they found a stash of orange brandy stacked case upon case. "I tasted it but didn't like it, so I gave it away to the enlisted men, who got skunked!" wrote Van Cleef.

Another who appreciated the move to Fritzlar was 1st Lt. Ed Lopez, who expressed his exuberance with a test hop over the field. "I took my *Sweet and Lovely* up to five thousand feet and did a high-speed dive, aiming right for the control tower . . . ." Lopez wanted to give the ground crews a thrill. Flat-hatting across the deck at more than four hundred miles per hour, he flew right at the glassed-in tower, at the last second dipping his left wing to miss it by inches. "I could see the men in the tower ducking . . . but I knew what I was doing and as long as I had control of the plane, they were not in danger."

But Lopez was. After landing he endured a royal chewing out by Stecker, who roared at Lopez that his demonstration had won him a week's tour of alert-fighter duty. Each morning at 5:00 a.m., the young hot-shot dutifully protected the field from enemy attack by sitting in a ready P-47, spotted at the end of the runway. "Lopey" was philosophical: "I got the feeling that he got a big kick out of my escapade, and wished he could have done the same. At heart the CO was a hot fighter pilot like the rest of us."

☆

The relative luxuries of Fritzlar were no protection against the dangers of combat. Returning from a strafing mission with the 388th on the 13th, 1st Lt. Graydon M. Whitford was just twenty miles from home when flames began pouring from his P-47. Major James E. Hill, leading the 388th, shouted the bail-out command over the radio, but Whitford didn't reply. The fire reached the stricken pilot's main fuel tank; the detonation blew the engine away from the plane as it plunged to earth. Lieutenant Whitford's mangled body was recovered soon after and buried in the Eisenbach temporary military cemetery.

Losses in combat and accidents were a constant for the men of the 365th, but losing a comrade so late in the war was especially telling. Major Bob Brooking of the 386th was a squadron commander; no matter what he felt personally about the loss of a particular man, he had missions to launch the next day. "I was concerned, but I wasn't a very passionate guy," he said about losing pilots. "It was just kind of the normal thing happening each day."

Most were not so detached. Major Jimmy Wells had watched his flight leader bail out over Normandy the previous June: "The parachute got wrapped around his legs . . . he went in headfirst. I lost a lot of friends over there. It hit pretty hard." Wells knew the routine: the squadron commander signed out a letter to the dead pilot's parents, while an administrative officer went through the man's personal effects and boxed them for shipment (removing any material that might embarrass those back home).

Captain Thomas E. Stanton of the 387th, who flew 121 combat missions and never got a scratch, lost his close friend, 2nd Lt. Mahlon Stelle, on June 7, D-Plus-One. "We graduated from Advanced together," said Stanton. "Stelle was married and had a new baby. I had to gather up his effects and get them shipped home."

Long before that chore, however, the pilots had divided up their friend's cigarettes, whiskey, and battlefield souvenirs—spoils of war. Often all that was left to send home were some impersonal items of clothing, odd bits of uniform, and a few dollars in cash.

Sam Lutz, a friend of Grant Stout's who was in the thick of the fighting in March and April 1945, said, "If you lost a friend, they'd send you up the next day. They didn't want you to dwell on it."

☆

Perhaps those who felt the losses the hardest were the crew chiefs, who worked personally with their pilots day after day, patched battle damage that had nearly killed them, gratefully accepted a share of the liquor ration, and watched them climb, shaking, from the cockpit after tough missions.

The part of this war a crew chief dreaded most was discovering his airplane and pilot had failed to return from a mission. Charles Johnson wrote the following lines on November 28, 1944, the day his pilot, 1st Lt. John Fitzsimmonds, took off on his eighty-fourth combat mission. A flak burst over Julich, Germany, shattered Fitzsimmonds' canopy. The pilot slumped forward, chin on chest, his P-47 entering a gradual dive. Leading the flight, the 386th's Bob Brooking watched, helpless, as the Thunderbolt steepened its descent and hurtled into the Belgian landscape. Back at Chièvres, Johnson had waited at the runway for Fitzsimmonds' return:

> All eyes as one surveyed the sight,
> Mentally counting. It can't be right!
> Where's the one that can't be seen?
> Where's the one to make sixteen?
> One by one, sighs of relief.
> I stood alone in disbelief...
>
> You sense the silence that's yours as you go.
> No words are said; the others know.

Yet the ground crews—like the fliers—couldn't afford to dwell on their losses. Technical Sergeant Don Shilling, a flight chief in the neighboring 406th Fighter Group, lost his pilot three days after D-Day. "You got over it in a hurry," he says. "You could not sit around and mope. You had to get [back] on the stick."

☆

The war was plainly entering its last days, yet the pace of flying accelerated. The Wehrmacht in central Germany fell back into fragmented pockets of resistance, backing to the Elbe, Berlin, and the oncoming Red Army. The Luftwaffe's remaining planes were being hunted down, caught on the ground for lack of fuel or trained pilots. On April 16 the Hell Hawks destroyed forty-three planes on the ground and damaged another fifty. The remaining German rolling stock and locomotives all fell under the guns of the Ninth Air Force's roving fighter-bombers. Dozens of locomotives were destroyed or damaged by the 365th's dive-bombing and follow-up strafing attacks. At a roundhouse near Plossig, the Hell Hawks caught twenty-five locomotives trying to scatter in all directions as the engineers heard the approaching planes. The pilots blew up nine and damaged eight, a typical toll in this target-rich environment.

Yet trains were never easy targets. Some harbored disguised flak cars, bristling with 20mm. Others were laden with explosives whose detonation could shatter a P-47 and knock it from the sky. On a spring day, late in the war, 1st Lt. Herbert L. Prevost took on a train hidden on a wooded stretch of track.

"Oh, boy, we're gonna' get us some trains today," remembered Prevost. He and his wingman, 1st Lt. Allen Mundt, pulled up high over the target, reversed, and headed back down to the deck. Flat out, at treetop height, Prevost opened up on the locomotive. "He just came out of the woods long enough, on an embankment, for me to get one squirt at him, 'cause I had to pull up." Prevost racked his P-47 into a tight, low-level turn, keeping his eyes on the engine. "I came in on him and he was out in the clear, moving. I started shooting. . . . I was hitting the top of him." Lower, lower, he nudged the stick forward to bring the tracers right into the guts of the boiler, and "the prop hit the ground!"

Instantly he hauled back on the stick, up over the train. "It was shaking like hell, of course," said Prevost. He radioed in that he'd hit the ground and would belly in. He searched the wooded area for a suitable field. There was a mile-long stretch of grass just in front, but nudging the throttle back up to maintain gliding speed, the bird kept flying. "It still shook, but it started flying . . . I was climbing at about 115 miles per hour, not very fast." Prevost got the P-47 across the next stretch of woods and called Allen Mundt down to cover his tail as the vibrating prop dragged the plane slowly higher.

He got the plane to one thousand feet, barely, but Mundt called—several times—to tell Prevost that he was headed straight for a 1,500-foot radio mast.

He steered around that obstacle, eventually climbing to five thousand. "I got my mask off, had a cigarette, but that tail was shaking, Al told me, up and down about two feet! About then the low fuel light came on." Fortunately he was nearly home. Prevost, now too high, dumped gear and flaps and flew an S pattern down into Fritzlar, pulling the power off on short final. With the bent prop and extra drag, the plane practically stopped; only a last-ditch burst of throttle lifted the gear clear of the perimeter road embankment. "I had to use practically full power to taxi . . . there was a horrible sound from this propeller; everyone within a mile was looking to see what was making that terrible noise," he recalled. He jumped out to see his propeller, blades twisted, its tips bent back. One of his squadron mates shook his head at the battered prop and the pilot who'd put it in the dirt. "You ought to have your ass kicked, Prevost." Perhaps so, but Prevost could still say that he was lucky.

That's what everyone hoped: that their luck would hang together long enough to get them home. First Lieutenant Sam Lutz noted in his log on April 11 that in two missions that day, numbers sixty and sixty-one, he flew seven hours and twenty minutes of combat time. He willed himself to add, "I'm so tired I can hardly write but still have to get up at 3:00 a.m. for duty pilot. It seems like this war will never be over, and I'm getting pretty sick of it all."

Chapter Nineteen

Reckoning

"**B**LUEBIRD, THIS IS STOWAWAY. Buzz the town . . . and make it a low pass, west to east. Do not fire. Repeat. Do not fire. Follow with second pass, south to north. Over."

"Roger, STOWAWAY, two passes as requested. Will hold fire. BLUEBIRD, out."

The 387th Squadron, Capt. Neal E. Worley leading, had fourteen planes in the air over Bernburg, Germany, southwest of Berlin. A company of Volkssturm, ill-trained national militia, were holed up in the town, and the 3rd Armored controller in a Sherman on the town's outskirts thought they might respond well to a little demonstration.

Worley strung out his three flights and single element in trail, four groups total, and swept in low over the town at full throttle, Pratt & Whitneys howling. The Thunderbolts peeled up from rooftop level and dove again from another quadrant, streaking so low that 1st Lt. Allen Mundt nearly lost a wing on a church steeple. Then Worley directed a rejoin, assembling a gaggle of Thunderbolts to circle the town in a menacing arc.

The Germans made no move to leave, but STOWAWAY was a patient man. He would wait ten minutes, he said, and then mark a target with a smoke shell. The Jug pilots circled closer, the song of their engines blanketing the town. Twenty minutes went by.

"BLUEBIRD, strafe the river at the center of town. Repeat, strafe the river only."

Worley sent a flight in, the P-47s now diving single-file for the River Saale. Black water churned and fountained as a hail of .50-caliber slugs struck the main channel, hugged closely by neat German shops and apartment buildings on each side.

"Do it again," called Stowaway. Worley sent in his second flight. The guns hammered out another demonstration of what awaited the defenders.

"Do it again," came the call once more. Tracer, ball, and API (armor-piercing incendiary) ripped the current from bank to bank. By the third firepower demonstration, civilians were streaming away from the waterfront in a panic, terrified by the low-level firing.

"Bluebird, Stowaway. Good job, boys! The town just surrendered. Thanks for the buzz job! Stowaway, out."

☆

By April 17 the American First and Ninth armies were drawn up to their objective lines in central Germany, holding position as the Red Army crossed the Oder River westward in their final offensive toward Berlin. The U.S. Seventh Army was pushing east for Munich, while Patton raced with the Third Army to meet the Russians near Linz, Austria. Wherever the 3rd Armored needed help, the Hell Hawks were overhead; the 365th also smothered the rail network southwest of Berlin and escorted Ninth Air Force medium bombers to their targets.

The 386th Squadron had just pulled up from wrecking a locomotive and forty-car train near Torgau, Germany, when their top-cover flight was jumped by a lone Focke-Wulf 190D. This long-nosed, up-engined version of the Würger was the fastest piston-engined fighter in the Luftwaffe inventory, and the 365th had a few impressive encounters with them in the closing months of the war.

The Focke-Wulf's bullets and cannon shells thudded into the P-47 of 1st Lt. Alfred Longo, and he dropped out of formation. Engine failing, he made a forced landing near Zorbig, and spent several harrowing days evading the enemy amid the chaos of collapsing Wehrmacht units before safely encountering advancing GIs.

When the 190 hit them, the top cover flight broke hard right, continuing the turn into the lone enemy pilot, who was diving again for another pass. First Lieutenant Charles G. Young pulled up and head-on into the attacker and fired two short bursts as the two planes whipped past. Young rolled left and pulled hard and down after the diving 190, now streaming a thick trail of gray smoke. Accelerating in the dive, the Philadelphia native pulled his tracers back through the Focke-Wulf's fuselage, raking the elongated engine compartment.

Fleeing on the deck, the German ran at full throttle, and despite a twenty-mile chase, Young and his wingman couldn't close to firing range again. The cagey Lufwaffe pilot escaped, and the Hell Hawks were grateful that they rarely encountered the high-performance Focke-Wulf.

Near Thurland on the 17th, the 388th's own 1st Lt. John Schneider was working as liaison with the 3rd Armored Division's 4th Combat Camera Unit. When one of the division's command posts was overrun by a German counterattack, Schneider hid in a barn overnight and successfully evaded a search by German soldiers. Flushed the next morning by a pair of German farmers, Schneider killed one of them before he was cut down by a machine gun burst as he dashed for cover. Charles Johnson wrote that the Chicago native "was a fearless man who would gamble his life against odds at any time." Schneider was far from the cockpit, fighting on unfamiliar terms deep in Germany, but gave his life doing his job as a soldier.

As if driven by the loss of their dead comrade, Schneider's squadron mates from the 388th downed ten Lufwaffe Bf 109s in air-to-air combat on April 18. Thirty miles southwest of Berlin, Maj. James E. Hill found a squadron of Messerschmitts scrambling to put down at a wooded, camouflaged airfield. Catching their adversaries low and slow, the eleven P-47s held all the cards.

One after another, the Hell Hawks—a mix of new and old boys—flamed and shattered the vulnerable 109s, some with gear and flaps down. Second Lieutenant Edward M. Snyder got two; 2nd Lt. William H. Myers bagged another. Hill and his wingman, 2nd Lt. John W. Rohde, each caught two 109s in quick, turning chases; and 2nd Lt. Thomas N. Threlkeld and 1st Lt. Lavern R. Alcorn downed a Messerschmitt each. Only one enemy fighter managed to shoot back at the P-47s. One German pilot leapt from his Messerschmitt on landing roll-out and sprinted for cover as his fighter careened into the trees. It was a lopsided victory.

On the same day, the 386th and Capt. "Curly" Rodgers jumped a truck convoy 120 miles west of Berlin: 150 to 300 vehicles went under the guns of the eleven Hell Hawks. They left more than seventy trucks blazing. A Wehrmacht company lost at least fifty men when the strafers caught them in the open nearby.

By the end of the day, the group had racked up a devastating score against German forces: twelve enemy fighters downed and 219 trucks, two tanks, three locomotives, two rail cars, three buildings, twenty-nine horse-drawn vehicles, four flak guns, and one gun emplacement destroyed. Additionally, they had killed more than 150 enemy soldiers. Ten Thunderbolts were damaged by flak, but all the pilots returned safely to Fritzlar.

☆

Second Lieutenant Gale Phillips earned a Distinguished Flying Cross on April 19 for pressing another attack on a German airfield at Oschatz. Phillips, who flew his first forty combat missions without putting a nick in his airplane, was hit seven times on missions forty-one through forty-seven. With the 387th that day he strafed both enemy planes and installations on the field. "Despite the severe damage which his aircraft sustained during the initial encounter," his citation read, "Phillips refused to withdraw from his course, and continuing to strafe, he destroyed numerous gasoline trucks, other aircraft and trucks."

Phillips would be in the air the next day when the 365th, encountering low clouds and bad visibility in their combat area, received a request from V Corps to strafe an ammunition dump thought to be in the woods near Zeithain, about thirty-five miles northwest of Dresden. Previous attempts by medium bombers to destroy the dump had failed because of decoys nearby, now surrounded by a shotgun pattern of raw-earth craters from the many bombs they had attracted.

The first pass went to the 386th Squadron, and their bullets located the target: "The whole forest seemed to erupt in a tremendous explosion sending debris 7,000 to 8,000 feet in the air," wrote Charles Johnson. Secondary explosions and flames shot skyward, tossing the heavy Thunderbolts and damaging one severely enough that the crippled craft barely made it back to Fritzlar.

Drawn by the smoke over Zeithain, the 387th Squadron arrived and picked out twenty Nissen-type metal huts dispersed in a field. The squadron unsuspectingly opened fire from low altitude at these sitting-duck targets, which at the first bursts blew up in their faces. Captain Elliott B. Beard's plane was struck by debris hurled from the detonations, but he returned safely to Fritzlar. Not so lucky was 1st Lt. Walter W. Irwin, who ran afoul of the flak defenses on his second run over the Oschatz aerodrome, ten miles west. Irwin wrote that:

> ...suddenly I caught a stream of tracers right into the old Jug's
> poweplant. The strikes were really zeroed in because the engine just
> flat froze up within seconds. I was right on the deck so I pulled up,
> made about a 90 degree turn to the right and bellied into a plowed

field adjacent to the airfield. It all happened so rapidly I didn't even have time to slide the canopy back.

The good old Jug bounced across the field and came to a stop about ten feet from a road bordered by a ditch. I could see a great number of soldiers all around the edge of the woods . . . I knew I was going to be captured. There was just no chance of running.

I got on the radio, which still worked fine, and called the rest of the flight to tell them that I was okay, but would be taken prisoner. ("I guess I've had it; here come four Jerry soldiers after me now.") I then slid the canopy back and stood up in the cockpit. As I stood up, a German farmer stood up in the ditch just a few feet away and raised his hands. I guess he thought the Americans had arrived; unfortunately it was only one American. . . .

I crawled out of the cockpit, shed my chute and .45 then raised my hands as about 50 German soldiers approached with guns leveled. They searched me then blindfolded me, which upset me somewhat. I had visions of being shot on the spot. I was also angry with myself for my stupidity in making that second pass. By the way, this was my 87th mission, so I did know better.

After ten days imprisoned in a Luftwaffe guard house and later the hellish POW camp nearby, he would escape and make a dash by bicycle into the welcoming arms of the GIs. But the April 20 attack had continued after Irwin bellied in, with another flight from the 387th back over Zeithain that same afternoon. The munitions dump was a huge military storage complex sprawling across a six-by-eleven-mile area, so expansive that its remnants are still visible on satellite photos today. Captain Russell E. Gardner attacked the ammunition bunkers dug into the fields and woods, strafing from a shallow dive. Two huts disappeared in a violent blast, leaving a dense cloud of low-lying black smoke and numerous secondary detonations.

The eleven Thunderbolts then spotted still more huts, unscathed from the earlier attacks. Gardner's wingman, Red 2, reported to the others that Gardner's radio was out. White Leader, 1st Lt. William B. Thompson, took over command of the squadron. With 1st Lt. Dick R. Schlegel on his wing, Thompson, who had joined the 387th in July 1944, set up a right-hand gunnery pattern over the ammo dump. The pilots peeled off one after another for their runs. Thompson bored in and threw tracers into the complex of two dozen or more storage sheds, blowing up one as the others followed, strafing.

Now Blue Flight, the top cover, joined the others for a second pass; there were so many planes wheeling above Zeithain that midair collision became a real hazard. "Space yourselves . . . I'm making a 360," called Thompson, careful to make room for the diving Blue Flight. He wanted to minimize the chances of fratricide, having one pilot run into the blast caused by the Jug in front.

First Lieutenant Samuel B. Lutz, flying his seventieth mission, had been worried about this target. He had no bombs, and he had seen another pilot break off his strafing run in the face of an intense 20mm flak barrage. His best chance, he thought, was to come in unusually low and fast; a last glance at his airspeed indicator showed 420 miles per hour. Roaring in on the deck over the POW camp, he began jinking to throw off the gunners' aim as he lined up his target.

As Lutz touched the trigger, someone's shells—no one knows if they were Lutz's, Thompson's, or another's—struck an innocuous-looking white bunker. "Everything disappeared in front of me in a mass of boiling flames and debris." The bunker had erupted in a shattering blast, and "all hell broke loose," said Phillips; at eleven thousand feet his Jug was knocked upside down by the detonation wave. Lutz had no choice but to fly through the fiery debris cloud: "I ducked my head and tried to be as small as possible," he wrote, but something smashed through the side of his bubble canopy and knocked him unconscious.

Lutz had trimmed the plane nose-up and selected 100 percent oxygen before his attack run, and so he came to with his Thunderbolt in a slight climb. He knew the ship was hurt badly. "Unable to see very well, I pulled my emergency handle [for the] canopy ejector, but the canopy failed to jettison."

Groggily, Lutz surveyed his situation. His airspeed indicator and most of his instruments were out. Dents and gashes marred the smooth aluminum skin of his P-47's wings. But he was still flying, if unable to see very well, and he found he could roll the canopy back electrically. "I . . . now figured on a belly-landing, a bailout, or even the hope of making it back to our home base . . . I called on my wingman to take me home."

To his chagrin, Lutz discovered that his wingman had neglected to bring his maps. The Beverly Hills High grad would have to manage that job, too. With the slipstream tearing through the cockpit, he struggled to plot a course from his own wind-whipped charts. Finally, Fritzlar appeared ahead. Lutz managed a decent landing and taxied to his parking spot.

He climbed down from the cockpit, uninjured except for that nasty bump on the head. Lutz recalled that he "stood on the ground to fill out the Form 1 report using the wing as a support—but I just couldn't hold the pencil." His crew chief quietly told the twenty-one-year-old that he'd take care of the job for him. For pressing his attack and getting his plane successfully back to Fritzlar, Lutz received the Distinguished Flying Cross.

Like Lutz, Bill Thompson had been right over the white bunker when it blew, and he'd also taken damage from the debris cloud. Dick Schlegel, who had split from Thompson when the latter called the 360-degree turn, climbed out of his second strafing pass and looked for his leader. He caught sight of Thompson again, heading west, alone.

Schlegel threw in water injection to catch him. His leader's canopy was open. Thompson spoke very slowly over the radio: "I have no aileron control, Dick." He was kicking in rudder, working the pedals to keep the wings level. Schlegel carefully slid below and around Thompson's P-47, looking for any damage. There were some tatters in the aluminum skin of the lower wing, but nothing appeared serious. The open canopy was glazed, as if frosted by some sort of explosion inside. The pilots had been getting a lot of flak from across the Elbe on the east; Thompson may have been hit.

Dick Schegel kept talking to his leader; he liked Thompson, who had always had a kind word for the new boys. "Bill, we're about a thousand feet up now. I'll get us a fix for home," said Schlegel, who went off frequency to obtain a radar steer. Back with Thompson, he called, "Let's climb in case of trouble," and the pair eased up to 6,500 feet. They were near the town of Bad-Langensalza, just a few minutes out from Fritzlar.

Watching Thompson's Thunderbolt, Schlegel spotted a stream of black oil from the engine cowling, streaking in ominous tendrils back along the silver fuselage. He gave the bad news to his leader; "My oil pressure just went to zero," answered Thompson, obviously struggling. "There's a brand-new dirt strip right underneath you," called Schlegel, "Want to try to land?" The 180-degree turn to the strip would be tough to manage with rudder only, but Thompson, true to character, was game: "Let's land."

Dick Schlegel hurriedly switched to an emergency frequency to check for a control tower below, but got no response. Switching back to Thompson, he heard the worst: "I've gotta get out . . . it's gettin' away from me." Thompson's barely controllable P-47 started a slow roll to the left, perhaps the intended start of a turn back to the field that inexorably took the plane fully and irreversibly inverted. "He pulled through into a split-S, trying to turn it around," said Schlegel, but in the attempt to pull out of the steep dive, Thompson's Thunderbolt entered an accelerated stall. His use of the rudder to level the wings led instantly to a violent snap roll, the plane corkscrewing wildly through the air. Its pilot was catapulted from the cockpit.

The Thunderbolt struck the ground and exploded. Schlegel was in shock. He glimpsed a figure in olive drab walking near the plane, and a remnant of parachute. "I hoped it was Thompson," he recalled.

He barreled down into the new strip he'd sighted and found American engineers just putting it into commission. Commandeering an ambulance and a flight surgeon, Schlegel was single-minded: "My flight leader just crashed . . . I need you to look for him with me."

Driving a half-mile to the southwest, back to the town and crash site, they stopped a GI at an intersection and asked if he'd seen the pilot whose plane had come down. "He's lying straight ahead in the village," the soldier gestured, adding that the flier's parachute had streamered in the fall, and now served as a shroud for the body lying on the cobblestones.

"The doc ordered me out of the ambulance at the intersection. Told me it was best he go get the body himself," said Schlegel. "He was trying to spare my feelings."

One thing about Thompson's death has nagged at Dick Schlegel for more than six decades: it was he, Schlegel, who after the oil leak suggested they return to the just-built airstrip and land. Thompson was able to handle the plane well enough going straight ahead. What if they hadn't turned back? They were fifteen minutes from Fritzlar; could his leader and friend have handled a straight-ahead belly-in once his engine seized? Would Thompson still be alive today if he hadn't radioed to the dazed pilot the suggestion to put the P-47 down on a runway behind them? Schlegel knows there will never be an answer.

First Lieutenant William B. Thompson, the holder of the Silver Star, the Distinguished Flying Cross, and the Air Medal with twelve Oak Leaf clusters, died on his 105th combat mission. He is buried in the Netherlands American Cemetery in Margraten. His last wingman, Dick Schlegel, has been there to visit his old friend.

☆

The 365th Fighter Group attacked the ammunition dump at Zeithain again during the afternoon, but the thick smoke and frequent explosions soon made strafing runs too risky. A British Army captain held in a prison compound four kilometers south of the ammunition dump had witnessed the Hell Hawks' attacks. The resulting explosions hurled debris into the prison camp, and the inmates threw themselves flat on the ground under the glare of a fierce red blaze, with rockets spewing and shells erupting in all directions. The fires and smaller explosions continued for more than twenty-four hours. The British captain called this the most effective attack he had seen in twenty months confined in the area. Polish prisoners told him later that the depot's two-thousand-man garrison had sustained severe casualties.

In late June 1945, Ninth Air Force headquarters notified the Hell Hawks of their second Presidential Unit Citation, this time for their combat actions on April 20, 1945. Major General O. P. Weyland commended the men for their extraordinary heroism in attacks against German troops opposing the U.S. VII Corps advance. "The results of this highly effective blow against the enemy's military power were 38 ammunition dumps and 40 buildings destroyed, 34 motor transport, 8 aircraft, and 5 barges damaged or destroyed," said the "Battle Honors" circular. Few actions illustrated better than Zeithain the devastating power of a Thunderbolt ground-attack group. The Hell Hawks were masters of that grim art.

☆

As the Hell Hawks were dismantling the ammunition dump at Zeithain, two of the group's "old boys" were dealing with their own set of airmanship challenges. Major Arlo Henry and Capt. Neal Worley of the 387th had taken a couple of warweary P-47s to central France to visit the recuperating 1st Lt. Joseph W. Faurot, liberated from a German prison camp by Patton's men a few weeks earlier. According to Worley, the 387th maintenance officer, Capt. Ralph Warshaw, told the two fliers not to bother bringing the Thunderbolts back (he could get replacements once the worn-out Jugs were crossed off his inventory).

Heading west through the hills around the Moselle River, Worley picked a likely graveyard for his Jug. "I bellied mine in deliberately," he wrote; he persuaded Arlo to pick him up for a tandem flight to their destination. Henry circled the field and expertly put his Thunderbolt down intact close to Worley's. The pair quickly ditched their parachutes. Henry, seated in Worley's lap, stood on the brakes, revved the tired Pratt & Whitney to takeoff power, and expertly pulled the big fighter out of the short field.

All was well until over the river at four thousand feet, Henry's engine inexplicably stopped, and Worley found himself the disconcerted copilot of a very bad glider. But he was far from worried. "I got a field picked out," announced Arlo. At 125 miles per hour, he carefully set the P-47 down, trees whizzing by on either side. Worley wrote later that "[Henry's] voice was soft and confident as ever. . . . I had so much confidence in Arlo's flying that I didn't even fasten the seatbelt until just before bellying into a freshly plowed German field."

They bounced to a stop near a young woman at the reins of a team of white mules. Worley had notched his second "forced" landing of the day (his third overall). Henry was bleeding from a gash where his head struck the rear-view mirror; Worley worked free and, with the girl, pulled his pilot from the derelict Thunderbolt, engine ticking as it cooled for the last time. "Neal! Don't let her cut all my hair off!" mumbled Henry, who then passed out. Patched and rested, the pair bicycled into the camp of some combat engineers, who bundled them back to the Hell Hawks. Worley's new nickname, "Dead-Stick," made it back to Fritzlar almost before he did.

☆

On April 24 the 388th Squadron escorted a group of B-26 Marauder medium bombers on a strike against the oil storage depot at Schrobenhausen. As the last element of twin-engined Marauders straightened onto their bomb run, four Me 262 jet fighters climbed out of the undercast on an attack run from astern. Whistling in from six o'clock low, they were spotted by the Hell Hawks escort. The first to respond was 1st Lt. Oliven T. Cowan, who had downed a 262 back on February 21. Diving at full throttle from seventeen thousand feet, he managed to put a couple of bursts into the right-most jet, forcing the four attackers to scatter before they could close to firing range on the bombers.

One of the jets turned for another pass at the tails of the B-26s. This time Capt. Jerry G. Mast spotted the Messerschmitt and executed a split-S from two thousand feet above, cutting off the enemy pilot, who dove sharply away. Picking up the chase was 2nd Lt. William H. Myers, who dove vertically at the jet at more than five hundred miles per hour. Myers, overtaking, waited for the jet to slow as it shallowed from its dive. When the Luftwaffe pilot began to level, he spotted both Mast and Myers closing from the rear, and pushed over again into a steep dive. It was a fatal mistake. Boxed in from above, the Messerschmitt slammed into the earth at terrific speed and exploded in a rain of flaming debris. Both Mast and Myers had to execute a punishing high-G pullout, Myers blacking out momentarily, to avoid the 262's fate. The rest of the squadron ran off the other three jets, which were unable to penetrate the 388th's fighter screen or hit a single Marauder.

☆

GIs from the American 69th Infantry Division and Russian soldiers of the 58th Guards Division, Red Army, met at the Elbe River near Torgau on April 25th. The Allies had split Germany on an east-west line south of Berlin. The pace of combat flying slowed dramatically as rumors swept Fritzlar that the Hell Hawks would soon be reassigned to the Pacific Theater. Colonel Ray J. Stecker's deputy, Lt. Col. John R. Murphy, had been promoted on the 23rd to command the 404th Fighter Group, also flying out of Fritzlar. Soon after, on the 27th, Stecker himself left for the States, replaced by Col. Robert C. Richardson III from IX TAC headquarters. Richardson picked the 386th commander, Maj. Bob Brooking, as his new deputy, while Maj. James G. Wells Jr. moved up to squadron command. The rapid changes in key personnel and the widening collapse of Wehrmacht resistance resulted in days of local training missions, as the new leaders met their commands and the pilots groused about "busy work" keeping them from getting some rest.

On the last day of April, another change of command with immense significance to the Hell Hawks took place. In the ruins of Berlin, Russian troops were less than a block away from the Fuhrerbunker. Inside his private study at just after three o'clock in the afternoon, Adolf Hitler put a pistol to his right temple and pulled the trigger.

Chapter Twenty

Final Mission

W HILE FLYING OUT OF FRITZLAR in April, 1st Lt. Donald E. Kark visited Buchenwald concentration camp, southeast of Nordhausen, where the 6th Armored Division of the Third Army had liberated twenty-one thousand inmates on April 11, 1945. The camp was about ninety miles east of Fritzlar. When Kark arrived with several other pilots, "we were given a tour of the camp by our troops. There were still bodies lying around, bones still in the ovens. . . . I didn't expect to see stuff like that. The barracks where they would sleep, they were just tiers, shelving, you might say, up to the ceiling . . . . they were sleeping on hay or straw, but stacked up so tightly you couldn't turn over. You had to sleep on your back.

"I'd never seen anything like that, of course. Buchenwald was the camp where the story was that the commander's wife made lampshades out of skin. I saw some of them in one of the buildings there."

☆

German forces in the West surrendered on May 7. The Russians received a second surrender on their front the following day, with hostilities ending on May 9. The shooting war was over. But a full understanding of the urgency and importance of defeating Nazi forces only came with time to reflect on the horrors Hitler's Reich had perpetrated.

Sam Lutz was the officer in charge later that spring at Nordhausen, halfway between Frankfurt and Berlin, escorting a team of inspectors searching for Nazi technology that might prove useful to the Allies. One object of Lutz's search was the Luftwaffe's new ejection seat that catapulted pilots from the cockpits of their stricken aircraft. The Allies had nothing like it, and Lutz, a fighter pilot in the 387th Squadron, knew too well how many P-47 fliers had died when they struck their Jug's tail on bailout.

Lutz had already visited a Messerschmitt factory and underground salt mines, stuffed with stolen gold and art, rooms piled with glasses, clothing, and suitcases. Riding in a jeep, armed with pistol and submachine gun, Lutz brought his team to Nordhausen, where the Germans' V-2 rocket assembly line had been housed in a subterranean factory called Mittelwerk. The laborers lived (and twenty thousand died) in the adjacent Mittelbau-Dora concentration camp.

A Dutch doctor showed Lutz how the camp and factory functioned. "There was a nice driveway that looked like crushed shells, maybe three to four feet high, and six feet wide. I commented on it to the doctor, and he told me that it was the remains of the bones from the crematorium, that many people were cremated each day," wrote Lutz.

His host was intent on ensuring the young pilot was clear on what had happened at the camp. They visited the dispensary. "When a person died, or was killed in this concentration camp, they would take everything off the body. There was a porcelain table with a drain hole at one end. There was a big wooden mallet on the wall, that they used to smash the face and extract the gold from the teeth. Around the room were meat hooks, and the bodies would be hung [on them and then] sent to the crematorium. That was one way the Nazis kept everyone working."

At the morgue, thirty bodies were stacked outside just like cordwood. "There were thirty prisoners a day still dying of starvation when we arrived," wrote Lutz. The doctor explained that even with treatment, some would never recover from the extreme malnutrition and mistreatment inflicted at the camp. Lutz, a seasoned combat pilot who had many times witnessed death, was overwhelmed.

"We went out the main gate. There must have been four sets of railroad tracks, side by side, where the supplies and the prisoners were brought in. On the opposite side of the tracks were a couple of German houses. I was in such a state of shock that I banged on the door of one of the houses. It was opened by a middle-aged German woman who was very polite to me. I just shouted at her. Her response was that 'We didn't know anything about it.'

"It was just an excuse. She lived on a major railroad siding with thousands of people coming and going, and just turned her back on it. Well, like they say, the hottest place in hell is reserved for the neutral. I saw humanity in its worst form."

Major Bob Brooking, now the group deputy commander, also visited the Mittelwerk factory. From the air he glimpsed V-2 tail sections and rocket bodies strewn outside the tunnel entrances. On the ground he was shocked by what he saw: "In the tunnel assembly lines, I saw how the workers had been chained to their lathes. Their living 'quarters' were just a straw mat, and a dish like a dog's." In fact, the inmates would have envied the life of even the mangiest mongrel. Brooking also heard local Germans tell him they knew nothing about the horrors of Mittelbau-Dora. Disgust still tinged his voice sixty years later: "Yeah, right."

☆

The war's end at Fritzlar had been marked by a long night of partying, with small arms, flares, and tracers from .50-caliber machine guns dancing across the dark sky. Charles Johnson wrote, "Bottles of champagne, scotch, cognac, calvados, wine, and home brew that had been carried across the Continent for just this occasion were taken out and dusted off, soon to be finished off." On May 8, with the surrender already taking effect across most of Germany, the 386th and 387th Squadrons took the takeoff flag just after 1:00 p.m. for their final combat mission of the war.

It was a debacle. The soggy runway at Fritzlar harbored several potholes full of standing water, and two Thunderbolts were slowed down so dramatically on their takeoff runs that both crashed and exploded at the departure end of the field. First Lieutenant James E. Murphy's aborted takeoff ruptured his belly tank, flames wreathing the wreck. His plane was a total loss, and Capt. Robert E. Robinson's P-47 bounced and skidded to a sad halt, nearly demolished. Both pilots miraculously escaped without injury, one last testament to their aircraft's rugged construction.

Captain William L. Ward of the 386th did make it into the air and with the remaining sixteen planes, completed an uneventful patrol over the GIs near

Leipzig. The first pilot to report in to the 386th Squadron in May 1943, Ward had flown with the Hell Hawks on their first day in combat, February 22, 1944. Now he was flying on their last. Perhaps remembering with grim amusement Col. Lance Call's boast that he would have the Hell Hawks home victorious by Christmas 1943, Ward landed in *Sally Flat Foot IV* at 3:28 p.m., May 8, 1945. With the Nazis crushed, the 365th Fighter Group completed its final wartime mission and concluded its combat operations on the Continent.

Fifteen months at war had made the men cynical in a "live for the moment" kind of way. Few expected that the end of the battles in Europe was the end of the Hell Hawks' fight. Most expected a swift transfer stateside for refitting and training, then a shift to the Pacific for the final, bloody struggle against the Japanese. Bored and annoyed at the steady pace of training missions that wrecked airplanes and killed a pilot on May 17, the group killed time at Fritzlar, flew to Mons to renew friendships with certain Belgian ladies, played baseball, and waited for orders home.

On June 10, General Eisenhower and Marshal Georgi K. Zhukov of the Red Army were in the reviewing stands at Frankfurt, eyes on the sky. The Hell Hawks joined 1,700 U.S. and British planes in an aerial parade meant to impress the Soviets with the potency of western airpower. The first rumblings of the Cold War were stirring, echoing in the roar of the 365th's Thunderbolts as they massed for one final mission as a group. More practice sorties followed, but five weeks later, on July 22, the Hell Hawks cranked up their big Pratt & Whitneys for the last time. The Thunderbolts departed Fritzlar at 8:30 a.m. for disposition at a central Ninth Air Force depot. The pilots returned by transport plane or truck, but the Jugs that had carried them safely though nearly fifteen months of deadly low-level combat were gone, never to return.

Some of the P-47s were transferred to the reconstituted French air force, but the majority were flown to U.S. Army Air Forces depots and scrapped. The combat-blooded aircraft were considered too "well-used" to be transferred stateside or to the Pacific, where the longer-ranged P-47N model was in wide use.

Departing Fritzlar in late July, the men survived three weeks of boredom at Camp New York near Rheims, France, then shifted northwest to Camp Top Hat at Antwerp, Belgium. Sailing on September 12, 1945, aboard the SS

William and Mary Victory, a new *Victory*-class cargo ship, the group endured a rough nine-day Atlantic passage, with even the iron-stomached fighter pilots falling victim to seasickness.

On September 20, 1945, whistles and horns sounded from fishing vessels and harbor craft in the port of Boston. An immense "Welcome Home—Well Done!" sign hung from a tug, and between the *William and Mary Victory*'s cargo masts stretched a thirty-foot banner reading, "365th Hell Hawks Fighter Group." The eager waves of some attractive WACs at the railing restored the men's spirits as they approached the dock. Many of the veteran ground crews and airmen wept unashamedly at the heartfelt welcome and the realization that after more than twenty-one months overseas, they were at last on American shores.

At Camp Miles Standish near Boston on September 22, 1945, Maj. James G. Wells Jr. under the direction of Lt. Col. Francis C. Robertson, the ranking officer present, signed the orders to officially deactivate the 365th Fighter Group. The Hell Hawks had folded their wings for the last time.

☆

"Few if any of the men in the Hell Hawks group relished being in the war, but circumstances beyond their control made them participants," wrote Staff Sgt. Charles R. Johnson, the 365th's unofficial historian. Major General Pete Quesada, who had commanded the Hell Hawks and the other fighter groups of the IX Tactical Air Command, noted in 1975 that "the young men of the Hell Hawks were a cross-section of our best. . . . It is not an accident that the men of the Hell Hawks had initiative, courage, ingenuity, imagination and loyalty. . . . Those who made the history . . . were and are a true reflection of America as it was and is."

The combat record of the 365th Fighter Group, representative of the eighteen fighter-bomber groups in the Ninth Air Force, demonstrates epic endurance, a single-minded commitment to victory, and a staggering toll of destruction levied against the Wehrmacht and Luftwaffe. From February 22, 1944, until May 8, 1945, a period of 440 days, the group flew 1,241 combat missions. Bad weather wiped out 123 of those 440 days, meaning the group put an average of four missions into the air every day it flew. When combat crises demanded it, pilots often flew two or more combat missions each day.

In those fourteen and a half months in combat, the 365th by its own tally made the following contributions to the destruction and collapse of the Third Reich:

	Destroyed	Probably Destroyed	Damaged
Aircraft (in air and on ground)	259	14	141
Tanks	190		170
Motor Transports	3,928		1,187
Locomotives	588		134
Railcars	3,356		1,857
Boats/Barges	62		43
Bridges	27		35
Flak Towers	5		5
Gun Positions	110		59
Horse-drawn Vehicles	521		52
Factories/Buildings	470		258
Marshalling Yards Attacked	280		
Rail Lines Cut	748		
Roads Cut	141		

At any given time, the Hell Hawks had about ninety to a hundred combat pilots assigned. Over the course of their fight in Europe, considering rotation and replacements, 280 pilots flew for the 365th. Of those 280 Hell Hawks, 109 were shot down. Five were shot down twice. Forty-six were killed in action. Twenty-two were taken prisoner, with five escaping. Fourteen more evaded capture while in enemy territory. Twenty-three bailed out or crashed in friendly territory. Nineteen were shot down by Luftwaffe fighters. The Hell Hawks shot down 151 enemy aircraft. Five of those were Me 262 jets, while no jets downed any Hell Hawks.

☆

In air-to-air combat, the group's kill ratio was thus eight to one, an impressive record considering the Hell Hawks' primary mission was air-to-ground attack. The 365th pilots were justifiably confident in their ability to deal with whatever opposition the Luftwaffe might throw at them.

Nearly 1,500 men served with the 365th Fighter Group during World War II. In addition to the 46 killed in action, 23 Hell Hawks died in accidents: in training, in non-combat flying, in vehicle crashes, and in the always-dangerous base operations supporting combat flying. The total of 69 killed is scarcely 5 percent of the total who served, but that fraction is deceptively low. Among the combat pilots, the loss rate was nearly 22 percent, or more than one in five. Among all eighteen Ninth Air Force fighter groups, a 1945 summary counted nearly 1,800 pilots and ground crewmen as killed, wounded, or missing.

☆

The Hell Hawks and the other Ninth Air Force fighter groups forged in combat a new weapon of modern warfare: airpower closely coordinated with ground forces. They learned from the blitzkrieg tactics of Hitler's Wehrmacht and Luftwaffe, expanded on the lessons learned by the Allies in North Africa, and took ground-attack operations to a level never imagined by its Nazi progenitors. The combination of skilled pilots, a rugged, capable aircraft, close and reliable communications between the air and ground teams, and the courage to fight a brutal, dangerous war at close quarters created an irresistible force that overwhelmed one of the most successful armies in history.

One Hell Hawk, former Cpl. Oliver T. "Tom" Massey of Memphis, Tennessee, expressed unabashed pride about his group's role in winning the war in Europe. A Thunderbolt armorer in the 388th Squadron, Massey wrote that "from a cost accounting point-of-view, the Ninth Air Force fighter-bomber groups were among the most effective units in the war . . . our pilots never got the credit they deserved. In my opinion, going down to fifty feet, at 350 miles per hour, and putting two five-hundred-pound bombs on a Tiger tank was a greater contribution to the war effort than shooting down an Fw 190; I was the armorer to a pilot who did both."

The legacy of that close partnership between American air and ground forces had to be revived in Korea, but in Vietnam and the Gulf Wars, near-seamless air-to-ground operations became commonplace. No American GI has lacked air support since the dark early days of World War II. The Hell Hawks helped establish and refine that tactical doctrine, now a given on the battlefield.

☆

The Hell Hawks were pioneers and then expert practitioners in the field of tactical air warfare. Yet their superlative record during World War II came at a steep human price. In the closing days of the war, 1st Lt. Gordon D. Briggs of the 386th Squadron penned "Memories of a Fighter Pilot," after the death of one of his closest friends, 1st Lt. John H. Wallace Jr. A few lines from his tribute suffice:

> How can we tell you how it was
> > To fight the war up there?
> Knowing we could meet our death
> > Anytime. Anywhere . . .
> We learned to live with danger
> > Yet somehow through it all
> The comradeship we learned to share
> > Is what we most recall.

True to their friendships among the living and the dead, the Hell Hawks grimly fought their war until victory was won. Crew chief and author Charles Johnson got it right: "That P-47 was one tough airplane, and I guess so were we."

Acknowledgments

T HE IDEA FOR *Hell Hawks!* originated when Tom Jones heard from his friend and Air Force Academy roommate, retired Air Force Lt. Col. Tim Hagan, about the wartime experiences of his father, Robert S. Hagan, with the 365th Fighter Group. Bob Hagan provided an introduction to the 365th Fighter Group Association and the many veterans and their families, leading to the research that generated *Hell Hawks!*

These first-person accounts of 365th Fighter Group Hell Hawks pilots and crews in combat are the result of 183 interviews and of research conducted over a four-year period. Any errors that appear here are the fault of the authors. However, this book would have been impossible without the help of many.

The following Hell Hawks combat veterans were interviewed for this book: Lavern Richard Alcorn, Guy Bauman, Alvin E. Bradley, Gordon Briggs, George Brooking, Michael Cannon, Oliven T. Cowan, Roscoe L. Crownrich, John H. Fetzer Jr., Russell Gardner, Milton S. Green, Robert Hagan, David N. Harmon, A. J. Harrington, Marion Hill, Donald E. Hillman, Russell C. Johnson, Donald E. Kark, Mitchell King, Ralph Kling, Carl Lindstrom, Edward J. Lopez, Frank Luckman, Samuel Lutz, Archie F. Maltbie, O. T. Massey, James L. "Mac" McWhorter, Joseph R. Miller, Owen Monette, Allen V. Mundt, Joseph Ornstein, Gale Phillips, Joseph "Pete" Piantino, Joseph G. Preston, Herbert L. Prevost II, Carl Riggs, Robert L. Saferite, Dick R. Schlegel, Glenn Smith, Thomas E. Stanton, Ross Turner, Paul

L. Van Cleef, William L. Ward, James G. Wells Jr., John B. Westwood, Eugene A. Wink, and Neal E. Worley.

☆

The following people also provided interviews and assistance for this book: Quentin C. Aanenson, Priscilla E. Beaudrault, Leslie Boze, John Caldwell, Oliven T. Cowan, Robert Day, Robert Essery, David Fry, Patricia Fry, Tom Glenn, Forrest A. Henry, Molly Smoak Jesse, Janice M. Johnson, Rich Jordan, Carrol Joy, Richard Kiefer, Paul Kraman, Bert Lok, Frank Mangen, John Motzenbecker, Peter Motzenbecker, Robert Reid, Hollie Henry Ritchie, Kemal Saied, Milton W. Sanders, Milton R. Sanders, Russell Sanders, Bernard Sledzik, Andrew Warren Smoak, Lyla K. Stout, Elizabeth Smoak Sykes, Michael "Skip" Ward, Ruth Ward, Warren Webster, Joey Wells, and Carolyn Smoak Wilder.

We also want to thank James Hornfischer, Richard Kane, and Scott Pearson.

Donald R. Baucom and Pat Condon, both retired Air Force officers of long service, provided early reviews of our work and added historical insight. Any errors that remain are our own.

We consulted on an almost daily basis *The History of the Hell Hawks*, by Charles R. Johnson and, with permission, quoted from this detailed but out-of-print history. A number of Hell Hawks and members of other P-47 Thunderbolt fighter groups wrote personal histories that we also used. With permission, we quoted from *Born to Fly*, by Gene Wink (Bloomington, Ind.: AuthorHouse, 2006). Another useful combat memoir is *Mangan's War: A Personal View of World War II*, by Frank Mangan (El Paso, Tex.: Mangan Books, 2003). We were strongly influenced by *P-47 Pilots: The Fighter-Bomber Boys*, by Tom Glenn (Osceola, Wisc: MBI, 1998). Other sources and recommended reading are found in our bibliography.

Tom Gregory, chief pilot of the Lone Star Flight Museum in Galveston, Texas, gave Tom Jones the opportunity to sit in the cockpit of the museum's P-47 and examine every inch of a flyable Jug.

Perhaps the most touching part of our work on this book, and certainly the most painful, was the loss of veterans who helped us with our research but did not live to see the finished product. They include I. Gale Phillips, William L. Ward and James G. Wells Jr. Early in this effort, we visited the Stephen F. Udvar-Hazy Center of the National Air and Space Museum to receive a guided tour of a P-47 Thunderbolt from Milton W. Sanders, Robert S. Hagan, and Quentin C. Aanenson.

Acknowledgments

Although they all flew the mighty "Jug" with different fighter groups, they offered many insights useful to our look at the Hell Hawks. Sadly, Milt Sanders, too, passed on before he could see the result of our labors.

Robert F. Dorr

Thomas D. Jones

What Happened to Them?

Valmore J. "Val" Beaudrault (May 18, 1923–March 8, 2000), the first Ninth Air Force pilot credited with shooting down a Messerschmitt Me 262 jet fighter, came home from war to marry Priscilla Pero on June 8, 1946. They were the parents of three daughters and a son. He went into the Air Force Reserve and became an original member of the New Hampshire Air National Guard in 1947, flying P-47s at Grenier Field near Manchester. Beaudrault left the Guard in 1950 as a captain and joined Eastern Airlines in 1953. Beaudrault spent the final fifteen years of his life in Weare, New Hampshire, retiring as an airline captain in 1983. He was active in the Experimental Aircraft Association and was president and vice president of the New England Aerobatic Club. He served on the board of directors for the International Aerobatic Club, 1983–84.

Alvin E. Bradley (June 10, 1917–), was working as a service station mechanic in Auburn, Georgia, in 1942 when he was drafted into the Army Air Forces. A crew chief with the 386th Squadron, he served as the A Flight chief, in charge of nine aircraft. After leaving the Hell Hawks in September 1945, he worked for General Motors, had a career with the post office, and then worked for an engineering company in New York. Bradley now lives in

Winder, Georgia, and occasionally speaks about his war experiences with the Hell Hawks. He remembers working before dawn on D-Day and seeing "the sky covered with airplanes."

George R. Brooking (April 18, 1919–) finished the war in September 1945 as the Hell Hawks' group commander. Stationed in Dover, Delaware, afterward with forty-six lieutenant colonels, he ran the motor pool, supervising forty German POWs. During the Korean War he wrote a joint training manual to set down the lessons on air-to-ground coordination learned at such cost in Europe. He served in Iran as the air attaché, flew F-86D interceptors and F-105 fighter bombers, and retired as the operations deputy for Twelfth Air Force in Austin, Texas. Brooking's second career was as chief of Austin's public housing authority. Bob and Anne, married since 1949, live there today. He has returned several times to Esch-sur-Alzette, Luxembourg, to meet and thank those who rescued him from the Wehrmacht.

Lance Call (May 18, 1909–December 9, 1981), the Hell Hawk commander who was relieved in the combat zone, remained in the Air Force and later Air National Guard. He commanded Luke Field, Arizona, from January 9 to April 14, 1945, and Kingman Field, Arizona, a facility where veteran aircraft were stored, later that year. Subsequently, he commanded Donaldson Air Force Base, South Carolina, and the 375th Troop Carrier Wing. He married his second wife, Harriett Clarell "Tuffy" Kenyon, a former Women's Air Force service pilot and qualified aviation accident investigator, on June 23, 1948. They are the parents of two sons and a daughter.

After a move to Pennsylvania in the early 1950s, Call reached the rank of brigadier general in the Air National Guard and commanded the 112th Fighter Wing at Pittsburgh. Call was manager and flight instructor at the eighteen-hangar, three-runway Connellsville, Pennsylvania, airport from 1959 to 1967. (Harriett was rated as a civilian flight examiner.) He was manager and flight instructor at Air Park South, Ozark, Missouri, from 1968 to 1972. He also ran a company called Lance Call World Aircraft Services. Said daughter Katherine Gonyo: "My parents were very passionate about flying. They had an exciting life living their dream."

Robert L. Coffey Jr. (October 21, 1918–April 20, 1949), was first encountered in this narrative flying over the D-Day invasion fleet. He led the 388th

Fighter Squadron, was later deputy commander of the Hell Hawks group, and was an air ace with six kills to his credit. He was called "cocky, debonair and fearless" by Hell Hawks historian Charles Johnson. To all who knew him, however, Coffey was more politician than pilot, and someone who might become president. Coffey resigned from active duty September 1, 1946, to enter politics but remained in the Air Force Reserve. In November 1948, he was elected to the House of Representatives from Pennsylvania. Seven months later, Coffey died in the crash of an F-80A Shooting Star while flying with the 4th Fighter Group on a deployment to Kirtland Air Force Base, New Mexico. Fellow Hell Hawk and former 386th Squadron commander William D. Ritchie was flying on his wing when he died. The House of Representatives recessed for one day to honor him.

Robert M. Fry (July 3, 1921–May 7, 1985) sailed the waters of Lake Erie as a youth and headed to Annapolis as a midshipman in 1939. Offered pilot training after Pearl Harbor, he left his classmates and joined the Army Air Corps. Fry rose to command the 388th Fighter Squadron and finished the war as the Hell Hawks' top ace, with seven victories (the Air Force reduced his official total to four after the war). Fry went on to fly F-89s, T-33s, C-119s, and B-57s before retiring as a full colonel in 1969. Fry married Betty Lou Shafer of Erie while home on leave on April 5, 1945. After raising two sons together, Fry lost Betty Lou in the early 1970s, but later married Patricia Nan Weber. The couple lived in Annapolis, where Bob Fry enjoyed sailing until his death in 1985. His son, David (a retired U.S. Marine lieutenant colonel) remembers his father's sentiments about the P-47: "It was well-protected and well-armed. I was happier than a pig in poop with that airplane."

Robert S. Hagan (September 19, 1924–) of the 386th Squadron was a typical Hell Hawk: he flew ninety-one combat missions, was shot down twice, earned the Purple Heart, and returned victorious to the United States one day after he turned twenty-one years old. After the war he went on to a long and distinguished flying career as a test pilot with the Cessna and Beech aircraft companies. He was first to fly the Air Force's Cessna T-37 jet trainer in 1954, and first to eject from one when the prototype wouldn't recover from a spin. He met his future wife, Fran, during P-47 training at Baton Rouge; hers was the name on the nose of Hagan's Thunderbolt. Bob and

Fran Hagan still live in Wichita, Kansas, and their son Tim became a career officer in the air force. Author Tom Jones and Tim Hagan were roommates at the Air Force Academy in 1976, thus providing an introduction to Bob and to the Hell Hawks story.

Arlo C. Henry Jr. (Mar. 22, 1921–Jan. 1986) of Dearborn, Michigan, was one of the stalwarts of the 387th Fighter Squadron. Awarded the Distinguished Flying Cross, his twenty-one oak leaf clusters to the Air Medal marked his one-hundred-plus combat missions. Not everyone found him easy to befriend, but Neal Worley said of Henry that "precision was in his blood . . . his voice was quiet but always imbued the listener with confidence." Henry returned to the Air Force shortly after the war and rose to colonel by the time he retired in 1967. Troubled with nightmares in Europe—his fellow pilots heard him call out in his sleep—Henry remarked upon the impact of once seeing the face of a motorcyclist he was about to strafe. At home with wife Alma, he displayed affection and humor. Recovering from minor surgery in 1986, Henry, apparently confused by medication, wandered from his hospital room into the winter night and died of exposure.

James E. Hill (1921–May 20, 1999) served thirty-two years in an Air Force career that saw him promoted to full general and commander of the North American Air Defense Command. General Hill was born in Stillwater, Oklahoma, and entered the U.S. Army Air Forces as an aviation cadet in March 1942. He completed pilot training in February 1943 and by December had joined the 365th Fighter Group en route to England. A Thunderbolt ace, he was credited with five enemy aircraft shot down while flying 127 combat missions. Following the war he commanded a P-51 squadron in the Oklahoma Air National Guard. Returning to active duty in 1948, he flew 128 combat missions in Korea as an F-80 pilot, downing one enemy aircraft. He graduated from the Royal Air Force Flying College and served in fighter-bomber wings in England through the mid-1950s. Following staff assignments, he was commander in 1964 of the 405th Fighter Wing, based in the Philippines, and later commanding officer of a pilot training wing. By 1970, Jimmy Hill commanded the 42nd Air Division in Strategic Air Command (SAC), overseeing several combat wings. General Hill later commanded the Third Air Force, served in high staff positions at the

Pentagon, and commanded Alaskan Air Command and SAC's Eighth Air Force. Before commanding North American Air Defense Command, he was SAC's vice commander. General Hill earned four stars, later retiring on December 31, 1979.

Donald E. Hillman (August 24, 1918–), a P-47 pilot, leader, and prisoner of war, made the difficult decision to remain in the Air Force after the war. He married Lloyd Pierce in May 1942; they are the parents of a son and daughter and have numerous grandchildren and great grandchildren. Hillman commanded the 94th Fighter Squadron, the famous "Hat in the Ring Squadron," from 1946 to 1948, flying F-80 Shooting Stars. During that period, he appeared on the cover of the December 9, 1946, *Life* magazine. Soon afterward, Hillman shifted from fighters to bombers after seeking a personal audience with Gen. Curtis LeMay to request the transfer. He was one of the first B-47 Stratojet pilots and, while deputy commander of the 306th Bombardment Wing, made the first reconnaissance flight over the Soviet Union in a modified B-47B on August 12, 1952. He later piloted the B-52 Stratofortress and commanded two B-52 wings. He retired in 1962 as a colonel, went to work for Boeing, and retired from the aircraft maker in 1980. Don and Lloyd live in Seattle.

Charles R. "Red" Johnson (March 11, 1922–October 19, 2003) enlisted in the Army Air Forces in September 1942, and was assigned as a Hell Hawk aircraft mechanic in June 1943. During his career as a P-47 crew chief, he earned six battle stars and a Bronze Star for his effectiveness on the flight line. He graduated from the University of Connecticut in 1950 with a mechanical engineering degree, and worked as an engineer with Pratt & Whitney in West Hartford, Connecticut, until 1979. Following World War II, Johnson became the 365th Fighter Group's unofficial historian, publishing in 1975 *The History of the Hell Hawks*, a 623-page documentary history of the unit's combat exploits. Charles Johnson always said that "everyone in the Hell Hawks wrote that book." He and Janice M. Johnson were married fifty-four years and had two daughters and five grandchildren.

Edward J. Lopez (July 17, 1923–) was born in Los Angeles and graduated from Beverly Hills High School in 1942. He enlisted in the Air Corps in August 1942 with a group that included Clark Gable. After a stint as a BT-

13 instructor at Chico, California, he joined the 387th Fighter Squadron in September 1944. In July 1945, flying a UC-64 Norseman in bad weather, he looked up to see a tree in the clouds *above* him. The crash broke both ankles, and the flaming engine nearly rolled over him as it tumbled down the hillside. Lopey recovered and went on to fly P-51s, L-5s in Korean combat, and the F-80 and the F-86 Sabre. He left the Air Force in the mid-1950s to start a photography business. Married in October 1956, he and Maria live in Arcadia, California, and have three sons. Ed Lopez has written *Roots of a Fighter Pilot*, a detailed memoir of his flying experiences.

James L. McWhorter (November 5, 1920–) was born in Eatonton, Georgia, and grew up in Umatilla, Florida. He joined the 386th Fighter Squadron in June 1944 and flew eighty-three combat missions in his P-47, *Haulin' Ass*. After the war he continued to fly in the new Air Force and retired as a major in 1962. He and wife Christine had four daughters; after Christine's untimely death, Mac married Dot in 1967 and became father to Dot's daughter. Prospering in Florida real estate, McWhorter marketed commercial real estate until his recent retirement. He lives in Sanford, Florida, and is the current president of the 365th Fighter Group Association.

John W. Motzenbecker (September 29, 1916–February 26, 1998) was an original Hell Hawks member who rose to command the 387th Fighter Squadron. One of nine children from a Newark, New Jersey, doctor's family, "Motz" was a business administration graduate of Georgetown University. He flew 113 combat missions in *Kelsey Balls* and discovered the German armored column in the early hours of the Bulge on December 17, 1944. He left the military in 1946 and worked for Prudential Insurance as a mortgage investment manager in Newark and Philadelphia. He married Margaret R. Eelman on February 8, 1947. They had seven children, six sons and a daughter. His sons say their father, a straight-arrow perfectionist, admitted to being frightened in combat, but believed he had a job to do. He retired in 1978 and lived in Venice, Florida, until his death.

Allen V. Mundt (October 19, 1922–), who flew combat missions with the 387th Squadron from Nov. 1944 through May 1945, is still fond of his P-47D, B4-M, *Wisconsin Witch*. Born in Menominee, Michigan, he earned his forestry degree from the University of Michigan after the war. Mundt worked as a park ranger until 1948, then joined the new U.S. Air Force, flying the C-47 and instructing in the AT-6. He became the Civil Air Patrol liaison for Nevada while at Stead Air Force Base in Reno, retiring as a major in 1966. He put in seventeen years as an aerospace education instructor with the University of Nevada, Reno, finally retiring in 1982. Mundt says that although he wasn't afraid to fly combat, he didn't think he'd survive the war. Flying with the Hell Hawks, he says, "taught me what the essentials of life were." Mundt lives in Reno and is an avid skier.

John R. Murphy (1918–January 13, 2000) was born in Minot, North Dakota, and attended The College of Notre Dame before receiving an appointment to West Point. He was commissioned in 1942 and earned his wings before joining the 365th Fighter Group. Murphy served first as a pilot, then, with the rapid expansion of the Army Air Forces, as squadron commander of the 388th Fighter Squadron and deputy commander of the Hell Hawks. He finished the war as commanding officer of the 404th Fighter Group, with 139 combat missions and 305 combat hours in the Thunderbolt. He later commanded a squadron of F-80 Shooting Stars, the first U.S. combat jet. In Korea, Murphy helped organize the tactical air control system for supporting ground forces. He first flew the F-51 Mustang in combat, then flew 89 missions as an F-80 fighter group commander. By 1957 he was director of operations for the Fifth Air Force in Japan. Lieutenant General Murphy completed his career as chief of staff, United Nations Command, and chief of staff, U.S. Forces Korea, with headquarters in Seoul, Korea.

Robert L. Saferite (December 27, 1922–), who had success fighting the Germans in both air-to-air and air-to-ground action, remained in the Air Force for eleven years before departing as a major. Saferite married Mary Emma Davis in May 1946, and she accompanied him on military assignments before being killed in a traffic accident in 1956. They had five children. Saferite's postwar flying included F-82 Twin Mustangs at Kearney Field, Nebraska, and P-47 Thunderbolts in Germany. Saferite married Evelyn Lacy Seymour, who already had three children, in 1966. They brought their families together, making them the parents of eight. Saferite has spent most of his life in El Dorado, Kansas, where he has enjoyed considerable success in automobile sales and in banking. As a civilian pilot, he flew most Cessna aircraft models from the 172 to the 310, and earned a DC-3 rating. He retired from flying at age fifty-three and from work at age seventy.

Dick R. Schlegel (March 4, 1922–) flew twenty combat missions at the close of the war, once returning to base with so many holes in his Thunderbolt that ground crews refused to let him taxi in. After serving in the occupation force, he left active duty in 1946, but flew C-46 cargo planes in the reserves until 1950. Schlegel married Maxine in April, 1943, raising two sons and a daughter. Schlegel earned a law degree at the University of Iowa, and was in active practice for fifty years. From 1994 until 2000 he served as the Senior Judge on the Iowa Court of Appeals. He and Maxine live in Ottumwa, Iowa, where he still plays in the municipal band.

Ray J. Stecker (July 26, 1910–September 19, 1967) commanded the 365th Fighter Group, the "Hell Hawks," from June 1944 to April 1945. He married Mathilde Ros, his second wife, in 1947. He flew jet aircraft briefly in the postwar period. His children remember Stecker retiring from active duty about 1950 and serving thereafter in the Air Force Reserve, where he reached the rank of brigadier general. They lived in Boxford, Massachusetts, for most of his postwar years and later in Marble Head. The Steckers were the parents of four children, including a daughter, Darcy Norton, who is named for Maj. Gen. Thomas C. Darcy, who was a West Point classmate of Stecker's (1932). Norton remembers Stecker conducting West Point–style inspections of his children, "lining us up and checking out fingernails," but adds that "He was a really good dad." He is interred at the U.S. Military Academy.

William L. Ward (February 21, 1923–October 12, 2006), who was the first pilot to report to the Hell Hawks and flew the group's final combat mission, was married (in June 1943) to high school classmate Ruth Thompson. When the war ended, he was "miserable" as a civilian and went back into the Air Force in 1947, flying P-51 Mustangs and P-80 Shooting Stars; he flew Mustangs in the Korean War. In 1956, Ward commanded a fighter-interceptor squadron with the F-102A Delta Dagger, which he helped design and develop. During the Vietnam war, he flew A-1E Skyraiders at Nakhon Phanom, Thailand. He retired as a lieutenant colonel at Sheppard Air Force Base, Texas, in 1971. Always an entrepreneur, Ward worked as an inventor, designing and manufacturing a hand tool, and did motivational speaking. He had a lifelong love of the game of golf and was an executive director of the Texas Golf Association. He and Ruth are the parents of a son, Michael, known as "Skip," an Air Force veteran of Vietnam who spent thirty years in broadcasting.

James G. Wells Jr. (June 7, 1920–January 11, 2007) was born in Houston, Texas, and served in the Texas National Guard beginning in 1940. Called to active duty after Pearl Harbor, he entered pilot training and flew 103 combat missions with the Hell Hawks from October 1943 through May 1945. After flying for twenty-three years in the Air Force (his favorite jet was the F-104 Starfighter), he retired in 1963 as a colonel. In Albuquerque he was a successful banker until retirement in 1980. His late wife, Mary R. Wells, was a pilot herself, a World War II WASP and later an Air Force officer. Colonel Ray Stecker once scolded Wells for his solo forays deep into Germany, looking for a tangle with the Luftwaffe: "I wanted to get that fifth kill so bad I could taste it!" Wells admitted.

Neal E. Worley (August 21, 1921–), from Emporia, Kansas, flew a bubble-topped P-47D-25 named *Mortician's Delight* with the 387th Fighter Squadron. He crash-landed five times, including two forced landings in one day, earning him the nickname "Dead-Stick." After the war he flew the F-84 Thunderjet with the 14th Fighter Group and instructed in the C-119 for Strategic Air Command. Worley retired from the Air Force as a lieutenant colonel in 1963. He once belly-landed his crippled Thunderbolt into a hedgerow of arm-thick yew trees. A farmer approached, saying "In a bit of a spot, aren't you, Yank?" then gave Worley a ride to his home in a red MG. He lives in Ukiah in California's Napa Valley.

Notes

Chapter One

Buzz bomb strike, May 3, 1944: Charles R. Johnson, *History of the Hellhawks*, p. 68; Wells interview, June 6, 2006.

"a pretty sturdy guy with black hair and a mustache": interview with William L. Ward, July 5, 2006.

"suave" and "debonair": interview with James L. "Mac" McWhorter, June 22, 2006.

"a railroad bridge southwest of St.-Sauveur-de-Pierre-Pont, a culvert at Couperville, and an embankment at St.-Sauveur": Johnson, *History of the Hell Hawks*, p. 100.

"daring flier" who smoked a cigar: interview with Gale Phillips, Sept. 15, 2006.

"stock" pilot who "ambled along": Ward interview, July 5, 2006.

Fetzer recollections: interviews with John H. Fetzer, Jr., Sept. 15 and Oct. 26, 2006.

"Henry dropped two bombs": Fetzer interviews, Sept. 15 and Oct. 26, 2006.

"He seemed to have a belief in fate": Interview with Ward, June 8, 2006.

Wells' D-Day return: James G. Wells Jr. interview, June 6, 2006.

Eisenhower notice: Johnson, *History of the Hell Hawks*, p. 101.

"Saferite looked down at Utah Beach.": interview with Robert L. Saferite, Nov. 6, 2006.

Chapter Two

Miller on D-day crash location: interview with Joseph R. Miller, Jan. 2006.

"depth of beachhead": Stephen F. Ambrose, *D-Day*, pp. 576–77.

"Bayerlein and scourge of the Jabos": Ambrose, *Citizen Soldiers*, p. 49.

Flakvierling 38: National Museum of the US Air Force, http://www.national museum.af.mil/factsheets/factsheet.asp?id=1018

Gardner encounter with JG 3: Russell Gardner interview, Sept. 15, 2006.

Malack and P-47 strike: John Malack letter to authors, May 29, 2005.

Jabo Rennstrecke: Johnson, *History of the Hell Hawks*, p. 109.

Hell Hawks' move to France: ibid., pp. 119–120.

Loss of DuPont: ibid., 127.

Hillman's June 25 dogfight: interview with Donald E. Hillman, Apr. 22, 2005; Johnson, *History of the Hell Hawks*, p. 128.

Arlo Henry's attack on the headquarters: ibid., p. 134.

"seven thousand Jabos": Ambrose, *Citizen Soldiers*, p. 48.

Chapter Three

Quesada's personality: Rebecca Grant, "Quesada the Conqueror," *Air Force* magazine, Apr. 2003

40 percent washout; 13,000 training deaths: Robert F. Dorr, "Dorr Field typified primary pilot training bases during World War II," *Air Force Times*, Dec. 4, 2006.

Pre-flight training: Donald L. Miller, *Masters of the Air: America's Bomber Boys Who Fought The Air War Against Nazi Germany*. New York: Simon & Schuster, 2006, pp. 164–65.

Wink in Richmond: Gene Wink, *Born to Fly* (Bloomington, Ind.: AuthorHouse, 2006), pp. 37–38, used with permission.

Browning M2: Warren M. Bodie, *Republic's P-47 Thunderbolt: From Seversky to Victory*. Hayesville, N.C.: Wide Wing Publications, 1994

thirteen pounds of bullets per second: Roger Freeman, *Thunderbolt: A documentary history of the Republic P-47*. London: Macdonald's and Jane's, 1978, p. 35.

Wink at Millville: interview with Gene Wink, Dec. 23, 2006.

Fetzer at Dover: interview with Fetzer, Dec. 28, 2006.

Training at Dover: Johnson, *History of the Hell Hawks*, p. 11.

Millville training: http://www.p47millville.org/

Call's wrath: Johnson, *History of the Hell Hawks*, p. 15.

Gene Wink is downed: ibid., p. 34; Wink, pp. 71–79.

Damon "Rocky" Gause and his death: Interview with Donald E. Hillman, July 6, 2006.

Chapter Four

Call's efficiency: Wells interview, June 6, 2006

Call's relief: Harmon interview, March 23, 2007.

Burning bodies: Aanenson web site, "A Fighter Pilot's Story," http://pages .prodigy.com/fighterpilot/

Newcombe's crash, July 11, 1944: Robert Essery, "They're Looking for Heroes." pp. 18–21.

Quesada's delay fuses: Stanton interview, September 2006.

Ernie Pyle watches the P-47s at Cobra: Ambrose, *Citizen Soldiers*, p. 82.

Bayerlein describing Cobra: Hughes, *Overlord*, p. 213.

Vitz shootdown and evasion: Johnson, *History of the Hell Hawks*, p. 165.

One bitter joke: "D-Day: A Luftwaffe perspective," Aeroplane, June 2004, p. 58.

Chapter Five

Lindstrom bailout: Lindstrom interview, Oct. 14, 2004.

Weather on August 5: Johnson, *History of the Hell Hawks*, p. 180.

Von Gersdorff and failure of Mortain counterattack: Isby, *Fighting the Breakout*, p. 129.

German withdrawal from Falaise Pocket: Johnson, *History of the Hell Hawks*, p. 195.

"There were Germans crawling around on their hands and knees": Fetzer interview.

Alcorn on August 13: Interview with Alcorn, Apr. 27, 2006

Stout on being wounded, moving to A-12, the British: letter written by Grant Stout, August 14, 1944.

Ninth Air Force toll on Aug. 13–14: Hughes, *Overlord*, p. 243.

Aanenson's aerial view of the Pocket: Aanenson interview, June 13, 2006.

Eberbach description of Falaise: Isby, *Fighting the Breakout*, p. 187.

Von Gersdorff on the Falaise battlefield: ibid., p. 225.

Buying a Mercedes in the Falaise Pocket: Smith, *Spitfire Diary*, p. 44.

Maltbie on August 19: interview with Maltbie Sept. 16, 2006.

1930 Army-Navy Game: "Football," *Time* magazine, Dec. 22, 1930.

Description of Murphy: interview with Frank Luckman, Sept. 19, 2006.

Arlo Henry's cigar: interview with Gale Phillips, Sept. 15, 2006.

Fry strafes a motorcycle: David Fry interview, June 14, 2006.

Chapter Six

Falaise summary: Hughes, *Overlord*, pp. 245–46.

Porter's strafing attack on Sept. 2: Johnson, *History of the Hell Hawks*, p. 218.

Porter's unusual kill on Sept. 5: ibid., p. 221.

Brooking shootdown: Brooking interviews, 2003; Johnson, *History of the Hell Hawks*, p. 225.

Kling shootdown: ibid., p. 244; Kling interview and written notes, 2003, 2007.

Hillman victories: Johnson, *History of the Hell Hawks*, p. 251.

Chapter Seven

Henry quote: Johnson, *History of the Hell Hawks*, p. 149.

Cholewinski and Jones: Ninth Air Force press release, July 1944.

Mangan quote: Mangan, "Mangan's War," p. 60.

Piantino quotes: interview with Joseph "Pete" Piantino, Nov. 20, 2004.

Piantino bomb release: Johnson, *History of the Hell Hawks*, pp. 99–100.

Glenn quote: Tom Glenn, *P-47 Pilots:* The Fighter-Bomber Boys, Osceola, MBI, 1998, pp. 148–49

Fetzer quote: interview with Fetzer, Mar. 6, 2007.

Charles Johnson preflight routine: Edgar C. Kiefer, *A P-47 Pilot's Recollections of his WWII Battles*, p. 8.

Mangan on killing from a distance: Mangan, "Mangan's War," p. 36.

Smith quotes: interview with Glenn Smith, Mar. 7, 2007

Bauman as crew chief: Bauman interview, Oct. 14, 2004.

Chapter Eight

Lutz' dampened mission: Johnson, *History of the Hell Hawks*, p. 259.

Kraman's ground view of the Hürtgen: ibid., p. 269.

GI's view of a P-47 attack: Max Hastings, *Armageddon*, p. 181.

Fetzer wounding: Fetzer interview.

Joy on battle damage: Joy interview.

Dronen and his crew chief question: Dronen oral history interview, December 4, 2002.

Hillman downing: McWhorter interview, May 9, 2005; Johnson, *History of the Hell Hawks*, p. 271.

McWhorter victory: ibid., p. 283; McWhorter interview, Apr. 4, 2007.

Brooking victory: Johnson, *History of the Hell Hawks*, p. 284; Brooking interview, Nov. 17, 2003.

Results of Hürtgen battle: http://www.hurtgen1944.homestead.com/02StorySummary.html

Lutz and a pilot's life expectancy: Lutz interview, July 9, 2007.

Chapter Nine

Wink quote. Wink, *Born to Fly* (Bloomington, Ind.: AuthorHouse, 2006) Used with permission.

First Ritchie quote: interview with retired Col. James "Mac" McWhorter, June 22, 2006.

Second Ritchie quote: interview with retired Lt. Col. Eugene A. Wink, Jr., Dec. 23, 2006.

Henry quote: from a report by Henry.

56th Fighter Group's kill ratio: Donald L. Miller, *Masters of the Air*, p. 237.

Galland's gripes: Miller, *Masters of the Air*, pp. 238–39.

Ten Grand: Joshua Stoff, *The Thunder Factory: An Illustrated History of the Republic Aviation Corporation*. London: Arms & Armour Press, 1990, p. 54.

250,000 U.S. pilots: Thomas A. Manning, *History of Air Training Command 1943–1993*. Randolph Air Force Base, Tex.: Office of History and Research, Headquarters, Air Education and Training Command, 1993.

German neophyte pilots: Miller, *Masters of the Air*, p. 284.

Stout quote: Stout's letters.

Hitler and the Me 262: Ian Kershaw, *Hitler 1936-1945: Nemesis*. New York: Penguin, 2000.

Lake quote: Interview with Jon Lake, Mar. 14, 2007.

October 21 dogfight: Johnson, *History of the Hell Hawks*, pp. 291–98.

Murphy quotes: Franck, *Winter Journey Through the Ninth*. p. 160.

Luckman dogfight: Luckman interview, May 23, 2007.

Hagan crash-landing: Hagan interview, Mar. 4, 2003.

Chapter Ten

Cornell's death: Johnson, p. 316.

Brooking's character: Hagan interview, Sept. 14, 2006.

Cornell's character: Brooking interview, Nov. 17, 2003.

Wells victory over Bf 109: Wells interview, June 6, 2006.

Battle of the Bulge, Dec. 17 air attacks: Sgt. Bill Davidson, "Even the Birds Walk," *Yank.* 1945, pp. 6–7.

Hagan strafing tactics: Robert S. Hagan interview, Mar. 4, 2003.

Dec. 18, 1944, air attacks on Germans: Johnson, *History of the Hell Hawks*, pp. 346–47.

Brooking attacks, Dec. 18: Brooking interview, Nov. 5, 2003.

Wells attacks, Dec. 18: Wells interview, June 9, 2006.

Jabo effectiveness: Stanley Weintraub, *11 Days in December: Christmas at the Bulge*, 1944. New York, Free Press: 2006., p. 110.

Mundt preflight experience, Dec. 18: Mundt interview, Sept. 13, 2006.

Worley attacks, Dec. 18: Worley interview, June 2007

20mm flak description: Danny S. Parker, *To Win the Winter Sky*, p. 227.

Move to Metz: Johnson, *History of the Hell Hawks*, p. 351.

Cowan air strike on Christmas Day: Cowan, Oliven. "Christmas Day 1944: A mission to remember." *Smoky Mountain News*, Waynesville, N.C. Dec. 19–25, 2001.

Heilmann quote on air attacks: Weintraub, *11 Days in December*, p. 111.

New Year's Eve: Johnson, *History of the Hell Hawks*, p. 363; Brooking interview, Jan. 13, 2005.

Chapter Eleven

Initial Hell Hawk missions, Jan. 1: Johnson, *History of the Hell Hawks*, p. 365.

Brooking, New Year's Eve: Brooking interview, Jan. 13, 2005.

German perspective of Metz strike: John Manrho and Ron Putz, *Bodenplatte*, pp. 233–45.

Surprise attack at Metz: Johnson, *History of the Hell Hawks*, pp. 365–72.

Hagan's dive for cover: Hagan interview, Apr. 29, 2003.

Hill wounded: Hill interview, Oct. 14, 2004.

Brooking during the attack: Brooking interview, Jan. 13, 2005.

Riggs wounding: Riggs interview, Oct. 14, 2004.

Piantino takes shelter: Piantino interview, May 9, 2005.

Lutz witnesses attack at end of runway: Johnson, *History of the Hell Hawks*, p. 369.

Gordon Briggs on German tactics: Briggs interview, Oct. 2003.

Catanuto heroics: Johnson, *History of the Hell Hawks*, p. 372.

Lawless and Holcomb heroics: ibid., p. 371.

Alcorn returns to Metz: Alcorn interview, Apr. 27, 2006.

Luftwaffe losses: Manrho and Putz, *Bodenplatte*, p. 273.

Galland quote: Hugh M. Cole, *The Ardennes: Battle of the Bulge*, p. 663.

Riggs on the attack's impact: Riggs interview, Oct. 14, 2004.

Chapter Twelve

Brooking and Kohl: Johnson, *History of the Hell Hawks*, pp. 366–67.

Spitfire funeral: Smith, *Spitfire Diary*, p. 148.

January 10 attacks: Johnson, *History of the Hell Hawks*, pp. 376–77.

Fry profile: David Fry interview, June 14, 2007.

January 16 dogfights: Johnson, *History of the Hell Hawks*, pp. 383–84.

Kraman victories: ibid., p. 386.

Fry and Hensley dogfights: ibid., pp. 387–88.

James Hagan quote: Hagan interview, Dec. 6, 2004.

Alvin Bradley quote: Bradley interview, Dec. 22, 2004

Details of German retreat under January 1945 air attack: Parker, *To Win the Winter Sky*, p. 482.

Bulge casualties: Roger Cirillo, *Ardennes-Alsace*. The U.S. Army Campaigns of World War II. CMH Pub. 72-76., p. 53.

Van Cleef strafing attack: Johnson, *History of the Hell Hawks*, p. 397; van Cleef interview, June 23, 2007.

Ardennes results for Ninth Air Force: Johnson, *History of the Hell Hawks*, p. 399.

Chapter Thirteen

McWhorter on Hillman: interview with McWhorter, June 23, 2006.

Hillman quotes: from interviews and a written report by Hillman.

McWhorter on McWhorter: interview with McWhorter, Apr. 19, 2007.

Kling quotes: interview with Kling, Apr. 9, 2007.

Chapter Fourteen

Sejtka DFC: Johnson, *History of the Hell Hawks*, p. 411.

Hagan dive-bombing technique: Hagan interview, April 29, 2003.

Wells dive-bombing instruction: Wells interview.

Wells returns in damaged P-47: Johnson, *History of the Hell Hawks*, p. 412.

Szymanski description: ibid., p. 437.

Preston shootdown: Preston interview, July 2, 2007.

Air support of attack across the Roer: Franck, pp. 212–15.

Stecker and Fry speak to Franck: Franck, *Winter Journey Through the Ninth*. p. 221.

Condreit's death: Johnson, *History of the Hell Hawks*, p. 431.

Hagan on flak dodging: Hagan interview, Mar 2003.

McHugh pilots a gliding P-47: Johnson, *History of the Hell Hawks*, p. 432.

Wells asks Quesada about going home: Wells interview, June 6, 2006.

Szymanski's death: Johnson, *History of the Hell Hawks*, p. 437.

Chapter Fifteen

Aanenson air controller experiences: Aanenson, *A Fighter Pilot's Story.* unpublished script. 37–39.

Lopez air controller experiences: Lopez interview, September 2006.

Henry's tank attack: Johnson, *History of the Hell Hawks*, 447.

Lopez jet encounter: Lopez, unpublished manuscript, 2007, p. 36.

Murrow excerpts: Johnson, *History of the Hell Hawks*, pp. 457–63.

Maltbie victory over Ju 88: Maltbie interview, July 5, 2007.

Chapter Sixteen

Smoak and the Me 262: e-mail message from Andrew W. Smoak, May 18, 2007.

Smoak and drinking: interview with his sister, Molly Smoak Jesse, August 7, 2006.

Peter Motzenbecker quote: e-mail message from Peter Motzenbecker, August 19, 2006.

Hitler and the Me 262: Kershaw, *Hitler 1936–1945: Nemesis*

Lake quote: interview with Jon Lake, Mar. 14, 2007.

Beaudrault kill: Johnson, *History of the Hell Hawks*, pp. 263–64; Beaudrault family documents.

Wray quote: Hugh Morgan, *Me 262 Stormbird Rising,*. London: Osprey, 1994, pp. 58–70

Cowan's jet shootdown: Johnson, *History of the Hell Hawks*, p. 426; Cowan interview, Oct. 2004; Cowan's encounter report, Feb. 24, 1945.

Chapter Seventeen

Kark versus Me 262: Johnson, *History of the Hell Hawks*, p. 446.

Lopez recollections: Lopez, unpublished memoir, 2007, p. 34.

Henry mission description: Henry memoir, repeated in Johnson, *History of the Hell Hawks*, pp. 447–48.

Grant Stout story: correspondence and interviews with Stout relatives.

Thunderbolt description: Van Cleef interview, June 23, 2007..

Bauman concerning William E. Rodgers: Bauman interview, Oct. 2004.

Brooking close call with bomb: Brooking interview, Nov. 2003.

Lutz napalm attack on Remagen area: Lutz, *Just One of the Boys*, pp. 58–59.

Loss of the two Millers: Johnson, *History of the Hell Hawks*, pp. 488–89.

Prevost map of Miller's loss: Prevost interview, Sept. 2006.

Chapter Eighteen

Lopez wounding and counterattack: Lopez manuscript, 2007, p. 37.

Preston training experience: Preston interview, July 2, 2007.

Wells initiation of new pilots: Wells interview, June 6, 2006.

Ritchie's tips on combat flying in the ETO tactics manual: Johnson, *History of the Hell Hawks*, pp. 276–80.

Thompson and *New Boy*: Mundt interview, Sept. 2006.

Thoman dogfight of Apr. 11, 1945: Johnson, *History of the Hell Hawks*, p. 516.

Okie invasion: Brooking interview, Nov. 17, 2003.

Orange brandy: Van Cleef interview notes, p. 30.

Lopez buzzes the field: Lopez manuscript, 2007, p. 38.

Brooking on pilot losses: Brooking interview, Nov. 5, 2003.

Wells on death of pilots: Wells interview, June 6, 2006.

Stanton on death of Stelle: Stanton interview, Sept. 2006.

Fitzsimmonds death: Johnson, p. 322; Brooking interview, Nov. 5, 2003.

Prevost hits his propeller: Prevost interview, Oct. 14, 2004.

Lutz tires of combat: Lutz, *Just One of the Boys*, p. 59.

Chapter Nineteen

Bernburg surrender to the Hell Hawks: Johnson, *History of the Hell Hawks*, p. 528; A. Mundt interview, Sept. 2006.

Schneider death in ground combat: Johnson, *History of the Hell Hawks*, p. 531.

Dogfights of April 17, 1945: ibid., p. 533.

Zeithain ammo dump attack: ibid., p. 538.

Irwin shoot-down: ibid., p. 539.

Lutz attack on ammo dump: Lutz, *Just One of the Boys*, pp. 61–64.

Thompson's death on April 20, 1945: Schlegel interview, Sept. 2006; Johnson, *History of the Hell Hawks*, p. 541.

British POW account: Johnson, *History of the Hell Hawks*, p. 541.

"Dead-Stick" Worley: ibid., p. 543; Worley interview, Oct. 2004; Worley letter, June 30, 2007.

Jet combat on April 24, 1945: Johnson, *History of the Hell Hawks*, p. 545.

Chapter Twenty

Kark at Buchenwald: Kark interview, Sept. 13, 2006.

Mittelbau-Dora concentration camps: Lutz, pp. 66–67; Brooking interview, Jan. 13, 2005.

Buchenwald: Kark interview, Sept. 15, 2006.

Deactivation of the Hell Hawks: Johnson, *History of the Hell Hawks*, pp. 561–68.

Quesada on the Hell Hawks: ibid., p. vii.

Briggs poem: ibid., p. 570

Bibliography

Aanenson, Quentin C. *A Fighter Pilot's Story*. Video production. Washington, D.C.: WETA-TV, 1999.

Aanenson, Quentin C. *A Fighter Pilot's Story*, unpublished script. Bethesda, MD. 1994.

Ambrose, Stephen A. *D-Day*. New York: Simon & Schuster, 1994.

—— *Citizen Soldiers*. New York: Simon & Schuster, 1998.

Ballard, Ted. *Rhineland: 15 September 1944–21 March 1945*. Washington, D.C.: U.S. Army Center of Military History, Gov't Printing Office: CMH Pub 72-25, n.d.

Bodie, Warren M. *Republic's P-47 Thunderbolt: From Seversky to Victory*. Hayesville, N.C.: Wide Wing Publications, 1994.

Brulle, Robert V. *Angels Zero: P-47 Close Air Support in Europe*. Washington, D.C.: Smithsonian Institution Press, 2000.

Chuinard, Remy. *A Stormy Sky Over Normandy: Summer 1944*. Granville: the author, 2000.

Cirillo, Roger. *Ardennes-Alsace*. Washington, D.C.: U.S. Army Center of Military History, 1995.

Cole, Hugh M. *The Ardennes: Battle of the Bulge*. Washington, D.C.: U.S. Government Printing Office, 1965.

Dorr, Robert F. "P-47 pilots were blue-collar workhorses of World War II." *Air Force Times*, June 2, 2003.

—— "Dorr Field typified primary pilot training bases during World War II," *Air Force Times*, December 4, 2006.

—— "Nephew's historical search highlights P-47 pilot's heroics." *Air Force Times*, September 1, 2003.

—— "Operation Bodenplatte was Germany's final attempt to win air war in Europe." *Air Force Times*, October 6, 2003.

Dorr, Robert F., and Thomas D. Jones. "Pilot's WWII tour had unexpected twist," *Air Force Times*, February 13, 2006.

Caidin, Martin, and Robert S. Johnson. *Thunderbolt*. New York: Ballantine Books, 1983.

"Football," *Time* magazine, December 22, 1930.

Franck, Harry A. *Winter Journey through the Ninth*. Tucson, Ariz: Prince of the Road Press. 2001.

Freeman, Roger. *Thunderbolt: A Documentary History of the Republic P-47*. London: Macdonald's and Jane's, 1978.

Gause, Damon. *The War Journal of Major Damon 'Rocky' Gause: The Firsthand Account of One of the Greatest Escapes of World War II*. New York: Hyperion, 1999.

Glenn, Tom. *P-47 Pilots: The Fighter-Bomber Boys*. Osceola, Wisc.: MBI Publishing, 1998.

Graff, Cory. *P-47 Thunderbolt at War*. St. Paul, Minn.: Zenith Press, 2007

Grant, Rebecca. "Quesada the Conqueror." *Air Force* magazine, April 2003.

Hastings, Max. *Armageddon: The Battle for Germany, 1944–1945*. New York: Knopf, 2004.

Hill, Marion. *A Personal Account of Service in World War II*. Unpublished memoir. N.d.

Hughes, Thomas A. *Overlord: Pete Quesada and the Triumph of Tactical Air Power in World War II*. New York: The Free Press, 1995.

Isby, David C. (ed.) *Fighting the Breakout: The German Army in Normandy from Cobra to the Falaise Gap*. London: Lionel Leventhal Limited, 2004.

Johnson, Charles R. *The History of the Hell Hawks*. Anaheim, Calif.: Southcoast, 1975.

Kershaw, Ian. *Hitler 1936–1945: Nemesis*. New York: Penguin, 2000.

Kiefer, Edgar C. *A P-47 Pilot's Recollections of his WWII Battles*. Boulder, Colo.: Richard Kiefer. 2000.

Lopez, Edward J. Unpublished memoir. 2007.

Lutz, Samuel B. *Just One of the Boys*. Santa Ana, Calif.: Words and Pictures Press. 2001.

Mangan, Frank. *Mangan's War: A Personal View of World War II*. El Paso, Tex.: Mangan Books, 2003.

Manning, Thomas A. *History of Air Training Command 1943–1993*. Randolph Air Force Base, Tex.: Office of History and Research, Headquarters, Air Education and Training Command, 1993.

Manrho, John, and Ron Putz. *Bodenplatte: The Luftwaffe's Last Best Hope*. Crowborough, UK: Hikoki Publications, 2004.

McManus, John C. *Deadly Sky: The American Combat Airman in World War II*. Novato, Calif.: Presidio Press, 2000.

Miller, Donald L. *Masters of the Air: America's Bomber Boys Who Fought The Air War Against Nazi Germany*. New York: Simon & Schuster, 2006.

Morgan, Hugh. *Me 262 Stormbird Rising*. London: Osprey Publishing, 1994.

Parker, Danny S. *To Win the Winter Sky: The Air War Over the Ardennes 1944–1945*. Conshohocken, Pa.: Combined Books, 1994.

Pitts, Jack. *P-47 Pilots: Scared, Bored, and Deadly*. San Antonio, Tex.: Pitts Enterprises, 1997.

Saied, Kemal. *Thunderbolt Odyssey: P-47 War in Europe*. Sand Springs, Okla. Stone and Wood Press, 1990.

Scutts, Jerry. *P-47 Thunderbolt Aces of the Ninth and Fifteenth Air Forces*. Oxford: Osprey Publishing, 1999.

Shook, Hal. *Fighter Pilot Jazz*. Huntington, W. Va. Humanomics Publishing. 2005.

Smith, E. A. W. *Spitfire Diary: The Boys of One-Two-Seven*. Austin, Tex.: Eakin Press, 1995.

Spires, David N. *Patton's Air Force*. Washington: Smithsonian Institution Press, 2002.

Stoff, Joshua. *The Thunder Factory: An Illustrated History of the Republic Aviation Corporation*. London: Arms & Armour Press, 1990.

U.S. Army, Military Intelligence Service. *German Antiaircraft Artillery*. Special Series 10. Washington, DC: War Department, Feb. 1943. Available at: http://www.lonesentry.com/manuals/german_aa/index.html

Weigley, Russell F. *Eisenhower's Lieutenants*. Bloomington: Indiana University Press, 1981.

Weintraub, Stanley. *11 Days in December: Christmas at the Bulge*, 1944. New York: The Free Press, 2006.

Wink, Gene: *Born to Fly*. Bloomington, Ind.: AuthorHouse, 2006.

Zemke, Hubert, as told to Roger Freeman. *Zemke's Stalag: The Final Days of WWII*. Washington and London: Smithsonian Institution Press, 1991.

Index